all the rave

▼

The Rise and Fall of Shawn Fanning's Napster

JOSEPH MENN

CROWN
BUSINESS
NEW YORK

Published by Crown Business, New York, New York.
Member of the Crown Publishing Group, a division of Random House, Inc.
www.randomhouse.com

CROWN BUSINESS is a trademark and the Rising Sun colophon is a registered trademark of Random House, Inc.

Printed in the United States of America

DESIGN BY BARBARA STURMAN

The version of Napster's logo on the cover was modified for the company by artist Tom Dolan from the more widely distributed original by Sam Hanks.

Library of Congress Cataloging-in-Publication Data
  Menn, Joseph.
    All the rave: the rise and fall of Shawn Fanning's Napster /
  Joseph Menn.
    Includes bibliographical references and index.
      1. Napster Inc. 2. Music trade. 3. Fanning, Shawn. I. Title.
      ML3790 .M43 2003
      025.06'78—dc21   20020142

ISBN 0-609-61093-7

10 9 8 7 6 5 4 3 2 1

First Edition

FOR SAMANTHA, MY LOVELY WIFE

Observe my uncle. If his occulted guilt
Do not itself unkennel in one speech,
It is a damned ghost that we have seen,
And my imaginations are as foul
As Vulcan's stithy. Give him heedful note,
For I mine eyes will rivet to his face,
And after we will both our judgments join
In censure of his seeming.

—Hamlet

Contents

all the rave

Author's Note

▼

I WAS NOT ONE OF THE THRONG OF JOURNALISTS WHO wrote dozens of stories about Napster during its peak from late 1999 through mid-2001. Like many, I figured that the exhaustive newspaper and magazine coverage was plenty. It was only in late 2000 that I met some of the talented people who worked at the company and realized how wrong I had been. Not long after, I came to the conclusion that Napster's real story could be told only in an investigative book, for three reasons.

First, for all of the surface coverage in the media, an astonishing amount of information was never made public. Most important, there was the unseen role of the man who incorporated Napster and essentially controlled it through its crucial first year, before the professionals took over. That man is not the enigmatic Shawn Fanning, the *Time* and *Fortune* magazine cover boy and the world's best-known hacker, whose message of free music eventually attracted as many as 70 million registered users. That man is Shawn's uncle John Fanning, who kept 70 percent of Napster's stock at its inception. John Fanning was a struggling but ambitious businessman with bad debts, a habit of mixing personal and company matters, and a confrontational style that brought him multiple lawsuits and a police record. By design, Shawn Fanning was pushed forward as the young spokesman for a computer-powered movement. But his uncle best represents what Napster became. And John Fanning was just the beginning. Other key employees brought in under his leadership were also well familiar with angry investors, the courts, and the cops long before Napster's landmark fight with the record industry. Their roles too have never been examined. All told, the undisclosed chaos, betrayal, and dissension within Napster made the record-industry lawsuit look like a friendly game of chess. And it is somehow fitting that the rapid development of this weapon for allowing consumers to take control away from the entertainment-industry giants also illustrates so dramatically the power that a few individual entrepreneurs can wield in a post-Internet society, for good or for ill.

The second reason that Napster merits book-length treatment is how different it was from all the other excesses of the Internet bubble. Napster wasn't selling pet food or baby products online. The fastest-growing business of all time, Napster had an innovative technology, true to the Net's roots, that fired up not only the computers of the music-craving masses but also the imaginations of CEOs at some of the biggest companies on the planet. And driven by leaders who kept doubling Napster's bet, it pushed the edge until it defined where the lines would be drawn on some of the most important political and economic issues of the day, including digital piracy, consumer rights, freedom of speech, and the future shape of the Net itself. As I write, the leaders of Hollywood and Silicon Valley, two of the most powerful industries anywhere, are jousting on Capitol Hill over whether widespread anticopying mechanisms will be mandated in the computers of the future. All that from the mind of an idealistic seventeen-year-old from Cape Cod who got some very bad advice.

The third reason nearly contradicts the second. While Napster was different, it also epitomized what went wrong at the hottest spot in capitalism in the historic boom at the turn of the century. It was exactly like everything else that was happening, only much, much more so. In Napster's case, billionaire venture capitalists were willing to put millions of dollars behind something that was not just foolish, as so many start-ups were, but something that they had *already concluded was illegal.* If the investment philosophy that powered Napster was badly overcharged, so were the characters that led it. But they too were archetypes of a remarkable era. A little rougher around the edges and a little more reckless, to be sure, but the sort of people who seemed almost genetically designed to take advantage of the mass mania that surrounded them. Read correctly, the story of Napster proves that the influx of investment money credited with spreading technology faster and wider than ever before also corrupted the evolution of that technology, provoking a brutal backlash.

This book is based on hundreds of interviews with virtually everyone who was important at Napster and many of the people they came in contact with, from their childhood years through Napster's dealings with media titan Bertelsmann AG and the company's bankruptcy. (Bertelsmann also owns the publisher of this book.) My dealings with John Fanning were more limited. They included authorized interviews with his company's lawyer and publicist, his hanging up the phone and shutting a door in my face, and his response to an e-mailed list of questions, an answer that consisted chiefly of his claim that the questions alone were grounds for a lawsuit.

My work is supported by police and court records from the states of California, Massachusetts, Delaware, Pennsylvania, and Washington. I also have relied on scores of confidential internal company documents, nonpublic depositions and other material from the legal battles, and thousands of e-mails from within Napster, the recording industry's trade group, and elsewhere. To avoid a mind-numbing excess of endnotes, you can assume that unless I say otherwise, when I refer to such a document, I have read it. Likewise, oral statements in quotes are from author interviews unless the endnotes say differently. Reconstructed speeches that are not from a court transcript or tape and that I did not personally hear are usually from the recollection of the speaker. There are some instances when a listener is the source. Whenever possible, these recollections have been confirmed by the other parties, and any conflicts have been resolved by the elimination of the material or by noting the discrepancy.

Because nearly all my reporting required substantial help from others, I owe almost everyone named in it a debt of gratitude. I would especially like to thank those who spent many days with me, some of them painful, to make sure I had the facts right, knowing that they themselves would not emerge unscathed. For exceptional bravery, I commend Napster's first Silicon Valley CEO, Eileen Richardson, founding developer Jordan Ritter, and cofounder Sean Parker, among others. Of the many good people still working for Napster when they spoke, I want to especially thank Shawn Fanning and Ricki Seidman, who prevailed on employees to meet me. My own employer, the *Los Angeles Times*, showed remarkable forbearance in giving me six weeks' leave at a time when not one but two of the Fortune 100 companies I cover were embroiled in public trials. I want to thank editor John Carroll, managing editor Dean Baquet, business editor Bill Sing, and senior technology editor Russ Stanton, who helped me in more ways than I can say. Thanks also to digital-music writer Jon Healey and the talented colleagues who filled in for me. And I am grateful to the readers of my early drafts, Anthony Effinger, Mark Saylor, and Samantha Zee; my editor, Doug Pepper, and others at Crown; my agent and friend Elizabeth Kaplan, who strides from mountaintop to mountaintop; journalist Dan Goodin, who raised the first questions about John Fanning; Celia Francis, for crucial introductions; and the queen of hospitality during my stay in Boston, Rachel Layne.

Prologue:
A Party out of Control

▼

NAPSTER FOUNDER SHAWN FANNING WAS FEELING GOOD. IN the limo on the way to a massive Halloween rave in Oakland, California, the eighteen-year-old had swallowed a tab of Ecstasy, and now it was weaving a pleasant cocoon around him. Inside the warehouse, the dancers swirled to the techno beat. Well-built and stocky from lifting weights, Shawn kept drinking water and trying not to grind his teeth. Normally shy, he was beaming at perfect strangers. Drugs aside, there was no reason not to: Shawn was surrounded by things that he loved. Good friends, youth culture at its antiestablishment best, and the music that was his passion. And it was for the right cause—his cause. Napster was a cosponsor of the festivities, and the new company's banner and stickers were on display. In the haze of that evening in October 1999, it didn't seem to matter that most of the other people there had never heard of his brainchild. It didn't matter that Napster's booth was slipshod and the last to go up. And it didn't matter that Napster's new chief executive was on Ecstasy too. That was sort of nice. "It was stupid. But it was a lot of fun," Shawn said later.

What did matter was that Shawn was a long way from his rough Massachusetts childhood—some of it spent on welfare, part of it spent in a foster home—and that he would never again face days like that. He was riding the Internet explosion that had transformed his new home, the San Francisco Bay area, into a pulsating mass of parties, easy money, and unlimited opportunities for hackers and hucksters alike. After months of demonstrating and explaining Napster to rich strangers, Shawn and his team had won funding for his fledgling company, now with about ten employees, some of them Silicon Valley pros. And the number of Napster's users was snowballing by as much as 50 percent in a single day. If that kept up, Napster would become the fastest-growing business in history.

It had been a blur to Shawn. Two years before, he was just one of a hundred seniors at Harwich High School on Cape Cod, where he was well liked but best known for the purple BMW Z3 that his uncle gave him. After Shawn learned to program computers and started tinkering with ways to find digital music files faster, Napster had sprung to life and spread rapidly by word of mouth well before Shawn could get all the bugs out. Shawn had moved to California the previous month at the insistence of Napster's first outside investor. In a whirlwind of cash wire transfers and quick decisions, he brought along Napster's nineteen-year-old cofounder, Sean Parker, now just as dazed as Shawn by everything that was happening around them. Driving one day in a car that an older employee had rented for them, Shawn had looked over at Parker. "What are we doing in California?" he asked.

The rave was a major break from their hectic routine, and the two teenagers would remember it as one of the high points of their breakneck adventure. Sponsoring it was a characteristically Parker idea. A hyperenergetic and business-oriented programmer from Herndon, Virginia, the severely asthmatic Parker had met Shawn on a chat channel for aspiring hackers while both were in high school. "He was one of the few people that would talk to me about stuff that wasn't technical—the meaning of life, consciousness," Parker said. Later, Parker was one of the first Shawn told about Napster. Parker used every business connection he had to get the project funded. It was an insane process, filled with double crosses and a sort of high-speed poker with investors, but Parker set the events in motion that finally brought the company its first, magical quarter-million dollars. Now most of Parker's time was spent strategizing, predicting what Napster needed to do next to keep growing and taking in money from investors. But while Shawn was busy writing code, Parker was more interested in making time for fun, and he was a longtime fan of electronic dance music. The Oakland party gave him something to be excited about that didn't turn him into a wheezing ball of stress.

There were thousands of kids inside the warehouse, and Parker had an all-access pass that came with Napster's sponsorship. The best part came when Parker stuck his head out a side door, where a hundred or more kids were clamoring to get past the guards, many claiming they knew someone inside. "They were all screaming. It was like slaves baking in the hot sun, all wanting water," he said. Scanning the crowd, Parker recognized the old school friend he had invited down from California State University, Chico, now a committed raver with his own friends in tow. Like a reigning rock star at an exclusive club, Parker let his acolytes in.

The third member of the original Napster troupe was in his element as well. Sporting spiky, dyed-blond hair and a pierced tongue, Jordan Ritter was older than Shawn and Parker, at the advanced age of twenty-one. Unlike them, Ritter had given up a real job and a real life to join Napster out West. Ritter had been a computer-security researcher in Boston, a dream assignment for a hacker who spent long nights breaking into networks just to see if he could do it. Coming from a trailer home in Florida, Ritter made it most of the way through to a computer-science degree at Lehigh University in Pennsylvania before joining online groups of hackers that straddled the line between taking advantage of security loopholes and issuing public warnings about them. It was in one of those groups, called w00w00 and pronounced "woo woo," that he met Shawn.

Shawn turned to that collective of young hackers, academics, and security pros for help in writing and improving the Napster program. Several w00w00 members served as testers, and Ritter took an especially active role. He kept pestering Shawn with questions about the workings of the server side of the system, the back end that connected one personal computer and its available songs to others. Eventually Shawn turned the server over to Ritter, who used his greater expertise to redesign it, allowing Napster to handle the traffic that surged when word leaked out and Napster started taking off. The first time they met in person was when Shawn stopped by Ritter's bachelor pad overlooking Boston's Christian Science Center headquarters and asked him to move to California. Ritter hesitated, reluctant to leave Boston and his job at BindView Corp. After weeks of negotiations, he took the plunge. On this night at the rave, he was glad he had. Improving Napster's design so elegantly that it could withstand tens of thousands of users without requiring more computer hardware than NASA was the challenge of his career. All three of them might get rich and famous. And in the meantime, he could hardly object to the rave.

Sean Parker had managed to convince Napster CEO Eileen Richardson that a sure way to get the attention of the company's natural constituency of young music fans was to blow $7,000 on a rave. Looking like a club diva herself, with a streak of magenta dyeing her wavy brown hair, Richardson loved a good party and loud music, and she was surprisingly easy to persuade. She wanted the Napster kids to have fun. And it made a certain amount of sense to market the brand at a rave. To Richardson, the best thing about Napster was that music fans could discover songs that they couldn't find in stores, and electronica was particularly hard to come by. "A rave is perfect," Richardson thought. "The kids there love this music, and it's impossible to get." Now she was beside Parker in the booth, her pupils dilated. Adorned with temporary tattoos in the spirit of the evening, they shouted at the sweat-soaked kids wandering by that Napster was giving away Rio portable MP3 players: Just put down your e-mail address to get in the drawing.

Richardson was thirty-eight, the grown-up in the outfit. But she was the sort of elder a teenager might pick for himself: "a den mother," said Parker. As a rising venture capitalist in Boston, Richardson led an investment in a company called Firefly, a service that recommends music based on user taste. Now living in the heart of Silicon Valley, Richardson heard about Napster from the company's first benefactor, investor Joseph "Yosi" Amram. "Oh my God," she said as she played with the service at home for the first time. If Firefly was an on-ramp to new tunes, Napster was the Autobahn. She agreed to join for six months as interim chief executive, working the line between Shawn and his young collaborators and the world of big-time Silicon Valley wheeler-dealers, the billionaires who had bankrolled Netscape and Yahoo!, Amazon and eBay.

Richardson loved her job. Instead of just investing in companies and coaching them from a distance, she was building a firm herself. For once, her teenage son understood what she did for a living. The kids at the company were inspired. And Richardson believed she could turn their invention into something the record industry would love—a way to market new music to potential fans, based on what they liked, for virtually nothing.

As the good feeling built up under the canopy behind Napster's booth, it was easy to forget that like the rave scene itself, the Napster movement was based on the unstable allure of illegal behavior. And it was easy for Shawn to forget what bothered him more than that: his blowhard uncle John. John Fanning had served as a surrogate father during much of Shawn's difficult childhood. He had hired Shawn to work at the online-games firm he ran in Hull, Massachusetts, and Fanning had even bought Shawn his first computer and that sports car in high school. But their relationship was far from perfect. A dropout from Boston College, the thirty-five-year-old Fanning fancied himself a successful businessman, destined to make the cover of *Fortune* magazine. His track record suggested that was unlikely, and the games firm was struggling when Shawn told his uncle about Napster. Fanning realized it could be huge and moved quickly to incorporate Napster Inc. with the Massachusetts secretary of state. And he took one more step, laying a minefield that would dictate every major direction that Napster would take in the crucial next year: Fanning awarded himself 70 percent of the company, leaving just 30 percent for his nephew. Shawn was stunned, but Fanning said that no one was going to fund a company majority-owned by an eighteen-year-old. He said that Shawn needed his business contacts and savvy. Since Fanning had taken care of Shawn before, the young man signed the papers.

Fanning's grab did far more than injure his nephew. It changed the balance of power at Napster to one favoring a completely different set of motivations. And it didn't take long before that shift started shaping Napster's destiny. Fanning's chief virtue, he told Shawn, was his business credibility and fund-raising power. Yet the majority of the potential investors looked at the technology and applauded, looked at Shawn and Parker and approved, and then looked at John Fanning and blanched. One near-investor explained that he thought he could handle what he predicted would be a serious legal issue, or handle a semi-involved uncle with too much ego and too much equity—but not both. After months of effort by Parker and Fanning, Silicon Valley investor Amram agreed to put in $250,000 for a sizable stake. Since Amram had been burned investing in the games company, he set three conditions: The company would move to northern California, where he could keep an eye on it. Fanning wouldn't be CEO—Amram would pick one instead. And there would be a three-person board: Fanning, Amram, and the new CEO. For the top job, Amram named Richardson, an old friend who had never met Fanning and had no idea what she was getting into.

At the time of the rave, John Fanning was thousands of miles away. Officially, he wasn't in charge, and he wisely kept himself out of the media circus that would surround Napster. But soon he would start meddling in every significant decision the company made. It was John Fanning, still the biggest shareholder, who decided that legal victory was a virtual certainty and that the company didn't need to negotiate with the record industry. It was John Fanning who vetoed venture-capital deals that might have transformed Napster into a legally sound business. And it was John Fanning, more than anyone else, who profited from Napster's meteoric but unsustainable rise. He kept a significant chunk of Amram's initial investment for claimed expenses back East, and he sold hundreds of thousands of dollars worth of his shares as more investors poured in.

Soon after the rave, power struggles would erupt as users of the Napster service soared into the tens of millions and made it the best-known brand on the Internet. Shawn would emerge as a household name and a generational icon, gracing the cover of *Time* magazine and testifying before Congress. He would also be crushed by court rulings that closed the door on the biggest theft of intellectual property in history. Much of Napster's wild trajectory can be traced to that early division of power, between a young hacker who wanted to see if he could solve an interesting problem and an uncle who recklessly aspired to riches. Yet the two depended on each other, personifications of the twin forces behind the dot-com explosion. For before even such a brilliant innovation could rise so far so quickly, it needed a hustler who could capitalize on the era's investor greed and naïveté.

Two years down the road, every member of the core team at the rave had departed Napster but Shawn, who quit briefly himself in a dramatic final showdown over the company's survival. He returned to help reshape Napster into a legal distributor of authorized music, only to see the company slide into bankruptcy. Yet the legacy of Napster's original technology is hard to overstate. The firm's pirate successors now combine for a bigger reach than Napster had at its peak. The record industry suffers from both declining sales and judicial scrutiny of whether its members conspired to suppress online distribution. Movie companies and others fear with good reason that they will be the next to be "Napsterized." And all manner of academics, start-ups, and giant firms are embracing what's known as peer-to-peer file sharing, hailed by Netscape Communications Corp. founder Marc Andreessen as a "once-in-a-generation idea."

For Shawn and his friends, it would be an incredible trip. But it certainly wouldn't be an easy one.

the rebels

THE RAVE IN OAKLAND CAPTURED NAPSTER AS IT WAS JUST coming into its own at the center of the Web boom's insanity and on the way to becoming the fastest-growing use of the Internet. The sometimes painful story of the quiet young man at the heart of the company began at another, far different party twenty years earlier, on the other side of the country. It was in a ramshackle old house in the hard-luck town of Rockland, Massachusetts, south of Boston. The sprawling home was barely big enough to contain the eight brothers and sisters of the Fanning brood, a diverse and struggling Irish family that this night invited half the neighborhood over to celebrate Eddie Fanning's high school graduation. The Fannings loved music and a raucous good time, and they had arranged for a band of local renown to play. MacBeth performed songs by better-known Boston rockers Aerosmith and sang its own material, even recording a 45 single. Coleen Fanning, sixteen, was especially impressed with the band and with eighteen-year-old Attleboro guitarist Joe Rando in particular. Hundreds of friends and neighbors showed up to enjoy the night. The next sibling after Coleen in the family, fourteen-year-old John Fanning, passed a hat and collected thousands of dollars to pay for the bash, his first entrepreneurial experience.

The band became part of the Fannings' social circle, and in time Coleen began dating Rando, who was smart, good-looking, and from a wealthier family. A couple of years later, after Coleen told Rando that she was pregnant, their romance ended. She kept the baby, and the young Shawn Fanning joined the already-overstuffed household in 1980, before it moved to nearby Brockton.

The first few years "were hell," according to Coleen, a small, freckled, blue-eyed woman who laughs a lot and speaks with a pronounced Boston accent. She moved from one tough area to another, then married an ex-Marine and truck driver named Raymond Verrier. The couple had four more children, and it wasn't the happiest of homes. "Money was always a pretty big issue," Shawn said. "There was a lot of tension around that."

They lived near Brockton's projects for a time, and Coleen could see her already-shy son withdrawing from what he saw happening around him. "He went inside himself real deep and said, 'I want to get out of this.' Even though it meant losing him a little bit, it's what I wanted for him," said Coleen, who was working then as a nurse's aide. During a split between the Verriers, when Shawn was about twelve, he and his siblings had to move for several months into a foster home until the couple reconciled. Always a strong student, Shawn tried to escape by concentrating on school and by playing guitar, basketball, and baseball. When the family was through the worst of the hardship, the Verriers moved to the small middle-class town of Harwich Port, on the elbow of Cape Cod. The new house was nice enough, if still crowded, and the neighborhood was full of pine trees and songbirds.

As Shawn kept playing sports, his mother encouraged him, thinking the whole time about scholarships to college. Shawn was especially strong at baseball, even though fear gripped him at each trip to the plate. He batted over .650 one year at Harwich High School, a small school with some very good teachers. As Shawn grew, Coleen wanted to give him more than she had had, more than she could give him directly. "We don't have much," she said. "He didn't get a lot of things that people get who come from money."

She saw that Shawn was motivated, and she turned to the person she knew best who could be a mentor of sorts, her business-minded brother John. John Fanning gave Shawn money for each A he brought home, and there were many. And he bought Shawn his first computer, an Apple Macintosh the Verriers could never have afforded. Shawn took to it immediately. Often he would be on the machine doing homework or chatting over the Internet through the evening. Every hour he typed, the radio blared. "I always knew from an early age he was going to accomplish things," Coleen said. Given her son's way of working, "it doesn't strike me as strange he would figure out a way to have music on computers."

John Fanning bought other presents for his nephew too. Nothing was more important than the car—a dark purple BMW Z3 that ensured Shawn made an impression at Harwich High. "He was a nice kid. Everybody liked him," said Tim Jamoulis, who played on the tennis team with Shawn. History teacher Richard Besciak taught Shawn in homeroom for all four years and remembered Shawn's unusual ability to focus intently on the task at hand. "A lot of kids can tune out, but he was right on track," Besciak said. "He was an A student without trying. He was a nice, generous, levelheaded young man." Harwich High had only about a hundred students in each grade, but around Shawn's time, there were several promising computer students. After Shawn became one of them, everything else fell by the wayside. "Once I started getting into programming, I pretty much quit all sports," Shawn said. A fellow hacker at the school said that Shawn's work on the machines "really seemed to consume him. There were those who were doing it just as a hobby, for games, or to cheat in school. Shawn went through that phase, but it was just a starting point. He was quickly beyond that, doing much more sophisticated things."

When Shawn was seventeen, John Fanning located Joe Rando on the Internet and asked his sister Coleen if she wanted Shawn to meet his biological father, who still lived in the area. Coleen had no hard feelings about Rando and had told Shawn the truth when he was seven, so she agreed immediately. "I knew Shawn had to get to know him. He was at the right age, and I knew it could only be good," Coleen said. "I know Shawn gets a lot of his good qualities from me," she said, laughing at herself. "But he gets a lot from the other side too." Still, when she first saw the two of them together, she couldn't get out of the car, she was so shocked. It was just that they looked so much alike, right down to the loping way they walked. Shawn and Rando hit it off, and they stayed in touch during all the craziness that Shawn was about to go through. Rando had done well for himself, earning a degree in physics and an M.B.A. He worked in fiber optics and tried his hand at running small software firms before settling in as a real-estate developer specializing in shopping malls. Rando discovered that he preferred working for himself to laboring at big companies or under the control of powerful investors. An Internet skeptic, Rando gave his son one major piece of business advice about Napster: to take the money as soon as he could. "I always told him, 'If you can cash out, cash out,' because the valuations I was seeing were mind-boggling," Rando said.

For more day-to-day guidance, Coleen continued to steer Shawn toward his uncle. Even though Coleen and John weren't close, John Fanning had ambition that she wanted Shawn to experience up close. "He's like Shawn in a different way," she said. "He wanted out of that situation he started in. It was the motivation to succeed that I wanted Shawn to pick up on."

John Fanning lived an hour away in blue-collar Hull, a 350-year-old fishing town halfway back to Boston from the Cape that was trying to survive on the tourist trade without offering much in return. Shawn saw his uncle's office, the home of his latest venture, Internet firm Chess.net, as a refuge. He worked summers there, learning to program and often sleeping on the couch. Fanning loved playing games, and he developed a serious habit with a computer video game called StarCraft. His favorite opponent was Shawn. Even when Shawn's hacking hobby started to look like a serious business, Fanning wanted to play. More than once, when Shawn's friends and collaborators needed him to work, he told them he couldn't: His uncle wanted to keep playing StarCraft. If he didn't keep playing with him, Shawn told them, Fanning wouldn't give him money for dinner. Shawn's friends believed that Shawn wasn't kidding, and that if his uncle was kidding, the humor was much darker than what they were used to. "I'm sure if he hadn't played StarCraft, he would have gotten fed," Napster cofounder Sean Parker said. "But John Fanning has a way of being really stubborn."

Shawn shared his family's love of a good time. But where Fanning could be boisterous, his nephew was inward-looking and serious. It was while he was working at Fanning's company that Shawn expanded on his early taste for computing. "I was just getting into programming, so I spent a lot of my time just fiddling with projects and hanging out. I have a really fond memory of that time, but I think I could have taken better advantage of it in terms of learning," Shawn said. "Eventually I transitioned into doing some programming for the Web back end. I built the Web store. I was doing a lot of network programming and Unix programming and stuff. I was around computer guys, so it gave me a chance to learn."

It was also then that Shawn discovered what would make him famous: MP3 digital music files he found through Internet Relay Chat, the hangout of choice for budding Internet programmers, hackers, and wanna-bes. Invented in Finland in 1988, IRC is a form of mass instant-messaging. In a channel, members type and send messages in real time to anyone who is monitoring that channel, and they can switch to private interactions. In the late 1990s, the IRC system spawned thousands of channels on every topic conceivable. Some were devoted to MP3s, where users traded music. Others focused on free software or pirated programs. Some of the channels were closed, while others were open to anyone who stumbled onto them.

— —

IT WAS ON ONE OF THE OPEN CHANNELS, devoted to minor hacker exploits and other things geek, that Shawn first ran into Sean Parker in 1996. As Shawn learned more and worked himself up the IRC hacker hierarchy, he got invited to join a private IRC channel called w00w00, which would play a key role in Napster's development. W00w00 was for hackers and others interested in security issues who knew what they were doing, having already cut their teeth elsewhere. It wasn't full of kids who pulled off hacking attacks by running scripts of code they had downloaded elsewhere. But it also wasn't for the established old-school hackers, who kept to themselves for fear of exposure. (The term *hacker* has two meanings. One is generally positive, implying technical ability. The other is negative, implying improper behavior. Many self-described hackers prefer to call those who engage in wrongful behavior as "crackers." But since that term is little used outside of hacking circles, this book adopts the word *hacker* in its broadest sense, without intending to give it moral weight one way or the other.)

Like New York nightclubs, IRC channels would rise and fall quickly in the esteem of others. Once too many people joined, the hip crowd moved on and started something new. W00w00 had been founded by a baby-faced high-schooler from Utah named Matt Conover, an impressive young hacker whose nickname in the channel was Shok. Shok had gained some notoriety for releasing detailed "exploits"—code that could be used for attacks—which is something that's extremely controversial in the computer world. Many big software companies say the practice is destructive and should be criminalized. Some security experts, however, argue that the threat of the release of such code is the only thing that forces companies to admit they have a problem and fix it. At present, some groups are attempting to form a compromise standard, such as a four-week warning before an exploit's release.

Shok's work is available on hacking sites today, including a "war-dialer" that bombards Unix computer systems looking for open modem lines, a key hacker technique. Another is a program to fake an IP address, a computer's location on the Internet. Shawn's nickname in the group was Napster, which he had picked up on the basketball court for the short, nappy hair he sported before shaving it off. Another mainstay was Dug-song, who was in reality a University of Michigan student named Dug Song. "The whole point of w00w00 was to have an environment that was open to all," Song said. "People could talk about the computer universe from both sides. I'm a 'white hat.' I'd never actually done anything crimi-nal. But there are definitely people interested in other things." He paused, searching for the right phrase: "Applied uses of the technology."

W00w00 drew from several other groups, including a black-hat outfit based in France called ADM, an acronym for Association de Malfaiteurs, or "association of evildoers." Another affiliate was el8.org, run by Evan Brewer. The name was a play on "elite," slang for sophisticated hacking experts. Brewer was a little darker than average on w00w00, and at one point in a channel chat he defended the man who was facing prison for writing and releasing the wildly destructive Melissa virus. "I don't see what's so bad about writing viral code," Brewer wrote under his nickname "dmess0r," short for "digital messiah." Shok gave a balanced rejoinder, writing: "It's fine until I'm victimized."

Another member was Seth McGann, who was brought into w00w00 while a computer-science freshman at Worcester Polytechnic in Massachusetts. Pale and shy, McGann was a stereotypical computer nerd from Hamden, Connecticut. "I was a hard-core Unix geek," he said. McGann had been playing around with vulnerabilities in instant-messaging systems, coming up with a way to make messages appear to have been sent by someone else. After he posted some additional exploits, including detailed instructions for cracking the Solaris operating system from Sun Microsystems Inc. with a common technique called a buffer overflow, McGann got an e-mail message from Brewer. Brewer praised his work, but suggested that it might be better to keep it out of the public eye. Toward the end of 1998, Brewer brought McGann into w00w00.

McGann wasn't much of a positive thinker, taking the nickname "Minus." But he was in awe of some of the people in w00w00 and ADM. He also appreciated the collaborative culture. Unlike seasoned engineers, who have solid grounding in theory and many different parts of the computer world, hackers are often brilliant and knowledgeable about one or two things, with huge gaps in the rest of their understanding. An IRC group like w00w00 allowed them to reach out for help when trying to write code in an unfamiliar area. In structure, w00w00 was the polar opposite of profit-driven Silicon Valley, where equity was all. It was a loose network of confederates who grouped together on projects, with leadership determined by charisma, the amount of work put in, and the quality of the contributor's ideas.

For most, the unifying interest was computer security, or the lack of it. Searching for open ports on computers was one of the key areas of the trade. Not coincidentally, it would also be a crucial part of the Napster service, which could attach itself to company systems in unfamiliar ways, tunneling through corporate firewalls to allow bankers, brokers, and even military personnel to use the program at work. "My main interest in computers, what really sucked me into it, was some of the security stuff,"

Shawn said. "I never really had the desire to break into machines, but the act of securing machines and understanding how at a lower level things worked, for the purpose of making them more secure, was something I was interested in. I kind of found people along the way that were both talented programmers as well as interested in security."

In his later congressional testimony, Shawn said nothing of his own hacking background—only that he was interested in programming and in listening to music. When Napster was international news, every story missed the fact that Shawn was an aspiring hacker who was at best a gray hat. He wrote programs that took advantage of Unix computer network flaws and bore such unambiguous titles as "faker.c Dalnet Address spoofer," which allowed electronic correspondents to misrepresent their computers' locations. "Napscan.c portscanner," likewise, was a tool for checking computers for open lines to hack through. And "orgasm.c Portscanner/Flooder," cowritten by Shawn, was a program for denial-of-service attacks, the type that has taken down Yahoo!, eBay, and the federally funded CERT institute for computer security, among other targets.

"That was just silly," Shawn said when asked about those early programs. "This guy showed me this basic program to connect to a port and send a little bit of data there, so basically I did everything you could possibly do with those functions until I had really learned them inside and out," he said. "None of that stuff really did anything interesting at all—it's just silly, really a test program. It was really just my version of 'Hello, world.'" It's true that Shawn wasn't big time, and it's unclear how many hackers used the programs he put his nickname on. But they were good enough to get him into w00w00.

W00w00 members would go on to populate Napster, BindView Corp., and several other well-known Internet security firms, and the ties among the group prompted some to joke about an Internet mafia and world domination. Before the dot-com boom pulled many of the collaborators away to more profitable uses of their energy, though, it was less like a mob than an unusually diverse social club. "Without w00w00, Shawn and [Jordan] Ritter wouldn't have met, and Napster might not have taken off," said group founder Conover, now a computer-security professional in California. "We had completely different sorts of people."

Around the time that Shawn got involved at w00w00, he graduated from high school. He badly wanted to go to Carnegie Mellon University, the superior computer-science school that was home to CERT and the alma mater of several of the young programmers at his uncle's Chess.net. But Shawn didn't get in, and in the fall of 1998 he enrolled at Northeastern University in Boston. The introductory computer courses were below his level, so he partied, had a good time, and didn't learn much. It was far more interesting to be in w00w00, meeting people like Dug Song and Jordan Ritter.

——— ———

RITTER WAS BORN IN 1978 in Northridge, near Los Angeles, the only child of a heavy-drinking mother and a drug-addicted father. Two years later, as his parents divorced and his father disappeared, he moved with his mother near Dallas. She ran a jewelry business and dated affluent men in the hunting-and-horse-jumping set, including one she would marry. Ritter played baseball and soon placed into advanced programs in school. His natural father reappeared when Ritter was in elementary school and would fade in and out as he moved around and battled various drug habits. Ritter believes his father was a good man with problems who was unusually vague about his past: He thinks his father worked for a secret government agency in Vietnam. His father's brother, Donald Ritter, found a more mainstream outlet for a similar drive, serving as a U.S. congressman from Pennsylvania for fourteen years.

At twelve, Ritter moved to the first of a series of homes in Florida, near where his father was living in a double-wide trailer and running a gardening business. Ritter stayed in Florida through high school and would visit his father every few weeks. One Christmas, perhaps angry that her thirteen-year-old son had chosen that day to visit his father, Ritter's mother called and drunkenly told him not to come home. Ritter was crushed, but his father was overjoyed, seeming to have been waiting for just such an opportunity. Ritter moved in with his father, staying close until he left for college. The pair had a loving but rocky relationship that sometimes erupted in physical fights. To keep the peace, Ritter went to stay in his own trailer next door.

In high school, Ritter threw himself into music, playing multiple instruments in multiple bands. He also devoured computer languages and began programming everything from games to a graphic user interface. When it came time for college, scrounging enough money for just the application fees was a real problem. Like Shawn, Ritter wanted to go to Carnegie Mellon in Pittsburgh, which had exceptionally strong music as well as computer science, and he was admitted with a small scholarship. But his parents directed him to Lehigh University, which awarded him a much larger grant and was nearer to his successful uncle Don.

Ritter left for Lehigh in Bethlehem, Pennsylvania, at seventeen, taking his computer with him on the Greyhound bus. Soon he grew bored with the computer courses and decided to work one summer at the lab of Terrance Boult, eventually managing the systems for the man who was founding chairman of Lehigh's computer-science department. "He's my god," Ritter said. "He turned me on to [free computer operating system] Linux, using free software. He turned me loose and trusted me." If Ritter appreciated his mentor's trust, he didn't always keep his end of the bargain. One Friday night, after smoking a nontrivial amount of marijuana, Ritter used a cable modem to take down three thousand university computers in about six minutes.

During Ritter's freshman year, his father died after open-heart surgery. When Ritter returned to college, school seemed less vital. He began spending more time online in hacker collectives, especially a group called Asylum. Like the shifting allegiances of soldiers in Afghanistan or spies in Vienna between the wars, the communities of hackers and security professionals are surprisingly porous. Ritter wasn't atypical in protecting Lehigh's computer system by day and taking it or other networks down by night. While there are plenty of white-hat security workers and black-hat malicious hackers, who assault large networks like Yahoo! for the thrill of it, the majority of people are in the middle, gray hats who create their own ethics. The debates within groups and among them are legion, and those arguments can be complicated by the entrepreneurial aspirations of the practitioners. Hacking for its own sake can be educational and amusing, a power trip for a bored but clever teen. One way to turn that skill into extra income is to publicly reveal a hole in a system, then offer a "patch" to fix it. The demonstration of expertise can lead to security jobs. But the timing and the publicity of the security two-step can change everything. If you just tell the company of the problem, implicitly suggesting that it hire you to resolve it, the step can be interpreted as extortion. If you give the company notice of the problem, then post the problem and the patch—or worse, just the problem—in an open forum the very next day, you get wider recognition but can be criticized for spreading the tools of darkness.

At Asylum, Ritter set standard rules for the hackers that congregated there online: no gov, no mil, no money. In other words, don't hack government or military computers or try to profit from the activity. As they trolled for computers to infiltrate, Ritter and his band often looked first for systems that had already been compromised, leaving easier access. Sometimes they stumbled onto other hackers still on the scene, be it a university computer in Illinois or a corporate machine in Sweden. Mini-wars would erupt for mutual entertainment, as each hacker sought to boot the other out of the system. Once, after bouncing through his customary three proxies to disguise where he was working from, Ritter engaged in such a dogfight with an unknown adversary inside a big computer network in China.

As Ritter honed his skills, he was invited to join w00w00, where he took the nickname "Nocarrier," after the automated warning of a failed modem connection. At the time he was also working part-time at AMP, a computer firm not far from campus. He wasn't challenged much more there than he was at school, and Ritter woke up one day and realized he was getting fat. He quit college, moved to Chestnut Hill outside Boston, and took a job writing security software for Netect Inc., which had operations in the United States and Israel. Soon BindView bought Netect and its code, firing most of the employees other than Ritter. BindView left him alone to do research, giving him what he considered a dream job at the age of twenty. "I just hacked day and night," Ritter said. At Bind-View, he excelled: One of Ritter's published articles revealed what became known as the Palmetto Bug, a vulnerability afflicting 60 percent of the world's Internet servers. BindView was publicly credited for the find by CERT, the top computer-security organization in the United States.

⸺ ⸺

IF BOTH SHAWN FANNING AND RITTER had tough childhoods, financially and emotionally, Sean Parker's was a paragon of normality. Born in 1979,

Parker grew up in the northern Virginia suburb of Herndon. His father worked as an oceanographer and his mother as a media buyer for infomercials. Parker had two younger sisters and was a strong swimmer at an early age, before his asthma grew worse and he had to carry an inhaler from place to place. In school, Parker described himself as a "highly variable student," with multiple As and Fs, depending on whether he felt like concentrating on an assigned subject or on something else. At home, he fooled around with his father's Atari and began learning to program.

Parker was torn about what to do with his life. He wanted to write books, and he was interested in philosophy, "but I was known as a computer guy, and that usually won out." He learned the computer language Basic, a little C, and some Perl. That was enough to pass as geeky in the high school population, but his entrepreneurial skills developed even faster. Parker tried to start a newspaper at age twelve; later, he grew fixated on the idea that anyone could make money simply buying things wholesale and then marking them up. "I went on a mission to find wholesalers" of anything at all, he said, and found one in the eighth grade that would sell him model planes in bulk. He resold the planes for a couple hundred dollars in profit. Not long after that, Parker started his own Web-design shop, then a security firm he called Crosswalk.

"Most of my productive time was spent either doing computer stuff or entrepreneurial stuff," Parker said. Some of the unproductive time was spent on Internet Relay Chat, though he chatted far less often than Shawn and Ritter. On IRC, Parker met Shawn and future Napster engineer Jordy Mendelson, both of whom joined Parker's fledgling Crosswalk. Crosswalk was one of the security groups that published advisories on the "man-in-the-middle" hack, which redirects Web servers to spurious sites that grab visitor names and passwords. It wasn't a bad hack, but Parker knew he wasn't the sophisticated engineer that some around him were turning into. "I never was as hard-core a programmer as others," he said. Instead, Parker was a brilliant talker, using what knowledge he had to spin business ideas.

Those ideas always took precedence, as far back as a Fairfax County science fair for high school students. Parker spent the majority of his preparation figuring out what would get the most attention. "My mom thought I was wasting my time, but I needed to come up with something that was really hot," Parker said. "The Net was just breaking." At the time, many were writing about software "agents" that would sift through the Web and return information to users based on their interests. Parker figured he could capitalize on the hype, and he wrote two simple algorithms, one that searched the Web broadly and one that searched deeply, showing that the former worked best to get information to people with low-bandwidth connections. More important, Parker learned that the same broad-and-shallow approach worked best in conversation. Most people in America, investors included, aren't technical experts. They are like the science-fair judges were, appreciating someone who could synthesize concepts and explain in English how they fit together. Years later at Napster, Parker's e-mail signature would append to each message a similar conclusion from science-fiction writer Robert Heinlein: "Specialization is for insects." Parker won $5,000, the first science-fair winner in years who didn't attend a magnet school for science. He got job offers on the spot and plowed the prize money into Crosswalk. The team there "bit off more than we could chew," Parker said, and Crosswalk burned through a couple thousand dollars before folding. "It failed because we didn't have a cohesive organization. It was hard to keep a bunch of sixteen-year-olds all over the country motivated and focused." Parker later recovered the money by selling the domain name "Crosswalk.com" to a Christian portal.

One day in 1996, Parker attended a local job fair and walked up to a booth set up by Freeloader, at the time part of northern Virginia's pack of hot Internet companies led by America Online and smaller Internet service providers like UUNet. Freeloader sold programs that "pushed" content to computer users with techniques like those Parker had worked up for his science-fair project. He found Freeloader's most senior employee at the booth, Jamie Hamilton, and bragged that he could have knocked off a version of Freeloader's flagship program by himself. Hamilton was more amused than offended. He offered an internship, during which Parker wrote Perl scripts and generally distracted other employees, Hamilton recalled. Rob Hoadley, then Parker's office mate, remembered him as more interested in Linux and hacking than in doing what he was supposed to. "He was a smart kid," Hoadley said, but Parker was tagged with the nickname "Sprout" all summer.

As graduation neared, Parker told his parents that he wanted to work for a year before going to college. That wasn't true: Secretly, he planned to work just long enough to hatch another business. During his senior year of high school, Parker heard about an invitation-only day of interviews for experienced managers applying to UUNet, the largest Net access provider for businesses and one that enjoyed a good reputation for innovation. He called the company and pretended that he had an appointment and was on the way, but had lost the directions. When he got there in his standard intern garb, he saw thirty people in suits. He got a lot of dirty looks, but each of the several UUNet staffers he met wanted to hire him. Parker was "cocky but creative and amusing," said Jonathon Perrelli, who headed UUNet's hiring at the time. Parker came away with an entry-level job writing internal software applications.

As at Freeloader, Parker networked and made one key contact, this time Perrelli himself, a recent Virginia Tech graduate who had run a small business before joining UUNet. Perrelli took Parker under his wing, and they became good friends. Parker would bounce business concepts off Perrelli or throw out ideas about how to do things better at UUNet. Parker "had the unique ability to accomplish a hell of a lot in a very short period of time," Perrelli said. "So the rest of the time he envisioned the future of connected networks, and usually he did that while he escaped his cube to my office." Once when Parker wandered in, Perrelli was trying to figure out how to process online job applications better. Parker took over the whiteboard, started drawing with markers, and helped Perrelli come up with a system that allowed UUNet to hire three thousand people in less than two years. In return, Perrelli built up Parker's confidence and dressed him in promotional UUNet gear until Parker resembled a fully outfitted "UUgeek." Parker stayed a year and a half, until February 1999—the longest he would hold any job, including his assignment at Napster.

Perrelli also would come to play a part in the formative months of Napster. And through him, Parker met other technologists and sales professionals who would circle around the revolutionary start-up. Among them were brothers Scott and Mike Shinn, hotshot engineers and security experts who developed database technology that complemented what Napster would do. In his other networking efforts, Parker kept in touch with a customer whose computer server he had configured—Ben Lilienthal, who nearly became Napster's first real CEO.

While Parker spun visions of how the Web could work better and who could help him realize those dreams, his friend Shawn Fanning was experimenting with code and tossing around technical ideas in w00w00 a few hundred miles to the north. In his freshman year at college, Shawn's roommate complained that nearly every time he looked for an MP3, the link to the digital file was dead and the music was gone. There had to be some way to fix that, Shawn thought.

2

a big idea

BY THE FALL OF 1998, WHEN SHAWN FANNING STARTED AT Boston's Northeastern University, digital music was still very much hit or miss. MP3s had become the standard, growing in popularity largely because they weren't encumbered by electronic straitjackets on their use. Many services offered lists of songs in the format, including MP3.com, MP3.lycos.com, and Scour.com. But more than half the time, the electronic links to those songs were broken—the song was no longer there. Other sites required passwords or knowledge of File Transfer Protocol commands for transmitting files. It was hardly worth the effort to try. "The index would become out of date because the indexes were updated infrequently," Shawn would testify. "I began thinking about ways to solve the reliability problems."

Shawn was coming at the issue in the same way that many Internet innovators had come at earlier roadblocks. The entire point of the World

Wide Web had been to make information available to people using whatever connections and computers they had, whenever they had them. "The system should not constrain the user; a person should be able to link with equal ease to any document wherever it happened to be stored," wrote Tim Berners-Lee, the Web's inventor. "The basic revelation was that one information space could include them all, giving huge power and consistency." When Berners-Lee was doing his pioneering work, the content available was static. Now content was changing more often, and Shawn was about to try an ambitious method to help the system's users catch up to it.

Digital music on computers had gotten off to a slow start, largely because narrow-band connections meant that it took too long to download anything containing as much data as a song. Some of the biggest early consumers were fans of the Grateful Dead, whose members had realized in the late 1960s that permitting bootlegs of concerts would help their paying fan base grow. (Dead lyricist John Perry Barlow, a prep-school friend of the band's guitarist Bob Weir, would later cofound the Electronic Frontier Foundation, which defended other music-sharing services in court, but not Napster.)

College students drove many of the next advances in the spread of digital music, including a turning point at the University of California, Santa Cruz. It was there in 1993 that Rob Lord and Jeff Patterson, two computer- and information-science majors and full-time music fans, tried various methods for posting songs from Patterson's band, the Ugly Mugs, to Internet newsgroups. The band spent $100 on software to compress the music using MP2 technology, the best then available. And they steered potential listeners to a free MP2 player, one made by a firm called Xing Technologies. They got a few enthusiastic e-mails asking for more music. The really exciting thing for Patterson was that some of the messages came from places like Turkey and Russia, where it was hard to get Western music.

Within a month, Lord and Patterson started what they dubbed the Internet Underground Music Archive. The idea was that IUMA, with the permission of the artists, would make available alternative music that wasn't getting mass distribution. With only limited compression from the MP2 format and slow dial-up modems, it could take half an hour to download a three-minute song. But IUMA drew fans nonetheless. Lord, who would later cross paths with Napster, took a very different approach from the one that Shawn would take. The first songs he encoded to the MP2 format, rare tracks by the Durutti Column and the Residents, he kept in his computer for his own use. In a decision that would come to appear quaint, and still later would appear to have been the right idea after all, Lord didn't distribute those songs over the newsgroups for the simple reason that he didn't have permission from the copyright holders. IUMA cadged free equipment from Sun Microsystems Inc. and Silicon Graphics Inc. and hired people from the Santa Cruz music scene, who by 1994 convinced other bands to pay in order to post their music.

When a newspaper article about IUMA appeared that year, the record labels took note. Yet despite some internal debate, they did little to encourage the new technology—or to fight it, since MP2s could also spread music without the copyright owner's permission. Things changed over the next three years. Connections to the Internet got faster. The World Wide Web and the Netscape browser spread at fantastic rates, making it much easier for people to find what they were looking for. And in Germany, research efforts to improve video-compression technology had spun off a vastly improved audio-compression technique. After approval by the International Standards Organization, ISO-MPEG Audio Layer-3 emerged, soon to be better known as MP3. The source code was made available, so that anyone could distribute the tools for encoding music to the new format. By eliminating data used to convey silences, the MP3 technique fit much more sound into many fewer bits, making transmission and storage much easier. And the developers hadn't bothered to include any system for locking the data to prevent copying.

The software for opening and playing such files on computers got better too, especially one called Winamp, cobbled together in 1997 by a nineteen-year-old college dropout in Sedona, Arizona, named Justin Frankel. A geek's geek, Frankel gave Winamp away and asked for a minimal payment on the honor system if the users liked it, a process for software known as shareware. Winamp wasn't the first MP3 player, but it brought together a number of features that quickly established it as the most popular. Winamp let users make the player look like whatever they wanted, and it could be customized easily to work with other programs.

Rob Lord left IUMA to join a music firm called N2K, which published a magazine, sold compact discs online, and put up websites for Madonna and other rock stars. As he kept a close eye on the MP3 scene, Lord made it one of his top priorities to get N2K into some kind of alliance with Frankel's tiny company, Nullsoft Inc. "I was kind of shrugged off" by N2K executives, Lord said. So he asked Frankel if he could join Nullsoft instead. "He said he wasn't very interested in turning Nullsoft into a [serious] business, but that he would listen to ideas." Lord had several. How about putting a picture of the product on the website? How about selling ads? Ads, Frankel mused. Okay, see what you can do. Lord went to ArtistDirect, another Web music retailer, and showed the company the immense traffic Nullsoft was getting to its site as people downloaded Winamp and other software. Lord returned to Frankel with a six-month advertising contract from ArtistDirect and a check for $300,000. A surprised Frankel asked his parents what to do. His father recruited an acquaintance as a business-development man and teamed him with Lord to write a plan. They returned with a white paper predicting that if Frankel continued on his own, he could build a company worth $1 million. With help, they said, it could be worth tens of millions.

Nullsoft hired both men. The company stayed very small, with five or six people working in separate offices in Sedona and communicating over IRC. They arranged advertising for the site and immediately began striking deals, including one to incorporate a modified browser that allowed Winamp users to buy CDs from Amazon. And they made new versions of Winamp compatible with the industry's secure digital formats as soon as they became available. "I'm not about piracy," Lord said. He even called the Recording Industry Association of America as a courtesy, explaining what they were doing and giving his phone number in case the organization had any questions.

The RIAA didn't have any grounds to go after Nullsoft, which was distributing a product that could be used legally or illegally. But the trade group certainly didn't like what was happening. The spread of the technology made it a simple matter for someone to buy a CD legally, rip it into an MP3 format, and post it for others to download. David Weekly, a Stanford University student, did just that—a lot—until Geffen Records executives complained and university network administrators, already upset at the massive amount of bandwidth that Weekly's visitors were consuming, shut him down.

Musicians were divided from the beginning. Unknown acts saw the MP3 phenomenon as a way to spread their music. Brand-name acts, which had more to lose through piracy, were naturally more conservative. But even some of them wanted to release the occasional track digitally, often having to fight their labels for the right to do so. When they won, the effects could be huge, as Michael Robertson found after he opened the website MP3.com in the fall of 1997. Robertson knew almost nothing about music, he had no technology of his own, and his business background was at best undistinguished. But he knew college kids were constantly searching for MP3s on the Internet. Robertson looked up the man who owned the domain name MP3.com, which the man had picked because of his initials, and bought it for $1,000. Robertson paid another $2,500, plus $500 a month, to take over the content of a Netherlands site that offered a guide to related software available for sale.

The day that Robertson's version of the site went up with just the software guide on it, he got ten thousand Web visits and a call from someone who wanted to advertise. "We didn't know anyone. We didn't even know, like, one person in a band," Robertson said. Instead, he displayed articles about MP3s, which in the early days he had to write himself, and posted links to where MP3s could be found. Small bands sent in clips, usually of singles, in hopes of generating sales of full CDs. Some big-name acts followed suit, including Alanis Morissette, who accepted pre-IPO shares in MP3.com and the firm's sponsorship of a tour supporting her second album.

One of the clearest displays of the power of MP3s in promoting acts would come in 1999, with Tom Petty's CD *Echo*. Trying to build buzz for his mature client among the younger set, Petty manager Tony Dimitriades spread the word that one song would be available as a free download at MP3.com. He had neglected to check with the singer's Warner Brothers label, which promptly chewed him out. But Warner allowed him to keep the song up for one day. And during that day, the single "Free Girl Now" was downloaded 156,992 times. There is no way of knowing how many of those downloads were later copied and spread to others; what is clear is that the gimmick helped *Echo* debut in the Top Ten. But even that would not warm the industry's heart to any kind of digital distribution. "They won't cede control," complained Thomas Dolby Robertson, of "She Blinded Me with Science" fame, who is a serious music technologist. "Right now, we have a great system for them and one that screws the artist."

——— ———

SHAWN FANNING'S BIG INSIGHT, like his instruction, came from his time on Internet Relay Chat. Similarly to the more prevalent instant messaging of today, IRC knows who is on a channel at any time. It has, in the jargon of the industry, "presence awareness." Search engines, on the other hand, may scan the Web only daily or weekly. Especially if the search results turn up a private person's files, instead of those controlled by a business, the content on the site may well have changed or be unavailable. "My idea was to have a real-time index that reflects all sites that are up and available to others on the network at that moment," Shawn said. The easiest way to accomplish this was to have a central computer server, to which everyone would connect. "Anyone who disconnected from the server would be immediately dropped from our index," he said.

In a way, the core of the Napster system was an index of other indexes, the lists of music files people kept in folders on their own machines. Like a telephone switchboard operator in the old days, the Napster system would take an inquiry for a specific song from someone, find another person who had a matching offering, connect the two, and then hang up to let them finish the transaction in private.

Shawn ran his idea past a few adults, who gave him various reasons why it wouldn't work. Too complicated, they said. Shawn listened attentively, weighed their arguments, and didn't buy any of them. "Somebody would say something negative about it, and some of that stuff really got to me at first. I definitely used that to motivate me," Shawn said. He believed from the first that Napster could be very important. Back then, he didn't worry much about legal issues, reasoning that individual users were taking responsibility for offering up every song. Shawn started by designing the search engine to scan the lists of offerings. Then he wrote a draft of the software that would run the server that connected everyone. Finally he turned to the "client," the application that the user would see.

"I wanted to make this software work, and to prove my concept for file sharing on the Internet," Shawn said.

The only real problem was that Shawn had never written a program to run on Windows, the computer system used by just about everybody. So he started cramming Windows the way his fellow students were cramming for exams, drinking caffeine-laden soft drinks by the gallon and banging away on his laptop. It took just a few weeks, and the first rough version of Napster was done.

The most elegant sociological element of what would grow to eighty-five thousand lines of code was that Napster both gave and took away. If you used the system to look for a song and then began downloading, the system would open your MP3 files to others at the same time unless you actively blocked it from doing so. Like magic, the more people who were seeking music, the more music would become available.

Another important innovation was the system architecture. Most huge stores of information are housed on databases controlled by a single computer server. While people can get access to that information from different places, the data is all mashed into one giant machine. With Napster, such a server would have been overwhelmed in minutes by all the space required for MP3s. Shawn wanted Napster to work more like such search engines as Google or AltaVista. Those search engines show you data anywhere on the Web that is reachable and that they can find, but they leave the data where it lies for you to retrieve. That meant Napster required central servers only to list who had possession of what, not to store the actual songs. At the peak in 2001, that would mean about 150 servers—not a number well into the thousands, affordable only by the biggest corporations.

From very early on, Shawn turned for help to his more experienced comrades on IRC. "I could always ask them a question about protocol design or just shoot a question to the channel and have somebody answer it. I wouldn't have been able to write Napster without IRC and without these groups of people," Shawn said. "The amount of time it would have taken me to find answers in books or find the resources I needed, I would never have finished it on time. I definitely owe it to a lot of people."

Most of those people were on w00w00, the IRC channel founded in 1998 by Matt Conover, the sixteen-year-old hacker using the handle

Shok. Among Conover's real jobs were stints at the RSI security firm and later, aided by Jordan Ritter, at BindView. A mix of white-, black-, and gray-hatted hackers, w00w00 kept its IRC conversations limited to members. But the group also maintained a public website. There it published some exploits and patches on a range of systems. In June 1999, the word "w00w00" was one of the top twenty most-searched-for terms on the Internet search engine Google. (Google was more of a search engine for Internet experts at the time, only later developing a mainstream following.)

Shawn was a regular on w00w00, and so was Ritter. Ritter was on the channel in early 1999 when the hacker he knew as Napster sent him and the others an application, telling them to check it out. It was the first version of the program, and Ritter wasn't blown away. "What are you going to do with it?" he typed. "Is it free?" The reactions of others in the channel varied. Seth McGann, known as Minus, was amazed. "I was pretty impressed. But a lot of people I showed it to didn't really get it," he said.

Members of w00w00 often traded pieces of code. They also swapped security exploits and the patches that would fix them, exchanged digital pictures of their girlfriends, and generally gave each other a hard time. While they made fun of it, the group frequently used the "elite" slang of IRC-speak, designed in part to outwit security programs that search for red-flag words like "hacker" but kept alive mostly because of the sense of in-group cool it promoted. As "halflife" once opined to the group: "napster is a darks1de mp3 warez hqr." "Warez" refers to pirated software: Thus, "Napster is a dark-side MP3 pirated software hacker."

— —

SHAWN KEPT W00W00 APPRISED of what he was doing, eventually sending out an improved "beta" version of his software every few days. Ritter and other senior w00w00 members like Dug Song helped by giving advice on the state of the art and steering Shawn to where he could learn more. Song, for example, pointed Shawn to prior work on ad hoc networking and routing. "He took it and ran with it," Song said. The Napster program came to dominate the w00w00 discussion after each improvement, so much so that a new "Napster" IRC channel launched with a handful of people from the w00w00 channel. Conover initially disapproved of the way others in his group had glommed onto Napster. "I was opposed to it," he said. "To me, it was leeching off the success of a member. It bothered me at the time." But he had no idea how important the program was going to be. If he had realized it then, Conover admitted later, he would have been right there debugging the code with the rest of them. "I didn't want to sell out cheap," he said. "Now I regret it."

McGann was one of the earliest testers of the beta version of Napster. At one point, he, Shawn, and two other people were the only ones using the program. The system was poorly set up back then, using no database software to house the lists of songs. It was buggy and would freeze up for no apparent reason. But McGann, who had little patience for tracking down MP3s on IRC channels, realized he still could triple his music collection in weeks. While he was testing the system, he sent Shawn a private e-mail. "Do you realize that this is going to change everything?" he wrote. "Yeah, I know," Shawn replied. McGann gave Shawn some sample code for recognizing songs by electronic tags. And he copied the system for his roommate, a nonhacker who couldn't believe his good fortune. It was just so easy to use, the roommate told others. And the smooth give-and-take of music could be almost hypnotic. The word kept spreading, and others logged on before Shawn's system was ready for them.

━ ━

OUTSIDE OF THE w00w00 CIRCLE, Shawn was chatting about his invention with his old friend Sean Parker on another IRC channel called "dweebs." And Parker, being Parker, immediately started thinking about how to make a business out of it, regardless of the fact that the code was still buggy. Shawn "had very little business acumen," Parker said. "He just wanted to code it." Parker had a point: With more and more people coming aboard, the system needed money for more servers.

Back in Boston, Ritter was getting more interested in Shawn's code from another angle. He peppered Shawn's e-mail address with one-line questions about the code. Finally, Shawn showed him what he had written. There were some obvious bugs, which Ritter fixed, and the programming was raw. Among other things, it was written in C++ with unnecessary complexity, because it didn't take full advantage of that language's advances over the more rudimentary C language, which Shawn understood better.

The server side of the program was another problem. W00w00's Evan Brewer managed the server system at first, but he loaded it up with multiple security programs. That would have made hacking the system harder, but it ate up memory and slowed the server to a crawl. After some harassment by Ritter, in late June Shawn turned control of the server over to him. Ritter wasn't getting paid anything, but he was expected to fix the system when it crashed, and he did. He was more interested in the program than the music; he doesn't remember what song he searched for first. Maybe something by Steely Dan.

Because the music itself was stored on client computers, Napster needed far fewer servers than it otherwise would. But the servers still had to route traffic and handle indexing and other complex functions. Ritter's solutions were elegant, according to Scott Shinn, the engineer Parker had met through Jonathon Perrelli at UUNet. "Shawn had the brilliant idea and prototyped it in a way that was practical," said Shinn, who had helped put the White House and the Securities and Exchange Commission online and held senior technical positions at many firms, including Cisco Systems Inc. "He was able to put it together and put it in front of his little sisters and his grandmother and they would be able to use it. Jordan took what Shawn had put together and made it scale up to five hundred thousand users. Those are numbers AOL has to compete with, and AOL needs acres of equipment. Jordan did some really brilliant stuff."

Shawn did some of the coding in his dorm at Northeastern during the week, then went full steam at his uncle's office in Hull on the weekends. He kept himself awake as long as possible to finish one piece or another of the Napster puzzle. One of the biggest challenges was an early attempt to link the multiple servers together, so that people could look for music, or each other, no matter which piece of the system they had signed onto. Shawn grew obsessed with figuring out how to do this, and he took advantage of a conveniently stored case of the ultracaffeinated soft drink Red Bull. (Ritter had another method for keeping the intense concentration needed for long stretches of programming: He took Ritalin, usually prescribed for children with attention deficit disorder.)

"We didn't have any money, and we didn't have Coke left, and I was literally trying to finish this," Shawn said. "And I looked at the Red Bull, and I'm like, 'It has caffeine in it!' I literally went through most of a case that time, and I was up two or three days. . . . The strange thing about Red Bull is that it has this really weird ability, and it's not just the caffeine, to keep you really sharp and focused, even though you've been up for two or three days. Usually [on caffeine] you get hazy and you're wired but you're tired, mentally not functioning. But [on Red Bull] you can focus, and you can think logically and clearly. You get tired, but usually it just gets you tired to the point where you're not likely to get distracted. You're just kind of a zombie, but you can focus and think, and it helped to do massive amounts of programming where I had thought of the design before, and I just had to do the programming." Red Bull abuse also has side effects, Shawn learned. "By the end of it, I called the cops because there was a car across the street the second night and I thought it was going to do something bad." Not people in the car, mind you, or even the people who owned the car, wherever they were—the car itself. "I was slightly hallucinating by then," Shawn said. "I remember calling the cops, and they said something about it not being in their jurisdiction, call somebody else. And then I realized I was kind of going crazy."

Shawn often worked alone, leaving fewer astonished witnesses to his intensity. In something that would seem strange to anyone but an IRC devotee, he never even met Ritter in person for two months after Ritter joined Shawn's cause, though they lived just a few miles apart. Finally, after an August evening of hitting parties, Shawn came by Ritter's apartment. Shawn's hacker friend, who would later join Napster, had been drinking too much to be deemed presentable, and Shawn made him wait in the car as he went upstairs. Shawn and Ritter chatted about the program, and Shawn said he would be moving west, to start the business. He asked Ritter to come. "How do I know this is real," Ritter thought. "Who is the management team? How are we going to sell it?" He was skeptical about other things as well, and he decided not to chuck his job and adult life. "I had lots of issues. He didn't really have answers." But Shawn's enthusiasm was boundless. "It's going to be fucking huge," he told Ritter.

3

birth of a business

JOHN FANNING TOOK TO BUSINESS EARLY, A BLUE-COLLAR
Sean Parker with more street sense and less polish. He bears little physical resemblance to his nephew, having smaller eyes, thinning brown hair,
and a bantamlike forward lean to his posture. Fanning graduated from a
vocational high school in Hanover, Massachusetts, in 1982 and took
courses at Boston College beginning later that year. He continued off and
on for eight years without graduating. Fanning worked in construction
and studied to be a contractor. His stint at Boston-based Fidelity Investments looked better on his résumé. Fanning said through an attorney that
he worked there as a "senior trader" handling high-risk investments and
also spent time in the "telecommunications group," which the lawyer said
dealt with holdings in the telecommunications industry. Fidelity said
something different. According to spokesman Vin Loporchio, Fanning

worked there two years with the title of national console representative, from which position he redirected incoming calls. Console representatives do not make trades: "They are responsible for watching customer call volume and routing customer calls appropriately," Loporchio said.

Wanting to run his own firm, Fanning was still in his twenties when he inquired about the struggling computer business of a man he met playing squash at Boston's University Club. Around 1990, Fanning bought Ed Walter's Cambridge Automation on credit. The company took in big general-purpose computers from manufacturers and resold them to laboratories and other customers. But the business models were changing then, and large computer makers started making more of their sales directly. Under Fanning, Cambridge Automation limped on for two more years. Fanning spent much of his time there trying to strike new deals with creditors, from the phone company to the computer suppliers that were the firm's lifeblood. When some businesses demanded their money, Fanning would call up and sound outraged, insisting on speaking with superior after superior until the creditor gave up and offered new terms.

"He learned how to look the big boys in the eye and not blink," said company manager Jack Martin. Fanning's style of running the company was unorthodox. "John was crazy," Martin said. "He would call a meeting for 6 A.M. on a Sunday, because that way he could tell who gave a damn." Martin brought in a friend, Jack Nevil, as controller of the company, a sensitive position given the firm's precarious finances. Nevil, who would also play a key role in Fanning's next venture, had made a lot of money in real-estate deals. But his history still left something to be desired. In 1985, for example, Nevil had been fired after three years as treasurer of Aunyx Corp., where the majority owner accused him of spending company money for a Cadillac used by Nevil's family and other conflicts of interest. He sued for wrongful termination. "Until the termination of his employment by Aunyx, Nevil engaged in a pattern of breaching his fiduciary duties," the company said in Nevil's lawsuit, which was dismissed by agreement in 1987.

That dispute was just a taste of things to come. In 1989, some of Nevil's real-estate deals went bad and resulted in massive defaults to lender Rockland Trust Co. Rockland won a judgment of more than $7 million against Nevil personally and collected more than $5 million from one of his codefendants.

At Cambridge Automation, Fanning, Martin, and Nevil weren't able to keep things going for long. Key supplier Unisys ultimately sued the company, winning a still-unpaid $700,000 judgment. The company dissolved without paying off the purchase loan, according to Walter. Yet even as the business was sinking, Fanning carried himself like a successful sales executive, dressing in good suits and driving expensive cars. "He took over a tiny company, and it continued to fail," said Duncan Audette, a Cambridge employee. "I didn't think he had much ability as a manager, but he liked to appear wealthy and flashy." Fanning also remembered his allies, even Nevil.

FANNING'S NEXT TRY AT BUSINESS success began with his love of chess, a game that drew him and many others into computers. Just like math and music, chess reaches some intuitively analytical part of the brain. All three areas have turned out child prodigies for generations. As access to computers spread, prodigies began showing up in that field as well. With such deep ties between chess and computers, chess players became rapid adopters of the Internet as a means for matching wits remotely.

Chess enthusiasts designed a computer server for those seeking fellow players. The free server moved from university to university until it arrived at Carnegie Mellon in the early 1990s with about fifty people logged in at any one time, enough to find a partner of roughly equal strength. One regular player was a CMU computer-science professor named Danny Sleator. Sleator enjoyed the system, but a number of bugs in it bothered him. And he didn't like the time clock, which turned some late-developing games into mad rushes at the end. He preferred a mechanism that gave each player a bit more time based on the number of moves they had made already. Sleator asked the people running the system if he could tinker with the system, and they agreed. In 1995, as the Web's popularity was increasing, Sleator decided to try to make some money back from his improvements. With his wife and two other online chess players, he formed Sleator Games Inc.

If he had it to do over again, Sleator said, he would have left the old, buggier version of what was called the Internet Chess Server up and running for anyone to play for free. Instead, he announced that anyone already on the system would have six more months for free, then have to pay the same $49 a year he was going to charge new players. At the time, very few sites charged for anything on the Internet, and some CMU students were outraged. They cobbled together another system, calling it the Free Internet Chess Server, and in the spirit of the open-source movement, they posted their code to the Web for anyone else to modify for their own systems. That effort took half a year. By then, Sleator's system had critical mass and could advertise that it had more players, better customer service, and stronger features than the free alternative. Sleator hired students from time to time, and others volunteered to help administer the system, which did business as the Internet Chess Club, or ICC. One of the helpers was Dmitry Dakhnovsky, an online chess player from a California high school whom Sleator had recommended for admission to the university.

John Fanning used the ICC service heavily and played at an above-average level. Today he has a U.S. Chess Federation rating of 1813, making him a Class A player in the federation's traditional rankings: That's better than Classes E through B but shy of Expert and Master. On the system, Fanning struck up a relationship with another of Sleator's players, the emotional and brilliant Roman Dzindzichashvili, who had twice shared the U.S. championship. Dzindzichashvili earned a small amount for playing games and giving commentary on Sleator's system. Fanning helped Dzindzichashvili produce a series of instructional videotapes on chess strategy, and he began looking for a place to sell them. According to e-mails from Fanning, in early 1995 he offered to buy Sleator's company for $50,000 plus future royalties. Sleator turned him down.

In December of that year, Fanning asked how he could advertise Dzindzichashvili's tapes on Sleator's system, and Sleator's wife and partner offered a package for $500 that would include a mass e-mail to members of the ICC. (Now known as ChessClub.com, Sleator's system is the most popular chess site on the Web.) Fanning didn't respond, Sleator said. He had figured out a way to get the e-mail addresses of the club's members on his own, and Fanning sent them all offers to buy the videotapes directly. Sleator sent Fanning a bill for the spam, which he didn't pay, and the argument escalated until the company kicked Fanning off the service and refunded the rest of his membership fee.

That got Fanning mad. He hired Dzindzichashvili and Dakhnovsky, Sleator's volunteer, who in turn helped Fanning recruit other Carnegie Mellon students, including Ali Aydar, who was working on the Free Internet Chess Server. The team used the code from the free project to start a rival service for Fanning, which he named Chess.net. And Fanning didn't stop there. In 1996, he filed a lawsuit against Sleator Games in Massachusetts, claiming that the firm had improperly barred him from advertising and thereby cost Chess.net $248,000 in potential profits. At first read, the suit appeared ridiculous. But it allowed Fanning to capitalize on resentment among chess players who had to pay to play on Sleator's network. Chess.net posted inflammatory statements like this one on its site: "Chess.net was started by International Chess Grandmaster Roman Dzindzichashvili . . . with the help of the company that produces Roman's instructional chess videos. . . . Roman was forced to do this by ICC, who prevented Roman from selling his video tapes on ICC." As the rhetoric flew in chess chat rooms and on bulletin boards, Fanning built a following by allowing free games and charging only for additional services. And in the legal process known as discovery, Fanning sought to learn all of ICC's business partners, a move that struck Sleator as a bid to obtain "a list of people they should contact if they want to run a chess server." The sniping and bad blood continued as the lawsuit dragged on until 1999, when Fanning's lawyers won court permission to abandon it: They told the judge that their client owed them $94,341.82 in legal bills.

For Chess.net, Fanning used a core of Carnegie Mellon students and graduates, including Dakhnovsky, Brian McBarron, Matt Ramme, and Aydar, a son of Turkish immigrants who was swayed by Fanning's claimed business connections. Because Fanning had paid Dakhnovsky so little for Chess.net work while he was finishing college, Dakhnovsky demanded an unusual price to move to Boston: a new BMW Z3. Much to his surprise, Fanning called his bluff and agreed. Dakhnovsky flew to Boston, and the two men picked one out. Fanning put an $8,000 down payment on the $48,000 car. The paperwork on the sale listed two buyers: Chess.net parent Multimedia Engineering Corp. and Dakhnovsky. But only Dakhnovsky's signature appeared.

Fanning and his young charges raised $500,000 in seed funding from a Salomon Brothers executive and others. The employees got small equity stakes, with Fanning keeping majority control of Multimedia Engineering. That was "an invitation to disaster," McBarron said. "He doesn't really inspire trust." Ramme said that the team was too inexperienced in business to know better and had initially been overly influenced by what they thought was Fanning's past business success. "We were working for free, essentially," Ramme said. Fanning "stopped talking to me because I was the least tolerant of his bullshitting." Ramme was the first to leave. When Dakhnovsky also quit, he left the new car behind, and Fanning gave it to Shawn. But Fanning also stopped making payments on the car, and the financing company came after Dakhnovsky, tarring his credit record to this day. After about a year, the car was repossessed.

Fanning was committed to the chess company, and he did some things right. The technical system was solid, Fanning hired other world-class chess experts, and he made a deal for referrals from America Online that brought in thousands of new players. The internal management was another story. The programmers soon discovered that the office rent, other bills, and even paychecks were going unpaid. Aydar in particular confronted Fanning about his concerns over where the money was going. "Obviously, the money was misspent," Dakhnovsky said. Fanning reassured the programmers that a good man was handling the books—none other than Jack Nevil of Cambridge Automation, Aunyx, and the $7 million judgment. Aydar wasn't impressed, especially after he went late one night with Fanning to bail Nevil out of the local jail.

Fanning also mixed his personal and business affairs. As late as August 2000, a lumber-supply company won a $1,934 default judgment against John Fanning in small-claims court after "MM Engineering" failed to pay what it owed. The judgment still hadn't been paid nearly a year later, according to lumber-firm president Bill Mischel. And billing records from 1997 show thousands of dollars flowing back and forth between Multimedia Engineering and the personal credit card of Fanning's wife, Coreen Kraysler, a portfolio manager at Independence Investment in Boston, shortly before the card was revoked.

The problem with Kraysler's credit card was unusual: Normally, Fanning insulated his wife from his business issues. The Hull condominium where they lived and the house he was rebuilding at 2 Summit Avenue were both in Kraysler's name, protecting the properties from any debt collectors going after him. Whoever the owner of record, the house was a source of pride for Fanning. The mansion overlooking the Atlantic was condemned when Kraysler bought it for $450,000 in 1996. Fanning threw himself into a dramatic overhaul of the wood-frame Victorian. By 2002, it had six bedrooms and four bathrooms and was valued by tax officials at $1.4 million.

But as Fanning's home improved, his business declined. The last straw at Chess.net came when Aydar demanded to see the books. Fanning took him to Nevil's home, and the records were in shambles. Aydar found suspicious checks from Multimedia accounts to building-supply firms and unexplained women. And the living conditions were so foul that each of the instructional chess videotapes Nevil was storing for shipment had a putrid smell to it. Only then did Fanning fire Nevil. The financial problems drove several employees away from Chess.net, including a young friend of Shawn's named Tarek Loubani. "I never learned so much about dealing with creditors" as then, Loubani said.

Numerous lawsuits from the late 1990s show that Fanning's money troubles extended well beyond Chess.net. In mid-1999, the year of Napster's birth, a court entered a default judgment against him over a $17,529 bank debt. Later that year, he lost another judgment for $26,759 owed to collection agency Creditrust. The first debt would prove enough to deter the first venture-capital firm that Napster courted, Draper Atlantic. And Fanning's wife was not immune. Her condominium complex sued her in April 1999 for unpaid fees over the unit she bought in 1988. That case was settled the following year. More serious was the 1998 collection case filed by Kraysler's credit-card company for more than $13,000. In April 1999, Household Bank of Nevada won a default judgment against Kraysler for the full amount.

In the summer of 2001, well after Fanning had come into money by selling shares in Napster, he finally responded to the two large judgments against him. But rather than simply pay off the debts, he fought back like a wolverine. Fanning hired lawyers who filed motions to vacate the judgments on the grounds that the creditors had his address wrong and hadn't served him with the paperwork. Fanning even countersued Creditrust for a host of alleged wrongdoing, including violations of credit-collection statutes and infliction of "emotional distress."

It was a stretch for Creditrust to agree that since Fanning had never been served, he didn't officially know about the suit against him. The firm had gone so far as to enlist the Plymouth County Sheriff's Department to hunt Fanning down and bring him to court. Normally when the Plymouth sheriff gets such a request, his department simply sends out a letter. That's almost always all it takes to get the defendant to appear in court when he or she is supposed to. Sometimes it takes a phone call. On a very few occasions, the deputies have to go out and look for someone in order to make a form of civil arrest. With Fanning, deputies would have to go out on foot—not once or twice, but a total of eight times, according to Plymouth sheriff's spokesman Mike Seele, all without success. "The guy was pretty good at hiding. We put a lot of shoe leather and effort into that guy," Seele said. A frustrated deputy reported to the Creditrust lawyer that he had done everything he could. "Defendant will not come into court," he wrote.

When Fanning's attorney filed the motion to vacate the judgment, the Creditrust lawyer was beside himself. Obviously Fanning knew about the case, as demonstrated not only by his efforts to dodge the sheriff but by the Creditrust lawyer's conversations with Fanning's lawyer. Nevertheless, without a proper service of the documents, Fanning was able to get the judgment vacated and start the suit over from the beginning. The other credit judgment was also vacated, leaving it to that creditor to file suit again. Neither case had been resolved by the time of this writing.

Fanning responded in a more conciliatory manner to the $13,000 judgment against his wife, whose wages were nearly garnisheed by her employer. In that suit, Fanning interceded with the bank and negotiated a deal. On September 30, 1999, a month after he raised the first outside investment in Napster and sold some of his shares, Fanning sent a check for $5,685 to the bank to fulfill the compromise settlement terms, and the case was dismissed.

——— ———

FANNING'S WILLINGNESS TO MIX IT UP with opponents didn't stop at the courthouse steps. "I'm a fighter," he told one interviewer. "I don't let people push me around." In January 1999, Fanning was charged with assault and battery with a deadly weapon—his shoes—after he kicked and punched the maintenance man at his condominium complex on the morning of December 31, 1998. The two men had a history of animosity over a junked convertible in the parking lot, which maintenance worker Robert Lynch said he had asked Fanning to move. On this morning, Lynch said he found a Christmas tree in Fanning's stairwell and a "nature trail" of pine needles. He knocked on Fanning's door, which Fanning opened and then closed without a word, Lynch said. Angered by the reaction, Lynch unwisely dragged the discarded tree out into the parking lot and put it on top of Fanning's old convertible.

Later that day, Lynch encountered Fanning and his brother David, and they beat him badly, according to the district attorney. "They seriously attacked me. John Fanning kicked me in the face," Lynch said. "They threw me into the wall. They got me really good." His cheek was fractured and the area around his eyes cut up. He needed stitches in two places and was laid up for a week, Lynch told the judge in the case. Lynch was charged with malicious destruction of property for damaging Fanning's old car but wasn't ordered to make any restitution. After he finished three months of pretrial probation, the charge against him was dismissed.

The criminal proceedings against the Fanning brothers continued for more than three years. After the beating, John Fanning moved out of the sixty-six-unit complex and into the big house on Summit Avenue. His brother David moved into Fanning's old apartment and was later charged with a new count, intimidating a witness, after he allegedly threatened Lynch and warned him to drop the case. "He came up to my car and punched on the window and tried to get in," Lynch said at a court hearing. Since all sides had been ordered to stay away from each other, Lynch couldn't roam the building and therefore lost his job, he told the judge. David Fanning, who like his brother had been charged with assault and battery with a deadly weapon, pleaded no contest to the reduced charge of assault and battery and was sentenced to two years' probation in February 2002.

John Fanning made out much better. The district attorney pushed for the same result his brother received—a no-contest plea and formal probation. But Fanning's lawyer stressed his client's business prowess and his growing family. After noting the existence of related civil lawsuits, the lawyer argued against a no-contest plea. "There are serious and collateral consequences to Mr. Fanning if Mr. Fanning were to admit to sufficient facts or be found guilty of any charges," he said. Instead, he asked the judge to impose a short pretrial probation, like that Lynch had been ordered to serve. Assuming no further problems, that would mean the charge against John Fanning would eventually be dismissed. With that, the lawyer said, "this matter can be concluded in the criminal courtroom, and Mr. Lynch can have his day in a civil session, if that's his desire." Over the objections of the prosecutor and Lynch, the Hingham judge agreed. John Fanning received six months of pretrial probation beginning in February 2002.

Six months later, the charge was dropped. But that didn't end the matter. Lynch was pursuing a suit he filed in late 2001 against Fanning, his brother, and Fanning's wife, who owns the $200,000 apartment. (Fanning has countersued for assault, trespass, and defamation.) And the condo complex workers' compensation insurer sued John and David Fanning for reimbursement of Lynch's $6,000 in medical bills and $45,000 in lost wages stemming from the assault. (Fanning countersued the insurer as well, claiming invasion of privacy and intentional infliction of emotional distress.)

All told, John Fanning's background certainly marks him as unusual for a leader of a firm on the cutting edge of technological innovation. He had the chance to become one only because of the happenstance of his blood tie to Shawn. But there is something deeper at work here as well. In its earliest days, the Internet was designed by nonprofit researchers working in the government and at universities. One of the most important differences between their work and what had gone on before, at such change-resistant places as the telephone monopoly, arose from the fact that the Internet's architects had no idea what the ultimate use of their creation would be and didn't try to direct that evolution. Instead, they designed it to carry almost any sort of traffic, without discrimination among different sorts of data. Build an application that runs on your computer, and it will work across the wires of the Net. Later, the World Wide Web itself could have been patented by Tim Berners-Lee. But Berners-Lee wasn't interested in getting rich. He just thought it would be a good idea if other people adopted his designs and communication improved, and he made it easy and free for them to do so.

Stanford law professor Lawrence Lessig and others have argued convincingly that the reason innovation happened so quickly on the early Internet was that so much of its design was open and not driven by the quest for quick profit. And Shawn Fanning fits into that tradition. He didn't release Napster's underlying code to the public, as Linus Torvalds did with the free operating system Linux, but neither was he driven by the goal of getting rich by any means necessary. "If Napster had magically had Shawn in charge, I think his attitude would have been to make a deal" and stay on the right side of the law, said Shawn's father, Joe Rando. "He started it because he thought it was cool. Then later, he thought maybe it was a way to make a living."

By the late 1990s, the ideals of the early Internet, as articulated by Shawn's intellectual predecessors, were giving way to something completely different. Microsoft's Bill Gates had shown that intense focus on business strategy could trump superior software. And the subsequent gold rush mentality of people seeking tens of millions of dollars in a hurry didn't include concerns about what was good for the overall development of the technology. By the time Napster came into being, the Shawns of the world were no longer running the show.

"Through 1996, most of what happened to the Web was driven by pure excitement," Berners-Lee wrote. "By 1998, the Web began to be seen as a battleground for big business and big government interests." A year after that, he might have added, the Internet was the playground of yet another new generation: people who spoke the hardball huckster language of Silicon Valley. People, in other words, like John Fanning. Their styles and their tactics varied one from the other. But deep down, there wasn't much of a difference between John Fanning and some of the venture capitalists with whom he would be dealing. "The unfortunate part of the story has to do with mania," Rando said. "Unfortunately, Shawn got taken along for that ride."

— —

IN THE SUMMER OF 1997, Shawn practically lived at Chess.net, sleeping on the couch in the living room of the crew's rented house as the firm grew to about a half-dozen employees. "He did more listening than talking," Chess.net colleague Brian McBarron said. "When he gets interested in something new, he dedicates all of his resources to mastering it, and then he goes beyond that. He just has a single-mindedness that made him proficient." Ali Aydar and Tarek Loubani both said they had seldom seen anyone as focused as Shawn. "I don't think people can appreciate how hard he worked. This was his way out of the 'hood, out of everything," Loubani said. Shawn gave up sports and pretty much everything else to program, blowing off steam only by playing the computer game Quake 2 with his friends. It was a life of full-time hacking with few frills or even decent meals. "We ate at Burger King four or five times a day," Loubani said. But Shawn was having a blast. Looking back on that summer, both Shawn and Aydar remembered what was probably just a coincidence and not a sign from God: Aydar drove Shawn to a Borders bookstore in Braintree, Massachusetts, and bought him a manual on programming in C++, the language he would use to build Napster. On the way home, thunder and lightning struck so fiercely that the two had to pull off the road in the shelter of an underpass.

At the end of the summer of 1997, after the last of the Carnegie Mellon crew had graduated and worked at least a few months at Chess.net, the group scattered. Dakhnovsky went to Moscow, Aydar to Michigan, and McBarron to Ohio. Aided by its promotion deal with America Online, Chess.net membership had been doubling every year. But the marketing went slowly; it was hard to convince the chess players to pay for lessons or other premium offerings. And the management was an obvious disaster. "I felt like we blew it," Aydar said. "I felt like John had no clue, and I'd been taken for a ride."

Because he stuck to programming when he interned at Chess.net,

Shawn said, he never realized the depths of the problems at his uncle's company. He had to have known some of it: He was close to the embittered employees there, and once he rode his bike to deliver an overdue paycheck to Larry Christiansen, one of the chess champions Fanning hired to play games online. But business strategies and management styles were never very interesting to Shawn. His focus was elsewhere.

WHEN SHAWN WAS AROUND his uncle during Shawn's freshman year in 1998 and 1999, it was mainly to pour out code for Napster. "The dorm was not conducive to work, so I would go back to the office, and then my cousin would have to drive me back to school and drop me off," Shawn said. "I started noticing my weekends would get longer and longer, and I would have to drag myself back to school. And one day, for some strange reason, I pulled up, and I think I had skipped a day where there was something really important, like finishing up something or finding bugs."

It was January 1999, and his cousin Brian Fanning had just dropped Shawn off for the week at Northeastern's campus. Shawn walked up to his dorm's front door and stopped. Then he turned around and walked back to his cousin's car. "I'm not going back," Shawn said. "You're crazy!" Brian told him. Shawn shook his head. "I gotta finish this. I gotta pick." Shawn was torn about the decision. If he had stayed in college, "I was going to do 50 percent of two things, and I wouldn't have ever been satisfied. So I just decided to go for it and left everything at the school and didn't talk to any of my roommates. Because if I had talked to them, they would have said, 'What are you doing, you're crazy,' and convinced me to come back or made me feel bad about it. So I basically disappeared for a few months. And then finally once I had launched it, and they saw what I was doing, they felt a little better about it. I think they could tell I was never happy—well, not not happy about school, but I never felt like I was supposed to be there."

Shawn did tell some people of his move, including computer-science professor Richard Rasala, who understood. "He felt strongly he had something to do in the world and that simply remaining an undergraduate was going to get in the way of that," Rasala said. Several of Shawn's friends, including Loubani, did try to talk him out of quitting Northeastern. Hardest hit by the news was Shawn's mother, who broke down in tears. All of her dreams for Shawn had been bound up in his graduating college, something she had never done. "It was tough," Coleen said. "I built this thing up about him going to college. He knew how disappointed I was." She asked why he was the one who had to go, why it couldn't be one of the other kids he was working with. But Shawn explained that if he didn't do it now, and someone else came up with the idea, he would always regret not having pursued it. Coleen fought back her feelings and thought about what would be best for her son. "I told him he should go with his gut," she said. Secretly, she was thinking, even hoping, that Napster would last six months or so. Then Shawn could come back and return to college.

John Fanning had a different reaction, one natural enough for an ambitious businessman with tens of thousands of dollars in debts: He saw his ticket to riches. As Shawn kept working on the system, Fanning told him he would help with the business end. Fanning drew up papers incorporating Napster Inc. At first, Shawn was pleased: It was a sign that his uncle believed in him, and that his project was becoming a reality. But then Fanning told Shawn that he would be getting only 30 percent of the company. John Fanning would keep the rest. Shawn was stunned. "Napster was his baby," Loubani said. "It was completely do or die." Fanning told Shawn that the company needed an experienced businessman like himself in charge, especially since when it came time to raise money, investors would want Napster controlled by a capable executive like himself. Besides, he said, when it came time to sell off part of the company to new investors, Fanning would sell some of his shares, reducing his percentage of the firm. Less emphasized was the obvious corollary: that Fanning would be the first to get money out of the project to which his nephew was devoting every waking hour.

It isn't unusual for an inventor, even one who starts with 100 percent of a company's ownership, to end up with 20 percent or less by the time of an initial public offering. Early investors and top executives are important to the process and often have equal stakes by that point. What is unusual, especially so early, is for more than half of a company to go to someone who is merely providing management expertise, even if he is world class—which Fanning clearly was not.

An interesting perspective on the matter comes from Shawn's mother. First, John Fanning is her brother. Second, it was she who steered Shawn to him. And third, she currently is making ends meet by cleaning Fanning's house for pay. Even she leaves little doubt that both she and her son were unhappy from the beginning about the split and what it led to. "My main concern was that he have the proper people to guide him," Coleen said. "When there's so much money involved, there's going to be people that don't have his best interest in mind. I would like to think that what [John] really wanted was for *Shawn* to succeed—what he really had in his mind, I don't know." As for Shawn, "he regrets that—giving so much control away," his mother said.

In May 1999, Shawn signed the paper that his uncle told him to sign. At the gym one day with Loubani not long afterward, Shawn talked about how he could get more of Napster back from his uncle. But he didn't see a way. "He never forgot that it was his uncle that did this to him," Loubani said. "From then on, the relationship became really strained." Always guarded about personal matters, Shawn himself has declined to criticize his uncle's actions in public. But there is unanimity in Shawn's circle about his real feelings. "Shawn was upset, and he continues to be upset" by the split, Jordan Ritter said. When Shawn told Sean Parker about it, Parker couldn't believe it: "What did you sign, exactly?" Shawn said he didn't know. In the next two years, Parker and others wondered if Shawn had legally turned over the rights to his creation or not. In private, Shawn and his uncle sparred, broke off contact, and eventually made some kind of peace. When it comes to his uncle, "Shawn is like a battered wife," said one former Napster official who knows both men well, referring to Fanning's unchecked sway over Shawn. It's just too hard emotionally for him to let go.

getting money

JOHN FANNING MAY HAVE SEWN UP 70 PERCENT OF THE ownership of Napster, but he wasn't the only one seeing dollar signs. As soon as Shawn Fanning had told his friend Sean Parker about Napster, the wheels began turning in the nineteen-year-old's head as well. And when Shawn said he was ready to move ahead, Parker sprang at the chance. He tallied up the investor contacts he had made by networking and simply hanging around the northern Virginia Internet scene. One of his first calls was to Ben Lilienthal, whose server he had configured more than a year earlier.

Lilienthal was a good man to know, and he was in a mood to listen. He had grown up in nearby Reston and attended Amherst College in Massachusetts, majoring in anthropology. Always interested in business, Lilienthal returned to Virginia and worked eight months at a small consulting firm, where he watched America Online and others in the area take off. "People were just awakening to the possibilities," he said. In 1996, Lilienthal founded Nascent Technologies to develop a Web-based e-mail system. Nascent gained traction but was caught off guard when Hotmail launched a similar Web system for free. Lilienthal deftly switched gears and began working on a PC-based version, and the company recovered.

By 1999, at age twenty-six, Lilienthal had sold eighteen-employee Nascent to CMGI, the Boston Internet holding company in the process of spending billions of dollars acquiring everything from the AltaVista search engine to the naming rights to the New England Patriots' football stadium. He was looking for something new when the phone rang. "Sean Parker called me up out of the blue and said, 'My friend and I are about to launch a really cool service for sharing online music,'" Lilienthal said. When Parker asked Lilienthal if he would help, Lilienthal asked a few more questions. He didn't get many answers. "You guys need a lot," Lilienthal told him. "You need a business plan, and you need investors." Don't worry, Parker told him. "We're working on it."

Lilienthal was intrigued, and he wondered if he should sign up to run Napster. "There was no question in my mind it was going to be huge," Lilienthal said. "There was just a question of was it going to be legitimate." He soon called a college friend who had been one of his early backers at Nascent, New York investor Jason Grosfeld, and told him what he knew. Grosfeld had analyzed investments for Black Rock Financial Management and then specialized in technology stakes for a hedge fund. He had just started his own fund and was looking for ways to take advantage of the trends toward broadband connections and increased desktop processing power. If Lilienthal believed in Napster enough to run it and everything else checked out, Grosfeld was willing to put up the seed money as an angel investor. (Angel investors usually invest less than $1 million of their own money in early stage companies, while venture-capital firms come in later and can put in tens of millions of dollars supplied by pension funds, endowments, and wealthy individuals.)

Within a week, Lilienthal and Grosfeld arranged a visit to the Napster office in Hull. Lilienthal came over from Martha's Vineyard, where he had been vacationing, and Grosfeld flew up from New York. A strange scene greeted them. The office was in what appeared to be a dilapidated former hotel on the wharf in Hull, which was itself not much to look at. Fast-food containers littered the place. Next to the old hotel lobby sat Tom Carmody, a former Reebok marketing executive who owned the house next to John Fanning's. To the left sat Fanning, wearing black Reeboks and pink Bermuda shorts. In the back was what appeared to be a card table, where Shawn sat coding away on his laptop. The entire Napster brain was in that laptop, connected to the Net by a cable modem.

Lilienthal wasn't looking for much. Mainly, he wanted to make sure that Shawn was a true hacker. Clearly, he was. Lilienthal's first impression of Shawn's uncle was altogether different. "We're going to have to manage you," he thought. Fanning knew he was on to something—more power to him. But he was somehow overexuberant. Lilienthal and Grosfeld took turns talking seriously with Shawn while the other occupied his uncle. "We sat there and listened to how impressed this guy was with himself. All I wanted to do was talk to the kid," Grosfeld said. When it was Grosfeld's turn to set the pick, Fanning started peeling through a stack of business cards on his desk, bragging about his contacts. Among the cards, he said, were those of Steve Jurvetson, of the well-known Menlo Park venture firm Draper Fisher Jurvetson, and Ben Rosen, the veteran venture capitalist who had founded Compaq Computer Corp., then the world's largest PC company. Grosfeld smiled appreciatively. "If Ben Rosen knows this putz, I'll eat my hat," he thought.

While Lilienthal and Grosfeld realized that Fanning was going to be a problem, they both took to Shawn. "He seemed pretty bright, and he had a nice way about him, an innocence," Grosfeld said. "I was looking for bright people, and I was looking for a competitive advantage, or something that had already gained such traction in the underground that it sort of had a momentum of its own. I got an inkling of what was germinating." When the two men who might soon be running the company asked about the legal issues, if Fanning had hired a lawyer, he brushed them off. "My first question was, have you consulted a lawyer," Grosfeld said. "They said no, but it's perfectly acceptable." Fanning turned on the hard sell, telling the pair that Napster needed money quickly to keep the momentum going.

Fanning seemed ecstatic about his new partners, at one point handing Lilienthal options to buy shares in Napster Inc. The documents hadn't been made effective, and they never would be. Lilienthal said he would get the core Napster machine moved to a server farm and see about getting venture funding. In the meantime, he and Grosfeld planned to research the legal issues.

Lilienthal considered himself already on the Napster bandwagon, and within weeks he called on an old colleague from Nascent to help design a logo for Napster. Sam Hanks, twenty-seven, met Parker, Shawn, and Fanning at a Herndon mall for lunch, and they explained how the service worked. When Hanks asked about the reason for the Napster name, Shawn didn't talk about his previous hairstyle. The group talked instead about a cat napping, and Parker suggested a logo with a cat running across a PC screen. Maybe a hip cat, a cat from the club scene. As Hanks worked on it for a few days, he was thinking of younger users and was probably influenced by the Japanese animation he had been watching. Hanks emerged with a drawing of headphones on a face with catlike ears, eyes, and a nose. At a second lunch he presented it, and the Napster crew loved it. Hanks thought he was done. But Parker called a week or so afterward, pointing out that the eyes and nose looked like a mustache and goatee. "So I stuck in a little smirk," Hanks said. Not long afterward, Parker called again. "Some of the venture-capital guys think it looks like Satan," he said. Hanks asked what Napster users thought of it, and Parker told him they loved it. "Well, who are you selling it to?" Hanks asked, exasperated. "The venture guys or the kids downloading the music?" Parker decided the logo would stay. Later, he thought that the cat image appropriately evoked stealth and thievery. Even more appropriately, he realized, cats are risk-takers who escape death. The finished symbol would rank among the most recognized symbols of a volatile new era. Hanks had never negotiated a payment, and it took him months to collect his due: $5,000, plus options that proved worthless.

GROSFELD AND LILIENTHAL WORKED WELL as a team. Typically, Grosfeld studied a business proposal in depth before committing money, while Lilienthal was more intuitive, willing to risk some time as a manager on something his gut told him was inspired. When both approaches led to the same conclusion, they felt comfortable doing a deal. "We usually came up between us with the right answer," Grosfeld said. Both were excited about Napster, but their minds didn't meet on one issue. The more-cautious Grosfeld wanted to cut a deal with Napster first, which would establish what their stake would be, what role Lilienthal would have at the company, and what would happen to both of those things if venture money came in. At a minimum, they should set a commission for bringing in venture funding if that meant they were forced out as a result. But Lilienthal was fired up to act fast, and he thought he could trust the venture investors he had in mind to do the right thing. "Let's get it done as quickly as possible," Lilienthal told his partner. Later, he said Grosfeld "ultimately had the right idea—cut a deal with them first." But securing the commission wasn't as important for Lilienthal, since he didn't plan on getting involved unless there were deeper pockets than Grosfeld's.

Against Grosfeld's advice, Lilienthal called John Backus at Draper Atlantic in Reston, Virginia. The small venture firm was the obvious choice for several reasons. One, Draper's partners prided themselves on moving quickly. Supportive quotes from entrepreneurs on the firm's website included one praising it as a VC firm that moved "on Internet time." A second reason was the firm's ties to Silicon Valley, through the stake in it held by the bigger venture firm Draper Fisher Jurvetson, backers of Hotmail and Sierra Semiconductor Corp. Most important, Lilienthal had earned Backus's trust. Backus had offered to fund Lilienthal's Nascent, and Lilienthal had turned him down, saying that he was likely to sell the company soon. That had spared Draper the hassle of a short-term investment.

In three days, Parker put together an outline of Napster's plan, and Lilienthal did minor editing. "The idea was, this was a user play," Lilienthal said. "We get as many people to use it as possible, then sell them ancillary stuff like concert tickets and music. Let's go after 10 million users. Then we'll figure out what to sell them." Parker and Lilienthal went in to meet Backus and Draper Atlantic managing partner Jim Lynch. "They loved it. They got it right away," Lilienthal said. The Draper team said that there might be legal problems, and each side said that it would study the issue before anyone committed to anything. But once again, no one felt like waiting. After just a few days, a meeting was set for the Draper men, Grosfeld and Lilienthal, Fanning, Shawn, and

Parker at Grosfeld's apartment a few blocks from the World Trade Center.

Parker took the train up from Washington and waited with the angel investors in the apartment. It was mid-July, and the temperature rose above one hundred degrees outside. They sweated as they waited for the venture capitalists, Lynch and Backus, who arrived late in their suits. The air-conditioning couldn't keep pace with the heat, and Fanning and Shawn still hadn't appeared, so the group adjourned to a gritty Irish bar nearby called Brady's Tavern.

The Fannings arrived more than two hours late: John had insisted that they drive down in style in a Z3 convertible with the top down and Napster's server in the backseat. Trying to ignore the smell of stale beer at Brady's, the men pushed together two tables in the back and ordered chicken wings and soft drinks. After the pleasantries, Jim Lynch surprised everyone but his partners. He whipped out a ready-made term sheet, a page-long summary of how much the firm would invest in Napster and under what conditions. Grosfeld couldn't believe it. The venture pros had moved even faster than he had. And now they were cutting him and Lilienthal out of the deal. "They weren't honorable," Grosfeld said. "They did something that I had never seen another investor do. They tried to take all of the action." He pulled his old friend aside. "You fucking idiot," he hissed at Lilienthal. "We didn't negotiate our commission." Lilienthal looked abashed. "I didn't really think about it," he said. "I thought they'd play square."

The saving grace, from their perspective, was that the term sheet required Lilienthal to be Napster's CEO, which gave them some leverage to negotiate their equity stake. And the deal was generous to a fault. It called for Draper to put in $500,000 and take only a minority position in the company. Fanning began hemming and hawing, saying it wasn't enough money for the stake they wanted. For the second time in ten minutes, Lilienthal was flabbergasted. "John, this is the most friendly term sheet I've seen in two years," he said. Fanning said he'd think about it, and the signals he gave turned positive. "I've got a bias for action," he told Lynch, and as the meeting broke up, it looked like everything would come together soon.

After the Draper team left, the rest of the crew went back to Grosfeld's loft, and Shawn showed Lilienthal the new *Star Wars* movie trailer on his laptop. Shawn and Fanning headed back to Boston, and Grosfeld and Lilienthal took Parker out for a celebration dinner at one of the fanciest restaurants Parker had ever seen, the chic Bouley. After staying the night at Grosfeld's, Lilienthal decided to treat Parker to his first plane trip, the shuttle flight back to Washington. Napster's server was going with them, destined for housing at Global Center's facilities in Virginia. On the way to the airport, Parker realized he had forgotten the inhaler for his asthma. Since he didn't want to make Lilienthal late, he decided he could make do without it. The two men missed the first plane they tried for, ran to the adjacent terminal, and missed the second plane. By the time they made it back to the first terminal, Parker was getting nervous about not having his inhaler, especially after all the running. Hoping that enough caffeine would open up his lungs, Parker slugged six shots of espresso as Lilienthal watched in disbelief. Out of the corner of his eye, Lilienthal saw a newspaper headline: The record industry had announced another step in what it called the Secure Digital Music Initiative, to encrypt music that wasn't in the MP3 format. "Too late," Lilienthal thought.

Finally on board a shuttle and taxiing down the runway with the Napster server in an overhead bin, Parker asked a stewardess if she had an inhaler. He didn't realize that the airlines have strict rules about asthmatics, since the air gets thinner at high altitudes. The stewardess ordered the plane to return to the terminal and told Parker to get off. Lilienthal lent the teenager $20 for cab fare to get back to Grosfeld's for the inhaler. As the plane finally lifted off with Lilienthal and the server, the entrepreneur shook his head and reconsidered Sean Parker. "Here's a kid who doesn't have any shares in the company," he thought. "But he has been responsible for all the things that have been happening. Now he's going to take on the recording industry. And he doesn't know how to fly on a plane."

——— ———

WITH FANNING AMENABLE TO the Draper Atlantic term sheet, all that remained was for Draper, Grosfeld, and Lilienthal to do their "due diligence." The phrase, something of a hollow one during the Internet bubble, comes from the legal responsibility of the parties to a deal to conduct a reasonable investigation beforehand if they want to preserve the right to claim later that they were misled. In Napster's case, the due diligence proved to be anything but routine. A credit check turned up the first of Fanning's two major overdue debts. The assault charge emerged as well. Though they troubled Lilienthal, neither item was a deal breaker for him. The bigger problem was U.S. copyright law. Grosfeld spent most of two months getting deeper and deeper into the state of the law and the prognosis for Napster. He hired the law firm of Weil, Gotshal & Manges to research the newly passed Digital Millennium Copyright Act and read the court rulings that would later prove crucial to Napster's chances for survival, rulings that had arisen from topics as diverse as VCRs and flea markets.

The outlook was not good.

In 1998, spurred by fears that the Internet had enabled both mass instantaneous copying of intellectual property and perfection in the quality of those copies, Congress had passed the Digital Millennium act. The law extended existing copyright protections into cyberspace. And it made it a felony to circumvent technical measures that protected copyrighted material, or to distribute programs whose primary purpose was to crack those measures. After intense debate, the law also included some exceptions designed to translate some of the balances of existing copyright law into the digital era. Among those balances were the fair-use doctrine, which allows critics to quote passages of a book or an article, and protection for libraries and their equivalents, which allow the public to peruse published work. And the law codified what had been worked out in some court cases, including one in which the Church of Scientology had sued not just disaffected church members who had published the church's sacred—and copyrighted—teachings on the Internet, but also the Internet service provider that had allowed them to do it.

The judge in the Scientology case had ruled that if the Internet service provider did not monitor what its users did, it was acting like a phone company, and therefore shouldn't be held responsible for what customers said to each other. The Internet provider was more like a library than a publishing house. As long as it responded to complaints by the copyright holder after the fact, it couldn't be liable for the content. Following that ruling, the DMCA gave explicit protection to Internet service providers that merely routed offending material, as long as that transmission was part of "an automatic technical process without selection of the material"; that the service provider didn't select the recipients of the material "except as an automatic response to the request of another person"; and that no copy of the material was maintained on the system in a way that left it available to anyone other than the intended recipient.

Another "safe harbor" was given to Internet service providers that listed hypertext links or otherwise indexed offending material. In order to qualify for that protection, the service provider had to be unaware that the material was infringing a copyright. The company couldn't have "actual knowledge," or be aware "of facts or circumstances from which infringing activity is apparent." Once it became aware, it would have to act to disable access to the material. In addition, the company couldn't benefit financially from infringing activity if it controlled that activity.

Two other cases came up in Grosfeld's research. One was the 1984 U.S. Supreme Court ruling that narrowly allowed videocassette recorders to enter the market after an eight-year legal struggle between Sony and Universal City Studios. A bare 5-4 majority of the court held that even though Sony's VCRs could be used to copy protected television programs and that those copies could be sold, unfairly diluting the profits of the program's owner, a "substantial" use of the machines would be for an innocent purpose: taping a program now for viewing later, with the ability to temporarily halt viewing while answering the door for the pizza delivery boy. "There is no precedent for imposing vicarious liability on the theory that petitioners sold [VCRs] with constructive knowledge that their customers might use the equipment to make unauthorized copies of copyrighted material," the court had written. "The sale of copying equipment, like the sale of other articles of commerce, does not constitute contributory infringement if the product is widely used for legitimate, unobjectionable purposes, or indeed is merely capable of substantial noninfringing uses."

Napster could, and would, argue that it was providing a similar technology, with substantial noninfringing use. But Grosfeld saw that it would be a harder argument than it was for VCR-maker Sony, judging by the way people were already using the Napster service. In theory, some people could use Napster to transmit their own home-studio recordings.

And there were plenty of older songs available that were no longer protected by copyright. It was just that most people were not actually using Napster that way, and they never would. And unlike Sony, which lost contact with its customers after they bought the VCRs, Napster kept watching exactly what its customers were doing.

The fact that one more case turned up at all is testament to the thoroughness of Grosfeld's research. *Fonovisa Inc. v. Cherry Auction Inc.* had been filed in 1993, when a Latin music company accused a Fresno flea market of improperly renting booths to vendors selling counterfeit recordings. Fonovisa argued that Cherry Auction was aiding and abetting those vendors' copyright infringement. The flea market claimed it had no responsibility to supervise what the little retailers were doing, and a federal judge agreed, tossing the case out of court. In 1996, however, a panel of the San Francisco–based U.S. Court of Appeals for the Ninth Circuit reversed that decision. Since the police had told the flea market's owners what was going on, the flea market knew about it. And it was improperly profiting by charging admission and selling concessions, the court found.

The common threads in the DMCA and the court cases were knowledge of wrongdoing and the ability to stop it. And that's what made Grosfeld nervous. Unlike the DMCA-protected Internet service provider that doesn't know who is posting what, Napster always knew who had what file and to whom they were transmitting it. And a claim that Napster was just "indexing" who had which songs, which might qualify it for the second DMCA safe harbor, wouldn't work if Napster got complaints about a given song file. The company would have to remove it, although another version of the same song was sure to pop up in no time.

The more Grosfeld thought about what was actually happening inside Napster, the worse it looked. Not only were the employees aware of "facts and circumstances" *suggesting* copyright infringement, by itself enough to ruin the second safe harbor, they were aware of the infringement itself. Napster's few workers "weren't anything like a service provider," Grosfeld concluded. "They were not in reality closing their eyes to the copyright infringement going on there—they bragged about it. My lawyer thought it was insane."

Contrary to Napster's later depiction of its founders as a couple of bright but naive kids, Shawn and Parker knew early on that they were pushing the legal envelope. Shawn just didn't think they'd get sued. Parker did, but he thought Napster had legal arguments that would be at least good enough to buy time until the industry opted to settle. "We understood where it was going to go. It was premeditated," Parker said. The game plan made Grosfeld very uncomfortable. And as for making money ahead of a record-industry deal, the law stressed the dangers of profiting from the wrongful behavior of others. Finally, avoiding that pitfall by avoiding profit didn't exactly strike Grosfeld as a solid business model. "If they profited, they were profiting from theft," he said. "We live in America, and that's punishable."

JOHN FANNING, ALSO WELL AWARE of the legal hurdles, was doing his own research. He called Andrew Bridges, a partner at the top law firm in Silicon Valley, Wilson Sonsini Goodrich & Rosati. Bridges might have been the best single person to call. An expert in intellectual property and cyberspace with a law degree from Harvard, Bridges was defending Diamond Multimedia Systems Inc., the maker of the Rio portable MP3 player, which had been sued by the Recording Industry Association of America on copyright grounds. Bridges won that case, which extended the Sony VCR decision to new devices. But he told Fanning that he wasn't interested in representing Napster. Instead, Bridges referred Fanning to a lawyer named Bruce Joseph. Joseph begged off as well, sending Fanning to Washington lawyer Seth Greenstein. Greenstein took Fanning's call, and the two chatted. As Fanning described how the service worked, Greenstein said it sounded like search engine Lycos's music service "on steroids." Fanning put the phone down and passed the compliment on to Shawn. Both laughed. At last—someone who got it.

Greenstein had worked for a number of Internet music companies, including RealNetworks Inc. of Seattle, and in 1998 he had cofounded the Digital Media Association and testified before Congress. Greenstein said he would be willing to help develop a legal rationale for Napster. Since his firm also represented some record companies, however, he said he might not be available for any litigation to come. Parker soon went to visit Greenstein in his office at McDermott, Will & Emery. Parker had never been in a law office before, and he was cowed by the posh trappings and towering ceilings in the conference room. Parker looked hopelessly uncomfortable in his suit and tie. "I said about five words and handed him a check," Parker said.

With the retainer, Greenstein drafted a twenty-seven-page memo spelling out what Napster's arguments should be. In what would become an almost-biblical text for Napster's inexperienced leaders, he revisited the cases Grosfeld had, pointing out a number of defenses. First, he said that in the flea-market case and others, courts had ruled that the companies were aiding infringement when they had direct knowledge of what was happening. Napster, on the other hand, could argue that since the files being sought by its users were not marked either as copyrighted or otherwise, it didn't know what was in violation. "When you look at cases that impose contributory or vicarious liability in the case of a service, it's because in those cases the defendant was actually able to exercise present control," Greenstein said. "For example, someone says, 'Make a copy' and hands a tape to someone to duplicate. That person is liable because they could see if it was suspicious. When you're looking at a service that consists of an automatic, technical process, that's quite different." In his memo, Greenstein wrote: "MP3 lacks any flags or other means that indicate whether copyright has been asserted over the music file and whether the music file may be copied with or without restriction."

Fanning would trot out Greenstein to explain the legal defenses, often by phone, for Draper Atlantic and other potential investors. But he didn't brag about two other points that Greenstein said he made orally. The first was that, as Greenstein saw it, the odds of a lawsuit being filed against Napster were about 98 percent. The second was that copyright law is a complex animal, especially when it comes to issues on the edge. Those are "the grayest of the gray areas in the law," Greenstein said. Sampling of older songs in rap music was one such battleground, a fight between fair use and infringement. The significance of the trend for Napster was that the eventual lawsuit was bound to be what lawyers call "fact-intensive." The ultimate ruling would almost certainly turn on Napster's internal conduct, the evidence produced from within about what it knew, what it should have known, and what it could have done about it. For instance, a court might inquire whether Napster's servers had the ability to check each file for some sign of copyright violation, such as the acoustic "watermarks" being developed by the industry.

A major warning in Greenstein's memo concerned the DMCA safe harbors for service providers. Napster's chances would rise dramatically if it could qualify for one, but it was far from clear that it could, Greenstein said. Companies that ignored obvious misuse wouldn't make the cut. "Napster should be able to meet the test for immunity from liability, but it is not a foregone conclusion," he wrote. "The knowledge standard required by this section is a 'red flag' of facts and circumstances from which it is apparent that infringing activity is occurring. In this case, the RIAA might contend that the red flag consists of thousands of MP3 files that were ripped from commercially available compact discs being made available through the Napster network. . . . This is the closest of questions presented in the memorandum." Greenstein concluded by recommending that Napster appoint a copyright agent, post a policy to ban users who infringed, and act on that policy.

But Greenstein hadn't been hired as a general counsel, someone who would work full-time at the company and monitor its behavior. He was hired only to provide an interpretation of the law that could allow Napster to win if sued. And while Greenstein believed in what he had written, he conceded that his counterparts in the record industry "probably see me as a wild-eyed radical."

GROSFELD, IN THE MEANTIME, kept visiting his friend Lilienthal's office in Washington and calling other intellectual-property lawyers. They didn't find many that shared Greenstein's qualified optimism. So Grosfeld and Lilienthal started kicking around new ideas for harnessing Napster's system. The technology itself was legal and a huge advance over what had gone before. Perhaps, they thought, the company should just stick with that, and license the file-swapping technique to others. The possibilities seemed real enough, but the men decided that they couldn't trust John Fanning to follow them down that road.

"If it was just the legal issue, that would have been okay," Lilienthal said. But the combination of that minefield with Fanning's behavior was too much risk. Lilienthal decided that if he were going to try to steer Napster out of its legal predicament, he would need to make sure Fanning was not in majority control, with veto power over anything Lilienthal might do. And so began weeks of tortured negotiations during the summer of 1999 as Lilienthal and Grosfeld offered Fanning more and more money, finally more than $1 million, to whittle his stake in Napster down to about a third.

If they had succeeded in cutting a deal with Fanning, things might have turned out differently. Lilienthal and Draper Atlantic both thought the legal issues could have been managed, perhaps even if Napster had stayed in the music-distribution business. "We were going to run this thing and then go to the record industry and cut a deal," Lilienthal said. "One side of me thinks the record industry was out to shut everything down. Then part of me thinks that at a certain point in the process, they would have been willing to cut a deal. I would like to think I would have been able to pull something off."

As the negotiations between Grosfeld, Lilienthal, and Fanning dragged on, Grosfeld pursued another angle as well—extracting Shawn from Napster Inc. Some lawyers Grosfeld spoke to believed that Shawn wasn't legally bound to give his invention to the company because of the haphazard way in which it had been formed. "He's killing you," Grosfeld told Shawn on one call. "You can start over." Grosfeld even looked for apartments where Shawn might live in Manhattan, away from his uncle's influence. Parker joined the debate, making similar arguments to his friend about the damage Fanning was doing to their cause, but he got nowhere. Shawn explained that his uncle had helped him when no one else would, that he had given him that first computer. "Shawn had an emotional attachment to him. He was the only real father figure," Parker concluded.

So the investors' talks with Fanning continued. At times, it seemed like Fanning had agreed to an offer, or nearly had. They got as close as two percentage points apart on what Fanning's remaining equity would be. Then, without warning, Fanning would turn into a car salesman. "How much do you have?" he asked Grosfeld at one point. "How much could you wire me today?" Fanning also tried to drive a wedge between

Grosfeld and Lilienthal, telling each that he wanted him involved more than he wanted the other. The pair ultimately realized that Fanning would never sign. "He was just negotiating for the sake of negotiating," Lilienthal said. Finally, Grosfeld and Lilienthal threw up their hands. Grosfeld moved on to investigate other possible investments, and Lilienthal went on a surfing trip to Peru.

NAPSTER KEPT ADDING MORE USERS and more music. A few hundred users became a few thousand, then ten thousand, then fifty thousand. Cash at Napster was tight, but Fanning didn't seem worried. He had plenty of other angles to play. He returned to Draper and said he needed at least some money right away if the firm was still interested. Spooked by Fanning's background, the legal worries, and the continuing lack of a proven CEO, Draper agreed to give Napster only a $50,000 loan. In return, Draper got the future right to buy more than 1 million shares, or about 10 percent of the company, at 20 cents apiece, which was the price then being bandied about with other investors.

Fanning went after more of Parker's connections as well, some of whom Parker knew through his UUNet guru, Jonathon Perrelli. One of those men was Scott Newlin, who had little technology background but had done well for himself as president of Sparks Personnel Services, a temporary-employment agency in Maryland. Newlin agreed to meet with Parker and John and Shawn Fanning to hear about Napster. Parker didn't say much at the meeting, but Shawn impressed Newlin by speaking passionately about the project while sporting a T-shirt and shorts. "Shawn is a very nice guy, just a natural kid," Newlin said later. The problem was that John Fanning would barely let his nephew talk. Fanning "did all the speaking, and I just felt it was too much of a control issue. It seemed like to him, it was a quick in, quick out. He just wanted to sell it quickly." Newlin decided to pass on the deal for that reason. Some time later, he and Perrelli talked about making a $1.2 million offer for the company that would leave them in charge. But in a replay of the stalemate with Grosfeld and Lilienthal, Fanning said he wouldn't give up majority control. "What makes you think you should have majority control when you're not going to be the CEO and you didn't put money in?" Newlin asked. "That's the way it is," Fanning told him. "I just said, 'I'm not going to waste my time,'" Newlin recalled.

Possibly the best choice of all for Napster would have been another Parker-Perrelli connection, engineers Scott and Mike Shinn. The Shinns were northern Virginia brothers in their late twenties who always worked as a team, from their internship at the White House, where they were in the same orientation group as Monica Lewinsky, to the U.S. Securities and Exchange Commission, where they worked on the well-regarded EDGAR system for putting SEC documents online. The Shinns began with the same sort of hacker/security background as Jordan Ritter, but they reached a bigger league at a company called WheelGroup Corp., based in San Antonio. WheelGroup gained widespread attention in early 1997, when it appeared on the cover of *Fortune*.

The magazine had heard WheelGroup executives boasting that its white-hat hackers could break into any corporate system in a day, then teach the company how to protect itself. To test the claim, *Fortune* found a large New York company that was proud of its computer security and that agreed to serve as a guinea pig as long as it was never identified and an auditor made sure secrets weren't stolen. The magazine then chronicled how WheelGroup's employees, many of them former information-warfare specialists for the government, used public data about the company's network structure and a wardialer program like that released by w00w00's Matt Conover to go around the company's $25,000 firewall. WheelGroup got in through a fax server and then broke into the company's tax department, where an employee had a popular remote-access program running on his computer. As a crowning touch, the hackers sent an e-mail to a division president that appeared to come from his deputy, suggesting a $5,000 bonus for the employee who had approved the WheelGroup project.

Basking in the publicity, WheelGroup was bought the next year by Cisco Systems for $124 million, making millionaires out of many of the firm's seventy-five employees, including the brothers Shinn. Cisco, the largest maker of networking gear, was pressuring the Shinns to abandon Virginia for San Antonio, and the brothers were looking for an excuse not to move. They knew Perrelli from UUNet's interactions with Cisco, and when Perrelli and Parker told them about Napster, they were receptive. They also knew something about digital music: Scott had decided he liked MP3s but had run into availability problems. Like Shawn, Scott had done something about it. He knocked out a program to search for MP3 files automatically and bring them back to his home computer. The big drawback was that the program didn't discriminate, and Scott didn't like most of what it came back with.

In June 1999, Parker brought Shawn and John Fanning to meet the Shinns in their basement in Centreville, Virginia. "I knew nothing about them," Scott said later. "Parker said, 'I got these guys I want you to meet.'" Scott agreed because he was curious and because the potential for a big payoff in digital music was increasingly obvious. America Online, the Internet-access behemoth based a few miles away, had just plunked down a total of $400 million for Internet-radio firm Spinner Networks Inc. and for Nullsoft, the small maker of MP3 player Winamp run by Justin Frankel and Rob Lord. That kind of money would certainly be enough to justify blowing off Cisco and staying close to home. The Shinns hit it off immediately with Shawn and Parker. As they talked, Scott mentioned that he had hosted Internet bulletin boards on a local digital-art network called Ice.org, on which Parker had chatted five years earlier as a precocious teen. And without knowing Shawn's real name, the Shinns had run into him as well, on IRC channels covering security issues. (Later, when Scott discovered that Ritter was involved at Napster, he had another small-world moment: He knew of Ritter by his reputation as a security expert and server architect.) Finally, Scott had heard about Shawn and Parker, again only by their IRC handles, after they had duped a friend of his who was unwisely running a multiuser game from his U.S. State Department computer. "They schooled my friend, who is pretty bright," Scott said.

"Do you like MP3s?" Shawn asked. "Yeah," Scott said, "check this out." Scott showed him the search-and-retrieval program, or "bot," and Shawn showed Scott Napster. Scott's first reaction was that it took too much work: You had to type in the name of the song you were looking for. But the idea was "pretty cool," he told Shawn. "I need to marry it to my bot." For half an hour, Shawn and the Shinns had a Vulcan mind meld. "We kind of geeked out on how it worked," Scott said. "I had seen some not quite peer-to-peer models, but something similar in IRC, without the searching. We talked about how to optimize it." By the end of the meeting, Scott decided he had heard enough. "This is the next logical step," he thought. "This is going to catch on big time." Just like that, the Shinns decided to quit Cisco and work for Napster.

The Shinns had $1.2 million to invest from the WheelGroup takeover, and John Fanning wanted it. But in the discussions over what their role at Napster would be, the Shinns grew concerned about John Fanning's outsize stake in the firm. "Mike and I said, 'This capital structure is kind of weird. Do you want to redo it?' and John Fanning said no," Scott said. "We were not convinced it was going to work, so we bowed out." The Shinns kept talking to Shawn, but in July 1999 they formed their own firm, along with Parker and Perrelli, to develop other music technology. ETantrum, as the firm was called, refined Scott's MP3-hunting bot and added a recommendation tool that analyzed the music that a computer user was listening to on his MP3 player. The bot would then go out and find similar songs. "We were always like technology cousins," Scott said of eTantrum and Napster. "What we were evolving into was the realistic business half of Napster."

ETantrum and Napster compared notes often, but the most dramatic moment in the two firms' relationship came later that summer. That's when the Shinns decided that Shawn alone was worth their million dollars, as long as he came without John Fanning. "We didn't want the uncle. We just wanted Shawn," Scott said. While Scott was chatting to Shawn over IRC, Mike called him on the phone. "I've got a million dollars," Mike told him. "I'll give you a million dollars if you come work for us." The phone went silent on Shawn's end as he tried to digest the offer and looked around for his uncle. "I have to call you back," Shawn said. Minutes later, he messaged Scott, worried that eTantrum would start its own peer-to-peer system. "Dude, you're not doing what we're doing, are you?" Scott told him no, and it was true. Besides wanting to avoid direct competition with their friends at Napster, the Shinns believed the record industry would soon be screaming for blood. They thought it would be safer if they worked on the recommendation service and incorporated a way to buy music. They would still have to make some kind of a bargain with the RIAA, they felt, but they wouldn't have to give away as much when they did.

Shawn didn't take the Shinns up on their offer. As eTantrum slowly evolved, even attracting acquisition interest from CMGI, the computer-security job offers were "falling out of the sky," Scott said, with hourly pay that could add up to $12,000 a week. The Shinns returned to anti-hacking work. Like the good geeks they were, instead of pulling the plug on eTantrum, they open-sourced the software and allowed others to adopt it.

Given what John Fanning had, which was 70 percent of Napster Inc., and what he *thought* he had, which was control of a company worth far more than what he was being offered, one can understand why he declined overtures from Grosfeld and Lilienthal, Newlin, and the Shinns. The harder thing to comprehend is why eighteen-year-old Shawn would turn down an offer from technically superior teams that would have net-ted him "a million dollars and a monster truck," as he laughingly described it later with a hacker inside joke: That's the nonnegotiable fee that hacking collective Cult of the Dead Cow demanded for handing over an advance version of its powerful Trojan-horse attack program, Back Orifice 2000.

It wasn't clear that Shawn himself understood why he had done so. "One, I didn't take them that seriously. Two, I didn't really know much about starting a business, and even at this stage we weren't really thinking about it. Three, my uncle was family. So I didn't. I mean, it could have been that I was just so out of it from working on the code that I didn't even want to think about it, even though those are kind of crazy numbers. But most of that period of time was a blur, and I just went for what felt comfortable and what felt right, and none of those felt right—the idea of taking a bunch of money and moving somewhere, even though I'd never seen close to that amount of money. . . . I can't even think of the thought process that I went through when stuff like that happened," Shawn said. "I wonder what would have happened if we had done that. I don't know. There are just too many variables."

⸻

JOHN FANNING CONTINUED HIS ceaseless quest for money on his terms, turning for help to his neighbor and adviser, former sneaker marketing executive Tom Carmody. And one of Carmody's connections seemed like a match made in heaven. Andy Evans was a San Francisco venture capitalist who was starting an incubator called Zero.net to nurture emerging companies. He was smart as hell, and his own connections could be summed up this way: He had managed money for Bill Gates, the richest man and one of the shrewdest businessmen in the world. Fanning, Carmody, Shawn, and Parker flew out to meet him in August 1999. It was the first trip to San Francisco for both teenagers, and they were in awe of nearly everything. "I was really excited. We were showing [Napster] to somebody who might be putting money into the company and help us buy servers," Shawn said. Evans's office was low-key, in the new-media style of the day. Evans himself was much less low-key. He bragged about running Gates's investments in the mid-1980s and about his multiple Ferraris. "Miraculously," Shawn said, the Napster demonstration went smoothly. Beyond that, he said, "I had no idea what was going on. It was a weird experience." Evans heard the Napster pitch, and suddenly he was thinking several steps ahead. Of course Evans would fund the company, he said, but then he might want to set up an alliance with another small firm that did market testing of new musical groups. After that, Napster could approach the record companies about an alliance.

Evans was so excited that he insisted that Shawn and Parker stay in California at a hotel he would pay for. He would wire investment money the next day. Fanning and Carmody, Evans said, could return east. The gambit sent up all kinds of warning flags for Fanning, who vetoed the idea. Even the deal-hungry Parker agreed. "There was something not right about him," he said. And Evans had misread Shawn. When it became clear that the Napster crew was going to head home that night, Evans called for a stretch limo to take Shawn to the airport. At that point, such conspicuous consumption only embarrassed Shawn and made him uncomfortable.

Evans still might have invested in Napster were it not for Jordan Ritter. Evans wanted to learn so much about the company that he asked to speak with the guy administering the back end. The Fannings called Ritter at his office at BindView and told him that Evans would be phoning and to answer his questions. But they neglected to tell Ritter that Evans was debating whether to invest. Ritter, thinking that Evans had already invested or was otherwise in the fold, held nothing back.

When Evans called, "he didn't misrepresent himself. He just didn't represent himself" as having any particular role, Ritter said. Evans asked who was running the server. Ritter said he was. Evans asked how stable it was. Ritter said it crashed every ten or twenty minutes. Evans asked how long it would take to get the server to be reliable. Ritter said a month at best, three months at worst. Evans asked how much Ritter was getting paid. Ritter told him zero, for the moment, and Evans laughed. (Fanning soon ordered paychecks sent to Ritter.) Evans called Fanning and used everything negative that Ritter had said for negotiating leverage, and the talks quickly collapsed.

Much of Napster's early life was marked by seasoned investors or managers looking closely at the company, consulting their lawyers, their common sense, or both, and walking away from temptation. A number of them might have set the young company on a different and viable path if John Fanning had let them. Andy Evans, on the other hand, was something completely different. His may be the single instance of an investor who actually could have made Napster's fantastic but doomed campaign into something even worse.

That day at Zero.net, Evans had talked a lot about Gates, who had served on the board of Evans's investment company and was godfather to his three children. What Evans did not talk about was his 1986 conviction for bank fraud. When, in 1993, questions about why Gates was relying on a felon for financial advice became too frequent, Gates broke most of his official ties. But by 1999, Evans was clearly a player in Silicon Valley, investing alongside the top venture firm Kleiner Perkins Caufield & Byers in such monster start-ups as Rambus Inc. and getting IPO shares from the top investment banks, Goldman Sachs and Morgan Stanley. Evans started Zero.net in May 1999, and one of its first investments was in discount perfume seller Perfumania's Internet division, which was spun off that September. One of Evans's investment firms bought a majority of the spin-off's shares. As the prices of the shares rose on the constricted supply, Evans's firm transferred them to Zero.net, fattening Zero.net's balance sheet and allowing the incubator to raise more venture capital. Lawsuits soon accused Evans of manipulating the stock and failing to make required disclosures to the SEC. The suits echoed previous accusations leveled at Evans, when he had been forced to sign a consent decree promising not to violate securities laws. And Evans's criminal past caused a major Zero.net investor to pull back $20 million it had pledged, leaving the firm with a negative net worth. More than twenty complaints were filed with the SEC about Evans affiliates, and the agency was still reported to be investigating two years later. Following its custom, the SEC declined to comment on Evans.

While much of the Internet boom can be characterized by an alarming lack of research by private and public investors into the companies they backed, including Napster, the Andy Evans case shows why due diligence is supposed to work the other way as well. Especially in the early stages of a company's life, entrepreneurs have a responsibility to check out their backers and act accordingly. It was too late for Shawn to do so with his uncle. But it wasn't too late to do that with Evans. If Ritter had been less accidentally candid, Napster might have wound up a piece of Evans's then-growing empire of penny stocks and alleged massive self-dealing.

EVANS'S INTEREST, HOWEVER, DID LEAD to Napster finally sealing a deal with its first real outside investor, a man who would be crucial to its destiny. That investor, Yosi Amram, sat in on the talks at Zero.net at the invitation of his old acquaintance, John Fanning. Amram saw that Evans was willing to invest even though Fanning was a problem. And Amram decided that if someone of Evans's apparent pedigree was willing to take a risk, he might do so as well. "I could see it was going to take off. I liked the idea, and it was getting some traction," Amram said. What he did not do was do anything approaching the due diligence put in by Draper Atlantic and Grosfeld and Lilienthal. He didn't even read Seth Greenstein's legal memorandum. Instead, he recalled, Fanning described it to him, and he spoke to a lawyer on the phone, though he didn't recall which one. "I made a quick decision," Amram said.

More accurately, Amram made a quick decision that reversed his earlier, more thoughtful one. He said no at first because he didn't trust Fanning with his money. "I was very reluctant," Amram said. He had one hundred thousand reasons to be skeptical—that's how many dollars he had plowed into Chess.net. By mid-1999, Amram knew he wasn't going to be getting any of them back.

Fanning had met Amram years earlier in Cambridge, playing chess in Harvard Square at the tables outside the Au Bon Pain café. Fanning loved all kinds of chess, often playing multiple games simultaneously. Amram favored blitz, a kind of lightning-quick chess in which each side is allotted a total of about five minutes for all its moves. In blitz, the regular rules of chess can be broken, as long as the player doesn't get caught before the next move. "You have to make quick decisions," Amram said in explaining his taste for the game. "To me, it's like the real world. Time is a fundamental part of life—you can't take time off to go and think about it." Most people probably don't see their lives as being quite so rapid-fire. But if there is a more exact metaphor than blitz chess for Silicon Valley in 1999, it hasn't been made public. And like the Valley's soon-to-be-obvious missteps in that period, Amram had already been tripped up by his penchant for the quick-as-a-blink deal.

Overall, Amram had been very successful. His worldview was part of what made him a strong investor; he also had serious smarts, a real technical education, and a wealth of contacts. Raised in Tel Aviv, the son of a chief financial officer and a schoolteacher, Amram did his three years of universal military service in the Israeli Air Force in the late 1970s. He rose quickly to the rank of sergeant major. Amram wanted to be involved in technology and to be an entrepreneur, and he headed to MIT in Cambridge, where he earned a bachelor's and a master's degree in electrical engineering and computer science in four years. Amram said he recorded a straight-A average at MIT, and those who know him don't doubt it. Deciding he liked business better than engineering, Amram went to Harvard Business School, graduating in the top tenth of his class in 1984.

Amram's first job after business school was in product marketing at Rational Software Corp. in Cupertino, California, where he held a variety of positions over three years. Returning to Boston so his wife could accept a professorship at Boston University, Amram set up shop at a venture fund, pursuing possible investments and trying to see if he could come up with his own idea that the firm's partners would back. The idea came to Amram soon, though the partners' funding did not. Amram went ahead anyway, founding Individual Inc. in his Boston bedroom in 1989. "I went about nine months without a salary, living off my savings, before the first angel investor came in," Amram said.

Individual was based on one of the big ideas of that era, the same one that later inspired Parker's high school science-fair project: smart agents. At the time, before the World Wide Web, there was a vast amount of information on the Internet that people had neither the time nor the ability to find for themselves. Individual went out and located information that would be useful to people or companies and delivered it to them by fax and e-mail. Individual did well, and in 1996, the year after Netscape's watershed initial public offering opened the way for Internet companies, Individual filed for its own $200 million IPO. By that year, the news-retrieval service, later known as NewsEdge Corp., had 200 employees, 138,000 subscribers, and more than $50 million in cumulative losses. It also had $16 million in rapidly growing revenue and significant investments from Microsoft, newspaper chain Knight-Ridder Inc., and the venture firm Kleiner Perkins.

Acutely conscious of the power of trend thinking in the Valley and on Wall Street, Amram developed Individual's products but also acquired companies that sounded hot. One of those companies was Freeloader, the firm at which Sean Parker worked as an intern. Freeloader had been founded the previous year in Georgetown by a young Wall Streeter named Mark Pincus and by an America Online engineer named Sunil Paul. After querying strangers in a local bar, the duo decided people would value software that surfed the Internet on its own while the computer user was away. In a restaurant, one of the founders overheard another young man spinning business ideas, butted in, and introduced himself, and Jamie Hamilton became the company's first hire. Together they made a prototype and struck deals with search engines like Excite Inc. and the online magazine *HotWired,* later known as *Wired News. HotWired* readers then could download the free software, which would scan the publication and other sites at preset intervals.

As the media began writing about Freeloader in 1996, Amram at first offered $25 million for the company. "Freeloader had a unique technology and brand that I thought could get us into the market much faster than developing things internally would," he said. Pincus suggested that Amram double the price, a fairly outrageous request given that the company had no revenue. Amram kept calling to chat over the ensuing weeks, and Pincus and Paul casually mentioned his interest during an exploratory meeting to discuss joint marketing with Yahoo! Inc. CEO Tim Koogle. Koogle said Yahoo! might be interested in making a counterbid, and Pincus may have implied to Amram that Koogle was even more interested than that.

The classic seat-of-pants hustling found a attentive audience in Amram. "Yosi's style was frenetic," Pincus said. "He was a man on a mission, never without a phone piece attached to his shirt. He was incredibly optimistic about the future, even talking about how we'd eventually go against Microsoft." Amram described the acquisition talks as "kind of a mad rush." He split the difference between his first suggested price and Pincus's price, arriving at a bid of $38 million, mostly in Individual stock. The deal was struck in June 1996 and greeted with ridicule in Silicon Valley, where the satiric daily webzine *Suck* called it "era-definingly irresponsible." Not everyone at Individual was quick to disagree. The board, which had overcome some initial reluctance in approving the deal, was surprised when just a few weeks later, Amram told directors that he was planning three more acquisitions. The deals would have cost in the neighborhood of $20 million in stock combined, Amram said. And some of them would have brought the company into entirely new areas. The directors felt that Individual should concentrate first on digesting Freeloader.

As Amram described some of his new acquisition targets for Individual, the directors "asked a few polite questions" about his views on integrating Freeloader first, one director said. Amram felt insulted, and he displayed a temper they hadn't seen before. "He did exhibit some crazy behavior," said Bob Lentz, the company's chief financial officer. "I don't think he was possessed by greed—I think he was possessed by dreams." Amram's version is different: He said the board had approved the term sheet for the acquisition of one new target, Beyond News. Then it backtracked and "tried to make me jump through a bunch of hurdles" before closing the deal. In retrospect, Amram said, he did some fundamental things wrong. "I became overly consumed with what the Internet meant, how it was going to change the world." Amram said he should have slowed down to keep the board behind him. "When the whole thing blew up, it was a pretty traumatic experience for me, and I got depressed."

In July, the company announced it had placed Amram on indefinite leave due to disagreements over the pace of the deals. "Yosi pursued a wide array of investments and acquisitions unrelated to our core business," said Bruce Glabe, an executive vice president. The stock fell 37 percent in a day. Two weeks later, Amram issued a highly unusual statement saying that he had resigned from Individual after the board turned down his idea to contribute company shares to Free Spirit Holdings, a fund he wanted to invest in media, entertainment, and health companies. And he attacked the board, calling for a special meeting of shareholders and the formation of a committee to evaluate the board's performance. Later that day, the board fired Amram, who said he would fight to regain his job. The escalating and very public dispute seriously hurt what had been Amram's shining reputation around Boston.

Even worse was what never became public. Before Amram's press release, the company had attempted to reach an agreement with him, and it invited him to discuss how he might return. When Amram showed up for the meeting with the company's lawyers, he brought along a chess-playing friend—John Fanning. He installed Fanning and a chessboard in a conference room. Amram would discuss his job with the directors, then wander back to the conference room to play chess, as if he were playing simultaneous games. "It was surreal," a witness said.

After Amram was fired, he returned to the Burlington, Massachusetts, headquarters to collect his things. Director William Devereaux asked him to leave. "He simply hit me, and as a result of that, I ended up on the floor on my back," Devereaux said. Amram denied that: Devereaux "puffed his chest out, and I pushed back," Amram said. "He pretended to fall. It was staged." Employees called the Burlington police. When an officer arrived, both men gave their version of the events, and Amram said he wanted Devereaux handcuffed, according to the police report. Devereaux said he didn't want to press charges and that all of Amram's possessions were in boxes that he could take away. "Mr. Amram stated he didn't think everything of his was in the boxes and wanted to check his work area for his belongings," the officer wrote.

"I escorted Mr. Amram to his work area, and I could see that there wasn't anything in this area but the desk and chair and trash bucket. Mr. Amram went into the trash bucket and found several paperclips and stated: 'See, I told you they didn't pack all my things.' Mr. Amram then went into another area, interrupting a meeting to look into the trash bucket in this room. I advised Mr. Amram that was enough, that now he had to leave. Mr. Amram went into the eating area of the company and wanted to remove several pictures from the wall. I advised Mr. Amram that if he wanted the pictures he would have to take this matter up in court at a later date. Mr. Amram appeared to be confused and on some sort of medication. He was becoming very uncooperative and had to be led out of the building with his items by officers." Amram denied having been on drugs of any sort, and he said the officer's reference to paper clips "should be to the computer disks" he found in his desk.

Individual directors and former loyalists under Amram debated whether their leader had fallen victim to a raging ego necessary for the success of many corporate leaders, from Larry Ellison to Ted Turner, or had suffered some kind of self-destructive break. "It's a sad story," one director said. "He's got a lot of energy, he's very well educated, and he's very bright. And he thought himself right out of the box. He built this racing car, we got it halfway around the track, and he suddenly made a right turn into the stands." Individual would eventually be sold for a fraction of what it had been worth at its IPO.

By then Amram had taken time off, moved to Silicon Valley, and joined a new company, ValiCert Inc., which specialized in authenticating Internet transactions, like the bigger company VeriSign Inc. From the meltdown at Individual, Amram learned to distance his feelings from the fervor that can surround business leaders. "It was a very deep personal change," he said. "The important thing for me was that I came out of it with significant revelations about staying calm in the heat of the battle." Amram would need that inner calm during his time at Napster. But his psychological evolution had a downside as well: Amram grew more inclined to forgive unwise behavior in partners who reminded him of his younger self.

Amram decided to do his future investment deals on the side, as an angel investor. When Fanning began calling his mentor in the summer of 1999, telling him that Napster was going to be big, Amram put him off. "I'm not going to invest if you're the CEO," Amram told him, as gently as he could. "I don't think you're effective."

But in August, Amram was impressed by Andy Evans's interest and by that of Draper Atlantic, a real venture firm that Amram believed would invest alongside him. He agreed to put money in on three conditions. First, Amram would name the CEO. Second, he and the CEO would form the majority of a three-person board, and therefore be able to outvote Fanning if need be. And third, the company would move to northern California, where Amram could keep an eye on it. Finally desperate for a deal, Fanning agreed. Amram wired $250,000 over Labor Day weekend for 1.25 million shares at 20 cents apiece, and Napster was set to move across the country. "Yosi saved our butts," said Tom Carmody, Fanning's neighbor and right-hand man.

5

going west

ONLY A COUPLE OF WEEKS PASSED BEFORE SHAWN FANNING
and Sean Parker packed their bags for California at the beginning of September 1999, as investor Yosi Amram demanded. "It wasn't even much of a decision, it happened so fast," Parker said. Excited, he took whatever he could carry from Virginia and went to the airport. Shawn Fanning was supposed to fly the same day from Boston, but he misplaced his driver's license and couldn't make the flight.

When Parker arrived at the San Francisco airport and discovered his partner wasn't there, he realized he was alone in a city where he had no friends, no support network, and no place to stay. Then he heard his name being called out over the public-address system. He picked up the phone to the voice of Roman Dzindzichashvili, the fifty-five-year-old chess grandmaster John Fanning had lured from the rival Carnegie Mellon chess network when he set up Chess.net. Fanning had phoned

Dzindzichashvili and asked him to put up his nephew and Parker. Dzindzichashvili gave Parker his address in Sausalito, across the Golden Gate Bridge in Marin County, and told him to take a taxi. Parker gathered his bags and arrived late at night, having traveled three thousand miles to a bizarre new world. A gruff, potbellied giant speaking in a thick Russian accent greeted him at the door. "Sleep in there," Dzindzichashvili said. "We talk in morning."

Shawn arrived a day or so later, exhausted from being unable to sleep on the flight. "I was in really bad shape, just from programming for eight months. I hadn't been exercising or lifting weights," he said. "I was going to a strange place. I didn't get a sense of what I was getting into or really much of an understanding for what it meant to start a company or raise money or any of those things." With the Internet bubble in full bloom, finding somewhere to live was close to impossible for anyone of modest means, let alone a teenager without a credit history. So Shawn and Parker lived with Dzindzichashvili for three months. Together, they tried to adjust to their host's strange ways. Among other things, he would order them to stay silent and in their bedrooms when his chess pupils came over. He was renowned as a chess instructor, and nervous parents would bring their children over in the hope that they had produced the next Bobby Fischer. The parents would wait tensed on the couch and staring as Dzindzichashvili played the children and coached. Dzindzichashvili was usually serious, and the humor he did display seemed equally black. Parker had never seen anything like it, but Shawn had: It was a Russian sense of humor, the same kind that Dmitry Dakhnovsky had shown at Chess.net.

Once, when both Napster founders were in their rooms, they heard a searing, maniacal laugh. Alarmed that something was wrong, they ran downstairs to the room where Dzindzichashvili slept. When they looked in, they saw the giant sitting in front of his computer screen, his face red, laughing so hard that it must have hurt. He kept pointing at the screen, where a programmed cartoon figure would dance when Dzindzichashvili clicked on it with the cursor. "He dances! Look at him!" he boomed, near tears.

The living situation was not the only logistical hurdle for the teenagers. There were also the matters of transportation and of meeting and adjusting to their coworkers. Before they showed up in San Mateo for their first day of work, they knew almost nothing about the two central figures who would be running Napster, though they assumed both were successful professionals. They knew that Bill Bales would be a vice president and had the impression he was a Harvard M.B.A. with repeated scores as a Valley business leader. They knew that their CEO was named Eileen. And that was about it.

Steeped as he was in the ways of Silicon Valley, Yosi Amram was far more connected than an outsider like Fanning could ever be. As he wired Fanning the money for his stake in Napster, Amram told his network that he needed a CEO and other managers to take a risk on an Internet music company that was growing rapidly through word of mouth. To help with the recruiting, Amram turned to Bales, an excitable business-development executive Amram had known for years. Bales had worked at Amram's Individual Inc., and Amram had backed Bales when he founded a video news service in San Francisco called ON24 Inc. Bales agreed to work at Napster in exchange for stock and signed on as a vice president, with a six-month mission to bring in more funding and more executives, including a CEO. Bales and Amram soon had a stopgap CEO in mind: an old friend, venture capitalist Eileen Richardson.

⬜ ⬜

As often happened in the Valley, Richardson presented herself by accident. She knew Amram from when both worked in Massachusetts, and she had called him to talk about another technology start-up she was working for, a company so secretive it was incorporated as the Palo Alto Coffee Co. Richardson met Amram for lunch to see if he would be interested in investing. She spent most of the time talking about the pseudo-coffee company, which in reality had developed a system for automated Web scheduling of consumer appointments with dentists, hairdressers, and the like. But Richardson also mentioned that she was interested in other tasks, as a sort of hybrid angel investor and executive. That way, she could gain operational experience and stay close to the beginning of a company, when the energy and the potential financial rewards are greatest.

Near the end of lunch, Amram told Richardson that he was backing a new company she might be interested in. "It's called Napster," he said. "Go check it out." When she went home, Richardson logged on to Napster's site. "This is the most unbelievable thing I've ever seen," she said aloud. If a company had been designed from inception to press all of Richardson's buttons, it would have been Napster. An intense music fan, she had attended house-music shows and other concert festivals overseas and had been depressed to find little she liked as much when she returned to American record stores and radio. A single mother of two children, she couldn't go out to smoky clubs every night looking for new acts. And much of her career had been spent in musical backwaters where she couldn't have found what she wanted to hear even if she had stuck the kids with a sitter. Then, as a venture capitalist in Boston, Richardson had supported Firefly, which recommended new music to listeners based on what they and others with similar tastes liked already. The firm was later sold to Microsoft, and while it was not the biggest financial win of Richardson's career, it was still the one she felt most passionate about.

If Firefly was a *Zagat* guide to music, Napster was Waiters on Wheels. It would bring nearly any dish you wanted from anywhere to your home, and it was free. Suddenly, just by downloading one program, Richardson could find thousands of songs to sample. She told Amram she wanted in, and he hired her for a six-month term. She was the first and only candidate he interviewed. Asked later why he picked Richardson for the job, Amram gave his familiar refrain: "I didn't have a lot of time." But he added that Richardson had "a lot of enthusiasm and passion for the business." Besides, he said, "the first task was building a management team and raising money. She had done that, and she was plugged into the VC community."

Richardson was a good choice for a more esoteric reason as well. With her warm and engaging personal style, she came across as far younger than her thirty-eight years. Yet she was fluent in the financial language of the Valley. The combination made her a near-perfect safari guide to bring the wide-eyed teenagers toward the billionaire VCs they would soon need to approach. "Eileen was a good person to have as a first CEO," Shawn said. "We got along really well. She was easy to interact with, kind of energetic, and kind of experienced in areas we were not. She seemed to enjoy the time as much as we did."

Richardson had weaknesses, though they were less pronounced than Fanning's style of blustery confrontation and Amram's attempts to catch up with the speed of light. One obvious shortcoming was her lack of management experience. She also had a habit of failing to focus methodically on the task at hand. And she could get overinvolved emotionally with the firms she invested in and those that worked there. "Either you love her or you hate her," said her sometime adviser, sometime employer, sometime backer and sometime boyfriend, John Lee.

Besides her immediate and intense attraction to Napster's technology and her own career ambitions, Richardson had a personal reason for wanting to take on her first CEO job. That reason was Lee, her on-again, off-again romantic partner. Lee was the CEO of the purported coffee company, which would soon emerge under its real name, Xtime. Even though the two were in an off period in their romance, they remained close, and Richardson had agreed to help Lee by serving as a vice president at Xtime Inc. Lee loved being an Internet CEO, which at the time struck many as the most desirable job in the world. Richardson, though, thought Lee was getting a little full of himself. She didn't feel she had much left to prove, having been a successful VC for years, but she was tempted to show him up close that she could run her own company, then have it run circles around his.

A lot of their mutual friends thought Richardson and Lee would one day get hitched. It was her most serious relationship since her marriage, which had ended in the late 1980s. No matter how many times the stormy duet had broken up, they always returned to one another. The problem, as Richardson saw it, was that they were too much alike. "We were both used to being the dominant person in a relationship," she said. Other friends questioned the wisdom of her getting involved at Xtime, thinking it was poor judgment to work for her ex. Their relationship had hurt her professionally once before, and in time it would prove a distraction at Napster. But Richardson had never done things the conventional way.

          ◻ ◻

SILICON VALLEY VENTURE CAPITALISTS come from an extraordinary array of backgrounds. Before the industry was nearly taken over by amateurs in the late 1990s, many of the top performers came from entrepreneurial or technology careers. John Doerr of Kleiner Perkins, the best-known VC in the Valley, had been the number one salesman at Intel Corp., once throwing in a lawn mower to close a deal in the Midwest. His partner Vinod Khosla cofounded Sun Microsystems. Each had a deep understanding of how rapidly growing companies function on the inside. Another reasonable choice for preparation as a VC would be a career as a serious investor in public companies. Since almost no one before 1998 listed venture capital as an early career choice, "the only honest answer for the question, 'How did you become a VC?' is, 'I got lucky,'" said Scott Sandell, of the venerable VC firm New Enterprise Associates.

That certainly applies to Richardson, who was one of many who got there quite by chance. But besides natural intelligence and ease with other people, two useful VC qualities, Richardson had a third, critical strength: a streak of independent thinking. Once everybody agrees that a given piece of technology or an idea is the right one, it's too late to make a killing. Richardson had independent thinking in spades, despite a traditional upbringing near Middletown, New York. Her dock-builder father had worked on the Verrazano Narrows Bridge before he was permanently disabled in 1973. Her mother had emigrated from Ireland at twenty-seven, and they were poor enough that as a young girl, Richardson worried about the family losing its house. Often, Richardson's mother emphasized the way out of poverty that had nearly worked for her: finding a good husband early. The lectures made an impression, and after high school, Richardson went to secretarial college, following her mother's plan that she get a job where she could try to marry the boss.

Richardson's first workplace superior, a seventy-year-old lawyer, wasn't marriage material. Vivacious and driven, Richardson got bored with filing and other routine tasks, and she began doing some of his legal work. She soon realized that she could do a lot more than type. She entered St. Thomas Aquinas College in Sparkill, New York, then met a cadet at West Point and married him at age twenty-one. Without graduating herself from Aquinas, she left with him when he graduated and transferred to the first of a series of Army installations around the country. In each new town, she took an office job—once at an advertising firm, another time at a title-insurance firm. She kept thinking she could do more, even as she cared for her two young children. After her marriage ended, Richardson moved to Boston and looked for a company that might pay for her to get an M.B.A. She found Atlas Venture, a VC firm that wanted a secretary with research skills.

It was 1989, and no one Richardson knew had any idea what venture capitalists did. She grabbed a book on venture finance and started reading. "I thought it was the coolest thing I had ever seen," Richardson said. She stayed at Atlas more than six years, promoted again and again until she reached associate, helping to bring in deals including Firefly and Vermeer Technologies, which developed what is now Microsoft's FrontPage publishing tool. "She was energetic and worked hard," said Atlas partner Barry Fidelman. Richardson's biggest value to the firm, he said, was her ceaseless networking. She spoke at university panels and garnered local press as a rare woman in venture capital. Her good looks and self-described flirtatious manner didn't hurt: They got her calls returned more quickly. The public attention brought more deals to Atlas. And it was at the networking functions in the early 1990s that Richardson met people like John Doerr, Intel cofounder Gordon Moore, and local technology star Yosi Amram of Individual Inc.

Richardson stayed in touch with Amram even after Individual blew up in 1996, and they met up that year at the Agenda conference, one of the top annual technology gatherings. With Amram at the meeting was another Individual employee whom Amram seemed to like a lot, a disheveled young salesman named Bill Bales. "I liked him personally," Richardson said of Bales. "He was so full of energy, and he was fun to hang around with."

That same year, a new Chicago venture firm recruited Richardson to join them as a partner. JK&B Capital was flush with money from investor George Soros and Charles Wang, the founder of Computer Associates International Inc. Richardson signed on as a full partner and the sole software expert. JK&B had hit after hit, funding Exodus Communications, Phone.com, and other then-stars. On one of Richardson's trips west, Bales tried to sell her on a small company he was working for called Quote.com Inc. She wasn't interested. But when he mentioned his other job, at a small Web content-management company called Interwoven Inc., she got very interested indeed and went to look at the firm's Los

Altos office in early 1997. There she met the man who would be her main investment contact at Interwoven, early employee John Lee.

Interwoven made software that allowed multiple people to collaborate on a document and track the changes. The company was one of Richardson's first picks at JK&B, and it would turn the firm's $3 million investment into $300 million. It made her reputation as a VC, and it made her and many of her contacts rich. Interwoven prospered because "it had a fabulous CEO, who then brought in a fabulous management team, and it had a tremendous market opportunity," said Kathryn Gould of Foundation Capital, a venture firm that invested after JK&B did. And Richardson had been well ahead of the curve in providing financial support. "She believed in our vision before any of the other VCs really saw it," said Interwoven founder and first CEO Peng Ong.

But the early days at Interwoven, out of view and before its initial public offering in October 1999, were far from fabulous, as was its second CEO, a gregarious salesman named Steve Farber. The company tried to raise substantial amounts of money before it had a working product and serious customers. Farber was besotted by the Web, and he focused on shifting Interwoven's software to the Internet instead of selling to large companies. Now chairman, Ong had problems with Farber, and eventually the rest of the board did as well. Richardson, an Interwoven director, often flew out to Los Altos to calm the troops. Farber "was focused on the wrong things—saving money, not leading or strategy," she said.

It was hard for Richardson to act against Farber, investors said, because she was one of the most active in inspecting the business and had developed a good relationship with him. JK&B chairman David Kronfeld said that one of Richardson's best attributes was her ability to form such close bonds with entrepreneurs. "She clearly had a very hands-on relationship with Interwoven," Kronfeld said. Her relationship with Farber was so good that he got the wrong idea, sometimes suggesting that the two of them run off together. Eventually, after a final blowup by Ong, the board asked Richardson to fire Farber, and she did. Interwoven went looking for both a new CEO and new investors, and wound up with winners in 1998: veteran software executive Martin Brauns and Foundation Capital, both of which agreed to get involved on the condition that the other one did.

By then, Richardson had begun dating Lee, who reported to the CEO. When the new Interwoven CEO found out that one of his lieutenants was dating one of his directors, he told the other board members even as Lee resigned. Three weeks later, Richardson was also asked to step down. With more-established venture firms coming in and more-experienced directors available, Richardson would have been on her way out anyway, she and another director said. "She just made it easier for us by screwing up," the other director said. "I'm not a hardcore moralist, but serious people don't do this sort of stuff. She was a complete amateur."

Ong said he knew about the relationship between Lee and Richardson before the new CEO did. He didn't act on the information because so much else was going on, including a fierce board debate about the company's direction. But Ong said it "absolutely" bothered him. "It really caught me off guard. It was so out of the norm for me. I would say things in executive staff I expected to be private, and other people would know about it. It caused problems at the board level." While Richardson had done good things for Interwoven, Ong said, he was relieved when she left.

In June 1999, Richardson decided to leave JK&B as well. She took two months off, then joined Lee at six-month-old Xtime in August. At the same time, she decided to play the role of mentor, investor, and early-stage executive at other firms as well, and she called a few people she knew. The meeting with Amram was the first of what she had expected would be a series of exploratory efforts to find the companies she would work with. After he told her about Napster, it would be the last such meeting.

━━ ━━

BY THEN, RICHARDSON HAD KNOWN Amram for nearly ten years. She had known Bill Bales for several years as well, and she knew he would be Napster's vice president of business development, often the second most important position at Valley start-ups. Amram told her that he thought John Fanning, who retained majority control of Napster, was a good entrepreneur, just not someone he wanted as a CEO. And Amram said that together, he and Richardson could handle any problems with Fanning. "I completely trusted Yosi. I took his word for that," Richardson said. "I wasn't going to fly to Boston to check him out. I didn't think Yosi would get involved if the guy was psycho." Richardson didn't stop to think about how big Amram's equity stake was, and if that might influence his judgment. She also didn't consider Amram's history of rash investments. And Bales's presence should not have reassured her. Farber had fired him from Interwoven for failing to remember where meetings were being held and for showing up to give sales presentations with nothing more than a crumpled piece of paper, according to both Lee and Ong. (Bales said he was fired because Farber believed he had spilled the beans about Farber's unprofessional conversations with Richardson. In a subsequent interview, Bales said he wasn't fired at all, but resigned.) And the thirty-four-year-old Bales had been forced out at two other companies, including one he founded, his fellow executives said. Within his first months as Napster's dealmaker, Bales would prove to be a divisive force there as well.

Even in San Francisco and neighboring Silicon Valley, where alternative lifestyles are embraced and neckties are scarce as snow, the rumpled and dark-haired Bill Bales was unusual. Outwardly laid-back much of the time, he could collapse in tears at a mistake or grow so frantically excited that he would slap himself to calm down. Bales loved the pace of the wheeling and dealing in the Valley, an atmosphere that could not have been more different from that of his days playing Little League baseball in rural Thomson, Georgia. Bales dropped out of the University of Georgia to work at a brokerage in Atlanta, but he was already thinking about how to make a serious splash. "I've always wanted to do something big in business. That's what had motivated me," Bales told Georgia's *Augusta Chronicle* in July 2000.

If Bales's southern accent made it clear he didn't hail from the usual background, he also didn't act much like the others once he had arrived. At Amram's Individual, Bales made overtures on behalf of the Massachusetts firm to buy Silicon Valley start-up Quote.com, which gave up-to-the-second stock-trading information even to users with slower modems. The deal didn't go through, but Bales later joined Quote.com as VP of sales. Later, he would identify himself as a cofounder of Quote.com, and he was described as such by the media. That was not, however, how founder Chris Cooper saw it. Cooper had started the company in 1993 with his savings years before he hired Bales. "The only founder was me," Cooper said. Bales worked at the California company for at least five months. Then, Cooper said, he began to have "integrity questions" about Bales, declining to go into detail. "I had to let him go." Bales said he was terminated because he held so much stock and because Cooper believed that Bales had told people about Cooper's 1982 drug conviction. (Cooper said the topic came up only afterward, when Bales "used the threat of spreading negative news about me as leverage to wrangle a settlement.") Quote.com was later acquired for $80 million during the peak of the Internet bubble, making Bales wealthy. By then, he had moved on to Interwoven, and that firm's IPO stock also would do him well.

Everywhere Bales went, he made an impression. After Interwoven, Bales began a new venture in 1998 with television reporter and close friend Nina Chen. The pair attended a class on Internet video production given by Csaba Fikker, a Hungarian immigrant living in the Bay area. After class one day, Bales and Chen approached Fikker about turning his postproduction facility into a new firm, and Fikker joined them at News Direct. The firm produced video press releases and then news stories about businesses, posting them online. Funded by Bales and his old boss Amram, who served as chairman, News Direct changed its name to ON24. Subsequent investors included former Netscape CEO Jim Barksdale, former Times Mirror senior vice president Ed Johnson, and Dataquest Inc. founder Dave Jorgensen, and the company hired Sharat Sharan as CEO. Bales stayed on as the salesman and dealmaker. "Bill is a dreamer, a great businessman," Fikker said. "But he can get way out of line. He never pays attention to details, timing, what costs what."

Bales's single-mindedness got him into trouble when his personal life crossed with the professional. At ON24, he was aggressively flirtatious with female colleagues, paying them excessive compliments on their looks and telling them unappreciated off-color jokes. With one of them, twenty-two-year-old reporter Alona Cherkassky, he may have gone further. Cherkassky was friendly but rejected Bales's advances. Just after the July 4 holiday in 1999, Bales told her how nice she looked that day. Then, Cherkassky said, he mouthed the words "I want to fuck you." Cherkassky was upset but in a precarious position at the company, nearing the end of her three-month probationary employment period and hoping for a regular staff job with benefits. "I was pretty freaked out," she recalled. "I was like, 'How am I going to get him fired—he owns this place.'" She went to her supervisor, and Bales was told to leave the office for good. "Bill does not understand the concept of 'no,'" Fikker said. "If he wants to get into a room and there's no door, he will go through the wall." Amram said that Sharan probably wanted to get rid of Bales anyway and seized on the incident to make his move. Bales agreed that Sharan wanted him gone beforehand—after all, he had suggested that the directors get rid of Sharan instead. As for the Cherkassky incident, Bales said he merely mouthed an off-color punch line to a joke. Chen said she could see both sides. "Bill's personality is somewhat erratic," she said.

Erratic may be a charitable way of putting it, if Bales's criminal record is any indication. In November 1992, he was charged with driving under the influence, registering an impressive .16 blood-alcohol content. Many young men get arrested for drunk driving: That's why many states have first-offender programs, which replace convictions and more serious sentences with education and probation. Bales pleaded no contest to the charge and was ordered to spend two days in jail, then join California's first-offender program and pay monthly fines while on probation. But Bales failed to enroll in the program. And when the judge ordered him to appear at a hearing, Bales skipped that as well. This time, the judge issued a warrant for Bales's arrest.

The docket sheet summary of the proceedings in the case goes on for eleven pages. Ordered again to first-offender program. Failed to make fine payment. Ordered to come to hearing. Failed to appear at hearing. Arrest warrant issued. Failed to appear at next hearing. Probation extended. Failed to make fine payment. Arrest warrant issued. Bales finally completed the first-offender program and paid the balance of his fine in July 1994. His car troubles continued into his time at Napster: Bales's California license was suspended in 1999 and remained that way more than two years later.

In 1994, Bales went to work in Massachusetts, taking the job at Individual Inc. After his return in 1996, it took less than a year for him to come to the attention of the police again, when a former girlfriend complained that he was stalking her and tried to break into her apartment.

According to the woman's sworn statement, she had dated Bales for three years before his move east. During that time, he abused alcohol; slapped, bit, and restrained her; and threatened her with a kitchen knife. The relationship ended with his move to Massachusetts.

On his return to the San Francisco area, Bales showed up unannounced at the woman's job and called her there and at home. She told him they were through. In May 1996, she took a new job at Sun Microsystems and moved from Burlingame to San Mateo. "I did not list my phone number in an attempt to prevent Bales from contacting me, and I gave strict instructions to my family, friends and co-workers not to give any information about me to Bales," the woman wrote in her declaration. "I was forced to change my lifestyle to hide."

It wasn't enough. Bales found out where her new office was and showed up there four days in a row. Then he figured out where she lived and began coming there as well, even though she wouldn't open the door to him. After midnight one January night, Bales's ex-girlfriend heard someone outside. She was on the phone with a police dispatcher when her bedroom window broke. She fled back to the bathroom and locked herself inside until the police came. By then, the prowler had left the scene.

"I have not stayed at my residence since that incident for fear that Bales will return and hurt me," she wrote three weeks later. "His stalking has become more brazen, and it is clear that he is becoming more violent. Bales has followed me, called me and harassed me for over a year and a half. I believe that Bales is not mentally balanced, and coupled with his abuse of alcohol, I believe that he is extremely capable of violent acts." A judge issued a temporary restraining order to keep Bales away from the woman and her family for three years. (Bales said the woman's statement contained exaggerations and that he doesn't have a drinking problem.)

In most walks of life, an estrangement from reality is not a good thing. Yet in early stage business development, in which the job is to bring money and talent to aid something quite small, it has some advantages. That is truer in Silicon Valley than elsewhere, and it was truer than ever there in 1999. Bales's friend Adrian Scott, an early Napster investor and adviser from San Francisco, had backed a Bales company before Napster and would do so again at Bales's next venture. "Bill is a challenge to work with," Scott said. "But in those first few months, you need to get momentum going among investors. You're selling them on how big something can be when you have nothing more than an idea and a few people. You have to create the perception that they're going to get pushed out if they don't get in now. That takes a huge amount of energy and nerve. You can't be focused too much on reality, because you're selling a dream."

——— ———

WHEN NAPSTER MOVED TO San Mateo to take its shot at the big time, Shawn and Parker weren't the only ones in the dark. Amram didn't know about John Fanning's or Bales's legal problems, and he hadn't read Seth Greenstein's lawsuit-defense memo before investing. Richardson didn't know anything about Fanning, and she knew far less than she should have about her friend Bales. She didn't know about the people who had looked at investing in Napster or why they had passed. And perhaps most regrettably, she didn't know much about the law.

Richardson said that her first question to Amram had been about the state of copyright law. Anything as powerful as Napster, that took away so much music without paying any money to the labels, had to be illegal, she worried. Amram assured her it wasn't, and he told her about the Greenstein memo. And that was enough to convince her. She was foolish for not doing at least a modicum of due diligence and speaking to a lawyer on her own. But it's also true that CD burners were rare at the time— they would soar in popularity later, precisely because of Napster. So to Richardson, downloading music onto her computer meant it stayed there, playable only through the low-quality speakers that were then typically sold for desktop PCs. Most likely, you would take only a song or two from a given artist, she thought. If they were good enough, you would go out and buy the CD.

Richardson bought 333,000 Napster shares from John Fanning at 30 cents each and joined him and Amram to form a three-member board of directors, with Fanning as chairman. Then she subleased some adjacent office space in San Mateo from John Lee's Xtime, where she still planned to work some days. With Napster, Richardson decided that she had to keep nearly as quiet as Xtime did about its plans. The office space was appropriately anonymous, on the upper floors of an aging off-off-white bank building in San Mateo's 1950s downtown. Richardson also decided to move fast to raise more money. After Napster's June release in a test version, it had been downloaded thousands of times within a few days. Over the summer, the number of users swelled to a hundred thousand. As college students returned for the fall term, Napster had the potential to turn into the ultimate case of viral marketing, with word of mouth spreading it faster than any advertising could. But the usage was already straining Napster's capacity, and the system kept crashing. If the positive buzz was replaced by griping about the crashes, Napster could die even before its first official release.

Soon after Shawn and Parker arrived in San Francisco, Bales drove to Dzindzichashvili's house to meet them. Accompanied by girlfriend Holly Shin and a large golden retriever, Bales took the two teenagers out to breakfast to learn more about the company he had just joined. Parker was used to explaining Napster by then, having pitched to so many investors and gotten mostly positive initial reactions. But even Andy Evans, who had promised money the next day, wasn't much of a preparation for Bales. As Bales got more and more enthusiastic, his voice rose to the point of screaming. After a struggle, he brought his voice down, speaking rapidly in a hushed tone and muttering, punctuating his outbursts by pounding the table. Parker had never seen anything like it. But then, he supposed, maybe that's what a VP of business development was supposed to be like: a half-crazed evangelist who could convince other executives, investors, and companies to come along for the ride.

After breakfast, Bales drove Shawn and Parker to a rental-car agency so they could pick up something to get around in. On the drive, Bales sat Shin in front and the golden retriever in the back, sandwiched between Napster's founders. The Valley's future stars explained that neither of them had credit cards and were too young to rent a car in any case, leaving Bales a bit bewildered about what to do. They suggested that Bales rent the car while they stayed out of sight, then turn over the keys. The ploy worked.

During their first two days in the office, Shawn and Parker began setting up the computers and other gear they needed to tend to the Napster system. A few times, a woman they took to be an executive assistant at Xtime greeted them warmly. "I've heard so much about you," she gushed.

"I hear you guys are great." Shawn and Parker were polite, shook hands with her, and scurried off. The third time they ran into her, someone else called out "Eileen," and the woman turned. In the next second, Shawn and Parker whipped their heads around to look at each other. Whoops, their eyes said in chorus. This is our CEO.

Their first encounter with Bales had been one surprise. Now meeting the CEO by accident was a second. By the end of the first week, as the surprises kept coming, Shawn and Parker began referring to them by name: the "what the hell is going on" moments. Most surprising of all, the stunners didn't abate with time—they grew more common. "The frequency of those moments was increasing at a geometric rate, in tandem with the growth of the user base," Parker said. "We didn't have any real-world experience to process what was happening to us. It really felt like we were in a movie, even back then. Something crazy would happen, and we'd say, 'That's going in the movie.'"

Had Parker been more experienced, he would have realized that the next thing that was supposed to happen in the movie was the formulation of a plan for how Napster would make money. But for different reasons, neither Bales nor Richardson seemed to think that mattered much. Bales, Parker said, was "gung ho but undirected," adopting new business approaches and discarding them as often as once a week. He was interested in raising money and hiring executives, including someone more experienced to replace Richardson. And Richardson wanted to leave the decisions about the right business model to the experts, the big-league venture capitalists she hoped to approach in a few months. They would have the best connections and their own ideas about how to proceed, she figured. It would be a lot easier to have John Doerr approach Edgar Bronfman Jr. at Universal Music's parent firm than to do it herself.

That's not to say there were no early debates about direction: There were plenty, and they were chaotic. Parker would call strategy meetings and use the whiteboard to explain what he thought the company's next steps should be. "I would put on a presentation for Bill and Eileen, and halfway through, she would start screaming and running around the office, saying, 'We have so much to do!' Bill would say, 'That's brilliant! We're going to be a $10 billion company!' And I would say, 'Wait, I'm not finished yet.'"

One debate was whether Napster should eventually charge a monthly fee or instead charge per download. Another possibility was to adopt a combination approach, akin to cable companies charging different monthly rates for basic and premium service, then adding pay-per-view revenues on top of that. A separate issue was who would keep whatever money came in. At one extreme, the Napster crew considered offering the record labels every cent from the sale of music, while Napster would keep the profits from selling items like rock-'n'-roll merchandise. But how to structure a legitimate and sustainable business was simply not the focus. Fanning's deputy, Tom Carmody, flew out from Hull once for an inspection. When he was done, he called everyone together. "A business is like a person," Carmody said. "Napster has a spirit. It has a body. But it doesn't have a brain."

One of the first sketches of the Napster plan was drawn in early October 1999, when it had 150,000 registered users and 22,000 simultaneous users. (Some people have questioned Napster's claims for the number of registered users it had, which is a natural reaction to a figure that eventually climbed above 70 million. Napster counted such users by their log-on names. Users could register more than once at Napster, but the most common reason people reregister at other Internet service firms is that they forget their passwords. Napster's servers stored users' passwords for them, so they didn't have to be remembered. A second reason for inflation would be users who were banned trying to get back on. But relatively few people were banned from Napster before the service went dark, and many families shared one user name. So the logical conclusion is that the highest figures were only modest exaggerations. Ritter and another engineer who kept tabs on internal traffic reports believe that the service had more than 40 million users at its peak.) The main author of the four-page strategy document, which was discovered in litigation later but kept out of the public court file, has never been established. Parker said it was the result of groupthink, the record of a written discussion in progress. Meant for internal eyes only, the conversational paper lays out a "road map summary" of the new company's goals, showing that even then, the point was to cash out, not to make money the old-fashioned way, improve the technology for its own sake, or make sure the law was being followed.

"CLOSE ANGEL FUNDING," one section all in capital letters begins.

"PROGRESS USER BASE TO X# OF CONCURRENT USERS. GET TOP TIER VC FUNDING. PERFORM TESTS TO DETERMINE DEAL PRESENTED TO SONY. DO A DEAL WITH SONY. DO A DEAL WITH OTHER LABELS UNDER SIMILAR TERMS. DETERMINE WHETHER TO BECOME A PORTAL OR INTERMEDIATE INFRASTRUCTURE. LATHER. RINSE. REPEAT."

The crew planned to target Sony first because the company's consumer-electronics base might tempt it to tolerate piracy more, Parker said. As much as any document that has emerged, the October plan also reveals a strategy that comes close to a dictionary definition of extortion—using threats to extract money. By exploiting the obvious Napster advantage—"users know that by connecting to Napster, they have access to any music they want, absolutely free"—the author explains that the record industry will eventually be forced to negotiate in order to reach Napster's audience and get data about its habits: "We use the hook of our existing approach to grow our user base, and then use this user base coupled with advanced technology to leverage the record companies into a deal. The fact that we grow to 4 or 5 million simultaneous users with millions of songs (through the inherently viral nature of the Napster concept) can hardly be ignored by Sony or EMI."

The paper also proposes a campaign of subterfuge. Napster should not attack the record industry directly, instead stalling it until the company grew big enough to force a deal. "The key is to co-exist with the record industry, at least temporarily," it says. "The record industry is essential to our efforts." And the deal itself would be a trap: The plan was to "make Napster key to promotion, allowing us to ultimately bypass the record industry entirely." The document makes plain that the key to getting rich was to get as many users as quickly as possible, and that the good news was that this was happening already. "We already know we can grow the user base. The direction taken after this point is trivial. We can sell our user base out to a portal for a few hundred million, or take the following steps to create a billion-dollar company." Those steps included hiring top managers and programmers and, again, getting top-flight VC funding.

There was one solid reason for not choosing a business model that aimed at profitability. Many of the copyright laws and their interpretations by the courts hinged on where the money went. Taping a record for a friend was okay; taping a record in order to sell hundreds of copies was not. Napster's board figured that its legal chances were best if it stayed profitless for the time being. Fortunately for that approach, the stock market and venture funders were more tolerant of red ink than ever before.

——— ———

SINCE USER GROWTH WAS HAPPENING by itself, Richardson and Bales set hiring and fund-raising as top priorities. Their first hire in California was Ali Aydar, the twenty-four-year-old former Chess.net engineer, who happened to be working just a mile away at his third struggling start-up. John Fanning called Aydar first, and Aydar didn't believe him when he said Shawn had won funding for his idea. But Aydar called Shawn, who said it was all true, and he met Shawn and Parker for dinner the next evening. "At first, I didn't get how big it could be," Aydar said. "But Sean Parker is a great pitch guy, one of the best I've ever met." Parker and Shawn ran through how they planned to grow, then face the labels and make a deal. Suddenly, Aydar did get it. He lay down in the booth and looked at the restaurant ceiling. "Oh my God," he said then. "I knew at that moment it was going to be huge. I was like, 'I will do anything to be part of Napster.'" Soon Aydar sat down with Richardson on a bench outside Napster and told her that he had one big concern. He knew John Fanning better than anyone, including Shawn. "Are you sure you can handle him?" Aydar asked her. She said she was sure, and he joined the company.

Aydar was a rarity on Napster's fledgling engineering team. He was a bona fide college graduate with traditional training, and he didn't go around stealing software or breaking into other people's computers. He was also less boisterous than Jordan Ritter, who was still helping from Boston, and slower to complain, perhaps because he'd been in the business world longer. Closer to the Napster norm was talented twenty-year-old engineer Jordy Mendelson, an enthusiastic participant in "warez" groups on IRC trading pirated software and a friend of both Shawn and Parker. "Jordy is eccentric and phenomenally brilliant, like [mathematician] John Nash," Aydar said. "He could go through a pile of papers by college professors and understand more in two hours than I could after a month."

A crucial hire was the man who would supervise the young troupe. Eddie Kessler joined as vice president of engineering on October 6, 1999. Kessler was a pleasant and bookish forty-year-old who had taken a wandering path to a technology career. As a Harvard undergraduate, he concentrated in psychology and music, graduating in 1981. At Stanford, his next stop, Kessler did graduate work in psychology, focusing on music perception without finishing his degree. Beginning in 1988, he worked for Frame Technology of San Jose for five years, ending as vice president of software development. He had a string of short-term jobs and consulting tasks until he was named vice president of engineering at Infoseek, the Web portal later bought by Disney, staying eleven months at that job. His claim to fame came more than a year after that, when Kessler cofounded ReplayTV, leading the engineering team that came up with the advanced VCR. Once again, he lasted only a year, departing in 1998 well before the first product shipped. "Eddie is a great engineer," said ReplayTV's principal founder, Anthony Wood. "We just kind of had different opinions and started to have some personality conflicts."

Kessler's official biography on Napster's website mentioned only ReplayTV and Infoseek. Among the omissions was a brief stint at Quote.com, where Bales had also worked. That's understandable: Kessler had been dismissed from Quote.com because the technical staff didn't respect him, said firm founder Chris Cooper. (Kessler said he clashed with others at the firm and then quit, though he acknowledged that Cooper "was definitely ready to get rid of me.")

Bales knew Kessler from Quote.com, and he introduced the engineer to Yosi Amram before Napster moved west. Kessler and Amram had a series of meetings about one business and another. When Amram and Bales described Napster, Kessler was reluctant to join, in part because he was alarmed that John Fanning had sold some of his personal shares to Richardson and others. Normally, founders are the last to cash out. "That was the thing that really bothered me," Kessler said. Kessler asked Fanning about it, and Fanning said not to worry, that the rest of the company would be worth $10 billion one day soon. And Fanning passed along Greenstein's white paper on the company's legal defenses. "My reading on John was that he was a sales guy, unrealistically optimistic to the point of exaggeration, and very in-your-face," Kessler said. Amram, Bales, and

Richardson visited Kessler and his wife at their Los Gatos, California, home and pressed him to join, telling Kessler that he wouldn't have to work constantly and could still spend time with his young daughter. That part of the pitch was probably even more unrealistic than Fanning's projected market value for the firm. But Kessler signed on nonetheless, eventually buying more than two hundred thousand shares and imagining himself on the road to riches.

At Napster, Kessler understood some issues very well, and he knew whom to call on other points. But as at Quote.com, Kessler developed few fans underneath him. Some complained that he took credit for technical work that they had done. In one emotional dispute, Kessler vetoed a decision by the rest of the executives to grant Ritter's wish and list him in the section of Napster's website devoted to the company's history. At one time or another, Shawn, Ali Aydar, and even Richardson tried to get rid of Kessler as he failed to meet deadlines to launch new versions of Napster. "I don't think any of them would say, nor do I feel, that I was the best vice president of engineering the company could have had," said Kessler. But John Fanning protected him, and Kessler would outlast Fanning's two successors as CEO.

—— ——

IN BOSTON, RITTER WAS STILL running the back-end server, and he was reluctant to gamble on a move west. After a series of talks with Richardson, he agreed to fly out and discuss the terms that could change his mind. On the plane, he tapped out the state of things on his laptop. "The current design, version 2.0, is in many respects a hack," Ritter wrote. "It was a prototype meant to prove a concept, but which unfortunately fell victim to its own success. It is not stable, not scalable in any real sense, and realistically not feature-complete. Version 2.1 has made great strides over version 2.0 in the area of stability. Numerous bugs have been found and squashed, but unfortunately as bugs are fixed, more introduce themselves. . . . The harsh truth is that, realistically, the current server backend is not scalable."

Ritter made it to the Napster offices about 11 P.M. on a Friday and was met in the conference room by Shawn, Parker, Richardson, Bales, Ali Aydar, Bales's girlfriend, Holly Shin, who was working as Napster's secretary, and Xtime CEO Lee, who was introduced as an adviser. As Richardson led the discussion, Ritter explained where things stood with the system. Bales talked about strategy. Shawn seemed happy but didn't act as if he was in charge. At first, Ritter resented the presence of Aydar, who seemed to share Ritter's mission of keeping the system running. But after the meeting, Aydar drove Ritter toward a hotel that Shin had booked him into, and Aydar was remarkably open.

Aydar was excited about Napster, and he told Ritter what he knew about what was happening behind the scenes. Most important, Aydar said that John Fanning was still calling the shots, albeit from thousands of miles away. The two stopped at a Denny's restaurant at 4 A.M. and began a friendship that would endure through everything that was to come. It occurred to Ritter that it didn't really matter who was nominally in charge of the company. He, Aydar, and Shawn were the technical leaders. If they grew unhappy enough to leave, there would be nothing left for the chiefs be in charge of. Ritter spoke to his boss at BindView and told him how torn he was, and his boss told him that if he turned down Napster, there would be other great opportunities ahead. But he added that if Ritter could make the critical difference at Napster, helping to turn it into something huge, he ought to try.

On Sunday, Ritter returned to work out a deal with Richardson. Ritter had one advantage: He had physical control of the server code, and he implied that he might not turn it over if he didn't get a decent amount of stock. Richardson left the room to talk to Amram on the phone and returned with an offer of options and a $97,000 salary, significantly more than Shawn, Parker, or even Richardson, who were each getting $60,000. Ritter accepted, quickly moving into a glamourless Residence Inn near the offices in San Mateo. After three months with grandmaster Dzindzichashvili, Shawn and Parker moved to the hotel as well.

As at most start-ups, stock and stock options were a major draw for many. As the first outsider to invest for equity, Amram had negotiated an especially good deal. He got 100 percent of a new class of Series A Senior Preferred stock, with special rights that would prove important years later. For those, he paid the company 20 cents apiece. Most of the other early employees and investors got Series A Junior Preferred stock. Amram got 1 million of those as well, direct from John Fanning, at the surprisingly low price of 2 cents each. When all the transactions closed and the dust settled, sales by Fanning and the company left Fanning with 4.9 million Junior Preferred shares, Shawn with 3 million, Chicago financier Jim Gidwitz with 896,000, and Bales with 733,000. Richardson, Adrian Scott, Aydar, and Chess.net consultant Brian McBarron brought up the rear, while Parker and Ritter got only options. (Later they got stock as well. Both Shawn and Parker would sell some of their shares to other investors, buying Mazda RX-7s with the proceeds.) Fanning remained chairman of the board and was not shy about giving advice to Richardson and the others. And he had the power to back up his words, since he still had enough shares to veto any new class of stock, which would be the standard method for bringing in a venture-capital firm.

═ ═

ONE OF KESSLER'S FIRST HIRES WAS contractor Daphne Dembo, a long-time engineer and Amazon.com veteran who had a son about Shawn's age. One of her first missions, in turn, was to hire still more people. In that effort, she had no shortage of eager applicants. "I got five e-mails a day from people willing to *volunteer.* I had never seen anything like that," Dembo said. Napster being what it was, the hiring boom produced what she called "a most unusual collection of people."

More than one of the new staffers appeared to be transgender, and at least one used first the men's bathroom and then the women's. Many were under twenty-one and looked it. The sight of odd-looking employees was so commonplace that when a few teenagers sporting Mohawk haircuts were hanging around late one night, the Xtime employees in the adjoining cubicles thought nothing of it. Later, they were compelled to explain their reasoning to incredulous local police: It turned out the punks were exactly what they might have appeared to be to outsiders—street thugs interested in stealing Napster's computers.

There was one new Napster employee who admitted that he was sexually obsessed with young boys. The confession disgusted the core people, but they were just too busy to fire him. Better hires included senior marketing executive Liz Brooks, a Bales recruit who had been director of A&R, or artist and repertoire, at Sony and Virgin. Under her worked an immensely built man named Mark Hughes, an M.B.A. who referred to himself as "Chocolate Thunder." He was a solid worker but was valued more for the comic relief he provided, which included decorating his cubicle with Britney Spears and 'NSYNC posters and displaying an assortment of teen-idol figurines. "It reminded me of high school," Bales said. "People really enjoyed their popularity, regardless of whether or not there was any substance to their person." As the team worked late into the night, often sleeping under their desks, some would sneak off to the roof to smoke pot or just stare at the mountains nearby, marveling at the world.

Despite Richardson's presence and the increasing number of Silicon Valley pedigrees, it sometimes appeared there were no grown-ups in charge. One day, Bales took Shawn, Parker, and Ritter to look at a house where they all might live together. But the real-estate agent pulled Ritter aside and told him that his credit record was the only one of the four that qualified, and he balked at signing the lease alone. There would be no MTV-style house to throw parties in. The foray wasn't a complete loss, however. Bales asked the real-estate agent if she knew any finance executives looking for work, and she produced the experienced and grandmotherly Lyn Jensen, who became Napster's first CFO and one of its steadiest hands. Everyone made his own living arrangement. Shawn and Parker moved into a nondescript two-bedroom apartment nearby. For a long time, there was no furniture inside except for a mammoth television set. "I don't know if we ever used it," Parker said. "We were too busy."

In San Mateo, the crew worked late, often ordering Italian food from a restaurant named Amici's. "Fun, early on, was going to 24 Hour Fitness at two in the morning and lifting weights," Shawn said. "I tend to be obsessive, so if I could get enough work done during the day, I would reward myself by going to the gym." Even when he had time to explore, Shawn said, "it's really hard to find a scene out here that's not a bunch of geeks." Instead, after some long programming sessions, the young men blew off steam with drinking games, throwing bottle caps into each other's beers. The habit of smoking marijuana upstairs became more regular after the crew discovered that the Amici's delivery boy doubled as a drug dealer. On request, he began hiding pot under the plastic prop in the middle of the pizza that kept the lid from being squashed down. Like average teenage pot smokers, instead of the founders of one of the biggest

Internet brands in history, the Napster gang developed an inside joke that began with asking the delivery boy if he could bring anything that would go in a bowl, referring to a pipe. Soon, they just asked him to bring soup. Most smoking was done on the roof, but once it went further, with Bales and Parker slipping into an office and closing the door. A telltale odor seeped out. "The entire office reeked," said Ritter, who admitted taking a hit himself. After a second incident, both Ritter and Shawn told Parker never to smoke dope in the building again.

The lack of a life outside the office also led to more than one romance, another classic side effect in the start-up world. Richardson had worked at Xtime since August, and she thought she could continue there while helping Napster. For about six weeks, she did. But Xtime, which was growing by more traditional means, wasn't nearly as much fun. And it didn't help her complicated relationship with Lee when he hired a voluptuous and sweet young recruiter named Jessie Garrehy. Lee began dating Garrehy, who also helped Napster's recruiting efforts. A messy and emotionally wrenching love triangle followed as Lee saw both women. Richardson had some rough days, and after one last misstep on Lee's part, she finally told him she was leaving Xtime to work exclusively at Napster. "I was still loyal to John, really, but I'm an extremely competitive person. I decided Napster was going to be a success no matter what," she said. By Thanksgiving, Garrehy had broken it off with Lee, too, and begun to date Ritter, whom she found brilliant and warm.

ONE THING NAPSTER OBVIOUSLY NEEDED in a hurry was a topflight lawyer. Seth Greenstein, who had provided the legal logic behind the company's copyright defense, was in Washington, and he didn't do corporate work. Fanning had found Greenstein through a chain of referrals that started with one of his first calls, to intellectual-property and technology specialist Andrew Bridges, of the premier Silicon Valley firm of Wilson Sonsini. Now that Napster had moved west, Fanning urged Richardson to hire Bridges, since he'd already laid the groundwork. Richardson knew others at the firm, which represents as many as half of the top companies in the Valley. She went in to meet one of her contacts and explained what Napster was about, and the lawyer seemed excited.

He said he would check with the intellectual-property lawyers and get back to her. After some days passed, Richardson tried again but learned that Wilson Sonsini wasn't interested.

She was floored. How could they turn down such a hot business, especially when Fanning already had a relationship with Bridges? She asked Amram and others if they knew had gone wrong and found out that one of the very first articles written about Napster, appearing on the ZDNet technology-news website in August, reported that Fanning had "hired the firm of Wilson Sonsini," even though Bridges had turned Fanning down. When the article appeared, Fanning called Bridges to deny having made the statement. Bridges thought the whole thing was unprofessional. Richardson blamed Fanning for the ZDNet story and felt she had looked foolish in approaching the firm without knowing the background. "That was the first time I ruined my reputation for Napster," Richardson said. "That's when I should have quit." Napster ended up with a decent law firm, Fenwick & West. But there would be no Andrew Bridges.

⎯ ⎯

As the hiring spree rolled on, Napster's board moved on its other top priority: raising money from angel investors. The obvious place to start was Ron Conway, head of Angel Investors LP and a Silicon Valley celebrity. Amram got the ball rolling with an October 7 e-mail to Conway and his partner, Bob Bozeman. "Napster, with its proprietary Music-Share technology, is pioneering a new way for music listeners to reliably find, share and download digital music over the Internet. Recently, 'MP3' has replaced 'sex' as the most searched-for term on the Internet," Amram wrote. After recounting the past problems with broken links and the breakthrough of having one giant, continuously updated mass library of music, Amram wrote that Napster already had two hundred thousand registered users offering 3.5 million files. All of that, without having spent a dime on marketing. "I think this would be an exciting opportunity for Angel Investors. The angel round seems to be highly oversubscribed, but if you move quickly I would like to try and get Angel Investor's [sic] in." It was a pitch perfectly geared for Conway—the company is growing fast, it's on the Internet, and other investors want in. Better move fast.

Richardson met Bozeman and gave a forty-five-minute presentation. He was ready to write the check before she was done.

It was a route that many other companies had taken and, at the time, a promising one: A mysteriously large number of Conway's angel investments got larger venture funding down the road. Yet by late 1999, it seemed remarkably easy to get a blessing from Conway—an unimposing middle-aged man in glasses who came across more as an agreeable frat boy than as one of the most important men in the Valley.

Conway's technology career started right after college, when he went to work for chip manufacturer National Semiconductor Corp., soon emerging as head of sales for the company division that sold chips to car-makers. Denied a raise, he left for a nine-person start-up called Altos Computer Systems, where he went on the road making sales calls. When the company went public in 1982, Conway's 2 percent stake was suddenly worth $5 million. Three years later, as Altos was slumping, Conway quit, spending his time on charity efforts and advising other start-ups, always taking a piece of the equity for his services. After briefly returning to Altos and helping sell it to another firm, a deal that netted him $2 million, Conway was itching to get back in the game full-time. He bought a majority stake in a computer-instruction firm called Personal Training Systems, took over as CEO, and resolved to either make it big or sell it. Building the struggling company proved hard, but at long last, as the company was running out of money, Conway pulled off another lucrative sale.

While trying to peddle Personal Training, Conway came in contact with more and more rising Silicon Valley stars. One was Kim Polese, a core developer of Sun Microsystems' Java programming language. He thought she was an up-and-comer, and when he read that she was starting a new company named Marimba Inc. he pestered her with uninvited advice for more than a year until she relented and allowed him to invest in the company's second financing round alongside VC kingpin Kleiner Perkins, which had backed Sun, Netscape, and Amazon.com. "He was very pushy," Polese told author Gary Rivlin for his 2001 book about Conway, *The Godfather of Silicon Valley*. But he was pushy "in an inoffensive way. In fact, in a rather charming way. That he cared about the human side was very clear." In fact, the human side was Conway's obvious strength. He was often described as a consummate salesman, someone who quickly put others at ease.

Conway rubbed elbows at the Band of Angels, an organized group of individual investors. In 1997 he struck out on his own, pillaging his Rolodex to raise a $4 million fund to invest at $200,000 a pop. But as he met more investors with good ideas, it didn't seem like enough money. In late 1998 he started over with Angel Investors, raising $30 million in what seemed like no time.

— —

CONWAY WAS SURFING A RISING WAVE of incredible returns for companies that went public with no profits and speculative ideas, a wave epitomized by the November 1998 IPO of TheGlobe.com, a profitless enterprise run by two photogenic recent college graduates providing free homepages and chats on the Web. TheGlobe.com shares rose from $9 to $97 the first day, spurred by day trading and chat-room hype. That day may have been the nadir of rationality, the bottom of a slide that had begun with the 1995 IPO of Netscape. Netscape's main product was also free, the most popular Web browser, but at least it was a major innovation.

With TheGlobe and its ilk, the traditional due diligence performed by angel investors and venture-capital firms became completely passé. With ridiculous companies making billionaires out of entrepreneurs and those lucky enough to get in early, it didn't matter whether there was a sound idea at the core or not. The rational thing to do was get into as many companies as possible as soon as possible, wait for the IPO, then sell and make a bundle. Just like the economics of the record industry, you needed only one monster hit to make up for a hundred no-shows.

Such lack of scrutiny made for some appalling companies. While there are now hundreds of examples, it is worth recalling a few for the sake of context. There was Pixelon, which claimed to have a new system for transmitting video over the Web. In fact, the firm's top-secret locked boxes guarded off-the-shelf goods bought from other companies. Michael Fenne, the entrepreneur behind Pixelon Inc., raised $30 million from investors, none of whom bothered to get a routine records check, which would have shown that Fenne was not what he claimed. He was actually one David Stanley, a fugitive from a Virginia embezzlement charge.

What really set Pixelon apart, though, was what it did with the money it raised. Fenne blew more than half of the take on one of the largest parties Las Vegas had ever seen, hiring performers such as the Dixie Chicks, Tony Bennett, and the Who to play. The concert was recorded, theoretically to be made available to Internet viewers for a fee. Instead, it became a good-bye party. The expenditure prompted a board inquiry that led to Fenne's ouster, eventual exposure, and arrest.

Another Internet video firm that qualifies as a paragon of the times was a Santa Monica firm called Digital Entertainment Network. DEN made it as far as an IPO filing on the strength of venture money from Microsoft, Intel, and Dell Computer. The plan was to offer series of videos for niche teen audiences unserved even by obscure cable television channels. There were a number of fairly serious problems with the idea, including the fact that studio production is exorbitantly expensive and the reality that Internet consumers weren't ready to spend money for much of anything besides pornography and stock trading. The idea of supporting such costly programming with advertising money was likewise ludicrous. Beyond those issues, DEN had a rather delicate management problem that a cursory check by the directors should have flagged. The founder and chairman of the firm, Marc Collins-Rector, was living with two of the company's top officers. One had been his sexual partner since both had worked at early Internet service provider Concentric Network Corp., when the partner was sixteen. The other, a good-looking ex-Disney child actor named Brock Pierce, moved into the house at age seventeen and was paid a $250,000 salary for unspecified duties at DEN. Even after a former Concentric employee filed suit alleging that Collins-Rector had molested him at age fourteen, DEN survived. "I knew it was the ultimate Internet scam, but I figured I could flip the stock in six months," one executive explained, neatly summing up the era's prevailing work ethic. Only after the *Los Angeles Times* reported that Collins-Rector had been living with Pierce since before Pierce reached the age of consent and that other young DEN employees had been pressured to take social trips with the trio did the company collapse, filing for bankruptcy as the three men fled the country. Collins-Rector was arrested in Spain in the spring of 2002, and the United States began extradition proceedings over federal sex charges.

Those cases were extreme. Most dot-coms were not criminal—they were just incredibly stupid ideas suddenly flourishing like weeds in an untended lot. More typical was Pets.com, funded by Silicon Valley's Hummer Winblad Venture Partners. Pets.com was the first online pet-supply store to make a national splash, in August 1999, but the battle was joined within months by PetSmart.com Inc., and brick-and-mortar-backed Petopia and Petstore Inc. A shining example of the grow-at-any-cost mantra espoused by one of its investors, Amazon.com, Pets.com blew an astounding $27 million on advertising in one year yet managed only $5.2 million in quarterly sales before an overpriced IPO that sent its stock out over a cliff and down. That collapse wasn't much of a surprise, since the sales Pets.com did close were at a loss. In retrospect, perhaps shipping twenty pounds of kitty litter by next-day mail at a deep discount wasn't the most sustainable of business plans, even if pets can't drive. Pets.com shut its virtual doors in November 2000, with its omnipresent sock puppet as one of its most valuable remaining assets.

THE DOT-COMS AS A WHOLE were little more than a publicly supported pyramid scheme, built on the long-true presumption that an even dumber investor was just down the road. With more finesse, Kleiner Perkins' John Doerr called the process "the largest legal creation of wealth in the history of the planet." And Ron Conway had the perfect strategy for taking advantage of the situation. At the height of the boom, as professional investors saw it, the entrepreneurs held all the high cards. If you asked too many questions or dawdled too long, they could walk down the block and get cash from someone else. Conway didn't dawdle. He used his prodigious network, always pressing for the latest gossip on what was hot and then investing quickly. Then he worked the all-too-receptive media to hype his finds. Sometimes, he tried both tacks at the same place. One of Conway's investments was in *Red Herring*, a San Francisco magazine covering the venture industry. Conway would give editorial director Chris Alden, who was an Angel Investors limited partner, an update on the fund's new investments. Then he would walk down the hall and pitch the magazine's news staff on his start-ups.

Silicon Valley investors lived in a clubby world, where personal relationships were paramount. Many VC firms wouldn't even look at a business plan unless the author had been vouched for by someone the firm knew, like Conway. What Conway did best was institutionalize the relationship process. He looked for who else was going in on a deal, then followed suit, sometimes with only a two- or three-sentence description of the product. The important thing was the pedigree of the managers and the other investors. If they were good enough, they should be able to get a later VC round. And if they got that, the odds were they could go public. The actual product or service was irrelevant. And the more start-ups Conway backed, the more people came into his orbit that he could pump for information. He became "the human router," in the words of Netscape founder Marc Andreessen, who took Conway's money for his infrastructure start-up Loudcloud Inc.

Conway mixed extra allure into his operation by making Hollywood connections, then bringing them to his Atherton house for charity events. That was easy enough: The entertainment industry's stars and producers were tired of getting upstaged by this newer, richer, and sometimes flashier elite to the north, and many of them wanted a piece. *Red Herring* publisher Tony Perkins introduced Conway to top agent Jeff Berg of International Creative Management. Before long, Hollywood stars Matt Damon and Ben Affleck, who were funding an Internet start-up of their own, auctioned off an evening with themselves at a Conway bash.

Most investors didn't put money in Conway's funds because of the star power. They put money into the funds, if they could get in, because it was the easiest way imaginable to make a killing. Steve Bennet, a software-industry consultant who taught a class on getting financing at the University of California, Berkeley, invested after Angel Investors' Bozeman spoke to his students. In retrospect, he said the problem with Conway's scattershot model was that "it only works as long as things are going up." With hundreds of firms getting Conway's money and only three other general partners running the fund, the whole thing would collapse if the mania stopped and the firms couldn't go public. "There's no way they can manage that many companies," Bennet said. Of course, that's exactly what happened. By the fall of 2001, the $150 million fund that Angel Investors raised two years earlier, Angel Investors II, was worth 50 cents on the dollar, according to confidential estimates that Conway gave his limited-partner investors.

But back in October 1999, getting Conway's fund on board was the first step for Napster to convince venture-capital firms that it was the real thing. And Conway and Bozeman told confidantes that Napster was the winner in all of Angel Investors II, the one that would multiply the fund's total investment many times over. Starting in late 1999, as Napster raised its second, or Series B, financing round, and taking two more bites the following year, Conway's fund spent $1.5 million on Napster stock. For months, he stayed away from the company's business. But twice in the future, when Napster's survival and his investment were at stake, Conway would come riding back.

Strategically, Conway's initial $250,000 investment was the most important piece of the $2 million Series B round that Napster closed in December at 80 cents a share. The other major financial participants were Korean investor Sung-Bu Kim, for whom Holly Shin had worked; Eddie Kessler; Excite executives Graham Spencer and Joe Kraus; Chicago financier Gidwitz; and Amram. Smaller amounts were sold to John Lee, Bales's friend Adrian Scott, and others.

━━ ━━

A NOTABLE ABSENCE WAS Draper Atlantic. The Virginia venture firm had won the right to invest at 20 cents a share in August, when it loaned Napster the emergency $50,000. But then it passed on the Series A round that brought in Amram and Richardson, largely because Fanning was still in charge, Amram said. But Draper's agreement with Fanning had been worded so poorly, from Napster's perspective, that Draper felt it still had the right to invest later at the same low price. "Our understanding is that we have the right to invest up to $500,000 at the Series A price of $.20, or 2,500,000 shares," Draper managing partner Jim Lynch wrote to Amram in December, during the Series B round. Amram was not happy: That would have amounted to the entire Series B round at a 75 percent discount. So Lynch offered Amram an alternative: He would swap the current purchase right for a warrant to buy just 1 million shares, still at 20 cents, at any time over the next three years. By that time, Lynch hoped,

Napster's legal worries might have been resolved and the company might have gone public.

Amram was stunned. "They were trying to string us along and retain the option, sitting on the sidelines. They didn't want to be associated with it because of John Fanning and the copyright issue." A half hour after Lynch's offer, Amram replied, copying Fanning, Richardson, and Tim Draper of Draper Atlantic's much bigger affiliate, the Draper Fisher Jurvetson firm in Silicon Valley. "Jim: I think we are miles apart," Amram began. "The company does not believe we have an agreement that was ever executed between DA [Draper Atlantic] and Napster. Even if there was one, according to the alleged agreement DA had the right to participate in the financing offering but chose not to do so." Amram said he could offer only $25,000 worth of shares at 80 cents, or perhaps at 20 cents, if he could legally do so without tripping over antidilution provisions protecting the Series B shares already sold.

Tim Draper didn't appreciate getting put in the middle. "Either don't involve me, or get me the documentation if you want me to mediate," Draper wrote in an e-mail to all sides. "It is the first time in 11 years of working with Jim Lynch that he has gotten this kind of grief for a deal, so signs point me at the entrepreneur."

The saga continued through the Series B and into February, when Amram tried to end it once more as the stakes rose. "Napster is beginning to approach [venture firms] for our next round next week and I think that having to discuss the DA history will not be beneficial to either of us," Amram wrote, relatively cordially. He was right about that: Reasonable VCs would be less eager to invest in a company with a large chunk of ownership still in dispute. Sensing a timing advantage, Lynch stuck with his most recent offer, warrants to buy four hundred thousand shares at 80 cents over the next five years, or 2 percent of the diluted stock. Amram came back with an icy rejection. "I guess we all have our own judgment and standards that we live by," he wrote, offering half as many shares. Without a deal, he said, Napster might sue and launch a public-relations war. And, Amram suggested darkly, individuals might sue Draper and its principals personally for defamation, misrepresentation, and "usury laws and unconscionable acts (I will let your imagination continue here)."

Amram heard no response for nine days. When he asked why, Lynch was quick to the point: "1. We don't respond to threats. 2. After discussing the situation, in detail, with Tim, our offer to resolve the matter has been withdrawn." Improbably, John Fanning now urged escalation. "They called your bluff," he wrote Amram. "Now we have to draft a complaint." Napster was hardly in a position to initiate new lawsuits, and it didn't, leaving the matter to fester for more than a year. Every time Napster closed new financing, it had to disclose the unpleasant experience with its first funder. While the dispute was never revealed to the public, gossip got enough circulation in the venture world that one enterprising investor later approached Draper Fisher and offered to buy Draper Atlantic's right to invest. Lynch declined to discuss the experience beyond this statement: "We have an investment right in Napster. It may be the best investment we've ever made. It may be the worst. Either way, it may be the most noteworthy."

6

fame

AS CRAZY AS IT WAS FOR SHAWN FANNING AND THE OTHERS
in the fall of 1999, the period provided many of the high points in their
adventure. John Fanning stayed in Hull most of the time, reappearing
mainly for board meetings. Nobody had sued anybody, and perhaps they
wouldn't. And no matter how messed up the business side of the
company was, the engineers managed to teach themselves just enough
new tricks to keep the system from collapsing as the number of users
soared into the millions. The crew was beginning to have a tough time
imagining what could stop Napster from becoming the fastest-growing
business in history. When there was time for fun, it was serious fun: The
Napster-sponsored rave in October was just one of the temporary escapes
from reality.

It was after another chemically enhanced rave that Shawn and Sean
Parker returned home and flipped on MTV. They caught a few seconds

of a news update about Napster—the first time they had heard the name of their company broadcast. "We weren't sure that we'd really seen it," Parker said. "We were pointing at each other and rolling on the floor. Practically all my dreams were playing out before my eyes." There were other causes for celebration inside Napster's offices. One of the best nights was in November 1999, when Ritter's team found a bug that had been keeping a lid on the amount of traffic on a single Linux server. For months, the number of users simultaneously connected to a server couldn't rise past a thousand. The problem was both a frustrating technical challenge and a serious issue of expense, since it meant that Napster had to buy more and more servers to keep up with demand. After the team finally figured out was wrong and replaced the bad code in the kernel, it was like wrenching the valve off a fire hydrant. The number of users and songs listed on a single computer doubled immediately. Another night, the fourth version of Napster's search engine once again doubled the amount of traffic each server could bear. Ritter, Shawn, and Ali Aydar blasted rapper Dr. Dre and danced on the tables, mugging for each other's cameras. Ritter called Jessie Garrehy to come join them, and she drove to the office in her pajamas.

The Napster youth named the servers after bands, appropriately reflecting the temperamental machines' personalities. Pearl Jam, Nirvana, and Radiohead all had their strengths and weaknesses. And in the e-mail signatures automatically appended to their messages, the employees said a lot about what they saw as Napster's role in the scheme of things and their roles within Napster. Shawn didn't use a signature. Parker used a stamp that identified himself as Founder. Ritter's and Richardson's read: "Napster—Music at Internet Speed." Many had Che Guevara screen savers on their PCs, and the hours many kept were rock-'n'-roll erratic, often starting at midday and running past midnight.

Napster's employees were far from the only ones in Silicon Valley who thought they were part of a revolution—it's just that they were among the precious few who were correct. Dot-commers sold groceries online, electronically coordinated weddings, and gave away free Internet access, and they all thought they were changing the world. The year after Napster's birth was the peak of the Internet frenzy and all the hype that went with it. And the hype was key. Perhaps no profession in those heady days was as overstuffed as that of the public-relations specialists who tried to outshout or outflirt each other into the minds of the nearly as alarming number of new technology journalists. Many PR pros straight out of college—some of them hired by start-ups that had yet to find a CEO—would harangue reporters even at tiny websites with offers of hot exclusives. Often those stories turned out to be the release of version 1.1 of an unknown piece of software or a vague partnership deal in which no money was changing hands. But the unprecedented amount of cash poured into dealing with the press made sense at the time. Given the speed with which angel and venture investments were taking place and the slim evidentiary basis behind them, a clipping or two in a publication that an investor had heard of—even a single sentence in such a clipping—could make the difference between a multimillion-dollar round of funding and the company's founders looking for work.

So it is all the more surprising that Napster had no in-house public-relations person at all until February 2000, well after the record companies' lawsuit. When a record-industry spokesman or executive would talk to journalists and condemn Napster as sanctioned theft, communism, or the work of the devil, the reporter would dutifully call Napster for a response. The secretary who picked up the phone at Napster would then tell the reporter that no one was responsible for dealing with the press. She would get a message to Eileen Richardson—would the reporter mind checking back later to see if Richardson had responded? When there was no response, the story ran without it. But Richardson had reasons for this unorthodox approach.

In part she was preoccupied with other concerns, including hiring executives, sorting out Napster's messy capital structure, and getting more funding to keep the servers running. She also didn't have good answers to the reporters' questions, since after reading up on the law, she was increasingly worried that Napster would lose in court. And too much enterprising reporting might turn up John Fanning's spotty background, the lack of a business plan, or the antiestablishment ethic in the office.

But mainly Richardson was sticking to the October strategy memo's playbook: bob and weave until Napster had something serious to bargain with. From early on, there was little need for PR when Napster was growing by leaps and bounds like the e-mail system Hotmail had, without making any explicit marketing efforts. And the bigger Napster got before the inevitable awakening of the sleeping giant that was the record industry, the more leverage it would have to cut a good deal. If everything kept going as it was, Napster would have an audience well into the millions, along with a database about music consumers' habits that far outmatched anything the record companies knew about their own customers. Napster would be able to tell Warner Brothers that the average person who had Cure MP3s on his computer was most likely to be interested in finding new music by the Violent Femmes. Oh, and here are all those users' Napster sign-on names if you want to reach them. In the best-case scenario, the deal would turn out to be a Trojan horse that would make Napster even more powerful, at least according to the October memo. So when the Recording Industry Association of America called, appointments were made and then broken. Conversations with the other side were ostensibly cooperative but kept noncommittal, both to forestall a suit and to prevent the RIAA from learning more about the way the system worked. And reporters were fed platitudes. "My initial plan was to stay under the radar and play dumb," Richardson said.

When a story did break, being one of the few start-ups without PR helped perpetuate the sense that Napster was a true underdog, appealing all the more to its fan base. "It was David versus Goliath, and we had David," Richardson said. She was smart enough to put Shawn forward as a spokesman. He came across as soft-spoken, intelligent, and good-natured, an ungeeky geek, and his baseball cap became a recognizable trademark. Even record executives found it hard not to like him. As Shawn's popularity grew along with his service, the vast majority assumed that he had control of the firm. With no disclosure requirements of the sort binding publicly traded companies, Napster did little to dislodge the misimpression.

Websites run by geeks and for geeks were the first to take note of Napster and post stories with links to the site. Some of them soon seemed to feature Napster every week. News sites that focused on the music industry's electronic side or MP3s in particular also spilled digital ink on the firm. One of the first broader-audience publications to write about Napster was the online spin-off of *Wired* magazine known as *Wired News*, which was following the MP3 scene more closely than most. A

November 1, 1999, article on the website picked up on the piracy problem in a big way. "New music software that aims to make finding MP3 files easier may work a little too well," the article began. It quoted such Napster fans as the head of ArtistDirect, a sales site for musicians like Tom Petty, and such critics as CEO Dave Goldberg of music site Launch Media Inc., who said Napster was "just a different way" of getting pirated music. It also cited copyright lawyers who said that Napster and its users could be in legal trouble. Even if Napster qualified under the Digital Millennium Copyright Act loophole for Internet service providers, it would have to take down infringing music as soon as it was notified, they said.

The article also featured John Fanning, who identified himself as one of two cofounders, along with his nephew. Fanning called Napster "a microcosm of what's happening on the Net." And Richardson laid out her claim that Napster wasn't violating the law because it didn't host the music. Indeed, she said, it was trying to encourage CD sales by exposing people to new songs. Napster "is much more about community. We're not interested in people doing anything illegal," Richardson said. Realizing the legal position was tenuous, she stretched the truth at least twice. First, she said, "We're going to follow all the laws to the letter, including the Digital Millennium Copyright Act." And second, she said the company was in talks with the RIAA. "We're committed to working with them."

As the number of Napster users neared a million, some journalists figured out that its office mate, Xtime, a normal start-up with legal technology, a conventional CEO, and a press person, would be a useful place to turn for access. They called Xtime spokesman Travis Murdock directly, or sought opportunities to meet people at both companies simultaneously. One such event was a joint Napster-Xtime marketing-and-recruiting party thrown at the Bubble Lounge, a swank San Francisco champagne bar nestled between the Transamerica Pyramid and the hipster hangouts of North Beach. Strange as it may seem years later, many people in those days saw parties as a perfectly legitimate means of conducting corporate business. For recruiting in conditions near full employment, it helped to show prospective workers that their future colleagues were fun. For public relations, it was an easy way to reach a lot of reporters with their guards down. And, of course, the people monitoring the companies' spending weren't exactly in a state of high alert: hence the rise of celebrity-emceed affairs and extravaganzas like the launch party thrown by revenue-deprived Respond.com Inc., which handed out full-size bottles of Veuve Clicquot champagne to all attendees.

At the Bubble Lounge that night, most members of the press in attendance listened to a few sentences about Xtime. What they really wanted was Shawn, and Murdock had assured many in advance that they could have some time with the wunderkind. After a while passed with no sightings of the prime attraction, Murdock went around looking. Alarmed to learn that he wasn't even in the building, Murdock asked some Napster executives and learned the harsh truth: Shawn wasn't coming, for the simple reason that he wasn't even close to twenty-one. If he was going to be in a bar, it sure as hell wasn't going to be with half the area's technology press assembled as witnesses.

IN MID-NOVEMBER, THE DIGITAL MUSIC magazine *Webnoize* said the RIAA intended to sue Napster. *Wired* confirmed the report, citing an RIAA spokeswoman who said the trade group had repeatedly sampled what was available for download on the service and found that "virtually all file traffic is unauthorized." And spokeswoman Lydia Pelliccia all but called Richardson a liar for implying that she was negotiating. "We made several attempts over the last few weeks to communicate," Pelliccia said. "Our urgent requests for a meeting were not taken seriously. We really had no other option but to file litigation."

Richardson retreated into "aw shucks" mode. She said that the threat of a lawsuit was unfair, since Napster hadn't officially launched yet and was just beta testing. "We are freaking four months old," she complained. Wisely, she stuck to strategy and refused to say how many users Napster had, since the figure would totally undercut the posture of a little start-up under attack by a mammoth industry. The pose helped recruit legions of Napster evangelists, who filled Internet message boards and chat rooms with anti-industry rants. Since many knew that musicians got a tiny percentage of the industry's take, they had an easy target. And with little grasp of the law or Napster's history, the firm seemed like one of the good guys.

The RIAA finally filed the lawsuit on December 6, 1999, in San

Francisco's U.S. District Court, and it painted a different picture for those who took the time to read it. Filed by Los Angeles lawyer Russell Frackman and others on behalf of every major record company, the suit accused Napster of contributory and vicarious copyright infringement. "In an effort to ensure its users a safe haven for piracy, Napster promises and delivers user anonymity, and even boasts that it does not maintain logs of activity or other information that could be subpoenaed to reveal the identities of its users," the suit said. And whatever claims Napster made about promoting the new music, "the sound recordings reproduced and distributed are not obscure recordings of unknown or unsigned artists. Quite the contrary, nearly every hit song by every significant recording artist can be found on Napster." In answer to the question of how Napster was profiting from others' illegal copying, the suit said the company was planning to attract advertising and investment money. "Thus, Napster is building a business on—and seeks to profit from—the daily, massive infringement it enables and encourages."

The industry came well armed with evidence. It showed how Napster was involved in every step of the process, tracking when users logged on and off and steering them to the desired file by artist, song title, and connection speed. If a song disappeared because its owner logged off, Napster would find another copy of the file and resume the download from there. Worst of all, the company had bragged to users that they could "forget wading through page after page of unknown artists." The suit attached a list of a couple hundred songs available on Napster, including cuts by Elvis Presley, the Beatles, Jimi Hendrix, Bob Dylan, and Bruce Springsteen. Since the statutory penalties for copyright infringement maxed out at $100,000 per work infringed, two hundred songs meant at least $20 million in potential damages. If the court determined that each copy of a given song was a separate infringement, the figure could reach the trillions of dollars. To early inquiries about its defenses, Napster said mainly that it hoped to settle.

Her protestations to the contrary notwithstanding, Richardson had been expecting the suit. And she correctly predicted that it would put Napster on the world map, teaching more teenagers and young adults where to go for free hit music. The number of users on the system at the same time grew from about 50,000 when the suit was filed to nearly

150,000 less than a month later, at the end of 1999. The number of songs available quadrupled in roughly the same period, to 20 million. And the more songs that became available, the more incentive there was for new users to come. Napster was turning into the perfect technological snowball.

— —

INSIDE NAPSTER, THE COMPANY's haphazard start devolved into galloping chaos. "All of the resources on the technical side went to keeping the servers up and running," Sean Parker said. "On the business side, everything was reaction. There was no time to recognize that there was something awry with the way the business was being run." Before long, the dysfunction at the top began bothering many of the original crew. At board meetings, Richardson clashed so badly with John Fanning over strategy, funding, and other matters that shouts and curses were exchanged, leaving Yosi Amram trying haplessly to smooth things over. The result was often a paralyzing standoff.

Shawn and the others compared notes. They accepted the fundamental hard-line approach against the industry, but there was little progress toward getting new executives, serious funding, or big-business allies. For the kids, the power struggles and lack of direction combined with their desire to lead by themselves, Ritter said. "Shawn Fanning aside, everyone had delusions of grandeur. [Vice President Bill] Bales thought he was God. Parker thought he could do better. And everyone knew John Fanning was poison."

Shawn, Parker, and Bales talked about quitting en masse and starting over, perhaps incorporating a new company as Napster.com Inc. All of them were for it. "There were threats daily," Bales said. "Shawn was constantly resentful that he only had 30 percent." Once, Shawn said of his uncle, "How could he do this to me?" But the revolt always died at Richardson's door. It hurt Richardson to refuse Shawn, but she told him that he had turned over the rights to his creation, that legally he couldn't leave and then do the same thing elsewhere. "Bill was a proponent, as was Parker. It was me that kept saying no," Richardson said. "Ethically, I couldn't do it. It wasn't right."

Shawn kept stoic about Richardson's rejections, for the most part. "I was just waiting for it to be over with and go back to work," he said. Besides, Shawn added, "we had this whole theory internally, the technical people. That all these questions about the business model and the legality—as long as we keep focusing on the technology and keep making the system better, it will pull through eventually, even if we make bad business decisions, as long as we keep the servers stable and have it growing. That's what we know how to do, so we'll focus on that."

When new legal, corporate-structure, or financing worries came up, Shawn would get distracted. Then he decided to stop bothering. "I finally ended up saying, unless it affected whether or not we could afford to buy a server to scale or buy a database server or something, I wasn't going to pay attention."

As Napster's new users passed on the word to others, they also spoke more and more to each other through chat rooms built into Napster's system. Organized by such topics as Alternative or Pop, the talk included both discussions about bands and a large number of questions about how to use the service. As Napster had only about twenty employees by the beginning of the year 2000, the company itself could reply to only a tiny percentage of user requests for information. So it relied instead on senior members of the chat rooms to guide other users. But as with open channels in Internet Relay Chat—or any minisociety with anonymity, no rules, and a young median age—there were bound to be problems. Users insulted each other, made sexual suggestions or racial comments, "shouted" by writing in all capitals, or flooded the channels with continuous streams of messages.

Shawn, Ritter, and Parker had seen plenty of that kind of behavior before on IRC, even joining in the fray by knocking other people off channels with secret programming commands. With so many new users who could spread either positive or negative descriptions of their chat experiences, the Napster crew decided to have as many of the chat rooms as possible "moderated" by loyal users. It fell to Ritter, who also was serving both as head server engineer and as head of security, to manage the process. The company couldn't afford to pay the moderators. But it could entice them with the opportunity to test new versions of the system and with the prestige of being at least somewhere in Napster's hip hierarchy. Napster staffers began watching the chat rooms and nominating the most helpful participants for moderator status. Those moderators in turn nominated others, and debates ensued in a new moderator e-mail list over who was qualified to give advice on the system and who was vouching for whom.

One recurring debate was whether chatters with backgrounds in the more complex world of IRC were necessarily better than others. But as in debates over admission in any self-selecting club, the discussions could get petty. At times, one moderator would oppose electing anyone sponsored by another moderator he didn't like. A code of conduct was distributed on the moderator e-mail list, requiring them all to be both helpful and circumspect. "As active participants in a revolution, you must be conscious of what is and is not the concern of others," the document said. "Internal Napster Inc. affairs are just that. You will not disclose information about the workings of the clients [user-side programs], including, but not limited to, the number of servers, server IP's [Internet locations, or] new clients in test." Moderators also got the authority to require users to change their on-screen nicknames from offensive handles. In the way of the Internet, this led to prolonged arguments about users who outsmarted the automated filters by using nicknames like "flulclkly-lolu." On the moderator mailing list, some argued against all bans. "This thread has kept me confused," a moderator named "interline" wrote. "I understand the majority of you are against the censorship the riaa is trying to force upon us. Is there a reason that we are banning 'badword' nicks? . . . let's fight censorship, not start it."

The subject was one of the few among the moderators that prompted Shawn to take a stand. "I totally dislike what is happening here," he wrote on February 18, 2000, noting that the filters would catch the worst abusers. "Are you telling me we have banned over 5000 people simply because they have cuss words in their username (even legitimate swears?) I'm sure the value of these users in terms of contribution to the community far outweighs the fact that their usernames may be offensive."

Three days later, Ritter stepped in as the grown-up. "Censorship sucks, but so do assholes," he wrote to the group. "I have personally observed a /much/ greater likelihood of abusive activity from folks with inappropriate nicknames. While I work, I generally sit with two or three Napster sessions open, watching chat, often times having to intervene because 'pussyeater' or 'assrammer' decided it would be neat to start flooding curse words in a public channel." Since it was taking months to hire enough trusted moderators, he wrote that "we have to seek additional alternatives to make the job easier, and understand that lesser evils often times still make reasonable solutions." Ritter and Shawn discussed the matter further in private and compromised: Users with foul nicknames would be prohibited from speaking in chat rooms, but could still swap music. The desire for growth won out over complete dedication to propriety, but not in an unreasonable way.

Participating in chat rooms at all could require the patience of a saint. This three-way chat earned "Blaxthos," who didn't know he was being watched, his elevation to moderator:

<DO85> do you know anything about the new mp3 players

<BLAXTHOS> which new mp3 players?

<DO85> the portable ones

<BLAXTHOS> oh heh

<BLAXTHOS> yea, there are lots of different kinds now

*Boyd117 (56K) [sharing 14 files] has joined.

<DO85> but do you think you could help me

<BOYD117> I can help you

<BOYD117> tell me whats wrong

<BOYD117> I'm hear for you

<DO85> how do you transfer the songs you downloaded on to the mp3

<BOYD117> I care for all of you

<BLAXTHOS> well, usually, the unit comes with a serial interface cable

<DO85> I have that

<BOYD117> that's not so hard

<BLAXTHOS> and a program to download mp3's to the unit

<DO85> and the software

<BLAXTHOS> then just hook the unit to your serial port

<BLAXTHOS> install the software

```
<BLAXTHOS> and follow the prompts on the software
<BOYD117> I think you should listen to me instead of the other person
    they seem really dumb
<BLAXTHOS> each software is probably different, and I don't own a unit
    personally
<BOYD117> yeah I said dumb what you going to do
<BOYD117> that's what I thought
<BLAXTHOS> boyd: instead of hurling insults, try to be helpful yo
<DO85> I have everything up and running its just that I don't know
    how to transfer the songs I downloaded onto the mp3
<BOYD117> i'm leaving now so cya all later
<BOYD117> k then bye
*Boyd117 (56K) [sharing 14 files] has left
<BLAXTHOS> bye boyd
<BLAXTHOS> is there a manual that came with it?
<DO85> yeah
```

Blaxthos, a Lucent Technologies engineer named Brian Jacobs, happened to have been the thirty-seventh user of Napster and a friend of Shawn's. But many other moderators were nearly that good.

Others were not. Some were themselves abusive, electronically muzzling users without cause from speaking in chat rooms or banning them from the service. Sometimes the moderators just didn't know what they were doing. In one painful episode, a moderator banned a range of IP addresses that included not just the target, a racist Napster user, but a number of innocents as well. One of them, a woman in Toronto, booted up Napster with her ten-year-old child and was greeted by the message: "Banned—RACIST." Days later, the child had some friends of various ethnic backgrounds over, and they tried again. Again, they were confronted by the message, and the guests turned to their host in wonderment. The mother eventually got a message through to Ritter, who discovered the overlarge ban and hit the roof.

"I can't even imagine the horror," Ritter wrote to the moderators list. "We will not have this! This could have been DISASTROUS from a PR perspective—this is disastrous /anyway/." Ritter stripped the offending moderator of his status, ordered checks on old bans, and changed policy to reserve the ability for massive bans to the next step up in the community hierarchy, the dozen or so administrators. The administrators reported to a supervolunteer named Martin Lathoud, who served as the manager of moderators, or MoM, and who took his orders from Ritter. At times, disputes among the moderators would bump all the way up the chain of the command until they were resolved.

―― ――

A RECURRING FLASHPOINT WAS A seventeen-year-old Haverhill, Massachusetts, high school student named Wayne Chang. Chang, the hacker son of the owners of two Chinese restaurants, knew Shawn from his earlier days as "Napster," the fellow hacker. He found out about Napster the program early and took to it with a passion. After being made a chatroom moderator, Chang suggested to Shawn that the company also host a message board on its website for discussions that would be open to everyone, no matter what server and accompanying chat rooms they were connected to. Shawn agreed and put Chang in charge of the message board, which was visible to any Web visitor. That exposure put Chang in an unusually sensitive position, since the messages posted by Napster users included tirades against the record industry and open support of piracy, statements that would come back to haunt Napster in court. In one, a user wrote: "We all know it's illegal. We just don't think it's wrong." And the messages sometimes included recommendations for Napster competitor Gnutella, which Chang deleted.

Like many good revolutionaries, Chang feuded with others whose devotion wasn't up to his standards. One frequent rival for the evangelism crown was Rick Fletcher, who had been running an unofficial Napster Frequently Asked Questions site on his own. The Napster FAQ was incredibly useful to novice users, and Ritter tried for months to get the company to purchase the site and give Fletcher a modest salary. He succeeded only after another dot-com made a bid for Fletcher and his work. Before that happened, and before Fletcher had made a dime from Napster for his efforts, he decided to make a little money by selling annoying pop-up ads on the Napster FAQ site. This outraged the puritans, and a debate raged on the moderator e-mail list over whether Napster should drop its link to Fletcher's unofficial page or take other action. Chang went even further in private, taking the argument to an administrator in an IRC chat, which was how most sensitive Napster business was conducted. "Napster himself isn't making any money off this, so why is rick selling out?" Chang asked. "He's not selling out," the administrator replied. Besides, "Napster makes plenty of money, if you're talking about the person." Chang wouldn't back down, writing that "banners from the site are unappreciated," and accusing the administrators themselves of "cashing out." The administrator called Chang a "kiss-ass," and Chang signed off with a cheery "okay sellout." When Ritter got wind of the exchange in March 2000, he ordered Chang to drop the matter "or else."

Rick Fletcher and several other moderators complained to Lathoud and Ritter that Chang should lose his moderator status for erratic behavior. Once, Chang got carried away with the new, white color of Napster's interface for users, which replaced the original black. Chang tried to get a rise out of the moderators on the e-mail list by sending a message touting "WHITE POWER—wayne of KKK . . . (even though im asian)." Fletcher wrote Ritter in April that "more or less all the admins are really wanting ttol [Chang's nickname] to be demodded," or demoted from moderator, for posting information on unreleased versions of Napster, the KKK joking, and "near constant bad judgment calls."

And Chang angered Napster executives by showing up too often in the press and saying the wrong things when he did. One incident occurred after the release of Wrapster, a program that allowed non-MP3 files to travel through the Napster system disguised as MP3s. Wrapster permitted users to hoodwink the system and share anything else they wanted—text documents, pictures, even movies. Since the bandwidth that Napster was eating up already clogged the networks at many companies, the advent of unrestrained video-swapping on such a scale could have caused such havoc that the government might have been forced to intervene. Inside Napster, executives decided to ignore Wrapster and hope it didn't get too much attention. But Chang was ready with a quote, accusing Wrapster of "ripping off" Napster and "taking it further." Chang finally lost his moderator status. But with no one else paying as much attention as he had to policing Napster's publicly accessible message board, the posters went nuts in early May. An average visitor saw posts like "I JUST TOOK A SHIT" and "WHY DO JEWS HAVE SUCH BIG NOSES?" and felt compelled to write to the company, begging for a new moderator. Ritter reinstated him, but Chang was eventually demodded for good after he took privileges away from another moderator. Napster lawyers later killed the entire moderator program after America Online's similarly positioned volunteers sued that company for back pay under fair-labor laws.

——— ———

AFTER THE INITIAL PUBLIC ATTENTION following the RIAA's December 1999 lawsuit, Napster's growth became epidemic on college campuses that offered free high-speed access from dorm rooms. Richardson had thought Napster could prove to be the biggest case of viral marketing in history. But she still had underestimated how fast word would spread in academia. Colleges saw their networks clog badly. When they investigated, they discovered that Napster was sucking up virtually all the available bandwidth. Typical was the University of California, San Diego, where Napster's growth rate stunned the network administrators. "The first effect of this saturation was that Napster became virtually unusable to those on campus, but more importantly, this also slowed all campus Internet traffic," the administrators wrote on February 1 to all campus residents. "The use of Napster has now begun to impair the vital functions (education, research) of our network to the point that some action MUST be taken. At this point, the only option is to block access to Napster from campus machines." UCSD set the ban that day, and more than a hundred other campuses followed suit, either because of bandwidth issues or pressure from the RIAA, which was tracking copyrighted music going to student machines.

The campus bans were hotly debated and provided irrefutable proof that Napster had become the fastest-growing application for the Net. That drew still more media to the story, with the *Los Angeles Times* putting Napster on the front page in February 2000 and the *New York Times* doing the same in March. Closer to the hearts of the young men at Napster was MTV, which brought a crew to the office that spring and turned Shawn and Parker into teen idols. Of all the media exposure that would come, sometimes two or three national media interviews in a day, the MTV segment proved one of the most difficult. Shawn was quiet and sometimes awkward. It was the glib Parker who wound up with the most airtime. But even he found it tough going. "We had to balance being excited about it with having to represent the company well. You wanted to have a personality and be seen as having a hot brand. But at the same time, there was all this pressure to act respectable," Parker said. "It was always a struggle. We were constantly censoring ourselves: Certain words couldn't be used. A lot of it felt very forced. We hadn't developed a really solid facade, and we hadn't really established who we were." The coverage alerted even viewers in remote areas to the desirability and ease of use of the program.

Napster didn't want any more enemies, so it largely stayed out of the fight with universities over access to the system. Instead, it hoped that students would do battle for it. "We can't help the fact that everyone lovez Napster," one moderator wrote to his peers. "No worries, after they block access to napster, they will hear about it from students/staff."

Many students, even those who had collected hundreds or thousands of MP3s on their computers, merely grumbled. But at Indiana University, where a ban took effect after Napster's consumption of campus bandwidth neared 85 percent, a computer-science sophomore named Chad Paulson did something about it. In early February, he started a group called Students Against University Censorship and launched a petition drive. With Napster secretly paying the registration fee, he took the Web domain name Savenapster.com. The petition quickly gathered twenty thousand signatures and may have prompted Indiana, Yale, and other schools to bring Napster back, though another factor was work on a more efficient second-generation Internet system. A natural politician, Paulson was effective because he used neutral language and criticized the universities in an area of historic sensitivity for them, casting the dispute as a matter of free-speech rights on campus.

"Universities often overlook the student when making crucial decisions such as the ban of certain Internet privileges," Paulson wrote on his website. "Higher education in America should be free of censorship and complete administrative control." In his press interviews, Paulson conceded that many Napster users were looking for copyrighted material, but he argued that the innocent shouldn't be punished along with the guilty. Paulson was also honest when he said he wasn't using the system for piracy himself. A member of several bands while in high school, he used

Napster to look for live performances by independent bands that didn't mind their music being distributed.

Paulson was featured in dozens of interviews from MTV to CNN as a young spokesman for the Napster movement. Unlike those inside the company, whose words were governed by public-relations and legal concerns, Paulson could speak his mind. Napster adopted him as a virtual poster boy, and Paulson had more than a dozen chats with Shawn, Parker, and Napster product manager Brandon Barber. Paulson thought Napster could evolve into an amazing promotion vehicle for bands that never got big contracts. But Shawn and the others didn't spend a lot of time talking about that, he said. They seemed militant about changing the industry as a whole. "I had my own agenda, what I thought Napster would be great for," Paulson recalled. "They had their own agenda, but they wouldn't tell me what it was. They were like, 'This is great, we're really sticking it to them.' I didn't really get it. They were definitely playing the role of victim, but Shawn was more interested in breaking down the system and seeing what happened."

━━ ━━

As with rock music itself forty years before, public opinion on Napster divided largely along generational lines. Older, more-established Americans generally saw it as a clear case of piracy. Students and music fans in their twenties often saw it as mildly illegal—or soon to be ruled illegal—but morally fine, like exceeding the speed limit by five miles an hour. Some of the more studious defenders pointed out that artists realized very little money from their recording contracts or that compact-disc prices were absurdly marked up. One student interviewed on MTV said the amount of guilt he felt varied by the artist: He decided it was fine to rip off a no-talent band, or one that was already wealthy beyond imagination. Others embarked on different varieties of philosophical hairsplitting and rationalization. By the million, they were willing to take legal risks and moral stretches that they saw as small, and some declared that they would never buy another CD.

Among users under thirty, who would make up half of Napster's eventual user base, the antiestablishment feel of the system dovetailed with the rebellious posturing of much of the music they listened to. (For the computer-savvy, it also fit the hacker and free-software ethics.) Richardson figured that the best way to keep those fans as evangelists was to reach them through the people they admired most—the rock stars. If enough big names weighed in on Napster's side, the record companies would lose a lot of the weight behind their moral and political arguments, if not their legal case. So she embarked on a sensitive campaign to get endorsements or investments from top acts. She spoke secretly to Madonna business partner Guy Oseary and to early online music enthusiast and Beastie Boy Mike Diamond, among others. Since many bands were afraid to anger the record companies responsible for their promotion, most of the discussions were never made public, and some rockers who were supportive could do little to show their feelings. Napster posted the public tributes it did win prominently on its website. Courtney Love, Prince, and Dave Matthews all had quotes lifted from news articles. And Chuck D of Public Enemy went further, writing in an April 2000 *New York Times* op-ed piece that Napster was "a new kind of radio—a promotional tool that can help artists who don't have the opportunity to get their music played on mainstream radio or on MTV." Napster quietly paid Chuck D $100,000 and made the most of his endorsement, offering $5,000 for the best pro-Napster lyric written to accompany "donated" music from Public Enemy. Techno star Moby was also a big help, saying that "most people I know who listen to a lot of MP3s will download a lot of different songs, and if they like the song they'll go out and buy the album. The record company doesn't want me to say this, but out of the millions of MP3 files that are out there, if someone chooses to download one of my songs or an album of mine, I'm very flattered." A key part of the underlying debate, whether file-sharing has helped or hurt conventional sales, has yet to be resolved. The federal judge in the major suit against Napster would rule that it hurt, rejecting some surveys suggesting otherwise.

Several unknown bands that had been through hell with their labels cheered Napster on, in part because of serious thinking about the future of the music industry and in part out of a desire for revenge. Michael Lawrence, a Los Angeles musician who had been with a big label, wrote to Napster that he was a new and enthusiastic user of the service. He complained that his label had taken back 85 percent of the advance money from his band's signing, leaving 15 percent to divide among the musicians, their lawyer, their manager, and their producer, who had been appointed by the label. Then it got worse. "The label put us on the road and halfway through the tour a new president took over. Without notice, they pulled all tour support and label advertising for new bands. . . . We went broke trying to get home," Lawrence wrote. "Napster has the potential to put the power of art and business back in the hands of an artist."

The furthest Napster went to ally itself with musicians was sponsoring a free Back to Basics tour in July 2000 headlined by Limp Bizkit. The tour cost a whopping $1.8 million but helped spread goodwill, and Shawn got to meet band frontman Fred Durst after the San Jose show. But Napster also embarrassed itself by using a heavy hand against another supportive band, a punk group called the Offspring. The band was one of many that decided it had no problem with Napster distributing its music. "The Offspring view MP3 technology and programs such as Napster as being a vital and necessary means to promote us and foster better relationships with our fans," the band wrote on its site. But it grew annoyed that Napster had never asked permission. Cheekily, it decided to take its support a step further, copying the Napster logo, plastering it on shirts and caps, and selling the gear through its website. The Offspring figured that since Napster was playing fast and loose with copyright law, it wouldn't be in much of a position to complain. The group might not have realized, however, that if Napster knew about someone else using its logo and failed to get a signed agreement, it could have lost all rights to defend the trademark elsewhere. Product manager Brandon Barber urged the press team to tread lightly, perhaps putting out a humorous declaration of shock and outrage. But the lawyers were by now in charge, and Napster fired off a cease-and-desist letter to the band, demanding that it stop selling the products. Napster was duly mocked for the hypocrisy of the move. After several days, the company and the Offspring struck a deal giving the band formal permission to sell things, with all profits going to a charity agreed on by Offspring singer Dexter Holland and Shawn. They chose the National Center for Missing and Exploited Children.

The Offspring didn't know that it had stumbled onto another of the odd business blunders at Napster, a mess that had its roots in the company's unprofessional beginnings and that would fester on through 2000.

Seeing the immense value of Napster's brand, several employees had suggested selling logo shirts and other goods as an uncontroversial way to raise money and promote the service. They also had wanted to give away the gear to recognize hardworking volunteers, including the moderators of the Napster chat rooms. Richardson had been reluctant to approve the clothing plans because they got into the sticky area of profiting from the service prior to a settlement deal. She felt that any revenue taken in before the suit ended would be used against Napster in court, and she was right.

One Napster moderator, Tarek Loubani, a Chess.net veteran and a friend of Shawn's, asked Shawn if he could go ahead and make shirts on his own. Shawn told him to go for it. Loubani, then a college student in Canada, didn't want to make shirts with just the logo: He wanted something that would capture what he saw as the politics of the movement. He made a series with revolutionary themes, including one alluding to William Wallace, the Scottish rebel who inspired the movie *Braveheart*. Another adapted the slogan of the French Revolution: "Liberte, Fraternite, Napsterte." Barber warned him not to sell the shirts at a profit, which was no problem for Loubani. But when the company found about the slogans, it decided it had another issue. "It was deemed by the higher-ups to be too risqué," Loubani said. "It really upset me." Eventually, the company sent him a cease-and-desist letter. Loubani correctly figured that the company had bigger worries than he, and he continued to distribute several hundred shirts. "Maybe just because of Shawn's past, he and some of the other people didn't find these copyright issues compelling. I was one of them. I worked for the masses." As the rest of Napster "became this inflated, corporate thing," Loubani dropped out of the company's community, one of many radicalized youths who grew disillusioned as they realized that Napster was more and more about the money.

Shawn didn't give up on the shirt idea. As fans began clamoring for merchandise on Napster's message board, he tried to press the point. In April, Shawn e-mailed marketing VP Liz Brooks, copying Parker and Barber on the message. "We NEED to get some Napster merchandise on the site," he wrote, pointing them to the posted chatter. "This is crazy." Brooks responded that she couldn't do anything yet, because she had been waiting for Napster's board to sort out a dispute over merchandising rights for three months.

It all went back to Napster's infancy, when John Fanning's neighbor, marketing executive Tom Carmody, was seeking more compensation for the help he was giving Napster. Fanning gave him permission to sell Napster shirts on his own, keeping some of the profits and giving the rest to Napster either immediately or after it felt legally safe in collecting it. When Richardson learned about the deal, she asked Carmody to submit a plan. Richardson said she got no details back from Carmody and so had nothing to take to the board for a vote. Brooks shared Shawn's frustration. "I am and have been waiting on a decision from the board as to what ownership Tom Carmody has of our merchandising rights," Brooks wrote him. "Tom is ready to go, and I am also prepared to do an outside deal with someone other than Tom, but this needs to be cleared up." Despite Richardson's claim that Carmody had given her nothing to review, a draft licensing agreement did emerge from Napster's files during litigation, where it remained out of public view. (Richardson said in her deposition that she had never seen it.) That agreement, which Napster never signed, appears to conform to the informal arrangement Carmody said he had with Fanning. Without any payment from Carmody, it said Napster would give his firm, Summit International, licensing rights in exchange for royalties equaling 20 percent of the revenue from goods sold through Napster's website and 10 percent of the revenue from goods sold elsewhere.

In May, Shawn sent Richardson, Brooks, and Barber yet another message, forwarding along a T-shirt request from someone he admired. "I deal with this ALLLLL DAY. Many of these people are talented engineers at big companies," Shawn wrote. "I understand that therez lots of shit going on, but what's the plan?" Brooks replied: "I have Tom Carmody coming up on Wednesday to show me designs, ideas and deal structures. BUT—I still need to know what our status is w/regard to his rights— and that is not my decision!!!!! I wish it were!!!!!!!! How can we move ahead when there is an outside entity claiming the commercial rights to our merchandise, and half the board supports him?"

While he knew that Carmody might have some right to sell merchandise, Shawn was shocked to hear that he might have exclusive dibs. It was yet another thing that his uncle, the board, or both had done to screw up the company. "You mean he claims to have exclusive rights to our merchandise?????? No WAY!" he wrote to the executives. Richardson tried to resolve the matter on the fly, replying the next day that there wasn't any need for a board decision. "Tom Carmody has NO rights to our merchandise, no contract, no commitment, no nothing," she wrote. She said that in October, she had been willing to let him handle the matter, but that too much time had gone by since. Glossing over the problems with taking in revenue, she suggested that Brooks take over the project and develop a merchandising plan.

In the meantime, Carmody got tired of waiting for Richardson to give him a yes or no. Figuring he had at least Fanning's support, Carmody decided to act on his own. "I just went ahead and did it," Carmody said. "Did I nail it down in a contract like I should have? No." In June, Carmody arranged for Indianapolis merchandise firm Sport Service Inc. to sell Napster brand clothing through a website called Napsterstore.com. Some Napster fans found the site, and the company sold more than $60,000 worth of gear, sending a cut to Carmody. Carmody said he put a chunk of the money aside for Napster. In a little-noted case in December 2000, Napster sued Sport Service for trademark infringement, and that company quickly pulled the plug on Napsterstore.

As NAPSTER WAS LINING UP rock-band support, the Recording Industry Association was doing the same. It pressed its member labels to get rock and rap groups to come out against Napster, and some, like Peter Gabriel, obliged. "The fundamental point is: no music, no Napster. This is obviously a big business that was built by taking stuff without the consent of the artists who created it," Gabriel said. "More and more people are going to download their music, and if it all stays free and there is no control over the payments, then it will be difficult for younger artists to make a livelihood. . . . We would first like to be consulted before our stuff gets taken, and [we'd like to] have some vote in deciding what's distributed for free and what isn't." Rapper Eminem was more blunt: "I'm sorry; when I worked 9 to 5, I expected to get a fucking paycheck every week. It's the same with music; if I'm putting my fucking heart and all my time into music, I expect to get rewarded for that. I work hard . . . and anybody can just throw a computer up and download my shit for free. That Napster shit, if that gets any bigger, it could kill the whole purpose of making music. . . . I've seen those little sissies on TV, talking about [how] 'The working people should just get music for free,' I've been a working person. I never could afford a computer, but I always bought and supported the artists that I liked. I always bought a Tupac CD, a Biggie CD, a Jay-Z CD. If you can afford a computer, you can afford to pay $16 for my CD."

The record industry's biggest public-relations victory came in mid-April 2000, when the long-standing San Francisco hard-rock group Metallica filed suit against Napster in federal court. Metallica accused the company not only of copyright violations but also of running afoul of the Racketeer-Influenced and Corrupt Organizations Act, known as RICO, through its repeated transgressions. Metallica drummer Lars Ulrich said the band had gone through "a grueling creative process" for each song since its 1983 debut. "It is therefore sickening to know that our art is being treated like a commodity," Ulrich said. "From a business stand-point, this is about piracy—aka taking something that doesn't belong to you, and that is morally and legally wrong." Richardson was quoted as saying that the band had never tried to contact Napster. If it had, she claimed, it could have learned about ways to "leverage" the Napster system. Rap star Dr. Dre, whom the Napster kids liked even more than Metallica, also sued and demanded that his songs be removed.

The Metallica suit, which named Indiana University, Yale, and the University of Southern California as additional defendants, succeeded in driving a wedge through Napster's supporters. But filing it was a costly decision, image-wise. Even most Metallica listeners sided with Napster, proclaiming that the band had sold out years before, perhaps when the members cut their hair. A few noted that Metallica's popularity had been built in its early days precisely through unauthorized tape-swapping. And someone hacked Metallica's site, leaving the words "Leave Napster Alone." An ex-fan of the group launched Killmetallica.com and called for a boycott of the band's products. The site was joined by Metallica-sucks.com, Screwlars.com, and Paylarstoshutup.com, which sarcastically asked visitors to use an online payment service to make donations so the millionaire rock star would go away.

Some hackers went even further. Probably the biggest contributor to a wave of "Save Napster" hacks was sixteen-year-old Robert Lyttle of Pleasant Hill, California, east of San Francisco. Lyttle, who used the handle Pimpshiz, broke into more than two hundred websites and left a pro-Napster diatribe on each. He also offered to patch the security hole he had come through, for a fee, and ended with a cheerful "Hi Mom!" Among his victims were sites run by NASA, the U.S. Army Materiel Command, and the French Bibliothèque Nationale. Lyttle reached Shawn and Ritter on IRC and told them what he had done for their cause. The two looked at each other in horror. "Are you crazy?" Shawn typed. Lyttle's run ended in December 2000 with a raid on his home. He later pleaded guilty to two of the counts against him and was sentenced to probation and ordered to pay restitution to the sites he defaced. He said he planned to raise the money by selling Internet security services.

Others began to feel uneasy about their use of Napster. The most important change of heart came from Chad Paulson at Indiana University, the head of Savenapster.com. Paulson had been listening to all sides in the debate, and he had boned up on copyright law. He had seen the press reports about Napster's moneyed backers, and he was angry about what Sean Parker had told him on the phone. When Paulson first began organizing, Parker told him that Napster wanted to promote new artists. Yet almost nothing had been done on that score, while songs that were obviously unauthorized were trading like crazy. When Paulson asked Parker again about Napster's plans to support independent music, Parker told him that wasn't a priority, Paulson recalled. (Parker denied saying that.) Paulson also saw too many televised news reports that featured him defending the service, then cut to arrogant students with hundreds of MP3s by artists who weren't getting paid. He felt he looked like a stooge. "I wasn't really thinking about user habits," Paulson said later. "I was kind of naive, to say the least." Parker didn't help matters when he came to speak at a digital-music conference held on Indiana's campus. The teenager spent two hours huddled with a public-relations person who coached him on what he should and shouldn't say. Taking questions from the audience afterward, Parker was coy to the point of appearing smug. The rest of the time, Paulson felt, he was interested in being the guest big shot at college parties. And Paulson realized his politics were very different from those held by many Napster fans. He got e-mails in support of his campaign that he felt were Marxist in tone, including statements opposing all property rights.

After a couple of weeks of talking about his concerns with Parker and Barber and getting nowhere, Paulson wrote an open letter to both Metallica and Napster on his website, explaining that his views had evolved. "There are many kids out there today that do not respect the fact that artists work long and hard to put out albums. They take quality music for granted and they don't fully realize that even though a musician may be popular and on the radio, it doesn't necessarily mean they are full of money. Even if they are, there is no excuse to break the law, and copyright infringement is breaking the law," Paulson wrote. "I saw much potential with Napster, yet at the same time I had many issues on how Napster was used as a haven for piracy, something that I abhor." Paulson said that he "got to know more about the music business, as well as the Silicon Valley way of doing things" and decided that "the company is knowingly facilitating the transmission of copyrighted material, and they are making a profit from that without any crackdown." Napster was giving the MP3 format a bad name by disingenuously issuing statements against piracy without doing anything about it. "I personally want to see a plan that explicates (in detail) what the company plans on doing about the rampant illegal use" that he estimated made up 90 percent of Napster's traffic.

Since Paulson had been newsworthy before, his about-face brought even greater media attention. Napster employees were livid. Parker phoned Paulson and called him a traitor as an employee screamed in the background that Napster was a revolution that couldn't be stopped, Paulson said. Brandon Barber sent him a fiery e-mail: "I'm struggling to understand your logic on this shit. Are you looking for new press angles to support? . . . Your negative campaigning is the least of our press worries—we have larger fish to fry. However, I think it's safe to say that the sentiment around here is shock, disbelief and betrayal. On a personal level, I vouched for your ass internally and now you've called my judgment into question." Barber signed off, "It's a small world. Have fun."

Wayne Chang, the seventeen-year-old self-appointed Napster standard-bearer, went much further. To start with, he urged the company to sue Paulson for using the word Napster in his domain name. "Who the fuck does he think he is?" he wrote to Barber. Then Chang did something else. He hacked into the infrastructure company that was hosting Savenapster.com and made Paulson's Web-hosting bill appear two months overdue. And he hacked the site itself, adding a new story to the press section bearing the headline I BACKSTABBED NAPSTER. Chang was proud of the feat, and he e-mailed Ritter to brag. After suggesting that Ritter try to visit the Savenapster site "while it's still defaced," he added: "I also changed the pw [password] back on the shell, so chad won't think it's a server problem. . . . ps: delete this message." Ritter stayed mum, and when Paulson complained to Napster about the hack, Barber wrote: "I give you my word that no one affiliated with this organization had anything to do with it. I apologize for what must be a very frustrating situation." Paulson complained to the FBI, which was unable to solve the attack. In an interview, Chang said he would neither confirm nor deny responsibility. Paulson later quit school and joined the small online music firm Listen.com, then moved to Los Angeles to join Capitol Records' digital efforts.

THE MEDIA CIRCUS AROUND Napster hit a climax on May 3, 2000, courtesy of Metallica lawyer Howard King, who vowed publicly to shut the service down. In a spectacle designed for the television cameras, King and Lars Ulrich arrived at Napster's San Mateo office in a limousine bearing thirteen boxes containing the names of hundreds of thousands of Napster users who were offering Metallica songs. King demanded that the users be banned from the service. With advance notice that Ulrich was coming, Napster gathered its own supporters to appear. Several held a banner that read "RIAA = Master of Puppets," a reference to the Metallica album of the same name. Others obliged the cameras by taking sledgehammers to Metallica's compact discs. Still more took advantage of the heavy media turnout by bringing posters touting Gnutella or other sites. The new generation gap got its loudest display when Ulrich spoke from the podium. Protesters shouted at him to shut up and called him a sellout. "Fuck you, Lars," offered one. "It's our music too!"

Showing up with a lawyer was about the least "rock star" a move that Ulrich could make, and from the moment he realized Napster was housed in the decrepit building over a bank, he grew more and more uncomfortable. After pontificating outside, Ulrich and King went in with a dolly hauling the documents up to Napster's offices. Xtime spokesman Travis Murdock happened to be riding up in the old, creaky elevator at the same time and saw that Ulrich looked miserable. When the doors opened at Napster's fourth-floor office, the employees came up to him and told him what fans they were and how they had gone to Metallica concerts in junior high. Ulrich seemed to slump. "I really don't want to sue you," he said. "All I want is for artists who want to get paid to get paid."

Shawn and Parker were quarantined on the fifth floor, away from the press, but they and Ali Aydar snuck out for peeks at what was going on. Some of the Napster crew were upset at what was happening. Others were more annoyed at Napster's leadership for doing a lousy job of explaining to the public what the issues were. "The bands don't get the money," Ritter thought, exasperated. "The record companies do." Napster eventually issued a statement saying that it would comply with Metallica's request to ban the users. On May 10, Napster blocked 317,377 users cited by Metallica. Fans complained that they had been tricked into downloading a new version of Napster that made the bans possible. Soon a section cropped up on the Napster message board entitled "Circumventing Napster Bans," with helpful hints about how to get back on. After a news website linked to the comments, Barber ordered moderator Chang to remove them. A Napster fan, crying censorship, got hold of Ritter on an IRC channel and complained. "We will go out of business for shit like that!" Ritter replied under his "Nocarrier" handle. "Delete the post, or lose the court battle, and you lose your napster! This is reality man!"

7

the industry

IN EARLY 2000, NAPSTER EXECUTIVES WERE SQUABBLING over how much money and effort should be spent trying to win the hearts of pop bands. CEO Eileen Richardson wanted to do the most. She envisioned a New Artist Program that would encourage users to sample unknown groups and bolster Napster's court defense about having significant legitimate uses, the same argument that had saved the VCR before the U.S. Supreme Court. The allegiance of fan favorites could keep the public on Napster's side of the war in the press and on Capitol Hill, if it came to that. And open support from established acts might bring pressure on the record companies to offer something reasonable. But Richardson and her marketing deputy, Liz Brooks, were the only top executives serious about the campaign. Brooks got Napster to sponsor the free Limp Bizkit tour to promote the company, and later she offered the band warrants to buy 2 percent of the company, appealing to something more basic than their positive feelings about spreading free music. Brooks and New Artist Program manager Stephanie Norton also had secret talks with bands like Korn and Matchbox 20, offering special placement on Napster's Web pages in exchange for their endorsements. Band promotions and an "aggregation of legit partners makes us look legit and makes every partner in the industry realize they need to play ball," Brooks wrote in an e-mail. The executives took pains to keep the negotiations confidential. As Norton noted in one internal message, "these bands are in a sticky situation with their labels for setting up meetings with us. We don't want to piss anyone off."

Always combative by nature, John Fanning couldn't have cared less about antagonizing the labels. And others in the company didn't see much point in spending money on free concerts or promoting certain bands on the website. The vast majority of Napster users weren't looking for obscure music, and touting selected acts might be seen as selling out. If Napster fans sensed the shift, that might work against the company and its phenomenal growth rate. And that, in turn, might make it harder to get quite as much money when the time came to *really* sell out, to the record labels. But the most serious reason for foot-dragging on the New Artist Program, according to Sean Parker, was a legal one. "Eileen definitely wanted to do it, and it went to the board. But it didn't make sense because it had a different interface" than the rest of the song-searching. Since all of the participating New Artists gave explicit permission for their work to be on Napster, the presence of a distinct piece of the system that had only authorized songs could tempt the judge in the record-industry lawsuit to order Napster to keep that part and disable the rest. "We were arguing that there were a lot of noninfringing uses with the main services," Parker said. "We had to stick to our guns with an all-or-nothing approach, so we didn't need a dog-and-pony show."

The internal arguments appeared vital to Richardson and Brooks. But they obscured a much more fundamental problem. None of Napster's directors had dealt with the record industry before, and they had horribly misjudged their opponent. Even if the board had gotten behind the New Artist effort or won widespread enthusiasm from big-name bands, it likely wouldn't have moved the industry. After all, the big record labels had a history of opposing most innovations in technology. They were used to bands complaining about their onerous contracts or lack of marketing support. They were even used to gripes from *legitimate* companies or individuals owed hundreds of thousands of dollars. A business strategy based on poking the record industry in the eye made about as much sense as one built on trying to blackmail the Mafia.

In fact, it nearly *was* trying to blackmail the Mafia. Organized-crime figures played a major role in the history of rock-music distribution and sales, as thoroughly documented by court records, journalistic exposés, and books such as 1990's *Hit Men,* by Fredric Dannen. Royalties were chronically and enthusiastically unpaid, leaving music legends unable to make ends meet. One story unearthed by Dannen involved Florida songwriter George McCrae, who had a number one record in 1974 called "Rock Your Baby." McCrae hadn't seen a dime of the more than $100,000 he was due, and he couldn't pay his rent. He went to visit label boss Henry Stone in his office and threatened to cut Stone with a knife. "You really surprise me, today of all days," Stone said calmly. He fished out a thick wad of bills, perhaps a few thousand dollars, and handed it to McCrae. "But that isn't all. You see that Cadillac? It's yours, George," Stone said, and gave him a set of keys. Stone had a guest in his office at the time, and the visitor couldn't believe that McCrae had fallen for the time-honored cheap-car trick. As soon as McCrae left, he asked Stone: "How much did that Cadillac cost?" Replied Stone: "What cost? It's *rented.*"

Morris Levy, founder of Count Basie home Roulette Records, was just one of the major industry players with close ties to the mob. Levy affixed his name to the copyrights of songs he didn't write—like Frankie Lymon's "Why Do Fools Fall in Love?"—and did business with New York's Genovese crime family. Before his sentencing for extortion alongside a mob underboss in 1988, Levy managed to get letters of support from the heads of all six big record labels. (The present-day Big Five, all with subsidiary labels, are Universal, Sony, Bertelsmann's BMG, EMI, and AOL's Warner Brothers.) Such tough guys were revered within the record business. As the labels grew more corporate, the rough-and-tumble of the business grew subtler. But it did not go away.

Take, for example, the matter of payola. Even before rock 'n' roll took hold of radio, bagmen routinely gave disc jockeys money to spin certain records. Levy, for his part, gave the most famous payola fall guy, pioneering DJ Alan Freed, a quarter of the stock in Roulette. After congressional hearings in 1960, payola was made its own crime, separate from bribery. But the law was so weak that no one was convicted for decades, and the U.S. Federal Communications Commission specifically exempted "social exchanges," a loophole that essentially killed the law's usefulness. What's worse, the payola exposures and the new law made the record executives get smarter. Instead of paying off radio programmers directly, they started funneling money to outside contractors called independent promoters, who did what they needed to do with cash, drugs, and hookers, leaving plausible deniability for everyone at the record firms' headquarters in New York and Los Angeles.

Joe Isgro, one of the most powerful independent promoters and a former Levy employee, bragged of taking in $10 million a year to break records on the radio, out of a reported $60 million paid to the core group of promoters known as the Network. Isgro's independent record label released hits by James Brown and other R&B acts, and his clout extended to Hollywood, where he served as a producer of the movie *Hoffa*. In real life, he didn't play one of the good guys. Isgro was charged with racketeering and payola offenses in 1989. Employees of three different radio stations testified that they had accepted cocaine, cash, or both from Isgro's business in exchange for airplay. The case was strong but was tossed out because the prosecution blew it: They hadn't disclosed contradictory testimony from the trial of one of their many witnesses. Isgro returned to living the high life in Beverly Hills until he was sentenced to more than four years in federal prison in the fall of 2000 for loan-sharking. As part of that case, the FBI stated that he was a soldier in the Gambino family of the mob, an accusation Isgro's lawyer denied.

How big a problem were the independent promoters for the record industry? A yearly tribute of $60 million might seem easily affordable to companies with collective sales of $15 billion. But profit margins are thin in the music business. After a failed boycott of the Network served to make the promoters only more essential to the business, top label CBS Records, later bought by Sony, was spending an estimated $17 million a year on promoters, according to *Rolling Stone*. In a decent year, that was more than 10 percent of the label's pretax profit. In a bad year, it was half. In the 1980s, the labels came up with an elegant solution: They began charging the cost of the unsavory promoters back to the artists themselves.

The big record companies could do that because they could do just about anything they wanted and still sign aspiring stars. While the labels defend their practices by pointing to the more than $2 million they may spend to promote a band that flops, the contracts resemble those that decades ago left coal miners in debt to the company store. Promotional fees became just another of what are called recoupable expenses, which get paid back from the artist's advance. For most bands, that advance money is all they ever see, and it can be a big number. But the advance is actually a loan that's forgiven if the record doesn't sell well. If it does sell, the band must repay that advance before it starts collecting any royalties. And the repayment comes out of the band's end of the gross sales—as little as 12 percent, some of which has to go to the producer, the manager, the lawyer, and the accountant. In a hypothetical example of a smash success worked through by record producer Moses Avalon, say a four-member band writing its own songs and with a big five-year, four-album contract breaks out of the pack and into the top 5 percent of big-label acts, selling 4 million records. At the end of it all, each member of the star group would net about $140,000 a year. The record company would gross $11 million before overhead.

The promotion system also had the effect of keeping new music off the airwaves unless a big-spending major backed it. With radio sewn up and most tours also paid for by the big companies, independent acts had few ways to reach the masses, or even connect with the niche audiences that might be interested in their music if they knew about it. "With the stranglehold in radio, new artists don't get exposed," said Ted Cohen, EMI's vice president of new media. "That's why everything sucks right now. It costs $1 million to have a hit record by the time you've greased all the wheels you have to grease." It was small wonder that the industry wasn't very interested in new and more democratic ways of distributing music: The current system worked for them, at the expense of new entrants. The essentially conservative nature of the label executives also explained their opposition to such new technologies as digital audiotape, which died, and the compact disc, which turned out to be a tremendous industry boon when music lovers went out and repurchased their collections in the new format.

The lack of access to new music would prove to be one of the big drivers behind Napster's explosive growth. Another factor for which the record industry bears responsibility is the collective disgust among consumers at the price of compact discs, which cost only about $1 apiece to physically manufacture and package. Since the product was so much cheaper to make than old vinyl records, many consumers assumed that the retail prices would come down as well, at least after their first few years on the market. Instead, the prices inexplicably began heading toward $20 for collections of material that often included only one song a consumer wanted. The U.S. Federal Trade Commission investigated why the prices were rising and ultimately came up with an answer. The clue came when some home-electronics stores began selling discounted CDs in order to bring in store traffic. The resulting competition drove prices down to $10 for many titles. And the industry decided to fight back in the mid-1990s by requiring retailers to agree to advertise higher prices in order to get millions of dollars in funds for joint marketing. The FTC accused the Big Five labels, which shared 85 percent of the U.S. CD market, of apparent collusion in violation of antitrust laws. In a 2000 settlement of the charges, the labels agreed to drop the practice, which the FTC estimated cost consumers almost half a billion dollars. A subsequent suit by thirty states seeking to recover that money was settled in September 2002 for $143 million.

The CD price-fixing lawsuits were not the industry's first brush with antitrust accusations, and they wouldn't be the last. Napster's last-ditch defense in its own lawsuit would be that it couldn't be found to be infringing copyrights when the labels themselves were abusing the copyrights by acting collectively to keep the music from digital use. That long-shot counterargument would be enough to stave off what had seemed to be certain death through summary judgment through at least 2002. The Justice Department also began investigating the issue. Yet it would be a mistake to view the five labels as a monolith, each company marching in lockstep with the others. In fact, there would be many times that the companies, which competed heatedly for artists and sales, were also at odds on issues of politics or philosophy. One of the five majors was owned by Sony, which hedged its record-industry bet by selling stereos and the like, including equipment that played pirated music. By the year 2000, Time Warner's label was owned by America Online. Not surprisingly, the country's largest Internet-access provider was more interested than stand-alone labels in making digital music broadly available to its customers.

Other serious differences of opinion came from executives within the same record company. Most labels had hawks, old-school leaders who turned purple with rage at the very idea of an MP3. And most labels had doves, frequently younger managers who saw the Internet as a way to reach fans that were being left behind in the all-consuming drive to get hits on Top Forty radio. The contrasts were at times startling to music outsiders from Silicon Valley who were trying this way and that to make friendly deals with the labels. They would be greeted enthusiastically one day and met with expletive-laced tirades the next. Overall, the hawks were in charge when the Internet began taking off in earnest in 1999. But the active encouragement of the doves was enough to keep the entrepreneurs' hopes cruelly alive.

So there were scores of digital-music companies in business by 2000, offering a multitude of strategies. There were streaming companies like Listen.com that allowed onetime listening and no copying. There were Internet radio companies like Spinner, which was bought by AOL. There were companies that offered short samples of songs and then invited the public to buy the CD electronically. And there were firms like Liquid Audio Inc., which offered their own secure digital formats for downloading in accordance with music companies' terms for payment. But to have much desirable content, all of those companies depended to some degree on cooperation from the big labels. And most of them didn't get the content they needed. Without that, most of the digital-music firms were on the ropes even before the advent of Napster. When Napster made everything available for free, it killed the majority of the legitimate start-ups in their cribs.

⬜ ⬜

THE MOST IMPORTANT DIGITAL DEAL by the labels turned out to be with RealNetworks Inc. That venture, which became known as MusicNet, was at first ignored by the industry, then embraced with a sudden urgency as Napster took flight. By then, the labels wanted something to counter Napster, and they wanted to show federal antitrust officials and such critics as Sen. Orrin Hatch, chair of the powerful Senate Judiciary Committee, that they were doing something to put content online. But the effort to get MusicNet and its companion site Pressplay up and running was a lesson in abject frustration for those involved in the project, giving a hint of what Napster would be up against when its time came to deal.

MusicNet began in the Seattle offices of RealNetworks CEO Rob Glaser, who refused to believe that the recording industry wouldn't change. Glaser was a visionary, and he tended to think that the CEOs in the music business were innovators as well. A Microsoft veteran, Glaser had walked away from a lucrative career at the software giant to run his own operation, developing the RealPlayer application for viewing videos over the Internet. As an afterthought, he worked on a version to play music. After RealPlayer became one of the most downloaded programs on the Net, Glaser figured that he ought to be able to interest the record companies in a plan that would allow them to charge users for each song they downloaded, with RealNetworks or a joint venture taking a small percentage of each transaction. Reasoning that media attention might give others the same idea or even scare the industry hard-liners away, Glaser worked on his plan in near-total secrecy before Napster hit the world stage.

Glaser's first recruit was Alan Citron, a former entertainment-industry journalist who had risen to become president of Ticketmaster/Multimedia in Los Angeles. After Barry Diller's USA Networks bought Ticketmaster, Citron was looking for something new to do, and all the prognosticators said that music was about to be the next killer application on the Internet. He took the job, with the basic mission to sign up labels for the project, promising each of them equity in the new venture alongside RealNetworks. The thinking was that even if they didn't like the idea of digital-music distribution, the potential IPO windfall would be too much to pass up. In October 1999, Citron rented an office in Universal Music Group's building in Los Angeles, figuring that he would charm the label's executives as he got to know them in the halls. "We'll be pals before you know it," Citron thought. In fact, Universal was in the process of moving its offices to Santa Monica. Citron should have taken it as a sign.

Glaser was brimming with confidence in November, when he divulged a little of his game plan at a digital-music conference in Los Angeles. By then, RealPlayer had 88 million registered users, and Glaser said there was no reason that more content wouldn't be coming to Real's format from the big labels. Acknowledging that the intellectual-property rights and payment issues were tricky, Glaser nonetheless proclaimed: "We've been making real progress." Tieless in a gray shirt and glasses, Glaser waved his hands as he painted a future with music streaming and purchases of digital downloads, as soon as the security issues could be worked out. "Imagine a record store open twenty-four hours, with every album ever made, no checkout stand, with instant delivery, that's never out of stock," Glaser said. "You would think that everyone would be excited about what it would do for the industry."

Not exactly everyone was, however. Citron made the rounds of the labels in Los Angeles and flew to New York every few weeks, telling record executives that Real was working on a new system—how could they make it worth the labels' while to participate? "Real was on top of the world, and people wanted to learn what we were up to, so they took the meetings," Citron said. "But there was no urgency to do anything." In one office or another, Citron would run through the options. "I'd say, 'What if we charge 50 cents a song?' and they'd say that would undercut the physical product. So I'd say, 'Well, how about a dollar?' and they'd say there would be piracy if it cost that much. Every time you answered a concern, they would come up with another one."

Citron was used to dealing with irascible entertainment executives, but he was still unprepared for the hostility he encountered on some of his trips. Al Smith, a top Sony executive he dealt with in New York, often came across as sweet and grandfatherly. But he was also a husky six-foot-three and a buddy of Sony's U.S. music chairman Tommy Mottola, an old-school record executive from Brooklyn who had once been on the brink of co-owning a label with Network independent promoter Fred DiSipio. That deal had been scotched in 1986, after NBC reported that DiSipio and a close associate, promoter Joe Isgro, had just met with John Gotti and other top mobsters at a New York hotel. Smith had his hard side, too, and sometimes would just start shouting, Citron said. "There were three or four meetings where I stormed out" as both men cursed, Citron said.

After continual redrawing of the business plan and marathon negotiating sessions, Warner Brothers finally agreed to a deal in April 2000. It was one of the happiest days of Citron's life. Glaser insisted on keeping the deal under wraps, hoping to get at least one or two more labels on board before going public with the news. Citron went back to shuttle diplomacy with a little more spring in his step. By then, though, Napster was getting too big for anyone to ignore. Even Citron's twelve-year-old son and all of his friends were using the program. As Napster grew, Glaser and Citron figured they couldn't just offer downloads for sale, but instead needed to turn MusicNet into something that permitted sampling of a wide variety of music. They decided to shift to pitching a subscription-based model like cable TV: $10 a month for the service and premium features on top of that. With work on anticopying tools continuing and Warner still patiently waiting for the business model to get hammered out, Citron made the rounds yet again. Napster had made the labels much more nervous about copying, but Citron argued they should allow at least a limited test. If too much of the test music got into the wild, they could say they had tried. The labels did get more receptive, even calling Citron on occasion before he called them. "They had to show their bosses that they had an answer to Napster," Citron said.

An emotional high point came when Glaser got Edgar Bronfman, CEO of Universal's parent company, to attend a summit meeting in New York. The executive's presence was an encouraging sign, as was the fact that Universal sent label CEO Doug Morris and producer Jimmy Iovine—real content people, not technology specialists. "Rob said, 'Let's get this done or go our separate ways.' The mood was really positive. It helped us focus," Citron said. It turned out that Morris and Iovine had been in New York anyway because U2 was releasing a new album. In the spirit of the day, they invited Citron and Glaser to tag along backstage as they watched U2 perform on MTV's *Total Request Live* program. They met the band, and there was a feeling of real camaraderie. After spending hours together, Iovine invited Citron to return to L.A. with him on the company's private jet. Citron eagerly accepted and spent the flight schmoozing and talking about the bright future of digital music. They scheduled a follow-up meeting for the next week at Universal's office. When Citron went in for the follow-up, it was as if New York had never happened. "The business guys blew the whole thing up," he said. By this stage, Citron was used to being disappointed by the industry. Now he was just puzzled. Why had they bothered to spend a whole day with him before reverting to the same old tease? "They saw it as an opportunity to teach us a lesson," he concluded.

Trying to make the most of what progress he had made, Citron returned to New York for a visit with Al Smith on the upper floors of the landmark AT&T building. In the conference room, Citron played a little harder than he had before. "We're close to a couple deals," he told Smith, who glared. "I don't think you can pull it off," he said. "We can, and we're going forward with you or without you," Citron responded. Smith started screaming, and he ordered Citron out of the room. "You won't get any music!" he shouted at Citron's back. "Yes, we will!" Citron shouted over his shoulder. "You won't get Ricky Martin!" Smith said, referring to one of Sony's top sellers of the day. "We'll get plenty!" Citron retorted, still walking. "You won't get Mariah Carey!" Smith yelled. Citron left, shaking his head. It was all so primitive. The industry valued tough guys, the more street-smart the better. "There were all these 'whose-is-bigger' arguments," said Citron. "It's people clinging to a way of life."

An entire year passed in haggling after Warner had agreed to do something with MusicNet. In April 2001, as Citron was resigning—and the day before congressional hearings on the record industry's snaillike digital efforts—Glaser announced that MusicNet was a success. Warner, Bertelsmann, and EMI had signed up, and when the technology was worked out, they would begin licensing music. Sony and Vivendi Universal went their own way, again joined by EMI, with the Pressplay service. When the two systems were finally opened to the public, at the very end of 2001, they were an undesirable mishmash, reflecting every bit of the struggle that had gone into their construction. With MusicNet, $9.95 a month brought the right to stream, or listen just once, to one hundred songs a month. A hundred other songs could be downloaded but were rendered unplayable at the end of the month. Pressplay was better, offering four different subscription plans. The top-of-the-line Pressplay plan, at $24.95 a month, did allow consumers to burn up to twenty tracks a month onto a CD, and the other downloaded tracks didn't expire so long as the user kept up the subscription payments. But both services lacked the best content, and listeners stayed away in droves.

— —

MusicNet and Pressplay aside, the doves in the record industry did many small deals, afraid as they were of piracy. But even the most liberal were flummoxed by Napster's approach. Two of the biggest doves, responsible for eighty electronic deals in three years, were Ted Cohen and his boss Jay Samit, an executive vice president at EMI and much more of a technophile than a record-industry man. Internally, they had to overcome fear that the music would be stolen and institutional resistance to new forms of distribution—a resistance so intense that when Samit worked on new media at Universal, his request to buy the domain name Universal.com for $5,000 was turned down. They also had to deal with an accounting system from the Stone Age. "Digitized content? None of the companies even had digitized contracts," Samit said. There was no way to sort out electronically who had which rights to what song.

Once they got past those hurdles, the men had to structure deals of enormous complexity. To begin with, songs carry with them multiple sets of rights holders. The label might own the rights to one performed version of a song. Someone else often has the rights to the underlying composition. And there was a complicating difference between performance royalties—paid for a concert and perhaps a digital stream—and mechanical royalties, which are paid for radio play and the like. Then there's the problem of the different laws in each country and the different rights that many contracts assigned, depending on where the sale or performance occurred.

"Let's say I download a song on my Nokia in Japan," Samit said. "It's by a German band. The master [recording] is owned in Hong Kong. Let's forget about sampling [songs borrowing from previous recordings]. But I'm paying with a U.S. credit card . . ." The issues go on and on. "It seems silly. But we're the deep pockets that get sued if something goes wrong." Still, Samit persevered. A patent-holding technologist who had created the laser disc, he believed that online connection with fans was an opportunity too big to be missed. "There are so many new ways to slice and dice the content," he said. Most production costs vanish, "and we can let you know when your favorite artist has a new record." Samit and Cohen, whom he hired in early 2000, did licensing deals for the play of EMI songs on Internet jukeboxes, in hotel rooms, for a digital-only single by Lenny Kravitz, and for a Pizza Hut promotion that sold eight hundred thousand CDs with songs picked by customers.

It was hard to imagine a more receptive audience for Napster than Samit. And the company had a terrific introduction to him from Ted Cohen. Cohen had started in the music business managing bands and putting on dances at his Cleveland high school. At Ithaca College, he spent so much time booking bands into clubs that he went on academic probation and eventually returned to a local school in Cleveland. There he became music director at the college radio station, which happened to be the only alternative FM station in the area. As a result, real acts like blues guitarist Johnny Winter stopped in. Cohen quit school to be a record buyer for a chain, then moved into the promotion business for Columbia and Warner Brothers. "I kept running away with the band, so they moved me to artist development," Cohen said. The next stop, in 1982, was Warner's new-media group, and it was there that Cohen turned tech.

When the Web took off, Cohen rode with it as a consultant, helping Silicon Valley's Liquid Audio and assisting then-little-known Amazon.com to get into CD sales. He built a portfolio of dozens of companies and groups that he advised, from Microsoft to the RIAA. In May 1999, when Napster had just been incorporated, Cohen saw its website. A box on the site invited prospective advertisers to send e-mail. So Cohen did, introducing himself. John Fanning called, and they chatted. Two months later, Fanning asked if Cohen would come to work at the firm, then still on the East Coast. Cohen demurred, saying he wasn't interested in working anywhere full-time. In September, Cohen heard from Fanning again. This time, Fanning said that he had hired Eileen Richardson and Bill Bales but wanted Cohen as a consultant. Fanning had Cohen fly to San Mateo, where the conversation with Napster's new executives led to an offer to be CEO. Cohen declined again but agreed to serve as an adviser.

Two months later, Cohen was chairing the Webnoize digital-music conference at the Century Plaza Hotel in Los Angeles, and he brought Richardson down to speak in a panel discussion. It turned into Napster's coming-out party, and it was a memorable experience. The panel had other digital firms on it but no one from the record companies. Richardson gave her music-discovery pitch: "We are working with baby bands, independent acts, and helping to build careers," she said. When someone in the audience asked what contact Napster had had with the RIAA about copyright permissions, Richardson said she'd love to talk to them, that she was surprised the group wasn't on the panel with her. "Shouldn't we be talking here about how this new medium can change the face of music?" In a bit of theater, she added: Is there anyone in attendance from the RIAA? As it happened, there was, a low-level employee named Karen Allen, whom Cohen helpfully pointed out. "Come on up here, let's talk!" Richardson said. Allen was nervous at being put on the spot in front of an unfriendly crowd, and she came across as less open to dialogue than Richardson was. The vaudeville helped Richardson cast Napster as the innovator, dealing with a dinosaur that wouldn't be reasonable.

That wasn't a fair picture at all, since Richardson had been playing dumb with the RIAA. And Cohen soon would learn how incomplete the picture was. He set up a meeting between Napster and Samit for mid-December. Bales came down for the get-together on the top floor of the historic Capitol Records tower at Hollywood and Vine. So, Samit asked him, how does Napster work? What's the business model? "Lay something out for me," Samit said. Bales explained that Napster didn't have a model yet—it was just letting people get music for free. "I explained that that was illegal," Samit recalled. "He didn't have any clue." Bales said he would get back to Samit once Napster worked out a business plan. He never did. "These guys were willing to discuss a deal, and Eileen didn't support any discussion with the labels at that time, so I had to drop the ball," Bales said.

Bales tried another approach with a Bertelsmann contact. Tom Gieselmann, an investor with Bertelsmann's venture-capital arm in Santa Barbara, California, called Bales at home, saying he thought Napster had tremendous potential. He wanted to meet to discuss investing, and Bales knew Richardson would veto the idea. So Bales went to Fanning and Amram, who told him to go ahead. Gieselmann caught a plane and met

Bales in the Mandarin Oriental hotel lobby in San Francisco. Gieselmann promised to introduce Napster to Bertelsmann CEO Thomas Middelhoff and others, and he began quizzing Bales about Napster's closely guarded usage and file-swapping numbers. "I had to give him something to make sure he stayed interested," Bales said. Gieselmann turned over an envelope and started doing the math. His face turned pale. "He was like a ghost," Bales recalled. "You guys are destroying the record industry," Gieselmann told him. "You've distributed more music than the whole record industry has since it came into existence." When Bales reported the conversation, Fanning told him to cut off further contact.

Cohen stayed in touch with Napster and coached the company for another few months. On his last visit to the office in early 2000, he saw whiteboards filled with legal arguments to deflect questions about the theft of music. "It just became apparent to me that their message was not to settle," Cohen said. In April he gave up trying to convince Napster to negotiate and took the job under Samit. "I still think Napster is the coolest thing I've ever seen," he said nearly two years later. "Had we been able to work it out, it would have grown the music market. But it just got so acrimonious. It's hard to negotiate with people who are publicly saying they are going to beat you. And the rhetoric from the labels has been just as intense."

SAMIT AND COHEN WERE AMONG the first record executives to get a close-up view of how Napster worked and the foolhardy executives in charge of it. Other label people had to be educated by the RIAA. Napster turned up on the RIAA's radar in the late summer of 1999, flagged by the trade group's Internet-piracy specialists. That team, which hadn't been in existence for very long itself, found Napster during routine searches for MP3s in chat rooms and on Internet Relay Chat channels. Some music trading was going on all the time, and the RIAA didn't have anywhere near the resources to stop it all. Instead, staffers were trained to dig a little more deeply. Who owned the site, and what kind of resources could they put behind it? How large was the repertoire? How many users did it have? And how easy was it to get a song quickly? "If it takes thirty minutes to get a song, I'm less concerned," said Frank Creighton, the RIAA's head of piracy enforcement. Napster set off Creighton's alarm bells immediately. "FTP sites [those using powerful File Transfer Protocol commands] are nongraphical, non–user-friendly, and you can't use them with a regular browser. IRC is really technical, but it's more interactive—you can query for a specific file. Napster combined those services and brought the best aspects together. It was very robust and efficient," Creighton said. "We thought it was really exciting."

Creighton's job had gotten a lot more complicated over his fifteen years at the RIAA. In the beginning, he was chasing counterfeiters of eight-track tapes. The bad guys weren't too hard to find—they needed a half-dozen employees, a warehouse, and specialized duplication equipment worth as much as $250,000. Piracy back then cost the record industry about $250 million a year, a level that stayed constant until the mid-1990s. Then, as unencrypted MP3s made high-quality sound transferable more quickly, FTP sites began springing up, mostly at universities. Creighton sent his first threatening letter to an Internet site in 1997, then many more. Usually, a letter did the trick. For all of the eventual criticism about the trade group's heavy-handed tactics, it filed fewer than a dozen lawsuits in the ten years before Napster. By 1998, Creighton was feeling good about the work he had done on FTP sites. Most of the high-speed Internet lines were at colleges, which were sensitive to threats about legal action and even the potential loss of federal funding for their communications networks. The Digital Millennium Copyright Act, written by Orrin Hatch's Senate Judiciary Committee, helped matters further that year by setting out the rules of the road. Now the RIAA could inform an Internet service provider of infringing content under its control, and generally the company would cut off access. "The euphoria lasted a brief period," said Creighton. IRC and other chat networks were multiplying, and Creighton had to hire more specialists to keep up. The RIAA office grew from thirty-five people to seventy in just a few years.

With Napster, Creighton began as he usually did, playing the good cop. "We didn't want to come across as antitechnology or anti-consumer," he said. John Fanning was the registered contact person for the site, and Creighton dropped him a reasonable e-mail on September 23, 1999. "I am writing to you to see if we could start a productive and mutually beneficial dialogue regarding your service and technology," he wrote. "As you may or may not be aware, your software, while exciting to both consumers and producers (including potentially our members) of sound recordings, unfortunately facilitates in many cases the unauthorized posting of our members' sound recordings." Maybe there were good ways to reduce the number of unauthorized listings, he suggested. And while there were legal issues involved, Creighton said, he "would prefer to focus on operational issues, and see if we can't create a productive working relationship."

Fanning exulted at Creighton's soft approach, which he interpreted as weakness. "He took that as a sign that even the RIAA thinks we're legal," Amram said. Fanning e-mailed a reply that he was interested in talking; he just needed to "coordinate things internally." Copying Amram and Bales on the message, Fanning said he would be back in touch the following week. Instead, four weeks went by. Creighton wrote again in October: "I hope you have had a chance to dialogue with your colleagues. . . . I would really like to move this forward as I am receiving much press interest about your service and would like to respond that we are in some productive dialogue." This time, Fanning replied that he thought such a positive statement to the media would be "an appropriate response." But he added that it was unlikely he would be the right person to represent Napster, saying he would let Creighton know who that person was. "Thanks for the response John, but this issue can't wait," Creighton wrote. "I need to speak to the appropriate person ASAP."

Hours later, Creighton got a phone call from Richardson. "She was very nice. She came across by her own admission as being very naive. She said she didn't understand the nuances of copyright law, and so she didn't know what I wanted and what she had to do." Creighton gave her a week to get up to speed. When he called the next time, she was full of information about the Supreme Court's ruling on VCRs and about why she didn't have to shut Napster down or filter out copyrighted songs. Still, Creighton pressed for a meeting, getting only the runaround. On October 27, RIAA president Hilary Rosen decided to raise the stakes. "I think we need a complaint drafted to be ready" to file in court, she wrote to the RIAA lawyers. "Frank is not getting very far with them." And Rosen encouraged a response to a local district attorney who had inquired about a possible criminal probe into Napster and its users. No one in the loop at

Napster could honestly claim to be surprised when the RIAA sued in December 1999.

— —

EVEN THEN, MANY RECORD EXECUTIVES didn't get it. That changed the day after the Grammy Awards in February 2000. At the regular RIAA board meeting at the Four Seasons Hotel in Beverly Hills, Rosen decided to try a little show-and-tell. It had been a good year for the industry, and people were feeling upbeat. "You know about Napster," Rosen told them. "But you need to understand it. This is going to be big, and the fact that we sued them is going to make it bigger."

Staffers downloaded the software and registered in front of the eyes of a couple dozen label bosses. Then Rosen asked the executives to start naming songs. Not just big hits, but tracks deep into albums, either brand-new or obscure. The record men took turns calling out more than twenty songs. The staffers found them every time, and fast. Soon no one wanted any more convincing that the threat was serious. As the crowd grew increasingly uncomfortable, a Sony executive tried to cut the tension. "Are you sure suing them is enough?" he asked. The capper came when someone suggested a hunt for the 'NSYNC song "Bye Bye Bye." The cut had been on the radio just three days, and the CD hadn't been released for sale yet. And there it was. Maverick Records executive Ronnie Dasher had seen enough. "This is too depressing," he said. "Let's move on to other business."

With the labels now enthusiastic backers of the lawsuit, they began thinking more about public relations. Worried about the bad press they were getting for attacking a nineteen-year-old, they redoubled their efforts to get their bands to speak out. "We want to do a national advertising campaign and will have a large coalition of interests that support it including artists," Rosen e-mailed top record executives in March. "I don't believe we will change behavior until there is more legal music online, but a campaign to raise consciousness is critical and as an industry, we must put our stake in the ground." Eventually, most big-name acts who took a public position were anti-Napster. But in the early days, it was slow going. When Metallica stepped forward, "they got crucified for it," said EMI's Samit. "You don't want to look uncool to your fans." Many artists were nonetheless alarmed, especially when they toured and heard fans singing along to songs that hadn't been released and were out only in bootleg versions. Others couldn't get too exercised over Napster because they never saw more than their advances. "I don't feel like Napster cut into my royalties, because I generally don't get royalty payments anyway," said Dean Wareham, guitarist and singer for the New York band Luna. Besides, "radio in this country is awful," he said. "So how else are you supposed to find out about music, other than a little harmless file-swapping?"

Some major bands were Napster believers—at least at first. The Beastie Boys was one of them. The members had developed an interest in things Internet as early as 1994, when software writer Ian Rogers, an old friend of singer Mike "Mike D" Diamond, showed him how the Net worked during the rolling Lollapalooza festival. In 1998, Rogers toured with the band and recorded performances through the mixing board, then posted the recordings to the group's website. "I started putting those things up, and it created a big stink for them. They had Capitol questioning them," Rogers said. Band manager John Silva helped the Beasties negotiate to keep the digital rights to their songs, and the band also kept ownership of part of their master recordings. That gave them greater freedom than most of their peers to experiment. Rogers kept close tabs on what was happening in both music and technology: By then he was working at Nullsoft, the tiny company that developed Gnutella. When AOL bought Nullsoft and suggested he move to San Francisco from Los Angeles, Rogers quit and joined the Beasties' own label, Grand Royal, as head of new media. Diamond was already a Napster user, both impressed by its reach and alarmed by its implications. Rogers told him he thought the system was obviously illegal but had tremendous potential for mass exposure.

Grand Royal was selling CDs through its website, and the band began releasing a track or two of each new record, downloadable for free. A link on the site sent Web surfers to the approved cuts on Napster, so Grand Royal could sidestep paying for the server space and bandwidth. "We would do promotions," Rogers said. "But the rest of the record, no. That's what we were trying to make a living on." After waiting in vain for months to see what sort of payment Napster would offer for the band's nonpromotional songs, the band gave up and joined others in ordering that the company take down the unauthorized files.

In the meantime, Rogers had gotten to know Shawn Fanning through mutual friend Dug Song, an elder statesman from Shawn's hacker group w00w00. "I like Shawn a lot as a person," Rogers said. "He was in this amazing place, because he had the skills to pull it off, but not the experience to tell him not do it. It got way further down the road than anyone could have imagined." Napster, Rogers said, was the product of a unique set of circumstances, the most important of which was the dot-com investment fever that hit at the exact moment when Shawn and the opportunists around him were setting out on their quest. If Napster hadn't started just then, he said, "the time could easily have come and gone where people would give you money to do something that is clearly illegal."

Alternative band the Offspring had a later but even more enthusiastic awakening to the power of the Web. In 1998, *Rolling Stone* printed the first of a new kind of pop chart: Most Downloaded Songs on the Internet. There, at number one, was the Offspring's new song, "Pretty Fly (for a White Guy)." "The whole thing surprised us," said band manager Jim Guerinot, who also handles Beck and No Doubt. At one point, the song had been downloaded 22 million times and the band had sold 8 million records. "If we had been downloaded 40 million times, would we have sold 16 million records?" Guerinot wondered. When Napster rose to become the Internet vehicle of choice, Offspring singer Dexter Holland became one of the service's most vocal supporters, touting it in concerts and crediting Napster with much of the band's success.

But like the Beastie Boys, the Offspring expected *some* sort of business model to be worked out *sometime,* or at least Napster to ask the band's permission, which would have been granted speedily. Even after the dustup over it selling gear with the Napster logo, the Offspring remained a supporter. The last straw didn't come until much later, when word circulated that Napster was seeking a settlement by offering its stock to the record companies. "Why didn't they come to the artists?" Guerinot asked. "Why not get in bed with the top one hundred artists? They were as bad on the corporate-investment side as they were on everything else. Their strategy was to sell everything out. We just became mortified and asked to withdraw our amicus brief" from the lawsuit.

Some artists who said nothing at all about Napster helped its cause indirectly. Generally speaking, the more obscure a band was, the more likely it was to applaud greater exposure through Napster. Midsize and larger bands, while less likely to be outright Napster supporters, were more likely to feel cheated by their long-term and unrewarding contracts with the major labels. Those acts now had two new things to be mad about. The first was their contracts. And the second was that Napster could be hurting their sales, and the labels weren't coming up with reasonable alternatives.

As they chafed under the dual pressure, some bands set up their own retail operations online. One was the cult band Ween, which hailed from New Hope, Pennsylvania. Ween recorded on Elektra for eleven years, with sales that kept rising until the band had sold a fairly impressive 1 million albums total. Yet by the end of its contract, Ween had not only never seen a royalty check, it still owed the label $1.2 million from its advances. On a lark, the band recorded a Christmas album independently and offered it for sale through its website. Total sales: about 3,000 records. Total income: about $40,000. But the band got to keep all that income. A big, fat lightbulb appeared over the band members' heads, and they considered running their own tiny label. But Ween was torn. Three thousand people aren't very many fans. "They don't want to be a clique for geeks," a friend of the band explained. If they go back to a major label, they stay poor, but more people will hear them.

— —

SO FOR ONE REASON OR ANOTHER, Napster's popularity helped prod more stars to speak out about the injustice of their contracts. And they did more than speak. Don Henley cofounded the Recording Artists Coalition, which raised funds with performances by a wide range of performers, including Billy Joel, Sheryl Crow, Stevie Nicks, and Dwight Yoakam. "I got signed to a deal with a company that was sucking my blood for twenty-five years," John Fogerty told the crowd at one benefit concert. "I just don't want that to happen to nobody else." More stars filed lawsuits for back royalties, and some of them won millions of dollars when the labels were caught using sleight-of-hand accounting. And the coalition itself filed a friend-of-the-court brief on Napster's side in the labels' lawsuit. The amicus brief focused on just one of the many issues in the case, asking the judge not to assume that the labels owned the master recordings in perpetuity under a disputed doctrine called work-for-hire. Under the work-for-hire interpretation espoused by the labels, the companies didn't need a specific contractual clause from the bands signing away the rights to the masters. And the companies said the bands had no right to terminate the contracts and get those rights back. The Napster court was one of the places where that argument was being aired.

A bigger and more immediate target for the Recording Artists Coalition was a 1987 amendment to a California law that had ended the old Hollywood studio system, which bound underpaid stars to movie companies for life. The original law said that performers could end their contracts after seven years and become free agents. Intense lobbying by the record industry won the later amendment, which partially exempted musicians. Because of that exemption, record companies could require seven albums in seven years but make that output virtually impossible to fulfill in time because of touring, videos, and other obligations. Then the labels could hold out the threat of a lawsuit to keep more albums coming well after the seven years were up. Now, state lawmakers in Sacramento were treated to visits by a new breed of lobbyist, in the persons of Courtney Love, Beck, and Carole King.

The more the bands bashed the record industry, the more Napster users felt as though they were justified in ripping off the labels, and the less inclined members of Congress were to come to the record industry's aid. In testimony before a Senate committee in Washington, former Eagle Henley was one of the few voices of moderation in the great Napster fight. He said that the Recording Artists Coalition supported the labels' copyright suit, but he complained that the musicians were being left out of the negotiations and most of the discussions about new laws. Forced digital licensing—with the artists sharing in the royalties—should be considered as a last resort, he said. Napster and its successors "flourished because the record industry has failed to be forward-thinking and has made it extremely difficult for legitimate companies to license the rights," Henley said. "The record industry fiddled on the sidelines while the digital revolution went on without them."

8

competition

THE WAR WITH THE RECORD INDUSTRY KEPT NAPSTER ON
the front page of newspapers. But inside the company, Shawn Fanning
and his crew spent more time worrying about other threats, many of
which most Americans never heard about. The team had good reason to
be concerned: Napster was at serious risk from competitors for many
months after its inception. It was vulnerable because Shawn's major contribution to the march of technological progress hadn't been a blinding
discovery or an invention that could be protected by patent law, though
the company would try. Instead, it was a brilliant insight—one that could
be copied by others, and was. In that context, Napster's pursuit of rapid
growth at any cost made far more sense. If the horde of competitors
caught up, Napster would have had far less to bargain with when it finally
faced the music, as it were. In the end, Napster dominated the market
both because of its damn-the-torpedoes approach and its flawlessly easy-

to-use technology. Only when it was crippled in court did rivals surpass Napster, and many users say that the system's successors have yet to match Napster's execution.

None of the current generation of souped-up file-swapping services were anywhere in evidence in the fall of 1999. Back then, Shawn, Sean Parker, and Jordan Ritter were alarmed by programs with names like CuteMX, iMesh, and Napigator. CuteMX was among the first real threats, developed in mid-1999 at a software firm called GlobalScape Inc. Like Napster, CuteMX had a hybrid peer-to-peer architecture, with a central index that referred visitors to content stored on users' personal machines. GlobalScape was known for its Windows applications, and the "client" features seen by the users were "gorgeous," Ritter said. As a result, "they had a following. They were neck and neck with us," he said. Users could share music and also movies, which were mostly pornographic at the time. CuteMX could have been bigger than Napster, but two things got in the way. One was that as the product of client-program specialists, the central servers were structured poorly. That meant it was more vulnerable to hackers, and it was even less stable than the early Napster. When demand grew, the CuteMX servers had a harder time keeping up. The other problem was more basic. GlobalScape was a real company with traditional executives. When the record industry called and warned them that they were facilitating copyright violations, the executives listened. The lead developer of the project left the firm, and GlobalScape pulled the plug.

The most consuming of the competitive worries came from an origin markedly similar to Napster's. That was Gnutella, the brainchild of another brilliant teenage hacker from the boondocks, Justin Frankel. So great was Frankel's underground reputation that Shawn and his team were terrified of Gnutella before they had any idea what it did or how it worked. An Arizona college dropout, Frankel had made his mark by writing and distributing the best-known MP3 player for personal computers, Winamp. Frankel's tiny company, Nullsoft, was then bought by America Online in June 1999, creating an unholy alliance of corporate distribution power with technical expertise. Frankel moved Nullsoft to San Francisco and became friends with Shawn, bonding mainly over their love of fast cars.

In late December, Frankel told Shawn that Gnutella was coming. Shawn ran into the Napster office and started shouting.

"Justin Frankel's working on something that's going to blow us away!" Shawn told Ritter and the other engineers. Shawn next demanded that the team bind all of Napster's servers together, making a more complete system that could stand up to whatever Frankel had in mind. "We all freaked out," Ritter said. By then, there had been a long-running debate inside Napster about whether to link the servers and how to do it. One of the existing system's weaknesses was that everyone who logged on to search for a song was sent to just one server, which in turn referred the user to others who were relying on the same machine. When the number of servers grew to fifty, say, that meant each user was only exposed to the one-fiftieth of all the songs available on Napster at that moment. So many people were on each server that the songs being sought still came up better than 95 percent of the time. But linking them all together could make the system many times more powerful than it was.

There were a couple of arguments against linking. One of them was voiced by Napster's legal team. The lawyers opposed linking for the same reason they opposed many other technical improvements at Napster: The step would make the company seem even more of a threat to the record industry, which could run to the judge already weighing the case. And it would offer another example of how involved the company was in directing people to songs. The more hands-off Napster was, the better chance it had when it argued that it was just like a telephone company or other automated service that couldn't be responsible for the content it carried. Those concerns were likely on technology vice president Eddie Kessler's mind when he sat for a sworn interview with the record-industry lawyers more than a month after Shawn started working on linking. Asked whether a plan for systemwide music searches was in the works, Kessler replied: "There hasn't been any discussion of plans to have the server that users connect to search across the names of MP3 files other than the ones that user is connected to." Kessler explained in a later interview that his denial had been based on semantics—"We didn't have a *plan* to do it," he said. The other case against linking, voiced often by Ritter, was technical. It was a serious challenge to tie the system together, and the whole thing could crash if it wasn't done right. The biggest hurdle for the coders was that the search technology wasn't fast enough, and it would create a massive logjam if the number of simultaneous searches multiplied by fifty.

Parker thought that linking the servers was crucial no matter what the risk—not so much for the extra music it would bring users, but to unloose chat and still-to-be-developed functions from the isolated machines. If you wanted to search the universe of all other Napster users, it was impossible without connected servers. With linking, Parker imagined, the system would allow users to post personal profiles, showing what music they had available, what they were listening to the most, and what they had been playing most recently. If another user downloaded a file from that person, they might want to see what else the person was interested in. With work, the system could develop in such a way that some users emerged as thought leaders, and others would habitually turn to them to learn what was new and good, just as people turn again and again to the same friend in the real world for advice on a given topic.

"Ultimately, Napster could have evolved into a bazaar, where subcultures discovered each other," Parker said. "You wouldn't find an isolated person, but a person who had an interest in different genres, with their own taste, who was part of a community, and that user was a destination in that community. . . . It could lubricate the social discovery of music and accelerate it and usher in, I thought, a new golden age of music." All of that would be possible only if all the servers were linked. And economically, linking would make Napster a natural monopoly. America Online's AIM instant-messenger program worked the same way. It capitalized on the so-called network effect, in which the strength of the network grows geometrically with the addition of each user. That makes it very painful for someone to leave the network. Because AIM doesn't interact with other instant-messaging systems, many users won't leave it unless they can get most of their friends to leave as well. If Parker's plan for a national system of music-community discovery worked, it would permanently lock in the company's advantage before even very good rivals could put their shoes on.

After hearing about Gnutella, Shawn summarily dispensed with all the counterarguments. "We have to do it now. Like tonight," he said. With Ritter still resisting, Shawn sat down to do it himself. "It drove me to stay up for two or three days and write," Shawn said. "That was kind of the peak, after programming for a year straight. I couldn't believe how much coding we did in one night. It was just unbelievable. That was critical." The first version of the linking software was buggy, and it was never implemented. But it made the staff members feel that they were at least doing something to ward off Frankel's attack.

When Gnutella appeared nearly three months later, Napster's engineers were nervous but impressed. The system was much more complicated than Napster's. Instead of relying on a central server, Gnutella allowed users to create their own, smaller networks for searches. A request sent to one small network hub would be relayed to more hubs, and the geometric progression would reach a vast number of computers. The major advantage Gnutella had over Napster was that there wasn't what engineers refer to as a "single point of failure": There was no one machine, or small set of machines, on which everything else depended. In this case, of course, the fear was not a technical malfunction—the fear was legal action. Once Gnutella was in the wild, there was little the record industry could do about it. Gnutella was "unstoppable from a technological perspective," Shawn e-mailed his colleagues.

Gnutella also gave Napster some reasons for relief. It was nowhere near as easy to use as Napster was. And because of its technical structure, Gnutella had tremendous speed issues as its usage grew. The problem was that each inquiry multiplied as it ran through the decision tree. As the network grew larger, so did the multiplication, clogging up bandwidth and slowing everything down. While Gnutella got wide press, the initial version never got above ten thousand or twenty thousand users, Ritter said. As for Napster's precarious political position, Gnutella was a tremendous help. Since there was no way for the record companies to control Gnutella, Parker thought the labels might be willing to do a deal that would legitimize Napster and thereby keep that audience from turning to Gnutella and escaping their reach.

"It was the best thing that could have happened," Parker said. "We had been trying to get Eileen interested in using this idea as a threat to get a deal from Day One." If Gnutella hadn't been invented elsewhere, Parker said, Napster might even have tried to do the same thing itself, officially or covertly. In fact, he suggested, "it's entirely possible that someone from Napster gave Nullsoft the idea." That's a fairly wild claim, and Shawn's earlier reaction gives evidence to contradict it. While Frankel declined to comment, others who worked on Gnutella dismiss any conspiracy. The concept itself was so obvious that any sophisticated engineer involved in music-swapping would have considered it at some point, said Nullsoft veteran Rob Lord. The hard part was writing the code.

Frankel had done some serious thinking before deciding to compete with Napster. The Nullsoft crew had played with Napster when it first came out. "We looked at it and said, 'There's no way this is legal,'" said Ian Rogers, one of the handful of employees at Nullsoft and a friend of both Shawn and Dug Song, the w00w00 security expert. Frankel, Rogers, and Lord discussed the issue again as Napster grew at a mind-boggling rate and staved off a court-ordered shutdown. They decided they had to hedge their bet. The consensus was "It isn't legal—but if it is, Winamp needs to do this," Rogers recalled. "If it's going to live, we wanted that functionality."

Gnutella would have had some major headaches, were it not for a bout of self-restraint and the bonds of friendship. Just as the early Napster work had been done over an IRC channel that grew from a few w00w00 members to seventy or so Napsterites, rival Gnutella began in a small IRC channel led by Nullsoft employees. Old Napster aide Seth McGann, known as Minus to his w00w00 friends, got into the Gnutella channel for a bit of opposition research, criticizing the architecture of the system and trying to learn more. Then he saw a posting from someone who appeared to be in-house at Nullsoft. McGann used the information he gleaned to hack the man's computer. Improbably, he succeeded in getting in, and from there he reached a server where McGann found encrypted source code as well as the names and passwords of early users. Debating whether to take the next logical step of the true black hat and try to steal and crack the source code itself, McGann hesitated. But he did begin boasting in the Gnutella channel about the access he had, offering up some of the passwords as proof. That provoked some excitement from the Gnutella developers, both those opposed to the breach and those who wouldn't have minded taking the code and splintering from the official effort. It also caught the attention of w00w00's Song, who studied McGann's account of what he had done and realized that he knew McGann's victim: It was Rogers, a friend of Song's from when they rode skateboards together as teens. Song warned Rogers to secure his machine and asked McGann to back off. McGann did as he was told. "I had hacked into Dugsong's friend's machine," McGann crowed, peacefully enough. "I felt good afterward." Ritter, who had pressed Minus to go after the code, agreed with the decision to drop the spy operation. "We would never fuck Dugsong," Ritter said.

The Nullsoft team posted Gnutella on the company's site in March 2000. America Online fielded a host of media inquiries about the conduct of its subsidiary, looked at the program, and gagged. It came to nearly the same conclusion that the Nullsoft team had come to about Napster: If it wasn't illegal, it was close. And it didn't help that AOL was in the process of buying Time Warner, owner of Big Five record label Warner Brothers. Aiding and abetting the theft of its acquisition target's intellectual property wouldn't go over very well. AOL ordered Gnutella deleted from Nullsoft's pages within days. Soon someone using Frankel's IRC handle "deadbeef" said he was wondering about "accidentally" releasing the source code. Gnutella-like code did emerge soon, to the delight of file-swappers, technophiles, and open-source enthusiasts. With Gnutella free for anyone to tinker with and improve, it got much better, overcoming some of the roadblocks to scaling.

If AOL's reluctance to embrace Gnutella delayed its emergence as a powerful Napster foe, a quieter bit of corporate politics helped stop another Napster rival from getting critical backing. IMesh was close to Napster in structure but had some advantages, including the fact that it was based in Israel, where it would be harder for the record industry to attack. And iMesh beat Napster to the punch on one technical front, known as segmented downloading. In segmented downloading, the system identified segments within each song. Users were then shipped the multiple parts simultaneously. The process "generally results in the fastest possible transfer rate and almost guaranteed file transfer success," Shawn wrote to his coworkers.

As a user innovation, segmented downloading was great. As a legal proposition, it was a more interesting question. It offered a possible legal advantage for the users, according to Dug Song, who was developing something similar and offered it to Shawn. If files were split among multiple clients, each user would have "plausible deniability," Song wrote in March 2000: "You can't sue anyone for offering illegal files when only a few encrypted blocks are available" at each computer. Even if they accepted that reasoning, Napster executives were more worried about Napster than about its users. And like linking the servers, they decided it would have exposed the company by showing that it knew too much about where songs were and that it had total power over the transactions. So Napster didn't adopt segmented downloading. Instead, it went after iMesh with a cloak-and-dagger.

The matter took on some urgency after Napster VP Bill Bales heard that AltaVista, one of the first big Internet search engines, was looking to get into music downloading by buying iMesh. That worried Shawn, who wondered if AltaVista's deep-pocketed parent, CMGI, might merge it with its own music start-up. Ritter went to work hacking the iMesh system, and he found some potentially useful problems. Among other things, the network put too much trust in its clients. Once a part of the system, a user could hunt for songs—or a lot of other things, including other users' passwords. "IMesh is a wanna-be hacker's dream," Ritter told Shawn.

Recruiter Jessie Garrehy, meanwhile, had nominated AltaVista's head of search technology, Don Dodge, for a job at Napster. Ritter went to dinner with Dodge to discuss the position and brought a hidden agenda: to kill any chance iMesh had of being acquired. Over dinner, Ritter casually ran through the state of Napster's competition, taking care to drop in a mention of the security problem at iMesh. Dodge took it all in, and AltaVista soon walked away from iMesh. Just to be on the safe side, Ritter sent the holes he had found to his former colleagues at BindView in Boston. He suggested that BindView issue a security advisory, which might have scared away both iMesh users and potential corporate acquirers. BindView's Benny Czarny, noting Ritter's conflict of interest, wrote back: "I do not find that ethical." The security alert was never issued.

━━ ━━

CONCERNED ABOUT THE THREATS from Gnutella, iMesh, and others, Napster tried again and again to link its servers properly. Shawn was getting anxious both about others gaining ground and about the slow pace of improvements to Napster's system, due to legal concerns, lack of staff, and the distraction of executives more worried about getting venture money. "Adding stuff was actually a big task," Shawn said. "I always had a big list of things to do and bugs to fix. But the major factors were the lack of people and some of the legal stuff. Not anything specifically, but just the fact that we suddenly got sued—there was just an aversion to changing it because we didn't know what the rules were. We had no idea."

In a rare all-points outburst, on March 23, 2000, Shawn e-mailed Eileen Richardson, Ritter, Parker, engineering boss Kessler, Liz Brooks, Brandon Barber, and another executive, Chris Phenner. "Hey, all, I'm sorry if this rant offends anyone—this is the stuff that has been KILLING me for the last few months," Shawn wrote. "While we are making great strides on the financing and legal fronts, the client and the community are lacking behind. We all agreed very early that this is the most important aspect of our company. We have a list of kickass features that have not been considered lately. We are about to do a release that's going to hurt us more than help us. . . . We need to start focusing on 'cool' features. . . .

"Also, I frequently hear people talking about us as if we are unstoppable and immune to competition. We are assuming we are immune because of our size—however our users do not reap the benefits [of] our content depth. . . . our concurrent user count increases as we add [server] boxes to the network, which in no way increases the amount of content available per server." Shawn listed three priorities, in order: linking, the ability to transfer not just music but other types of content, and a redesign of the user interface. "The current production client is still using my prototype design from a year ago . . . :(," he wrote.

The technical team had already achieved some remarkable results, considering the originality of what they were trying to do. They were particularly proud of the search engine, which Jordy Mendelson and Ali Aydar had developed. Unlike Google or AltaVista, the mechanism had to cope with a constantly changing index. "From the time Google crawls a website to the time it actually shows up in a search window can take weeks or months. We had to do the same thing in microseconds," Mendelson said. Shawn and Aydar made early passes at the system, and Mendelson took it home to simplify it and make it faster. "I ended up waking up in the middle of the night, writing out the initial implementation for the final algorithm in an e-mail to Ali, and promptly went back to sleep," Mendelson said. "We ended up with a search engine that was small, elegant, and so efficient that we stopped optimizing it because sending the search results to the user took so much longer than performing the actual search."

By April, Richardson was convinced that the company's very survival depended on a server-linking system that worked. In the middle of that month, product manager Barber reported to her and to Kessler that the engineering team was close, after thousands of hours of work. He said the project might be completed in just ten to twenty days. Instead of a quicker Band-Aid solution, in which only searches unsuccessful at one server would be bounced to the next, Barber urged the executives to wait for the full solution. "It's safe to say that Napster as a company is experiencing tremendous pressure from the outside, media, industry, legal and financial concerns making demands, and it's important to react to them," he wrote. "However, I think it's incredibly important to make decisions that will help benefit not only these variables, but our users (read: our business)."

Instead, Richardson demanded the final linking method within days. "We have tried at least two other times with implementations that did not work," Richardson wrote to Barber and the engineers. "We cannot and will not take a chance like that again. . . . LET ME BE CLEAR: THERE WILL BE NO BUSINESS TO WORRY ABOUT IF WE ARE NOT LINKED BY NEXT WEEK, NONE!" Soon enough, Ritter and Jordy Mendelson did lash together Napster's servers into two massive clusters. In late May, Ritter told the marketing and customer-service people that he had gone even further, linking together those two clusters. For the first time, if a user was looking to see if a friend was logged on, the user could find him or her. And users could see what songs the friend was sharing through a feature that had worked poorly in the past, called HotList. "You know your friend is logged onto Napster somewhere, and his username is 'hillary_rosen_sux_cock,'" Ritter e-mailed the group. "All you have to do is add him to your hotlist, and then click his username to see what files he's sharing. Brilliant!"

Ritter assumed a press release would trumpet the dramatically enhanced features, presumably using a less antagonistic illustration. But Richardson checked with the company's lawyers and decided against it. Why give out any more information than necessary about the company's technology? Besides, it might provoke the record industry, which wouldn't help Napster's increasingly crucial search for new funding. Users would just have to stumble on the upgrade by themselves. The disappointed engineering team tried to drop the public some hints. Each Napster user's screen included a box displaying how many users were logged in and sharing that user's server. Once a week or so, Ritter or a colleague would flip a switch for a few minutes, and the display would show how many users were on the entire cluster. The number would jump from about eight thousand to about four hundred thousand. Most users probably thought the figure was a bug and ignored it. The engineering team's single greatest triumph wouldn't be acknowledged in the trade press for another six months, and the mainstream press never noticed at all.

THE NAPSTER TEAM HAD A DIFFERENT sort of politics to worry about when it came to some of their other competitors. Napster's chief asset was its software, and it was duly protective of its source code. But some of Napster's biggest technological fans thought it should release the code. They subscribed to the same widespread ethic as the original Napster crew—pursuing hacking for fun and knowledge. But they also belonged to the subsidiary ethic of the open-source movement, in which the code is available for public inspection. The open-source movement was becoming increasingly important in software development, and it is best known today for using unpaid and widespread collaboration to turn Linux into a viable alternative to Microsoft's Windows operating system. From time to time, open-source enthusiasts would harangue Shawn and the others to share the Napster secrets. Some of the more ambitious used technological clues about the way Napster worked to reverse-engineer and clone both the Napster client program seen by users and Napster's back-end program for running its servers.

Among the first client clones was a buggy contraption called Gnap, written by a teenager. After the author announced its existence on Napster's IRC channel, Ritter and Shawn quickly got hold of him in a private chat. They told him they didn't mind if he released the client program, but they begged him not to post the source code for at least a couple of weeks. The problem wasn't the competition, they said; the problem was that others could use the source code to develop bot programs that automatically connected to all of Napster's servers and repeatedly searched for the same song. Ritter, Napster's security chief, had been too busy to write software that would weed out such bots. The teen assured them that he would hold onto the code. "The next day, that prick released it," Ritter said. And the author added insult to injury, posting rhetoric about Napster's betrayal of the open-source movement.

Sure enough, bots soon started to scan Napster, straining the system and allowing contractors like NetPD Ltd. to search methodically for users offering certain songs. NetPD, run by a man named Bruce Ward out of Cambridge, England, was the firm that provided Metallica with the screen names of the more than three hundred thousand Napster users offering up the group's songs. NetPD had arguably violated Napster's user agreement, which banned bots, and Ward and Ritter engaged in a months-long hacking dogfight as Ritter figured out where abusive searches were coming from and shut them down, plugging holes in the dike as they appeared.

More useful for garden-variety Napster users was a program written by software engineer Chad Boyda called Napigator. That program impersonated a Napster client when it contacted the real Napster system, but it could also hop from server to server before Napster linked them. Napster rejiggered its system to foil Napigator, and Boyda retooled Napigator to fool the new system. Napster changed again, and Napigator changed again. "They did what they should have done in the first place, and then we couldn't stop it," Ritter said. Privately, Shawn thought that Napigator was a good thing, as was Wrapster, which allowed people to swap movies or documents over Napster by disguising them as MP3s. "Why are we fighting napigator?" Shawn asked one Napster volunteer. "If our users want it, our users are right. If somebody wants to make something that makes it easier to navigate the network, more power to them. . . . Same thing with Wrapster; people want to share additional content types. Why fight it? We have to embrace what people want or we lose."

A far more serious threat to Napster came from an open-source proj-

Napster founding developer Jordan "Nocarrier" Ritter, Matt "Shok" Conover, and Napster founder Shawn "Napster" Fanning in Ritter's San Mateo, California, apartment. The three met online in a hacking and security group that Conover founded in high school.

From left to right: Seth McGann, Andrew Reiter, Dug Song (flashing a sign for Matt Conover's computer-security group, w00w00), and Jan Koum at the DefCon hacker convention in 1999. Several members of the group, including McGann and Song, helped Shawn Fanning develop Napster. Later, McGann nearly stole the source code for chief Napster rival Gnutella, backing off only when he learned the computer he broke into belonged to Song's friend.

Business-minded Napster cofounder Sean Parker, with FreeNet founder Ian Clarke in the background, at a San Francisco dinner for the digital elite. (Photo courtesy of Edge Foundation Inc.)

▲ Future Napster chairman John Fanning (center) playing chess with former U.S. cochampion Roman Dzindzichashvili outside the New York Open chess tournament in 1996. Standing to the left is Dmitry Dakhnovsky, the first Carnegie Mellon student Fanning hired for his online chess firm.

▲ John Fanning's house in Hull, Massachusetts. While he turned the condemned house into a million-dollar mansion, his employees sometimes went without pay.

Eileen Richardson, Napster's first CEO in Silicon Valley, was a veteran venture capitalist, but she had no idea what she was getting into.
(John Todd for the *Los Angeles Times*.)

Yosi Amram, Napster's first equity investor, had been hurt before by his taste for rapid-fire deals. He was stuck mediating between Richardson and John Fanning.

Napster vice president of business development Bill Bales in the Napster office. Responsible for raising money and recruiting top executives, Bales added to the internal strife by developing a back channel with John Fanning.

▲ Napster engineers Ali Aydar (left) and Jordan Ritter clown in the Napster office after fixing a bug that limited the number of users able to connect to each server. Their best work was never publicly acknowledged.

▲ Napster's anonymous-looking building in a Redwood City office park in 2002. It was an unlikely headquarters for a revolution that would pit the powerful entertainment and technology industries against each other.

◀ Recording Industry Association of America president Hilary Rosen was the most prominent Napster critic, demonstrating the powerful program for alarmed label executives and pushing for a lawsuit. Behind her is the group's lead attorney in the case, Russell Frackman. (AP/Wide World Photos.)

◀ Napster supporters rally outside the company's first California office in San Mateo in May 2000 as Metallica delivered thirteen boxes with the names of Napster users who were offering Metallica songs over the system. The banner refers to the record-industry trade group and the Metallica album *Master of Puppets.*

▶ Metallica drummer and spokesman Lars Ulrich on the same day. The San Francisco band's lawsuit against Napster earned it attacks on its website and charges that it had become a stooge for the big corporations that reap most of the profit from music sales. (AP/Wide World Photos.)

Shawn Fanning and Napster CEO Hank Barry, who succeeded Eileen Richardson, exult at the July 2000 ruling staying an injunction that would have shut the company down. (AP/Wide World Photos.)

Hank Barry, Bertelsmann AG electronic-commerce chief Andreas Schmidt, and Bertelsmann CEO Thomas Middelhoff play with Shawn Fanning as they announce Bertelsmann's stunning alliance with Napster in October 2000. The move infuriated other record companies. (AP/Wide World Photos.)

▲ Rock singer and record-industry foe Courtney Love presents Shawn Fanning with an award in October 2000. She introduced him to ceremony attendees as her future husband, then sat on his lap. (Photo by Lats Latvis.)

▲ Motion Picture Association of America president Jack Valenti (left) warned that if Napster survived, Hollywood would be endangered. He speaks at a panel in 2001 beside Konrad Hilbers, who had just been appointed as Napster's last CEO. (AP/Wide World Photos.)

▲ LEFT: The *Red Herring* magazine cover in August 2002. John Fanning finally made the front of a business publication, which credited him for "creating" Napster. His nephew and other Napster loyalists were incensed. ▲ RIGHT: The *Time* magazine cover in October 2000. Shawn Fanning became the best-known hacker in the world, but said as little as possible to the press. (Time Pix.)

"I swear I wasn't looking at smut—I was just stealing music."

▲ From the *New Yorker*, February 2002. Napster became the most-searched-for term on the Internet, as tens of millions of users decided that it was morally acceptable to download digital music from strangers.

ect called OpenNap. It was what Ritter had been trying to fend off as long as possible: a knockoff of Napster's server system. With some technical sophistication, users could go to an OpenNap server instead of Napster's, and there would be no way for Napster to make a dime, should it survive the lawsuit and start charging for something. The development of OpenNap's server and client unfolded before Ritter and Shawn in a slow-motion nightmare they were powerless to stop. Developers working on the effort did so openly, often communicating through an electronic mailing list called NapDev. Programmers would ask each other what they had gleaned about one aspect or another of Napster's workings, and they would trade advice about variants of the Napster client program for non-Windows operating systems, including the Macintosh, Linux, and Be. (Among the names these knockoff efforts took were Macster, Knapster, and even Crapster.) Ritter and Shawn quietly subscribed to the mailing list, keeping their nervous eyes on the rearview mirror.

Both Ritter and Shawn felt conflicted about the open-source threat. Napster was about tearing down the fences around intellectual property, and now its own fence was under attack. It was particularly hard on Ritter, who had long contributed to open-source projects in other areas. He could easily imagine himself on the other side of the battle. And pride made it even harder for both to keep silent on the mailing list as the open-source developers figured out why Napster had done something—or thought they had figured it out—especially if they concluded that it was simply poor design. Finally, a University of Washington student named Evan Martin went too far, dismissing a piece of the system as "shoddy programming." Ritter couldn't take it any more.

In early January 2000, Ritter wrote an open letter to the NapDev open-source effort, making clear that he was speaking only for himself and not Napster. It was a mixture of self-respect and moral defensiveness, reflecting a need to explain himself to people whose worldview he largely shared, stock options or no. "We at Napster Inc. have our jobs to do, and you have yours. You don't know why we implemented the things we did, and we're not going to explain them to you, mainly because it's not public information," Ritter wrote. "You can sit at your computer, possibly between classes, or maybe during a company lunch break, or whenever, and ponder the meaning of why certain things are as they are at Napster. You'll form an opinion, and one usually laced with some variable amount of disdain, as past experience has shown. And of course it will be wrong, because you have no idea what goes on behind closed doors, and you assume that we're all idiots, as past and current experience is also showing.

"Then you'll post it to this list, or to some other forum, and by the hand of some perverse irony, it will suddenly become fact and spark discussion. Soon after, it will have spread all over IRC or e-mail lists or Webboards or Bulletin Boards, and the world will go on, as it always seems to, unresponsibly saturated with one more piece of misinformation. We're not going to correct you. Yes, we hold the answers. Yes, you'll eventually find out most of the answers—no one's debating that (especially since we're not trying to stop you). Reiterating that point over and over is a waste of breath and bandwidth, and often times serves only to antagonize us.

"We can't give you any information because Napster is not some garage organization working off of some cliché Pentium and 486 laptop, but rather an incorporated company with a development team, marketing team, bizdev [business development] team, and an executive management team. Hypothetically speaking, if I were to have a strong desire to give you all the information you needed to write a complete client, I couldn't. It's not mine to give any more, it's the company's. . . . Oh yeah, and it would be nice if you didn't assume we were all stupid, which is ignorant, and a gross underestimation. Almost all the Napster developers are also open-source developers."

Evan Martin wrote an immediate and public apology. "I didn't know anyone would be offended. I didn't even know that anyone was listening!" he e-mailed. "I'm sorry this has caused you so much grief. I'd like to reiterate that everyone who's taken the effort to get to this point has demonstrated their dedication and respect for your product. Most of us just find it fun to hack." Once the outside programmers discovered that Ritter and Shawn were listening, they would occasionally ask polite questions about why the Napster team had done the things that they had, or if they were working on fixes to certain problems. Torn between protecting their work and feelings of hypocrisy for protecting it, especially given everything that was going wrong at Napster, the young men sometimes gave answers that helped the other side. And Napster Inc. took something back from the dialogue as well, eventually hiring the team that developed Macster for use on Apple machines.

The struggle against open-sourcers still flared up from time to time, most notably in the case of Stanford University senior David Weekly, who had briefly alarmed the record industry earlier with his mass MP3 postings. Weekly reverse-engineered the Napster protocol and wrote code mimicking it that he posted on his website. Engineering vice president Eddie Kessler decided that Weekly had violated the terms of Napster's license for all users, which forbade reverse engineering. Kessler wrote to Weekly and ordered him to take the posting down. Weekly did so, then helpfully e-mailed the NapDev effort instructions on how to find copies of what he had written. "I'm not going to let them bully me!" Weekly wrote. "And remember: linking to documents is perfectly kosher. Looks like someone's already made a copy at http://lovenapster.tripod.com."

The open-source Napster effort became a natural place for fairly sophisticated discussions about nontechnological matters, including morality and ways to avoid copyright liability. After many Napster users were banned for offering Metallica tracks, some of them blundered onto the NapDev mailing list as well in their quest to get reconnected. "Is there any other way to get back on or where is another MP3 sharing site?" one young AOL user asked. That ticked off a number of the hard-working open-source programmers, one of whom shot back: "This is a developers list, not a piracy assistance hotline." But someone else did tell the requester what to do.

After it emerged that the Napster protocol temporarily recorded individual users' computer addresses, called IP addresses, a debate in the group ensued over whether Napster was putting its user base at risk for legal action. "I think it's a damned huge security flaw," wrote NapDev subscriber Ian Brown. "If the Recording Industry Association of America decided to really go after Napster, it would be a cinch for them to write some software that automatically trawled all clients logged in to a given server for illegal content, then start legal action against the person."

What Brown and the others didn't know was that Napster was worried about the same thing. Looking for an answer, it had begun talking with Zero-Knowledge Systems Inc., which made software for anonymous e-mails and Web surfing. Zero-Knowledge's system was fairly ingenious. It designed each request for information from a Web surfer like an onion, with layer wrapped around layer. When one of Zero-Knowledge's servers received the request for information, by necessity revealing where the request was coming from, the server peeled off that information in the first layer and sent the rest on to another server. That second server had no way of knowing where the original request had come from. The process was then repeated, making communication untraceable.

Napster tried to make a deal with Zero-Knowledge that would have given its users absolute invisibility. Even more provocatively, it would have allowed Napster to keep reaching users at corporations and campuses that had banned Napster access. "As more and more institutions block access to our service, finding a way to continue delivery of our service becomes more and more urgent," Ritter wrote in January to a Zero-Knowledge executive. Inside Napster, Ritter pressed Kessler to help put the deal together, using Shawn's desire for continued hypergrowth as a mild threat. "Shawn (napster) and I are both getting very fidgety over the blocking of our service at various institutions, and would like to at least see something happen," Ritter wrote. A minute later, he added: "And you know Shawn, if something doesn't happen soon, we're likely to see a cowboy roaming the halls." The talks with Zero-Knowledge failed because the demand for bandwidth from millions of users would have been too large for the architecture to handle.

CONSUMERS HUNTING FOR FREE MUSIC and hackers looking for something to do were not the only groups inspired by Napster's innovation and raging popularity. Big companies also took note and began to respond, in some cases by striking alliances with hackers barely older than Shawn. Peer-to-peer, they realized, was a very, very big deal. Longtime Intel Corp. chairman Andy Grove, the head of the world's largest microprocessor maker and a man not known for hyperbole, declared: "The whole Internet could be re-architected by Napster-like technology." Intel wrote its own programs for allowing employees to grab files from one another. With improved network flow and cheaper storage off the main servers, the program cut costs by 10 percent, according to Intel vice president Doug Busch. Intel alone poured millions of dollars into peer-to-peer research, and other blue-chip firms such as Sun Microsystems worried that they were missing something huge. They began a rapid search for the next logical step after Napster.

In Sun's case, the search led to a fresh UC-Berkeley graduate named Gene Kan, whose improbable rise to success on the peer-to-peer band-wagon was at once faster, easier, and far more lucrative than that of his friend Shawn Fanning. When Gnutella first burst onto the scene from Nullsoft, the Napster team had been surprised to see Kan quoted more than anyone else, including publicity-averse Justin Frankel, the lead writer of the software. If Kan had truly become the lead developer on the project, Napster's engineers thought, maybe they could relax: Just months earlier, Kan had asked for a job with Napster, and he had bombed by dint of personality.

Kan had applied at Napster as a server engineer, boasting in a group interview about some of his previous technical accomplishments. When Jordy Mendelson pulled out a calculator and reported that the math in one of his claims didn't make sense, the obviously talented Kan grew defensive. He declared that he had been a software developer for a dozen years and knew what he was talking about. Since Kan appeared to be in his early twenties, Ritter was incredulous, impulsively asking how old Kan was. Kan immediately warned that the question was illegal and that he could sue. One of Napster's personnel chiefs pulled Ritter out of the meeting and told him that Kan was correct, that Ritter had unknowingly put the company in danger. So the team decided to keep the interview going just to build a case for not offering Kan a job on other grounds. That wasn't difficult to do. The engineers sent Kan to see supervisor Daphne Dembo, who gave many job candidates brainteasers to see how they were at problem solving. When she posed one to Kan, he said he wouldn't answer it because it was insulting, and that was that.

Kan's route to fame and fortune began later, at a lunch for car enthu-siasts in Sunnyvale. He emerged from the meal to find a young man leaning on Kan's treasured and heavily modified Mazda RX-7. The pos-ture first struck Kan as offensive, but it was intended to show respectful interest. The young man, who appeared to be in his late twenties but was only nineteen, was Cody Oliver, most recently from Alabama. An unrepentant car freak, Oliver was also a programming ace working as a contractor at Nullsoft. Kan and Oliver became friends and eventually roommates, just two of the large number of peer-to-peer elites, including Shawn Fanning, who would be brought together over RX-7s.

"I've always liked cars, but I got into RX-7s because of the guys at Nullsoft," Shawn said. He wasn't content with his first RX-7, so he tried to sell it on eBay. That became a news item for the website CNet, which embarrassed Shawn with speculation that things must be going badly for him and Napster financially. So Shawn delisted the car and sold it to Oliver. Shawn bought another in Florida that didn't quite suit him either, and sold that. "I was just trying to find one I really liked, and I finally found the silver RX-7 that I'm in love with," Shawn said. "I mean, it's a Mazda, and it's pretty fast stock, and if you fix all of the weird flaws with it and do a few minor changes to it, they're pretty fast cars."

Car-club meals and late-night drag races on Fridays and Saturdays brought out Nullsoft coders like Frankel and his Gnutella coauthor Tom Pepper, Oliver, and some of the Napster crowd, including Parker, with an occasional appearance by Shawn. Almost every weekend, the crew would meet at office parks abandoned by workday's end in Milpitas, Santa Clara, or other spots. With an average age around twenty, the young men had unlikely amounts of disposable income and a lot of workplace tension to get rid of. At a racetrack near Sacramento, Shawn joined in the drag racing, where speeds exceeded one hundred miles an hour. "I like accelerating, but that was the first time I could actually open it up and really learn the limits of the car," he said. Trouble with the police wasn't unheard of. "Some of the top people have been arrested," said Oliver, naming no names. Oliver had the most reason to be annoyed when the police ended an evening's festivities, since he usually won the races even when he loaded up his car with spectators.

Nobody cared who worked for which company. "There was no rivalry. Everyone had a lot of respect for what everyone else was doing," Kan said. "Nobody had any kind of an attitude. We had fun." Through his new roommate Oliver and the other people at Nullsoft, Kan kept tabs on the development of Gnutella. After AOL shut it down, the Gnutella program itself was released in the wild, but not the underlying code. Programmers outside of Nullsoft began collaborating to reverse-engineer, recode, and improve the program. As they made progress, the twenty-three-year-old Kan offered to help. "I was late to the game," he said. But when an Associated Press reporter contacted some of the real leaders of the project, they referred the reporter to Kan. A photographer showed up to take his picture, and Kan suddenly became the face of what was being hailed as the most likely Napster successor.

Kan stuck around the open-source Gnutella effort for a few months. In addition to his unofficial-spokesman role, Kan's personal connections at Nullsoft are extremely likely to have enabled him to help the other programmers. Giving away the source code developed on AOL's nickel would have violated Frankel and Pepper's obligations to their employer. It also might have opened them and the company to massive liability if the record industry sued over the program. While Kan insisted in an interview that the open-source Gnutella code was redesigned, not leaked, there is an area in between, filled with helpful hints, suggestions, and carefully worded questions about what methods the new developers were trying. Asked if the Nullsoft team at least gave the open-sourcers direction by means of winks and nods, Kan remained wordless. Then he winked, and he nodded.

<hr>

ALONG WITH SOME TECHNICAL DRAWBACKS to a decentralized system like Gnutella, there was a profound economic one: There was no clear way for the creator of a system of ad hoc networks to make any money off of it. So Kan and others who were more business oriented began rethinking the entire issue. Kan spoke with Oliver and another friend about how to overcome that problem and avoid the "bad rap Gnutella was getting because it was associated with piracy and porn and all these kind of muckraking things," Kan said. During two weeks in June 2000, the three came up with a prototype product and called it Infrasearch.

Based on the Gnutella framework, Infrasearch was a search engine and sharing service that allowed all types of files to be swapped. In a demonstration, Kan's team linked together a calculator, a database of pictures, a collection of news stories, and a website that tracked stock prices. Typing in "cat" as a search term returned a picture of a cat, a price quote on Caterpillar Inc. (ticker symbol CAT on the New York Stock Exchange), and stories about kittens. There were also big challenges, including scaling and the security problem inherent in trolling an unregulated Net that could return viruses to the searcher. But now that Napster had paved the way, investment dollars were laughably easy to get. Kan's status as a public figure in tech publications brought the fledgling Infrasearch site some press, and within days venture capitalists began calling. One would-be investor simply had his secretary call Kan and ask for the address so he could send a check. Kan asked Netscape's Marc Andreessen to check out the site, and Andreessen, who had described peer-to-peer technology as a "once-in-a-generation idea," became an early enthusiast. With the rush of investor interest, Andreessen "helped us sort out what to do," Kan said.

Among the callers were VC firm Redpoint Ventures and Ron Conway, who was never one to let an opportunity go by. Redpoint listened to a presentation about Infrasearch, which didn't include much of a business model. "We just wanted them to pay our bills for a while, to see where it went," Kan said. Redpoint offered to invest with a number of conditions that would make the start-up more serious. Conway was less concerned about the road map. He took the Infrasearch crew out to dinner and offered money right away, with no strings. Young CEO Kan accepted and shook hands on the deal. Kan thought that was it, that now his team could get to work while the check was en route. But with competing investors still sniffing around, Kan soon got a call from Conway's more-organized partner, Bob Bozeman. "Ron wants to get married," Bozeman said. "Ron wants to get married *today*." Bozeman dragged Kan to a lawyer's office, where the contract for the $2 million deal was signed. "There was no specific business model," Bozeman recalled. "Gene was getting some good notoriety in the press, so we knew there would be a lot of people circling." Andreessen also invested, as did two of Napster's advisers, early Excite Inc. executives Joe Kraus and Brett Bullington.

Kan and his coworkers hired more than a dozen other staffers. And they did develop a plan to make money: They would charge websites to be listed in Infrasearch's service. A screaming endorsement came from *Red Herring* magazine, named for the preliminary prospectus before an IPO. *Red Herring* had cozy ties to Conway, who owned a piece of the publication, and to the rest of the VC establishment. It put Infrasearch on its cover in December 2000 with a headline blaring that the tiny firm would be "bigger than Napster." The article noted that Infrasearch had no revenue to date, little technology that others couldn't imitate, and a swarm of competitors in the exploding post-Napster field. But by then, media and VC frenzies had erupted over peer-to-peer, and the corporate world was paying close attention to all of it. Perhaps the only thing more surprising than *Red Herring* crowning a Napster successor so early was what Sun Microsystems did about it. Urged on by cofounder and chief scientist Bill Joy, a legendary engineer for two decades, Sun in March 2001 swapped about $10 million worth of stock for Infrasearch, hiring Kan and his car-happy colleagues in the bargain.

Joy had been working on a system of ground rules for peer-to-peer transactions, dubbed Jxta and pronounced "Jucksta." He folded Infrasearch into the project and launched Jxta weeks later. There would be no charge to download Jxta and join in its searchable network. And Sun made the project open source, releasing the code for others to improve as long as Sun approved. Dozens of companies agreed to participate in the effort, and thousands of software writers downloaded the code. But more than a year later, the technology was still far from ubiquitous, and it wasn't clear how anyone could make any money from it. Kan, however, got a pile for himself and his employees, and they got to work on things that interested them at Sun. Asked later why more hadn't happened with Infrasearch and Jxta, Kan pointed to the book *Accidental Empires,* by Robert Cringely. The moral of some of Cringely's technology stories is the same as that in Clayton Christensen's subsequent bestseller *The Innovator's Dilemma*: Innovation comes from those with no stake in the status quo, which necessarily means smaller companies. When big companies take over efforts at innovation that were successful elsewhere, they assign the projects to managers unskilled in innovation. The managers lack that ability because they have risen using a contrary set of skills, those needed for surviving in a corporate hierarchy full of entrenched systems. The effort to keep innovating almost always fails. Tragically, Kan also incorrectly saw himself as a failure. After a long battle with depression, he killed himself in June 2002.

Napster had started everything. It had proven that its technology worked and that it was vitally important. So it is surprising in some ways that major corporations were only pursuing ideas like Kan's and not offering to buy Napster outright as well. Once in charge, such buyers could have let the courtroom gamble ride, adapted the system for different uses, or licensed it to other companies to apply as they wanted. Back in the already long-ago summer of 1999, entrepreneur Ben Lilienthal had wanted to do just that. But by now, it was simply too late. Millions of consumers would have howled if the switch had been turned off. Big companies weren't conditioned to risk losing a mammoth verdict, which might have been applied even for wrongdoing before they took control of the firm. And when there were expressions of interest, Eileen Richardson was reluctant to do much talking: If she had, the big companies could have figured out how to copy what Napster had done. Instead, the besieged firm would have to make its own way, raising money from the professional risk-takers, the venture-capitalist kingpins of Silicon Valley.

9

venture games

FROM THE BEGINNING, CEO EILEEN RICHARDSON'S MOST important mission was getting venture funding. Eventually, she would be in good shape to secure it. By the spring of 2000, the market was at an all-time high, and many venture firms were drooling over Napster's unbelievable statistics—more than 10 million users. But before Richardson could get what she thought was the right firm and the right terms, she would have to battle John Fanning more fiercely than she had at any time since the two met in October 1999.

Ahead of that first meeting, employees warned Richardson that Fanning was a big problem who had hustled his nephew Shawn and was out for only himself. Ali Aydar, her first hire, told Richardson in all seriousness that his mother would kill him if she found out he was working for another John Fanning company, since Aydar had been taken advantage of so badly at Chess.net. But as the time neared for Fanning to fly out and inspect the operation, Richardson began getting warnings of another, unexpected sort. "You're going to love him," Sean Parker told her. "He's incredibly charismatic."

Sure enough, when he appeared, Fanning was charming, telling Richardson how thrilled he was that she was running the company. "I was surprised he was so likable," Richardson said. "I tried to be nice and listen to him." Richardson made a distinct impression on Fanning as well: As soon as she was out of earshot, he turned to Parker and whispered, "She's hot!" But the honeymoon was brief. As soon as Richardson dug into the books at Napster, she found herself in unfamiliar territory. For starters, Fanning and his marketing deputy, Tom Carmody, were each drawing monthly salaries of about $5,000 through December 1999 despite having no executive positions. "It was so far out of what I was used to," Richardson said. Yosi Amram's initial $250,000 investment also went to Hull and was under Fanning's control for far longer than Richardson had expected. Fanning told her he was paying office expenses and salaries. Then he stalled her, telling Richardson that the rest of the money had been transferred to San Mateo. Finally, after Amram stepped in and insisted, Richardson got control of Napster's money and cut off the payments to Fanning and Carmody. By then, $62,000 was gone, she said. Amram said he doesn't recall how much Fanning spent in Hull.

It wasn't even easy to sort out who owned how many shares in the company. Amram had bought the entire issue of Series A Senior shares, which had special rights, while the others had mainly Series A Junior shares. Amram paid 20 cents for his shares, while Richardson and Bales said they paid 30 cents, both to Fanning's personal account. And Amram got another million shares of the Series A Junior direct from Fanning for what Amram said was 2 cents each, a mystifyingly low price. In declining order of their stakes, Napster's junior holders included Fanning, Shawn, Amram, Jim Gidwitz, Bill Bales, Richardson, Aydar, and Brian McBarron. It remains unclear exactly how much John Fanning made by selling his shares through the course of Napster's life. But a capitalization table reflecting the state of things after the Series A round shows him with fewer than 5 million shares, down from the 7 million he took when he incorporated the company. Based on what Amram, Richardson, and Bales say they paid for those 2 million shares, Fanning made more than

$300,000 just on the move to San Mateo. Richardson and Parker believe he eventually cleared roughly $1 million, a figure that Aydar and a major Napster investor confirmed was in the ballpark.

Amram's extra million shares, the ones Fanning sold him at a bargain-basement price, were "the chess move John made to get Yosi on his side" during disagreements among the directors, Richardson later concluded. Bales figured Fanning needed to do something special for Amram to get him involved at all, since Amram had lost money at Chess.net. When the weekly board meetings had a key issue, Amram "didn't really vote with John, but he would try to mediate. It meant nothing got decided," Richardson said.

Amram said he wasn't unduly influenced by the cheap shares. But he agreed that he was stuck in the middle on many topics. "I don't think [Napster's problems were] either John or Eileen's fault," he said. "It was a combination of their personalities. [Napster] blew a number of opportunities by zigzagging. It didn't have strong, clear leadership with a mandate."

Fanning sometimes directed Richardson to sell more of his shares, with the company bearing the administrative expense of the transactions. Richardson believed that was improper. Kirk Hanson, executive director of the Markkula Center for Applied Ethics at Santa Clara University, agreed that for such expenditures to be appropriate, either board approval or a written agreement would have been required. Fanning's private sales of Series A Junior stock were at a range of prices. So were Napster's sale prices, but they rose in a more conventional manner, from 30 cents a share in the A round to 80 cents in the B round that closed in December. In some of the disagreements over his personal stock sales, Fanning found an ally in Amram, who was inclined to support anything that would reduce Fanning's equity stake. Amram was spending most of his energy raising money for and running ValiCert, which authenticated Internet transactions. Some of the stock transactions there were enough to raise eyebrows as well when ValiCert went public in 2000.

ValiCert filed for an IPO early that year, eventually raising $40 million in the fall. The prospectus for the IPO revealed a Byzantine capital structure similar to Napster's, with Series A Junior preferred stock, Series A Senior preferred stock, Series B, and Series C shares. It also showed a loss of more than $17 million in 1999, a reverse stock split, and the resignation of PricewaterhouseCoopers as the company's auditor. The most intriguing bit was buried in a footnote to the financial statements. It showed that the Series A Junior shares had been sold three times, in March, April, and October of 1996, at prices "ranging from 0.8 cents to 7.5 cents"—a spread of more than 800 percent. John Coffee, one of the most widely cited securities-law experts and a professor at Columbia University Law School, said such sales are legal as long as they are disclosed. "Antifraud rules might be violated if you fail to provide material information," Coffee said. "It may be material to investors buying at $5 that it was available to another investor at $2 a week ago."

ValiCert's Series A sales occurred before Amram joined the company. But he was the one who took the heat for them from angry investors. ValiCert angel investor and entrepreneur Gary Kremen confronted Amram, even threatening to sue over the variable pricing, but Amram told him he'd regret it: "Maybe you're right. Maybe I'm right. But if you sue, none of the venture capitalists in the Valley you want to talk to will ever do business with you again." Kremen backed off.

Even with full disclosure, selling the same class of shares at different prices, as ValiCert and Fanning did, is outside of the norm. Steve Humphreys, a CEO at three companies, an associate of Amram's, and an angel investor in Interwoven and other firms, said he steered away from that sort of hustle. "I wouldn't do it that way. But that's why I wasn't enough of a hypester for the environment," said Humphreys, who now heads the firm ActivCard SA. "It's weird, and it's not the right way to do it." Humphreys wasn't involved at Napster, but he said the company's payments for stock transfers, salary for John Fanning, and other questionable practices weren't atypical for start-ups in their earliest stages. "Traditionally, it happens in the first two or three years of a company's life, and it gets cleaned up in the next four years, before you go public."

During the bubble, that kind of evolution was so telescoped that the cleanup phase often disappeared.

FANNING AND RICHARDSON ARGUED often during his visits and board meetings in which he participated by phone. After Richardson stopped the company from footing the bill for transactions involving Fanning's stock, Shawn asked her for advice on how to sell some of his own shares, and she gave him the name of a lawyer. During the next board call, Richardson mentioned that Shawn was using an outside attorney, just as she wanted Fanning to. Fanning seemed incredulous that his nephew had consulted Richardson instead of coming to him. "I find that unbelievable—that he would ask you for help," Fanning said. Richardson, listening along with other Napster executives in the company conference room, drew in her breath. "John," she said. "Fuck you."

The pair also argued over what stance to take against the record industry. Richardson wanted to keep them at arm's length, while seeming to be cooperative. Fanning didn't even want to pretend to cooperate. "Fuck the record industry," he said during one meeting, according to Richardson. During another fight, she took Fanning into the conference room and told him he was making her sick to her stomach. She said she was trying to do what was right for the company, including lining up the right venture firm. "You know what you're worried about? John fucking Fanning," she told him. The next day, he came in and gave her flowers.

Vice President Bill Bales said that he had tried and failed to get Fanning to back away from trying to manage the firm. "John is an egotist," Bales said. "He's a wildcat." But Bales said that he didn't like what Richardson was doing at the company, either, and that she handled Fanning the wrong way. "She was becoming almost obstreperous. She didn't use psychology," he said. Once, when Bales suggested that Richardson tell Fanning she was sorry about something, she said, "'I'm not going to apologize to him for anything,'" Bales recalled. "Maybe it was integrity. I don't know."

Unfortunately, Bales contributed to the problem. Already averse to taking direction, he argued with Richardson and went behind her back repeatedly to complain to both of the other directors. Sick of the armed standoff between Fanning and Richardson, at one point Bales told Amram that one or the other had to go. "He didn't agree about that," Bales said. "He was like Switzerland. That could have been a mistake."

Bales and Fanning developed a back channel, frequently e-mailing each other about a range of ideas, Napster and non-Napster, with Richardson remaining oblivious. As his relationship with Fanning deepened, Bales felt more comfortable doing business the way he saw fit, including in his efforts to recruit new executives. High on his list was Rob Lord, the young director of online strategy at Nullsoft, maker of the Winamp MP3 player. Lord had first heard from Napster when John Fanning called him during the summer of 1999 and proposed an alliance, since most Napster users already relied on Winamp software to play their songs. Lord looked at the site and discussed what Napster was doing with his handful of colleagues. "We agreed very quickly that they would be sued off the planet," Lord said. In October, Lord's name came up as a possible hire in an executive staff meeting at Napster. Richardson was worried that Nullsoft was more likely to be a competitor than an ally, and she wanted as tight a lid as possible on what Napster was doing, since Napster's system wasn't that hard to imitate. The important thing was to maintain the critical mass that came with being the biggest provider, she felt. Led by Richardson, everyone at the meeting agreed not to go after Lord.

Yet Bales went ahead anyway, swearing Sean Parker to secrecy and taking him along to meet Lord. Parker, aware that Bales had his own relationship with Fanning, wasn't sure what to do and elected to keep quiet. Lord told Justin Frankel and the others at Nullsoft that he had no interest in leaving but would agree to a meeting to see what Napster was up to. Richardson found out about the get-together later and came to a second dinner with Lord to close the loop. There she made Lord sign a nondisclosure agreement, and to the extent that Lord's real mission had been to gather intelligence, he was soon frustrated. "They weren't being forthcoming enough to even recruit me. Which made me think the situation was even worse than I'd imagined," Lord said. "If they had given me a great story, I might have been interested, but I didn't hear it." Lord also showed less optimism than the Napster crew did about the company's prospects. "What about the lawsuit?" he asked, long before the record industry acted. Richardson looked stunned. "What lawsuit?" she asked. The lawsuit that is obviously going to be filed, he replied. Richardson was embarrassed. "He knew a lot more about copyright and intellectual-property law than I did," she said.

The dinner didn't lead anywhere. But Shawn developed his own relationship with Lord and with Frankel, the wunderkind who later unleashed Gnutella. Using instant messages, the young men would discuss coding a little, cars and women more often. A year later, when Napster was in its darkest hour, Lord was at his grandmother's house when he got nearly simultaneous instant messages from Shawn and Frankel. His grandmother didn't understand how both had traced him to her house. Lord patiently explained that messaging systems were based on log-ons, not physical location. Then she asked who his correspondents were. "Well," he said, "they're both my friends. This one has always done what he liked, building tools for listening to music on the Internet. And he just sold his company for $100 million. And my other friend—he also did what he wanted, building tools for listening to music on the Internet. And he's being sued for the gross national product of Europe." Noting that his grandmother seemed concerned, Lord explained some more. "See, this is what the Internet is all about. When I was in college, the worst thing that could happen is you could throw up in your dorm room and get kicked out. Now, with the Internet, you can be up $100 million or down billions."

⸺ ⸺

ONE DAY NEAR THE END OF 1999, after the recording industry had indeed filed suit, Bales called New York investor Jason Grosfeld. Napster was raising its second round of financing, Bales said. Since Grosfeld had nearly invested when the company was back in Hull, Bales wanted to know if he still wanted in. If so, now was the time. Grosfeld was intrigued but skeptical, given the history and his dealings with Fanning. During the call, Grosfeld realized that Bales and Richardson didn't know how close he had come to being the lead backer of Napster that summer and what had gone wrong. He guessed that Shawn and Parker had kept quiet about the early financing quest so as not to spook the new managers. Grosfeld said he would consider coming out to San Mateo for a meeting if Bales gave him the capitalization table, the list of who owned what share of the company. A basic document, the cap table is essential for funders because it makes no sense to invest without knowing how much of the company you're getting. Yet in all his dealings with the first incarnation of Napster,

Grosfeld had never seen one. Bales put Grosfeld off, saying he couldn't work up a cap table yet because he didn't know who was investing in the new round. Grosfeld said that was fine; Bales could just show him the one reflecting the status quo. Bales, himself a large shareholder, said he ought to be able to put one together if Grosfeld came out to visit. Or, he said, John Fanning would fax Grosfeld one. Right, Grosfeld thought. He laughed out loud.

With low expectations, Grosfeld nonetheless decided it was worth the trip to see if Richardson and the others had wrested control from Fanning and if they had sorted out the legal issues. Parker picked him up at the San Jose airport, and on the way north through Silicon Valley, he filled Grosfeld in on the events of the previous three months. "These guys are totally in the dark about Fanning," Grosfeld thought. "Eileen and Bales have no clue." When he arrived at Napster, Bales still didn't have a cap table to show Grosfeld, who assumed the worst. "I don't think you understand the ownership of this company," Grosfeld told Bales and Richardson in the conference room. He said he wouldn't invest unless they gained control of Napster in the new round, and Bales assured him they would. Grosfeld said he didn't believe them, and he recounted Fanning's negotiation games. "I kind of spilled the beans about my experience," he recalled. When he was through, Richardson just stared, her jaw literally hanging open. Bales got up and walked to his nearby office, put his feet up on his desk, and dropped his head in his hands, not emerging even to tell Grosfeld goodbye. Grosfeld drove to see Amram before leaving, and they chatted amicably. "Keep me in mind if you get things straight," Grosfeld said, and he flew home.

There was a natural tension in Bales's job, even if he did it correctly. In addition to seeking investors, he was on the lookout for a CEO that could replace his boss. It was a delicate proposition, made all but impossible when Bales mixed the two overtures. If he was interested in a potential funder whom he also saw as a potential CEO, he was essentially asking that person to invest in a company whose management needed changing—not the most assured of come-ons. And at times Bales may have overstressed the point about the need for a new CEO. One of Bales's multipurpose targets was Peter Macnee, who headed a New York Internet firm called FortuneCity.com Inc. Like dozens of its competitors,

FortuneCity had gone public at a time when investors didn't care about profit. Even though the company was losing money, it had raised nearly $100 million in an IPO. Like TheGlobe.com, FortuneCity offered users free homepages on the Web. It had added other services as well, including places for users to store digital music in private or public libraries. So there was some logic behind Macnee considering putting the company's money, or its high-flying stock, into Napster. In late 1999, Macnee fielded separate calls from both Fanning and Bales. Fanning "was being very coy," Macnee said. "He said everyone and their brother wanted to invest, and he was going to be very choosy." Bales was more persistent, calling repeatedly and coming to meet Macnee in New York. Bales went over Napster's prospects and confidently predicted that the company would win in court. "Bales struck me to be, for his times, a very shrewd entrepreneur," Macnee said later, "but sort of made for the time: a wheeler and dealer made for the up market." Bales never offered Macnee a job, "but I sensed him recruiting me. It was clear he had no love for Eileen," he said.

Macnee was interested enough to fly out to San Mateo, where he met Richardson, technology chief Eddie Kessler, and, briefly, Shawn, who was wearing a black Napster baseball cap. Macnee wasn't impressed by Richardson, who was "all over the map," he said. Later, Macnee checked with his firm's lawyers and a former RIAA executive to get their take on the lawsuit. He came away thinking there was a much greater risk of Napster losing than its executives let on. He asked if the company would indemnify FortuneCity if the firm invested and Napster lost in court, and they told him no. That turned out to be the deal breaker. "For us to take on a legal battle like that would have been nuts. We just said, 'Let's stick to what we know about,'" Macnee said.

Another CEO candidate, Ernst & Young technology strategist Yobie Benjamin, wasn't deterred by Bales, Richardson, or even the legal dilemma. He was gung ho through all the interviews until he spoke by phone with John Fanning. When Benjamin asked Fanning about the financial might of Napster's enemies, Fanning told him: "I'm going to buy Universal. I'm going to buy Disney." Benjamin came to his senses and dropped out of contention for the job. "It was a total megalomaniac view of the world," Benjamin said. "This will be the ultimate business school case study: How do you fuck up the greatest opportunity on the planet? It's a tragedy bounded by greed."

Whatever else Bales was, he was a true believer. He had plowed a lot of his fortune into shares in the company, even borrowing $100,000 from Amram to invest more, and he worked without a salary. "I gave everything I had to Napster," Bales said. He met with some potential Napster investors without Richardson knowing. When he was found out, he begged Richardson not to fire him. More than once, Bales broke down in tears as he asked Richardson to give him another chance. Still a soft touch, she did each time. His continued presence was hard on many of the Napster faithful, including Jessie Garrehy, who sat a dozen feet from Bales in the Xtime office. Bales was spreading a rumor about an evening of excess shared by Garrehy, Richardson, and John Lee. After Garrehy found out and confronted Bales, he cockily told her that since it was true, it didn't matter. Back at her desk, Garrehy picked up a full mug of coffee and hurled it at Bales. The mug struck the wall between Xtime and Napster and exploded in pieces.

Richardson was outraged by Bales's schemes and by the gossip. But the final straw came only after Ali Aydar and Ritter had too much. The engineers told their boss, Kessler, that they would quit if Bales wasn't gotten rid of immediately. Kessler had already warned Richardson that Bales and Fanning were plotting to get rid of her, and Aydar and Ritter convinced him that now was the time to act. "If he doesn't leave, I'm leaving too," Kessler told Richardson. Informed of the situation by Richardson, Bales figured Ritter was a hopeless case, since he was dating Garrehy. He thought his best shot was to turn Aydar around, which might sway Kessler.

Bales blasted off a desperate e-mail to Aydar, copying Richardson, John Fanning, Amram, Shawn, and Kessler. "I was told by Eileen that you were walking if I didn't leave the company by 5 P.M.," Bales wrote just after that hour on Friday, December 17. "I've gone back over all my e-mails with you, and they stand as proof of my feelings for you. It was a shock to hear Eileen say this . . . but I'm open-minded enough to hear your side of the story." Then Bales attacked the company itself, voicing legitimate gripes shared by others but also displaying much of his special mind-set. "I keep asking myself the question over and over and over again . . . why is this stuff happening at Napster? Why does the place smell like a rotten egg? If it's going to stink like this my vote is to flip it and move on. You absolutely cannot build a business around an environment so loathsome."

Shawn, who normally kept away from personnel explosions, was stunned at the public airing of Bales's grievances. Copying the entire board was inappropriate, especially since Bales lashed out both at the long-suffering Aydar and at the general atmosphere. And it was never a good idea to give his uncle more temptation to swoop into action. "DUDE," Shawn fired back immediately to Bales alone. "Why did you forward a message of this nature to everybody? Was this a mistake? If you intended upon finding out Ali's story you probably should have cleared it up with him alone before broadcasting this message. This is just wrong!"

Richardson finally sided with Aydar and the others and told Bales he was fired, that he wouldn't be working through the end of his six-month term. Bales didn't take the news well. Others in the office were concerned enough that they called Kessler to warn him that Bales might be headed his way. Kessler, in turn, took the threat seriously enough that he called the police. Bales never showed up at Kessler's house. But soon after, Richardson was shopping near home in a Fry's Electronics store and turned around to find Bales up close and staring at her. "He'd been following me. It was freaky," she said.

━ ━

JUST FIRING BALES WASN'T ENOUGH to stop him. Since he believed Fanning still held the real power at the company, he launched an audacious bid to take over the most important aspect of Napster's efforts, from his own view and Fanning's: getting money fast. In an e-mail sent in January, Bales wrote again to Fanning and Amram. "This should not be forwarded to anyone," he began, "but please note that it is for the record. Bottom line: is it fair to ask Eileen to bring a VC?

"I don't Eileen [sic] has the courage or experience to get us a VC, or even understands the process of raising money from VCs. . . . I will be disgusted if we don't get a VC and we let the momentum dissipate with our current options. . . . Get me involved and I will be accountable to YOU for bringing the financing issue to a close. Yosi, what about providing the value of VC introductions? John, please do a better job of managing the board. This is critical . . . the fortunecity deal is a longshot. We must keep our options alive."

Fanning was inclined to go with Bales. He responded to both Bales and Amram: "I totally agree. I am flabbergasted at the notion that I brought in professional management with the specific focused goal of getting the company venture financed, hopefully by KP [Kleiner Perkins]. It's been 5 months and we are no closer today than we were then. I'm really disgusted by the lost opportunity. John."

Amram, stepping in once more as mediator, then added his opinion: "I don't think saying we are no closer today is fair." Fanning replied with the last word, saying that in his view the problem was exacerbated because Napster had grown too valuable. "Not to be argumentative but we may in fact be further away," Fanning wrote. "If the companies [*sic*] value has risen out of the range of most top tier VCs then we have the problem Bill outlined. John."

⸺ ⸺

EVEN WHILE WAGING HIS rearguard action at Napster, Bales was talking to Fanning about new ventures, including some that would be potential competitors to Napster. In ordinary times and at ordinary companies, such discussions could be considered a conflict of interest for Fanning. The idea that Bales spent most of his post-Napster time on was something he called AppleSoup. It was another hybrid peer-to-peer system, meaning that it would keep central control of content that was housed on users' computers. But instead of swapping music, users would swap short films or animation. And it would come with a rights-management system, so that the creators of the content would have to approve each transfer and viewing. Since Napster at times considered expanding from music into other media, a conflict could have arisen. But that didn't stop Bales, Fanning, or even Amram. By the time Bales unveiled AppleSoup in the summer of 2000, his announced investors included both those Napster directors, entertainment executive Frank Biondi, and the son of MPAA head Jack Valenti, who had testified against Napster. After Apple Computer sued over the name AppleSoup, Bales changed it to Flycode. The suit was easy press, and Bales said then that Apple had done the little-noticed start-up a favor.

Bales and Fanning also had frequent discussions about Fanning's attempt to get into distributing Internet videos, which Fanning called NetMovies. NetMovies was part of what Fanning was describing as an Internet incubator, NetCapital, which claimed Napster as just one of many ventures, another being an Internet-games firm evolved from the old Chess.net. Early in 2000, Fanning hired a Bain & Co. entertainment-business consultant named Martin Kay to help him start NetMovies. Together they called Kay's old boss at Bain, who had left to take control of Artisan Entertainment Inc., a movie studio best known for the raging success of *The Blair Witch Project*. Mark Curcio was interested in leaving Artisan, and he was vacationing on Martha's Vineyard in Massachusetts. Fanning and Kay flew to the island and spent three hours talking about NetMovies. Fanning said that NetMovies would be similar to Napster, only with fees for usage and copyright control. Curcio thought he was being snowed. "It wasn't clear he had any money whatsoever," Curcio told another entertainment-industry figure. And when he went to inspect the operation in Los Angeles, "it was two guys in a closet. It was like the Wizard of Oz." The code wasn't even written yet, and Curcio passed.

The two guys in the closet were Csaba Fikker and Gerald Bagg. Earlier in 2000, Fanning had called Fikker, the old production expert from Bales's ON24, and asked him to help. Fikker was still kicking himself for not following Bales to Napster, so he signed on as VP of operations, and Bagg joined as CEO. Fanning raised money from Napster investors Jim Gidwitz and Sung-Bu Kim, a contact of Bales's through his girlfriend, Holly Shin. Bales also met with some prominent Hollywood figures, including actor-director Danny DeVito and Jon Avnet, the director of *Fried Green Tomatoes*. Fanning and Bales wanted money for NetMovies; the directors wanted to reach Napster's audience to test scenes or promote new releases. "John promised DeVito he would be able to deliver a Napster deal," Bales said. When he couldn't, one director who had invested demanded and eventually got his money back.

With a skeleton crew working near Los Angeles in Marina Del Rey, Fanning approved a contract for engineers in San Francisco to write the program for the movie player. The result "was a piece of crap," Fikker said, not nearly good enough to release. But Fanning didn't seem to mind. "He would say one thing today and something completely else tomorrow," Fikker said. "Gerald was the only one who could communicate with him." Far worse was Fanning's idea of how to build the business, Napster-style. He went out and bought a bunch of copyright-protected DVDs at the store and directed the NetMovies staff to duplicate the content and put it on the server, without getting permission from anybody, Fikker said. That certainly would have gotten NetMovies attention, and very likely a lawsuit. But Fanning evidently felt that the same negative attention paid to Napster had done wonders. "The plan was 'Let's have it up on the servers, open the gates, and then we'll figure it out later,'" Fikker recalled. "It was like a lunatic idea." The only reason NetMovies didn't go through with the gambit was that the technology wasn't working well enough, Fikker said.

Bales moved on to Flycode, and a May 2000 article about some of Napster's competition mentioned it and identified early Napster investor Adrian Scott as the firm's chairman. Shawn sent a group e-mail around Napster asking about Flycode's plans. "What's the deal?" he asked. "I believe Bill Bales is the CEO." Ritter responded to the same group: "Once a scumbag, always a scumbag."

— —

AT NAPSTER, THE QUEST FOR venture funding by then dwarfed all of Richardson's other projects. Getting Ron Conway on board in December in the Series B, which raised just over $2 million, had been a good start. But Napster still had no revenue, and it was spending millions of dollars on legal expenses, on servers to handle the still-bulging traffic, and on improvements to the service. And only a venture round would get rid of the last of Fanning's control.

Richardson's first call was in January 2000 to the established firm of New Enterprise Associates on Sand Hill Road in Menlo Park. Her contact there, the VC and *Fortune* magazine columnist Stewart Alsop, had good reason to listen to Richardson. She had courted him to invest NEA money in Interwoven, and he had passed. If he had listened that time, "I would have made hundreds of millions of dollars," Alsop said.

When she called this time, Alsop had already heard of Napster and had just invested in another digital-music company. Alsop came to Napster's office, meeting with Shawn, Parker, CFO Lyn Jensen, and Richardson, and they explained the company, including the legal issues and the unpleasant role being played by Fanning. But they were so vague about the business plan that Alsop never got around to thinking seriously about the other problems. He reported back to his partners that it wasn't so much that Napster had no business plan: As he saw things, it didn't have a business. A business implies customers, Alsop said. And a customer—derived from the word "custom," as in a tax or a duty—is someone who pays for something. Even when his partners encouraged him to look harder, Alsop said, "I couldn't see a business at all." Richardson gave a presentation to a committee of NEA partners, but the pitch went nowhere without Alsop's support. Later, Alsop wrote in *Fortune:* "Here's the sad truth about Napster. The company's legal argument is untenable, its business model is terrible, and its software isn't even all that good."

Napster's money kept flowing in the wrong direction. The company spent $1.6 million in the first three months of 2000, including a half-million dollars on legal bills and the same amount on research and development. Richardson and marketing VP Liz Brooks honed their financing pitch, putting together a PowerPoint slide show in February. It included a flow chart of the management structure, short biographies of Richardson, Brooks, Kessler, and Jensen, and eye-popping statistics on Napster's growth—still as much as 35 percent in a day. The presentation gamely tried to make the lawsuit a plus, arguing that it had put the brakes on more cautious competitors. The business model resembled a smorgasbord. Under "revenue assumptions," the slides listed advertising sales, CD sales, subscription revenue for premium content, and even direct e-mail marketing to consumers.

When the number of users, already passing 5 million, multiplied a few more times, Richardson and Brooks said, it would be in the industry's best interest to settle. The record companies spent millions of dollars to promote new bands, most of which disappeared without a trace. On its computers, Napster was building the world's premier database of who owned what kind of music and what songs they were seeking next. Richardson figured that the industry would accept very small payments for their digital copyrights in exchange for being able to market new bands to those users who were statistically most apt to go out and buy those bands' CDs. "It's very expensive to acquire an end user," Richardson told potential investors. "Napster takes that problem away."

Kleiner Perkins Caufield & Byers was the pick of the litter on Sand Hill Road, having backed Sun Microsystems, Netscape, and Amazon.com. It heard Richardson's retooled pitch first and assigned partner Doug Mackenzie to weigh the deal. Mackenzie wasn't impressed by the argument that the lawsuit was a good thing. "Doug assessed it and concluded that they were liable," said top Kleiner partner John Doerr. "They were breaking the law, and it wasn't a prudent risk." Worse, Mackenzie concluded that Kleiner itself—and even Kleiner's limited partners—might be found liable as well. "It could go back to our limited partners, the Stanford endowment," Doerr said. "We didn't want to put Stanford at risk."

But the opportunity was so big that Kleiner couldn't bring itself to walk away completely. Doerr liked Richardson, and Kleiner had backed Amram once before, at Individual Inc. At the end of the pitch meeting, Doerr gave Richardson a hug. "This is so exciting," he told her. Soon, Richardson asked for a more concrete show of support if Kleiner wanted to stay in the running—a bridge loan of $1 million. She got the check the same day. But at the rate Napster was burning through money, that wouldn't last even until June. Just as Alsop had done for his partners, Mackenzie agreed to look deeper.

When he did, Mackenzie thought he saw a way out of the jam that Napster was in, and he suggested that Richardson talk to another small Kleiner-backed firm called Gigabeat, which was working on a system for recommending songs to customers. Richardson loved that idea—it was similar to what she had tried to do with Firefly, years before in Boston. Her heart set on Kleiner, Richardson redoubled her efforts. She met with Gigabeat's young CEO, Erin Turner, and began to discuss a merger. Turner was a rising star in the Valley. She had been working toward a master's degree in engineering at Stanford when she met two doctoral candidates and they began talking about digital music. Turner drew up a business plan for Gigabeat and won a competition with it, at the same time winning funding for the plan.

For Turner, the prospect of a deal with Napster was thrilling. Napster had all the users, and Gigabeat had good technology without an audience. It seemed like a great fit for Gigabeat, and "from Napster's perspective, they realized they had taken off so fast that the ship was shaking and barely holding together," Turner said. The two companies began a long series of meetings between each other's engineers, executives, and shareholders. Turner even met John Fanning at Palo Alto's Café la Dolce Vita, where the pair had chocolate cake and Fanning explained why Napster was worth $1 billion. Afterward, he went to his Jaguar to get Turner a Napster T-shirt.

Richardson and Turner agreed on the outline of a deal designed to protect Kleiner in the event the lawsuit went the wrong way. According to Turner's e-mails from that time, the investment was to go into an escrow account, which could have been returned to Kleiner if Napster lost the looming fight over a preliminary injunction. "Our legal team was not optimistic," Turner said. "They anticipated Napster potentially paying damages." Another scenario would have simply subtracted a stream of those payments from the company's future revenue. Those amounts might be huge, the lawyers told Turner. In her notes from the meeting, she wrote: "OPEC vs. Jed Clampett."

The investment deal could have helped Napster, at least, by providing a legitimate music-discovery service akin to what Richardson had long been promising. And a new CEO might well have taken a friendlier tack with the record industry, since Kleiner had concluded that it would be backing a losing legal position.

Richardson returned from a meeting with Turner late one night with good news for Amram and a plan. The two companies would combine, with Napster stockholders getting two-thirds of the resulting firm, and then Kleiner would invest $15 million. The deal would value the merged firm at more than $150 million. Napster would get the Kleiner stamp of approval, and it would get a $100 million valuation—not bad for a six-month-old firm with fewer than thirty employees. Richardson e-mailed Amram that she wanted to huddle first with him, then with Mackenzie at

Kleiner, before finally combining forces with Amram to try to sell Fanning on it. "I'm planning to 1) strategize with you, 2) Meet with Doug, 3) if we have a deal, call john with you," Richardson wrote.

When Amram responded in the morning, he was enthusiastic. And he called for a full-court press on Kleiner to extract the most money. He urged Richardson to get a term sheet from Idealab, a southern California Internet incubator that had been interested in investing, in order to show there was competition to get in. And since Redpoint Ventures' Geoff Yang was interested but wanted to invest alongside Kleiner, Amram suggested that Richardson give Yang the go-ahead to call Kleiner. He didn't think that Kleiner would want to share the deal, but he figured that it would spur the firm to act quickly to cut Yang out. "I suspect it will get those two more competitive when he calls and KP gives him the finger. It will also put pressure on KP," Amram wrote.

Amram was also interested in tweaking the structure of the deal so that it could aid Napster in other ways. Among the possibilities was to turn it into a sale of assets, rather than a straight merger and investment. If an asset sale left Napster Inc. behind as an empty shell, the trick might have complicated the record industry's legal assault: Napster could distribute the sale proceeds to its shareholders and promptly disappear. And the gambit likely would have extracted Napster from its grief with Draper Atlantic, which was still claiming the right to invest at a bargain price in any new investment round. Technically, an asset sale wouldn't be an investment round, Amram mused. "Would it help w/riaa? certainly would help w/DA," Amram wrote to Richardson.

The meeting at Kleiner went off as planned, and Doerr told Richardson the deal would get done. She and Amram girded themselves for the big talk with Fanning. Since he had sold many of his shares, Fanning no longer had an absolute majority of the stock. But under the company's refiled incorporation papers, approval by 67 percent of the Series A Junior shares was needed to issue a new class of stock, the class that would go to a venture firm. And Fanning had 41 percent of the Series A Junior shares, enough to block anything he didn't like. In a tense and sometimes circular two-hour conference call, Richardson and Amram urged Fanning to support the Kleiner deal. "This could jump-start Napster," Amram told him. "This can change the game." Finally, Fanning capitulated.

After they all hung up, Richardson held her breath. Just as she feared, only an hour passed before Fanning told her that he had changed his mind. He said Gigabeat was getting too much of Kleiner's money. Richardson thought another reason was that he feared—correctly—that Kleiner wouldn't want him to stay on the board.

Just like that, the deal died.

Strategically, Napster's last best chance went down with it, according to Richardson and her confidant, Xtime CEO John Lee. "They wanted him off the board. That's where the battle was lost," Lee said. "Either John Fanning gets off and they get real financing and legitimize themselves, or he doesn't. . . . He didn't care about the kids. He was a greedy bastard."

Without Kleiner, Richardson worried that everything she and her team had worked so hard for would fall apart. At two o'clock one morning during the funding crisis, she sent a long e-mail of encouragement and exhortation to the troops that spoke to those fears. "Fellow Napsters, our company has come to a critical stage," she began. "What attracted each and every one of us to Napster is the chance to change the world. A chance to make things better for consumers, a chance to change the life of an inner-city kid by letting him make a living as a musical artist. A worthy goal for sure, but a long, hard road lies ahead." She listed all the ways Napster could blow it: executing poorly, making bad decisions, failing to get the New Artist Program running, and infighting. She asked the staff to work harder, stay focused, and be nicer to each other. "Someday we will be basking in the glory of having created the fastest growing, most successful company in the Valley. And you, the first 25 employees of this company, will be the ones who created the foundation for success." She signed the memo: "Your Sometimes Fearless, Sometimes Freaked-Out Leader, Eileen."

Having no alternative besides resigning and leaving Shawn and the others flat, Richardson trudged on. Her next stop on Sand Hill was Mohr, Davidow Ventures. Another well-established firm, Mohr, Davidow had backed Rambus, Sierra Semiconductor, and Vitesse Semiconductors Corp., all thriving chip firms. And it wasn't afraid to make selective software and Internet bets, though it had wisely avoided dot-com retailers. It had supported Viant Corp., the big Web consultant, and Critical Path

Inc., the e-mail-management company. Mohr, Davidow partner George Zachary heard Richardson out and was intrigued despite the legal risks. Then something strange happened: After Richardson's presentation, he got a call from John Fanning, who asked to come in and make his own case. Fanning went in and told Zachary that Napster was worth $1 billion, a staggering claim for a company with no revenue defending against an epic lawsuit. But Zachary would be lucky to be allowed a piece, Fanning said. What's more, Napster was just part of a broader plan. Fanning was starting his own incubator, NetCapital. Mohr, Davidow should invest in that as well, he said.

Since Fanning had the power to veto a Mohr, Davidow investment in Napster, the double pitch implied an audacious swapping of favors that once more called into question Fanning's loyalty to Napster shareholders. "He was superaggressive," Zachary said. "It was an 'I am CMGI' type of pitch," referring to the holding company with stakes in more than a dozen firms. Mohr, Davidow passed on NetCapital, but it did offer to invest in Napster. A term sheet dated March 23 called for an infusion of $20 million for a fifth of the company. Like Kleiner Perkins, Mohr, Davidow wanted Fanning dropped as a Napster director. At a Napster board meeting with Richardson and Amram, Fanning again voted no, saying this offer too didn't value Napster highly enough.

Other firms also got mixed messages. At Benchmark Capital, which had launched eBay, the partners were interested enough in Napster to talk price before the negotiations ended without a deal. Along the way, the partners were informed that Fanning would part with the technology for swapping music, but wanted to keep the rights for swapping video and other content. "It was insane," a Benchmark partner said. "But that's greed for you." Fanning also kept the rights to the unused Napster.net domain name, which he has to this day.

Richardson gathered herself to make still more calls. As she did, the stock market reached its historic high and began sliding down. Venture-capital firms, while outwardly calm and even welcoming of a modest correction, began recalculating. The further the market fell, the less chance companies had for a lucrative IPO. The less chance for an IPO, the less money venture capitalists wanted to put in new companies. Napster was finally out of money, and now it was running out of funding options as well.

——— ———

ONE OF THE last VC firms to keep the door open was Hummer Winblad Venture Partners, which had made an initial offer that spring valuing Napster at more than $100 million. Fanning had his usual problems with the deal, principally that there wasn't enough money in it, and the talks dragged on for months. As they did, Angel Investors chief Ron Conway was getting nervous. Conway went to the annual Webby Awards in San Francisco, a campy but star-studded gala where winners from websites judged the best in a variety of categories are limited to five-word acceptance speeches. There Shawn collected an award and the only standing ovation of the night. Conway cornered Shawn and Parker at the party afterward. The two teens had been well out of the loop in all the talks with the venture firms, but they knew something was going wrong. "We were going to run out of money. It was complete chaos," Parker said. "We had been forced to the sidelines. Shawn was in his own little world, and I was dealing with legal stuff." Now, Conway got their attention. Time was running out, he said, and he needed them back in the mix.

"If Hummer Winblad doesn't invest, the company is going out of business whenever the next payroll is," Conway told them. "We have to solve this, and we have to solve this quickly. If this funding doesn't happen, there are no more backups." Shawn tried not to take it too seriously. "He's just a big kid," Shawn said of Conway. "He was just so dramatic. It was a serious time, but we were just trying to figure out what he was all about." What Conway was saying echoed the exasperation Shawn saw in Richardson's face. "Eileen had planned on coming in and being the interim CEO. She was getting frustrated with the process of interacting with the labels, of trying to establish a business model," Shawn said. "She was constantly looking for someone to take her place and help build the company."

Conway met with Richardson as well, and he lobbied Hummer Winblad partner Ann Winblad, warning her that she was going to miss out on the biggest Internet company of all time. Winblad listened. In April, her chief partner, John Hummer, and another VC at the San Francisco firm drove to see Richardson at Napster's office. She walked them through the PowerPoint slides and introduced them to Liz Brooks and Lyn Jensen. It took about forty minutes. Later, another Hummer partner, a former intellectual-property lawyer at Wilson Sonsini named Hank Barry, came over, and he spent about fifteen minutes with Richardson and Kessler. And a third time, Hummer associate Alicia Morga came to look at documents. There were some phone calls, mainly between Barry and Richardson, and then a draft term sheet appeared like an answered prayer on April 22. Hummer would put in $13 million, along with another million from Conway's fund and $500,000 from elsewhere. After a month of dithering, Napster was worth not $100 million or more but $65 million. "Hummer had us over a barrel," Richardson said.

A confidential term-sheet draft called for Hummer Winblad to have two directors' seats and approval of the CEO, who would also serve as a director. Hummer Winblad wound up with two out of three seats, with Fanning keeping the third. The venture firm had one more provision, though. In the event of a merger or acquisition offer, Fanning wouldn't get to play roadblock again. He and the other big holders would have to promise to vote their shares the way the board wanted.

Letting Fanning keep his board seat was a huge concession, and Richardson prayed that it would be enough to get his support. But both she and Hummer Winblad were worried it wouldn't be. So the venture firm pored over Napster's shareholder agreements, bylaws, and incorporation papers, looking for a fallback plan. Fanning's 41 percent of the junior shares still meant he could veto a new series of shares issued to a venture firm. But if Fanning were suddenly not on the board, Hummer Winblad concluded, the remaining directors might be able to do a deal unanimously without calling a vote. "If John Fanning is removed and Hank appointed then can do a unanimous written consent," the plotters wrote in a two-page memo with the improbably bland title "Mechanics."

In a scheme worthy of a Shakespeare play, they saw a way they might be able, just barely, to get Fanning removed. Since one director was electable by the combined number of Series A Junior shares, some 11,750,000, and the 536,860 common shares, a majority of the two classes together could replace Fanning in that board seat with Hank Barry. "Then new board members Yosi, Eileen and Hank can vote to expand the board and elect John Hummer," the memo said. Fanning had 4.6 million shares. So the Hummer Winblad team and Richardson counted and recounted the votes. The Gidwitz clan had 895,000 Junior shares and were likely loyal to Fanning. But if Conway's fund called in a $250,000 loan to Fanning, for which he had pledged 312,000 shares as collateral, the odds improved. Richardson and Barry figured they could get Shawn's 2.7 million shares, Ali Aydar's 80,000, and the votes of Kessler, Parker, Ritter, and a handful of others. They calculated they could get to 6.39 million votes, 247,596 more than they needed. But there was a catch: They couldn't get there without Bill Bales and his 1 million shares. And Richardson had terminated Bales, who had then started business dealings with Fanning.

Richardson thought she could still swing Bales, who was oblivious to his role as potential kingmaker. But it was a conversation she didn't want to have. And it wasn't clear the scheme would hold up in court. Instead, she and Amram talked to Fanning over and over in the next few weeks to persuade him to support the Hummer Winblad investment. His vetoes had cost Napster offers from the other firms as the market was at its peak. Now that things were sliding, even Fanning began to see that Hummer might be the last chance for him to cash out. He agreed orally to the deal.

As the lawyers for both sides worked on the final contract, Richardson still worried that Fanning was out looking for something better. And on the May day that the Hummer agreement was set to close, she believed, he was in Los Angeles negotiating with potential investors, though she never found out for sure. Richardson didn't know how to reach Fanning, and she was afraid he would reverse himself again, just as he had with Kleiner Perkins. She grabbed Shawn and Parker and shoved them toward the conference room. "Find your uncle!" she ordered them.

Panicked but used to being panicked, Shawn and Parker agreed on a strategy. They would have to flatter Fanning, telling him he would prove himself a visionary by agreeing to the Hummer deal. They needed him to feel essential, and they would stress that unlike the other deals, Fanning could stay on the board. "We had to convince him that he was a seasoned entrepreneur and a respected, benevolent leader. At the same time, we somehow had to get his subconscious to understand he would be missing out on the money if he didn't do it," Parker said. Shawn got his uncle on the line, the blood pounding in his ears. "We just tried to convince him," Shawn said. At last, Fanning succumbed. The deal closed, giving Hummer Winblad about 20 percent of Napster to Fanning's 15 percent and Shawn's 9 percent.

With Fanning's simple scrawled signature, a feeling of immense relief flooded through Shawn. At last, he was free. His uncle was all but gone from his life. He could go back to coding. His company had an official valuation of $65 million. And a respected intellectual-property lawyer believed so strongly that Napster would win in court that he was staking his career on the prospect. "I was excited when Hank came and got involved and understood the legal side, which needed some attention," Shawn said in his usual understatement. An IPO and immense riches seemed more likely than not.

⸻

HAPPIER THAN HE HAD BEEN in many months, Shawn didn't have to wait long to celebrate his new status as a legitimate player in Silicon Valley. That very night, Ron Conway was holding one of his regular over-the-top charity-and-networking bashes at his home in Atherton, where the median house sells for north of $3 million. Shawn and Parker were on the three-hundred-person guest list, right there with billionaire investor Warren Buffett, Netscape founder Marc Andreessen, and Sun cofounder Bill Joy. With Hummer Winblad's vote of confidence, Shawn almost felt as if he belonged with the others drinking champagne and munching on scallops wrapped in pancetta. Almost, but not quite. "It was like a circus. I was very awkward going there. I had no idea what I was supposed to wear," Shawn said. The charity auction was emceed by comedian Dana Carvey and benefited a host of good causes, including the Boys & Girls Clubs and the *Red Herring* Community Fund. The San Francisco 49ers cheerleaders raised spirits around the backyard swimming pool. Among the items for sale were Arnold Schwarzenegger's Humvee, a tennis lesson from Pete Sampras, and a dinner with Andreessen. The highest bid of the night, $650,000 from a Network Appliance Inc. executive, went for a single round of golf with Tiger Woods. Napster's Chris Phenner introduced Shawn to Andreessen, who asked how many users Napster had and offered words of encouragement. "Controversy can be a good thing," he said, "as long as you know how to navigate it."

"I was trying to figure out if these types of things were normal for this area, or if Conway was just a madman," Shawn said. "It was all for a good cause, so it was cool, but it was a scene. Definitely a scene." For a time, Shawn and Parker just stood and watched the street as arrivals emerged from one amazing car after another. "I thought maybe this happened weekly," Parker said. "We thought we had been inducted into this inner circle, where everyone you bumped into was worth $50 million."

Richardson's toughest assignment had come to an end. Originally having signed on for six months, she had needed nine. She wanted nothing more to do with the firm, and Hummer Winblad was ready to put in Hank Barry as her temporary replacement. She resigned with a clear conscience. "There was nothing more I could do," Richardson said. "The suit needed attention, and in some ways, who better than Hank Barry for that?"

It would be hard to exaggerate the contrast in personality between Richardson and Barry. Richardson was a den mother and a cheerleader, sometimes energetic to the point of ineffectiveness. Barry was a corporate lawyer only recently turned venture capitalist, with no real way of bonding with the kids doing most of the actual work at Napster. Yet Barry harbored a rebellious streak that was unusual for one in his position. Once again, it was all about the liberating feeling of music. Not too many big-firm lawyers or VCs had spent seven years playing rock 'n' roll. Those times were well behind Barry, now a breadwinning family guy driving a minivan. But Napster was giving him a chance to recapture that side of himself. Mr. Barry, Silicon Valley lawyer turned private investor, would be transformed magically back into Hank the Cool Drummer, He Who Brings Music to the People.

One of five children in an Ann Arbor, Michigan, family, Barry played in bands in high school and during his first two years at the University of Michigan. It was a lot more fun than studying, and Barry dreamed of drumming for real. Deciding to take the chance while he could, Barry quit school, supporting himself with a radio day job while he played in bands five sets a night, six nights a week. He cut records with some of the groups, most of them bad, and toured constantly, hitting after-hours spots to unwind and then flopping in hotel rooms. Seven years passed, and Barry still wasn't a rock star. One day he awoke and smelled his clothes from across his hotel room. It wasn't the kind of life he wanted to be living when he was thirty-five. Barry decided it was time to change course dramatically. He returned to college with a much greater focus than most of his young classmates, then entered Stanford Law School at twenty-nine.

Barry gravitated to entertainment law, keeping his hand in what had been his great diversion. But when he headed to New York for his first job at a big firm, it took only a few weeks before he realized that most entertainment law consisted of haggling over details in contracts that all looked the same. He returned west for a shot at some technology work in the mid-1980s, when Silicon Valley had perhaps five hundred practicing lawyers. Barry worked on mergers, technology contracts, and copyright deals, where his clients included record giant A&M—the record label that by virtue of the alphabet would serve as the lead plaintiff in the land-mark lawsuit against Napster. Barry was unusual at his last firm, the top-drawer Wilson Sonsini, because he did both intellectual-property and transactions work, where the stimulation was greater. "He liked being closer to the actual business decision makers," a colleague at the firm said. "There was more action, and he was a very good dealmaker. He liked being in the limelight." Barry worked furiously as the venture boom expanded, and it began taking a toll. By 1999, there were three thousand lawyers in the Valley, all working flat out. In return, they were getting decent salaries—but not the pots of gold that were popping up all around them. Barry was drafting IPO deals for people who were about to make tens of millions of dollars, when all he stood to gain was tens of thousands in legal fees.

Two venture capitalists Barry knew asked him to join them at Hummer Winblad, and Barry accepted. On September 9, 1999, by coincidence a week after Napster moved to San Mateo, Barry joined Hummer as its fourth full partner. He had led just one other investment for the firm in the seven months before Napster made its pitch; he was still learning how to do what he did. What Barry saw in Napster was what everybody else saw—a terrific application with an incredible rate of adoption, something that had potential if you could make it work for everybody, including the record industry. Barry wanted to try right away to sell a deal to the labels. But he didn't plan on being too generous, because he was in the minority that truly believed Napster would win in court. When it did, he reasoned, it could drive a much harder bargain. If it lost the case before a deal was reached—well, that would be that. The assumption was that if Napster lost the case, there wouldn't be any business.

Hummer Winblad naturally deferred on the legal question to Barry, its in-house expert. For Barry, the investment was a serious break from his past representing copyright holders. And it was a slap in the face to one technology client in particular, Silicon Valley firm Liquid Audio, which made software for streaming authorized music to listeners. At Wilson Sonsini, Barry had helped Liquid Audio go public. And the venture firm that had backed it was none other than Hummer Winblad. Before Barry made the final decision on Napster, he called Liquid Audio chief Gerry Kearby as a courtesy. What happened in that call is a matter of dispute. "I said, 'I think it's a really bad idea,'" Kearby recalled. "It screwed the musicians. He didn't care. He was fully erect." Asked if Kearby had indeed advised him against Napster, Barry first said he didn't recall that. Then, in ascending order, he said Kearby's version was counterfactual, made up, and a lie.

Whatever the reasons, Barry decided to take a huge gamble on Napster as the investment's leader, a company director, and the next interim CEO, a job that he told his wife would last six weeks. Most of his previous colleagues, while impressed with his legal acumen and work habits, didn't see him as well-suited for a job as the visionary leader of a chaotic revolution. But Barry didn't mind making a splash. "He thought the current laws shouldn't apply to new technologies, and that maybe an adjustment should be made," a former colleague said. "When he believes in something, he would go all out. A lot of things Hank does, he does in a big way."

THE REST OF HUMMER WINBLAD had another motivation for approving Barry's decision on Napster. Whether one viewed the risks as insurmountable or merely enormous, it was clear that *if* Napster won in court, the payout could be massive. And Hummer Winblad wanted a home run very, very badly. While the firm had garnered a reasonable share of respect and press since its founding in 1989, Hummer Winblad was well on its way to becoming the venture-capital joke of Silicon Valley.

The first partner on the nameplate, six-foot-nine John Hummer, had gone from Princeton University to the NBA, playing six years before retiring and collecting a Stanford M.B.A. From there he went straight to venture capital without running a company himself. His partner, Ann Winblad, had a more traditional VC background, building software firm Open Systems Inc. from nothing and then selling it for $15 million. She consulted for IBM Corp., Microsoft, and others. But she was best known in the Valley for having dated the bête noire of the Valley, Bill Gates, who was revealed as a Hummer Winblad limited-partner investor in 1999.

At first, the firm focused on software companies, producing decent results. But Hummer Winblad missed the early Internet revolution while lesser-known firms racked up hundreds of millions or even billions of dollars in profits from start-ups. Hummer's third fund, raised in 1997 ahead of the big boom, had returned only 42 percent of the $99 million invested by October 2000, according to Steve Lisson of InsiderVC.com. (By the end of 2001, the fund showed a 10 percent total gain, making each dollar invested worth $1.10; similar funds raised by three other firms in 1997 by 2001 showed 180 percent, 400 percent, and 660 percent gains.) If John Hummer and Ann Winblad had come to the Internet religion late, their conversion made them die-hard proselytizers. Their fourth fund, worth $315 million, went almost entirely to Internet start-ups. "It's like the entire portfolio was made up of dot-com, swing-for-the-fences deals," said one Hummer Winblad limited partner.

Hummer Winblad's debacle would soon be memorialized in one of the best-read magazine articles in the Valley, a snarky January 2001 piece in *eCompany Now* entitled "Bonehead Safari: My Hunt for America's Dumbest VC." The winner, by a nose, was Ann Winblad. For a venture fund, IPOs were the ultimate goal—a sudden infusion of liquid money that could be distributed back to the limited partners, who could hold on or sell if they chose. Acquisition by another company, also a "liquidation event," was choice number two. There really wasn't much of a third choice. In the two boom years ending in the fall of 2000, Hummer Winblad could boast of precious few IPOs. Of those, many were or soon would be below the IPO price. Liquid Audio had gone public at $15 and was headed down to $4. Pets.com, where Hummer had put in as much as $7.55 a share, was below $1. The Knot Inc., a wedding e-commerce site, was falling from a $10-a-share IPO to $3, and expense tracker Extensity Inc. had caromed from $20 to $823.50 and back to $19 in October. And those were winners, ones that sold stock to the public. The others included Gazoontite.com, a me-too allergy-drug seller that forced a $15 million write-off; eHow Inc., an advice site that went bankrupt; Home-Grocer.com Inc., which was bought by Webvan Group Inc., itself headed for bankruptcy; and Respond.com, best remembered for the free bottles of champagne it gave away at its launch party.

The dot-com shakeout aside, Hummer Winblad also demonstrated a remarkable tolerance for conflicts of interest, a recurring problem at VC firms that go so far as to mate one of their start-ups with another, à la Kleiner Perkins, Gigabeat, and Napster. (Kleiner also presided over the disastrous marriage of two of its biggest offspring, portal Excite Inc. and cable Internet-access firm @Home Inc.) After the Hummer Winblad takeover, Napster signed a pact with Liquid Audio when Kearby's firm was coming up short one quarter. And Napster did little-noticed deals with two other Hummer Winblad firms as well, both at Barry's insistence, according to senior Napster employees. Engineers from the first firm, Boston's LavaStorm Inc., proved useful. At the second, it was a different story. Barry used $300,000 of Napster's money as an up-front payment to struggling Mountain View, California–based start-up Envive Corp., which evaluated website performance. Core Napster staffers, including engineering VP Eddie Kessler, weren't involved in picking Envive and never even learned that the money changed hands. Envive tried and failed to come up with a way it could assist Napster. "Eventually it just fell apart," said Envive cofounder Joe Hsy. Hsy said his firm kept the money anyway: "They never asked for it back." Even Napster's office furniture was supplied by a Hummer-backed firm.

The Envive deal was like most VC-related conflicts of interest in that it got swept under the rug. Private firms have few disclosure requirements, and entrepreneurs are loath to sue VCs for fear they will never again get venture funding. But John Hummer never backed down from a fight, and that trait exposed the conflict dance at a small investment company that Hummer Winblad had funded with $4 million, Zero Gravity Internet Group. Zero Gravity, whose smaller shareholders included Marc Andreessen, ON24 CEO Sharat Sharan, and MP3.com's Michael Robertson, came to life in November 1999 at the hands of one Steve Harmon, an Internet stock-picker and the author of a popular book on raising venture rounds, *Zero Gravity*. Harmon had garnered profiles in the *Wall Street Journal* and elsewhere, and a large following of day traders watched his weekly stints on CNBC. When he started his new firm, he sought investments by a number of CEOs whose stocks he was publicly touting, and at least two of them invested in Zero Gravity. Then Harmon put a Hummer Winblad–backed firm, Net Perceptions Inc., on his list of top picks, helping send the stock up 100 percent in ten days. By the summer of 2000, CNBC became concerned enough about Harmon's multiple hats that it canceled his contract. And Zero Gravity's board suspended Harmon for poor management, then fired him for falsely telling the SEC he had a college diploma. An embarrassing situation, to be sure. But instead of backing Zero Gravity's board and trying to put the pieces together, John Hummer sided with the loyal Harmon. As lawsuits flew, Hummer converted his firm's stake into voting shares, took control of Zero Gravity, announced he would bring Harmon back, and installed Hummer Winblad associate Alicia Morga as a special executive running the firm. All of Zero Gravity's other employees quit.

Even some Hummer Winblad allies began having problems with the firm's strategy. Seattle venture capitalist David Johnston was one. He introduced Ann Winblad to a firm he had helped found and was investing in, a sports site called Rival Networks Inc. Hummer Winblad promptly invested as well, and Ann Winblad joined the board. "Their reach is unbelievable. And it's sticky," she said at the time. But Johnston grew alarmed at lavish executive spending that brought monthly individual credit-card bills of more than $100,000. When he complained to the board, he was invited to leave the meeting. "Their whole mantra was 'Don't worry, we're going public,'" said Johnston, who had to sue for access to corporate records. Instead, Rival Networks' formidable burn rate forced it out of business. Well before then, Johnston decided he'd never invest alongside Hummer Winblad again. "In the bubble, everyone made some mistakes. Hell, I did Pets.com with them. But their greed and their drive for notoriety caused them to make bigger mistakes."

More than his peers, former basketball center John Hummer took obvious relish in big battles in front of the crowd. "I am the record companies' worst nightmare," he proclaimed in July 2000. "The fireworks are just beginning. Before they close Napster, they'll have to pry it from my cold, dead fingers." In his case, the revolutionary fervor penetrated to a remarkable level, considering that his primary duty was to return profits to his investors. As he told *Fortune*, "When I decided I was willing to lose my whole $13 million investment rather than change Napster, a wonderful feeling of peace came over me."

Hummer Winblad's limited partners can be forgiven if they didn't get the same rush of well-being. In the fall of 2000, about five months after the Napster deal, Hummer was forced to write what must have been one of the most painful letters of his life, explaining how badly the latest fund had fared through the quarter ended in September. By then, Gazoontite and Pets.com were gone, and the $25 million in post-IPO losses in the latter "were the biggest losses we have ever taken," Hummer wrote. "In fact, they are larger than all of our losses ever, in the aggregate. It is an understatement to say how bad we feel about this." Other IPO shares that had not yet been distributed to limited partners included the Knot and HomeGrocer.com, which had racked up another $29 million in losses for the firm's third and fourth funds. While most business-to-consumer Internet stocks were trading at fractions of their earlier values, Hummer said that was no excuse. The firm's performance was truly extraordinary—it was a well-positioned venture operation in Silicon Valley that hadn't been able to cash in on the biggest investment extravaganza of the century.

Hummer concluded his letter by saying that the firm needed to focus on execution by its surviving companies "as well as manage valuation risk in the follow-on financings." Even better, it would seek bailouts through acquisition. The effect on Napster was subtle but unmistakable. Instead of injecting new money as needed, fighting the record industry to the end, and aiming to cash out in an epic IPO, Hummer Winblad was already looking for help.

10

hummer winblad

A WEEK BEFORE THE HUMMER WINBLAD INVESTMENT CLOSED, the May 15, 2000, issue of *Business Week* featured Shawn Fanning on the cover, along with the other four "most influential people in electronic business." Napster executives were ecstatic. "It is so amazing and so cool," CFO Lyn Jensen wrote to her colleagues. John Fanning had a different take: "I hope Shawn is going to introduce me to his 4 new friends," he e-mailed the group. He also noted with amusement that his nephew was the only one not smiling. "The faces are great! Happy (Yahoo) Happy (eBay) Happy (Softbank) Very Happy (Amazon) and Don't #$%$ with me (Shawn Fanning)." By then, 73 percent of college students were using Napster at least monthly, according to *Webnoize*. On Monday, May 22, Jensen invited all employees to come eat and drink champagne at noon to toast the Hummer Winblad deal at Spiedo Ristorante in San Mateo, a short walk away. The staff felt incredible relief. Hummer's cash infusion and management takeover came just in time. The stock market, tumbling since March, appeared headed for a long vacation from its nosebleed highs, hurting IPO prospects and slowly endangering all the less fortunate companies without deep pockets.

Getting a seasoned lawyer as interim chief executive also struck many as an excellent idea: Napster had just lost the first battle in the record industry's lawsuit. The company had argued strenuously that it was protected under the Digital Millennium Copyright Act and that the suit should therefore be thrown out before a trial in a summary judgment. The movie, recording, and publishing industries had lobbied intensely for the DMCA, afraid that they couldn't keep pace with hackers who broke through whatever encryption schemes the industries put in place. Congress obliged and passed the law in 1998, making it a criminal offense to help others get around encryption. In a limited concession to free-speech advocates, librarians, and others, the DMCA created "safe harbors" for some types of companies. Napster argued that it qualified for at least one, and possibly two, of those exemptions. The first was for passive "service providers" that serve as conduits for others who transmit information. The second exemption covered services that merely index or otherwise point the way to a variety of information.

The Napster case was the first to test the meaning of those exemptions. Putting off a final decision on the second safe harbor, U.S. district judge Marilyn Hall Patel spent most of her time trying to sort out the poorly worded breadth of the first harbor, which limits copyright liability for service providers "transmitting, routing or providing connections for material through a system or network controlled or operated by or for the service provider." After much hair-splitting, Patel ruled on May 5 that Napster wasn't covered because it wasn't doing the transmitting: It was pointing users to one another, who then transmitted MP3s. It was a close call. But even if Napster had overcome that hurdle, it would have stumbled on another of the requirements for all the safe-harbor exemptions: that the companies have "reasonably implemented" a policy to terminate repeat copyright infringers.

Technology VP Eddie Kessler claimed that Napster had adopted such a policy in October 1999, but the company hadn't bothered to tell its users about it until the following February, two months after it was sued.

And when Napster did terminate users before Patel's May ruling, it did so by changing their passwords, not blocking their computer IP addresses. An expert witness didn't have much trouble erasing the traces of his past Napster account and creating a new one on the same computer. Napster's claim that it couldn't easily block infringers' IP addresses didn't carry much weight, since the company had managed to shut out the IP addresses of bots like those used by NetPD to search for songs mechanically.

Summary-judgment fights are always an uphill battle. The party trying to end the case on the spot must show that there's no disputing its essential version of the facts, and that the law is on its side. But that was little consolation when Patel declined Napster's request for summary judgment in its favor. More than just rejecting Napster's argument, Patel had highlighted the ineffective copyright policy. And now the labels could conduct much deeper discovery of evidence through sworn interviews and demands for paper and electronic documents. New Napster CEO Hank Barry had no idea what the discovery process would turn up, having done less-than-exhaustive due diligence into the legal mess before investing. If he had done more, he might have paused in his rush to embrace the company. Among other things, he would have seen the e-mail discussions among Napster's chat-room moderators, where the outwardly poised Shawn had shown himself to be less than innocent. After one of the volunteers wrote that "we might not want to actually say that we know" that users were breaking the law, another chimed in that at least some of the MP3s were legitimate. Shawn then urged the parties to "try to avoid discussions similar to this . . . you should all be very aware of what you say." Sean Parker's words were far worse, Barry would soon learn.

Napster was up against a team of serious lawyers who were relative novices in Internet law. In a way, it was fitting that both the record industry and its attack dogs belonged to another era. Russell Frackman, the fifty-five-year-old Los Angeles attorney leading the suit against Napster, had until then never used e-mail, learning only during the course of the case. Frackman didn't even use a word-processing program, instead dictating his legal papers to a secretary, herself the last holdout from the days when shorthand was required of the firm's assistants. Like many label bosses, Frackman retained the essence of a Brooklyn accent, which faded a bit after he graduated from Columbia Law School and moved west, taking a job in 1970 with the L.A. firm of Mitchell Silberberg & Knupp. Soon after that move, Frackman paired with partner Howard Smith, an early force in filing record-company lawsuits against unauthorized duplicators. There weren't too many of those, since the duplicating required massive investment. So Smith led the way upstream, going after retailers that knowingly sold pirated goods and were easier to collect damages from. In the years after that part of the firm's practice began, Mitchell Silberberg developed a close relationship with the record dons, and one of its partners served as the Recording Industry Association of America's acting head of litigation during the Napster case. After Smith retired, Frackman became the industry's go-to man.

While the RIAA developed a reputation as a bully among Napster aficionados, the group rarely filed suit. When Frackman took the call from the RIAA to file against Napster, it didn't take long for him to conclude that he had a winner. "I looked at it as a copyright case, not a technology case. I thought it was very good," Frackman said. More than anything, the facts reminded him of one of his greatest triumphs, when in 1996 he had argued successfully before the Ninth U.S. Circuit Court of Appeals that a flea market could be held responsible for letting vendors sell pirated recordings. After Napster lost its bid for summary judgment, Frackman drafted more associates to help him as the timetable accelerated. They would have just a few weeks to plow through scores of boxes of Napster documents and change the momentum of the case.

A week after she left Napster, at the end of May 2000, Eileen Richardson went in for the sworn interview known as a deposition. She had never been through the grueling process before, and the Napster lawyers told her the cardinal rule: Say as little as possible. But as CEO, she had already said too much. Frackman put an article in front of her. "I'll read this to you and actually give you a copy if you want," he said, then recounted her words: "'Maybe I know about this band just in our local town, and you know about them too. I can share that with you directly. It's not about known artists like Madonna.'" Richardson acknowledged that she had said something to that effect. Frackman then presented her with a printout of a directory from her laptop computer. "There are, it seems to me, one, two, three, four, five Madonna MP3 music files on this page. Do you see those?" Richardson did see those; there they were. And she admitted it was likely that yes, they had been downloaded from Napster. Other Napster executives' hard drives didn't help the cause. Liz Brooks had seven Beatles songs, five Led Zeppelin songs, and seven Bjork songs, among others. Lyn Jensen was evidently a Shania Twain fan, with five cuts. At least Kessler's practice was close to the official line on Napster's mission to aid the discovery of new music, boasting three obscure Irish folk songs in addition to a track from the Dave Matthews Band.

Frackman also made Richardson eat her words about "collaborative filtering," by which, she had told reporters, Napster would recommend music based on what users liked and on what people with similar tastes liked, just as Amazon.com does for books. No such system had been put in place during her nine months on the job, though it would have been with Gigabeat. And Frackman hammered on the New Artist Program, which had taken so long to finally reach the website, in a fairly unusable form, just a month earlier. In the program's first phase, bands could fill out profiles about themselves, giving information about influences that was supposed to be searchable in later incarnations. In the interim, however, it was just a list of songs and artists, with no navigational guide.

In fairness, Richardson had been serious about the New Artist Program—she just couldn't get much support for it from the board or her fellow executives. Adrian Scott, the Napster investor brought in by Bill Bales, remembered discussing strategy at the office the previous fall with Shawn, Parker, Bales, and adviser Brett Bullington of Excite. Midway through the meeting, Richardson walked in, "and she was on a totally different plane," Scott said. "She was talking about unsigned artists. And we were like, 'hello?'" The balance of power on the issue didn't go Richardson's way even after the lawsuit began. VP Liz Brooks, in trying to defend the stripped-down New Artist Program as more than window-dressing, gave a typical response in an April e-mail to a critic in the music business: "There will always be a mass of people who only want to hear the current pop hits. Our job is not to force a musical education on these people."

But it wouldn't have done Napster any good for Richardson to say she had tried and failed, so she held her tongue. After Frackman ran through her lack of a college degree and internal documents that touted such potential Napster revenue streams as CD sales and advertising, he asked Richardson whether Hummer Winblad had estimated how much it stood to earn from Napster. She said she doubted it. How, then, did Hummer decide that Napster was worth $65 million? "Unfortunately, there is no science to venture capital," Richardson said. "It's an art, if you can call it that. It's gut."

Frackman was just getting started: The next day was Shawn's turn. As they had with Richardson, Napster's lawyers gave him basic lessons in how to survive the process, even playing him a videotape of a simulated deposition. Tell the truth, they told him, but volunteer nothing. Other than that, the only thing out of the ordinary Shawn did to prepare was to get a decent night's sleep. Frackman walked Shawn through Napster's early days, paying special attention to who held what title. "You said at the beginning that one of your titles is 'founder' at Napster. Are there other people who share the title 'founder'?" Frackman asked. "John Fanning," Shawn said. Anyone else? "Sean Parker does occasionally, but it's not clear as to whether or not he is a founder," Shawn said. Answering a follow-up question, Shawn said it wasn't clear because Parker had started work a few months after the project began. Neither Parker nor his uncle had contributed to the code that made the Napster system, Shawn confirmed. So before the move to California, Frackman asked, who had helped write the software? "Jordan Ritter. I believe that's it," Shawn said.

Shawn's testimony, given out of public view, didn't stop his uncle from claiming that he played a vital role in the development of Napster's technology. One of Fanning's lawyers was still repeating that claim well after Shawn's deposition. And Fanning went to some lengths to get the record to reflect it. As Napster was preparing to file for a patent on its technology, it drafted a description of the work and attributed it to Shawn alone, with Fanning's name in brackets. Asked why that was in his deposition, Eddie Kessler told his inquisitors: "His name is in brackets because at times John has made statements that he was—that he contributed to the design and technology of Napster, but that claim has been refuted by Shawn Fanning." Because Napster's lawyers worried that the entire patent could have been jeopardized if Fanning was excluded and then later claimed involvement, Napster filed its final application listing Shawn,

Fanning, and Kessler as the inventors. "We didn't want to have a fight with John," Kessler said in an interview. "It didn't make sense."

With Shawn, Frackman launched on a long series of questions about what MP3 files he had downloaded personally, from which service, before and after Napster came into being. Shawn pleaded to having a bad memory. He said he couldn't recall the song names, the artists, or even the type of music. One live Led Zeppelin track was all he could remember clearly from before Napster, he said. As Frackman pressed on, Annette Hurst, an attorney there to protect Shawn personally, grew nervous and began objecting that Shawn's personal actions were irrelevant to a case accusing Napster of contributing to users' copyright violations. "What you're trying to do is build a direct claim of copyright infringement against this young man," she complained. Frackman scoffed. "You're saying I can't do that?" he asked. "Whether the man who created Napster himself has committed copyright infringement is not relevant?" The legal fencing continued until the two lawyers agreed to take it up with the judge later on.

In the meantime, Shawn testified that the rap songs on his Napster-issued laptop were ripped from CDs he owned. Frackman appeared incredulous that Shawn had neither searched the Napster system for other tracks by Snoop Doggy Dogg and Ice Cube, nor offered his ripped MP3s for sharing. "Part of it is the bandwidth," Shawn said. "We don't share things from the office." Pressed about his knowledge of copyright law, Shawn said he didn't understand it very well, and he conceded that might be another reason that he refrained from sharing music himself. "I would say it concerned me some, so I was cautious personally," he said. He said that he was also concerned about the potential for piracy on Napster, and that the removal policy was intended to address that. The climax of the daylong interview should have been the early brainstorming documents about Napster's strategy and problems. But when Frackman showed Shawn one of the most damaging papers, asserting that "Napster brings about the death of the CD," Shawn said he didn't recall seeing it before. That was a good answer: Patel later wrote that the lack of positive identification forced her to disregard the document, which she called a "smoking gun." After the deposition, Shawn felt he had done his part well. "It's safe to say I was nervous about it, but once I got there it was pretty straightforward," he recalled. And he hadn't found Frackman intimidating. "Either they went easy on me, or it wasn't too bad," Shawn said. Music publishers' lawyer Carey Ramos, who participated in the deposition, agreed that Shawn had acquitted himself admirably. Afterward, Ramos thought: "Here's a nice kid who just stumbled into all this attention. He got surrounded by people who wanted to make a buck, all these handlers that wanted to make him into a poster boy."

▭ ▭

PARKER WAS ENCOURAGED BY Shawn's mild experience, but he still had reason to be nervous. He had written most of the early strategy documents, while Shawn had been busy coding. And instead of Frackman, Parker drew an unknown quantity as his interrogator—Frackman's partner George Borkowski, a brusque and pointed questioner with a gleam in his eye. Borkowski had been working until near midnight the previous evening, combing through the boxes of documents Napster had just turned over. Then he hit on what looked like one of the best pieces of evidence he had ever seen in a copyright case. And then he found another, just as good. They were nothing less than open admissions that the company was deliberately helping its users pull off the largest piracy job in history. In one e-mail from Parker to Fanning, Napster's cofounder had stressed the importance of anonymity this way: "Users will understand that they are improving their experience by providing information about their tastes without linking that information to a name or address or other sensitive data that might endanger them (especially since they are exchanging pirated music)."

In the other damning document, Parker used the same poor word choice in laying out the essence of the Napster gamble: "Many of the strategies I mentioned above (harping CDs, recommendation engine, etc.) will put us in a much better bargaining position with the RIAA when they see that we are not just making pirated music available but also pushing demand." Borkowski stopped reading. "It is the kind of thing you don't see every day," he recalled. He took the papers and walked down the hall to one of the attorneys for the music publishers who had joined in the lawsuit. "Boy," he told lawyer Jeff Knowles, "this is going to be a fun deposition." As he read the documents, Knowles's eyes grew noticeably larger.

Napster's lawyers had met with Parker beforehand and gone over what they thought would be the worst documents to surface, prepping him on his responses. Later, Parker said that they had missed the two that were the worst of all. In the same San Francisco law office where Shawn had breezed through his own deposition, Borkowski sat down and ran through Parker's abbreviated education and career history. As soon as he got to Parker's role at Napster, Borkowski sensed him growing evasive. Asked for his job title, Parker said he had never had one. "Let me ask you this," Borkowski said. "Do you have a Napster business card?" Parker said yes. "What does it say on it?" "It says 'founder,'" Parker replied. Asked if the title were appropriate, Parker hedged. "It's the most fitting title at this point, for lack of a better one," he said.

More and more, Parker's nerves began showing through his stoic exterior. "As part of your duties for Napster," Borkowski asked, "have you been involved in any drafting of any business plans or proposals?" "It's possible," Parker said. "But do you recall doing any of it?" Napster lawyer Laurence Pulgram butted in to establish an objection: "Vague." Annette Hurst chimed in as well: "Overbroad." As if following a cue, Parker asked: "What's 'it'?"

"Drafting or being involved in the drafting of any business plans or business proposals," Borkowski said with building irritation.

> Hurst: Compound, vague.
> Parker: Could you rephrase the question?
> Borkowski: What about it are you having trouble with?
> Parker: Could you repeat the question?

The court reporter read it back.

> Parker: What do you mean by "involved in?"
> Borkowski: Participate in any way.
> Hurst: I still think it's vague as to business plans or business proposals.
> Parker: I don't recall contributing anything to any business plans.

Like Shawn, Parker had a hard time recalling any specific downloads of MP3 files to his own computer. And he said he didn't remember discussing Napster copyright issues with anyone, even though he had been designated as the copyright agent for the company, the person to whom complaints should be directed under the Digital Millennium Copyright Act. During the lunch break, Pulgram assured Parker that he was doing fine. When they returned, Borkowski placed a printout of the text from one of Napster's earliest Web pages on the table, then pushed it forward to Parker meticulously, using two fingers from each hand. Was it Parker's handwriting, Borkowski asked, that suggested adding the sentence, "And no more wading through page after page of unknown artists?" Yes, Parker said, it was. And yes, that suggestion did make it to the website. That wasn't so bad, Parker thought—the word "unknown" had been picked deliberately because it could mean unknown only to that particular user.

But Borkowski had saved the best for last. As he placed the printout of Parker's e-mail to Fanning on the table and began pushing it across, the corners of his mouth turned up. The involuntary, evil-looking smile reminded Parker of Dr. Seuss's Grinch. He reluctantly read his own words about the strategies for making the RIAA see that Napster was "not just making pirated music available." *Pirated music.* What in hell had he been thinking? How could he explain it away? "Did you write that?" Borkowski asked, in his clipped and precise tone. Pause. "I believe I did," Parker said. The best defense he could muster was that he had been using "pirated" in the sense the RIAA meant it, that all MP3s were illegitimate. "I did not write that *I* felt that Napster would be making pirated music available," Parker said. By the time Borkowski's colleague Jeff Knowles got to ask about the user-anonymity document, it seemed like so much piling on. The damage was done. Founder or not, Parker's name disappeared from Napster's website.

― ―

ARMED WITH THE NEW EVIDENCE and Patel's refusal to grant Napster a safe harbor, the RIAA moved in for the kill. On June 12, just a few weeks after Hummer Winblad's investment, the labels filed for a preliminary injunction that would shut down or cripple the Napster service. "Napster has been aware from the moment of its creation that its service offers little but pirated music, and that rampant infringement of the most commercially popular music in the world is the very foundation of its system," the lawyers wrote. Once more, the filing tarred Napster with the now-regretted exuberance of its youthful promotional copy, since replaced: "You'll never come up empty handed when searching for your favorite music . . . and you can forget about wading through page after page of unknown artists!" Even Napster's more recent "sanitizing of its Website" and its addition of boilerplate warnings about copyright misuse, the record industry said, were accompanied by winks and nudges about the anonymity of the service.

A preliminary injunction is nearly as hard to come by as a summary judgment. In order to win one before a trial, a party to a suit must show that it is likely to win at trial and that either it will suffer irreparable harm in the interim, or that it will suffer more without an injunction than the other side would with one. So the well-funded record-industry team now trotted out a raft of studies showing that it was already suffering serious losses. Compact-disc sales, while increasing nationwide, were falling among college students, one reported. And near campuses with higher-than-average Napster use, sales were declining even faster. The most damaging study was that by Ingram Olkin, a Stanford statistics professor. The industry hired Olkin to find out what proportion of Napster users was offering music illegally. Olkin picked 1,150 Napster subscribers who were offering files and downloaded all of their available MP3s. Any percentage above 50 would have presented a big problem for Napster, showing that the majority of its users were violating the law. Any figure above 90 would make it hard for the company to talk about any substantial noninfringing use. Olkin's study found 100 percent were offering pirated music—every single one of the 1,150 users in the survey. And while some probably had at least a few files that were authorized, a minimum of 87 percent of the songs weren't kosher.

If the facts were bad for Napster, the law wasn't much better. Judge Patel had already ruled that the biggest safe harbor in the DMCA didn't protect Napster, in part because its policy for banning users wasn't tough enough. The labels now made a strike against the smaller exemption, the one for indexing and search services that steered users to inappropriate material. That exemption, Napster said, meant only that it had to take down links to offending material after it was notified about the material—something Napster also said that it was impractical to do, since the links popped up and then disappeared again as users logged on and off. Unfortunately for that defense, the exemption didn't apply to companies that were "aware of facts or circumstances from which infringing activity is apparent." As the industry lawyers put it, "The DMCA's safe harbors protect innocent infringers, not those like Napster, that deliberately build a business based almost exclusively on piracy."

———

AS SOON AS THE INDUSTRY filed its attack, it was obvious that the labels stood an excellent chance of winning. Ritter started reworking his résumé and wrote to his mother: "The end of Napster may be upon us." Hank Barry knew that if he couldn't stop the injunction, almost everything else he wanted to try would be useless. Discouraged by the previous legal team's losses, Barry called the biggest gun he could think of, ace litigator David Boies.

Raised in rural Illinois, Boies had kept his midwestern twang through his years at Cravath, Swaine & Moore, representing the likes of IBM and CBS Inc., and seldom losing. After starting his own New York firm, Boies cemented his reputation for brilliance by deconstructing Microsoft and Bill Gates on behalf of the U.S. Justice Department. When Napster called, Boies was out of town. He had never heard of the company and wasn't inclined to take on new clients anyway. But his twin thirty-two-year-old sons took the phone call and lobbied their father hard to take the case. Boies was interested mainly because the case was on the cutting edge of the law. "The first thing that struck me was that this was an important case not only for the music industry but for the whole of the Internet," he said. "Here you have a new technology, in terms of peer-to-peer sharing of information, and if that technology is going to work, you must allow people to have central indexes." With an injunction hearing already scheduled for the following month, Boies threw staffers onto the case and soon discarded most of Napster's old and failing arguments.

While still maintaining that Napster should be protected by the

DMCA, Boies spent most of the time and pages allotted to him on two new tacks. The first and boldest argument was that Napster's users weren't doing anything wrong. Boies cited the Audio Home Recording Act, which established that noncommercial copying by consumers—in those days, making tapes from purchased record albums or other tapes— was legal. If Napster users weren't breaking the law, then Napster wasn't either. The second major argument harked back to another new technology that at the time had been attacked as ruinous by the entertainment industry—the VCR. Motion Picture Association of America president Jack Valenti said at the time that "the VCR is to the American film producer and the American public as the Boston Strangler is to the woman alone." In a 1984 decision, by a vote of five to four, the U.S. Supreme Court had held that VCRs were legal because even though some consumers might use them to copy and sell videotapes of movies and television shows, the machines were "capable of substantial noninfringing uses." Many viewers, the court held, would use VCRs just for "time-shifting," taping shows to watch at another time. Later, the VCR provided an entire new revenue stream for Hollywood as tape rentals soared.

Napster's dire straits also helped Boies and Barry recruit major Web intellectuals to the cause. Along with his opposition to the preliminary injunction, Boies filed statements by John Perry Barlow, Lawrence Lessig, and a handful of musicians, most of whom suggested that the record industry was more interested in maintaining absolute control of the means of distribution than it was in protecting the rights of artists. Barlow brought an unusual combination of credentials to the fight. He had been a lyricist for the Grateful Dead for more than twenty years and was affiliated with Harvard Law School. He was also the first to apply science-fiction writer William Gibson's term "cyberspace" to what was actually happening on the Internet. And in 1990, he had cofounded the Electronic Frontier Foundation, which was to the Net what the American Civil Liberties Union was to free speech in the physical world. The EFF had wrestled long and hard over whether it should give Napster significant legal help. In the end it opted not to, both because Napster already could afford some of the best legal minds available and because the facts were so weak that the suit might end up producing case law that hurt the larger cause of cyberfreedom. "We agonized over it, but they were doomed," an EFF staffer said.

Privately, Barlow blamed Napster for much of its predicament. "They blew it by not being Napster.org," he said, referring to the domain-name suffix generally reserved for nonprofit organizations. "There was no possible business model." But because Barlow worried that the case would set a horrible precedent, he filed a supportive affidavit with the court. So did Lessig, a Stanford law professor known for assisting a Washington court in the Microsoft case and for writing the book *Code and Other Laws of Cyberspace,* which explained how Internet protocols were a series of choices that would shape society. The book argued that the engineers who were making collective decisions about the Internet had better choose wisely if they were to avoid provoking the government into imposing harsh restrictions on cyberspace. Lessig felt that even when technologists went astray, as they might have with Napster, courts should not be in the business of extinguishing revolutionary developments.

In a long essay that was more legal advice to Judge Patel than expert testimony, and was therefore deemed inadmissible, Lessig said that the early architecture of the Internet was both a serious threat to copyright protection and an unprecedented boon to free speech. And he said that people on both sides of the argument had overlooked work in progress that could give copyright holders more protection than they had ever enjoyed. New technologies were making it possible to track and control what recipients did with digital works. In the interim, before those new technologies took hold, Lessig said, courts should proceed with extreme caution before killing new systems like Napster.

Even if massive copyright violations had occurred, Napster dramatically improved on previous search engines, which couldn't keep up as more Web pages changed dynamically. "It would be a mistake," Lessig wrote, "to ban a technology based on its initial use, even if significant violations of copyright were enabled. If that had been the test, then many of the early Internet technologies would have been banned. Likewise would the VCR have been banned, and possibly even the Xerox machine." Instead of trying to crop a new technology to fit a preexisting business model like that of the record industry, Lessig wrote, "it has been the practice of the Supreme Court to leave to Congress the task of redrawing an appropriate balance."

— —

As the preliminary injunction hearing loomed, Napster CEO Hank Barry went on a public-relations and political offensive. He echoed Boies's radical contention that swapping MP3 files was legal, and he testified in Congress on July 11, 2000. Appearing before the Senate Judiciary Committee, Barry reported that Napster had amassed nearly 20 million registered users in a single year of operation, a milestone that took America Online ten times as long to reach. He stressed that the users were acting out of the love of music, and that the biggest draw for them was the chance to sample music before buying it. Barry was surprised at how appreciative his audience was. But senators know how to count votes. Napster's determination to grow no matter what—designed to keep its advantage over competitors, to prepare for potential ad revenue, and to entice the record industry—now had borne unexpected fruit. Napster's users now could amount to a major political force, one that could lobby elected officials, vote them in or out of office, and participate in mass civil disobedience if they thought the law was wrong. "We should not brand as thieves the 20 million Americans that enjoy the Napster services," Barry declared, striking an unaccustomed pose as a corporate lawyer and fledgling venture capitalist turned populist crusader.

Napster had been generating as many as ten thousand e-mails a day to Congress, and the record industry was on the defensive. But the RIAA's Hilary Rosen was still optimistic. Among other reasons, in terms of star quality, Hank Barry was no Shawn Fanning. "The more vocal they became, the clearer it was that these guys were talking out of both sides of their mouth," Rosen said. "They started talking about promoting artists, but they didn't want the artists to get paid. Then they said they did want the artists to get paid, but they didn't have the mechanism. Clearly it was about money, not consumer rights."

Rosen's inside information also suggested that the Napster camp wasn't as confident as it used to be. She heard from an executive at AOL Time Warner, Jonathan Sacks, that Hummer Winblad was soliciting a takeover bid. AOL's concern was how to avoid becoming liable for a judgment itself. Rosen told Sacks that she would be willing to give AOL a break only if it bought Napster and immediately shut the service down. But even in that case, Rosen wouldn't give up the right to go after the previous Napster management, including Hummer Winblad. Without the guarantee of immunity for itself, Hummer Winblad lost interest in the sale, Rosen said. AOL's Sacks said his company coveted Napster's massive user base but would have passed on a deal even if it had stayed on the table. "We never supported the idea that copyrights should be infringed or that music should be free," Sacks said. "We always knew the transition from stolen music to purchased music would be challenging. We quickly decided Napster had no future."

Inside Napster, where the AOL talks and other sale attempts were well-kept secrets, the big news not coming from Patel's courtroom was Barry's hiring of Napster's first chief operating officer, Milton Olin. Yet another lawyer, Olin had been senior vice president of business and legal affairs at A&M Records, one of the plaintiffs in the Napster case. Olin left the record business after his company was acquired by Universal, joining an Internet start-up that offered previews of music and movies. Some at Napster speculated that his chief credential, beside his onetime membership on the RIAA's legal committee, was his old friendship with Barry. Buttressing Napster's argument that it would be impossible to sort out which users were offering infringing content and which weren't, Olin testified in a deposition that even inside the record business, it was often unclear who owned what. But Olin didn't make an impressive witness. Asked if he had ever in his career tried to determine who owned a copyright to a work, he said that he had not. Asked if at A&M it had ever been necessary to find out who had the rights to a music composition, he said he didn't know.

Movie-industry spokesman Jack Valenti may have had a dramatic impact on Napster's evolution without realizing it. As part of a package of affidavits submitted with the labels' motion for a preliminary injunction, Valenti had written in June that a multiple-industry group he chaired called the Copyright Assembly was deeply worried about where Napster-like technology was headed next. "If the courts allow Napster and services like it to continue to facilitate massive copyright infringement, there is a grave risk that the public will begin to perceive and believe that they have a right to obtain copyrighted materials for free," Valenti wrote. "If Napster can encourage and facilitate the distribution of pirated sound recordings, then what's to stop it from doing the same to movies, software, books, magazines, newspapers, television, photographs, or video games?"

Actually, very little would stop it. Shawn had called for expanding Napster to other media months before, and now Napster was considering doing so. As things stood, Napster recognized only MP3 files. But the engineers had tweaked the system in tests to allow swapping of Microsoft Word text documents and Adobe Acrobat graphic files. If a new version of Napster was released with that capability, usage could have doubled, and an entire new front in the battle would have been opened. Ritter, who ordinarily supported enhancing functions no matter the risk, in this instance disagreed. It wasn't because he didn't think people should be able to share whatever they wanted. It was just that he understood the lessons from aggressive search engines like Scour, which often turned up documents from computers whose owners didn't realize that the material could be seen by others. "I think these format types are a big mistake," Ritter wrote on June 26, weeks after Valenti's declaration. "Napster is hyped and misconstrued enough; the above types are excellent fuel to an already unmanageable fire." Barry killed the plan, probably influenced more by Valenti than by Ritter. As the former AltaVista executive Don Dodge explained it to Ritter three days later: "Hank decided yesterday that we would not release the non-music file types. . . . As with most decisions these days, it was a legal call."

Other legal calls kept Napster documents out of court and out of the public eye. Almost all corporate litigation includes minor but time-consuming and expensive disputes about who is entitled to take depositions from whom and which documents they get to see. When enough arguments pile up and can't be resolved through compromise, the judge gets stuck having to make rulings on such minutiae. A hearing on several of those flaps was held June 19 in what would be one of Napster attorney Laurence Pulgram's last turns in the leading role before Boies got up to speed. Most of the issues were of little consequence. But one of them, a request for Napster documents, was so clearly legitimate that Patel didn't understand why Napster was resisting. The documents, like most of those in the case, would be subject to a protective order, barring them from appearing in the public court file or the press. There were two sets of documents at issue. One included the contract for Shawn's initial transfer of the rights to his invention to the company. Shawn had testified at his deposition that he knew he had signed something of the kind, but "he was generally unable to articulate precisely what it was," the record-industry lawyer said at the hearing. The other documents recounted John Fanning's sales of his stock. Pulgram argued that the two documents weren't relevant. "All this is is an effort to try to get to Mr. Fanning personally, to get private information about to whom he sold stock," Pulgram told Patel. Pulgram didn't give another logical, though legally insufficient, reason for fighting the request: The documents would show just how little Shawn had received, and how many hundreds of thousands of dollars his uncle had made from the piracy of others. Patel ordered the documents turned over.

Other documents went the way of the shredder. Napster was moving to new offices in Redwood City, and on the eve of the move chief financial officer Lyn Jensen sent a companywide e-mail telling employees to keep copies of documents that might be required for court. All the others, she wrote, should be dumped in the "large locked bins that have the words 'shred works' on the side." Moving offices added to the stress of the Napster team. Most of them thought their lawyers would defeat the attempt at a preliminary injunction, but they couldn't be sure. Napster's users weren't sure, either, and they poured onto the system in numbers that as much as doubled every few weeks. On July 24, one of Napster's outside public-relations staffers, Jill Mango, e-mailed a bulletin to her colleagues. "We have finally reached full pop culture saturation," she wrote. "I just got a phone call from the fact-checkers at Who Wants to be a Millionaire. Q: Dr. Dre and Metallica recently filed lawsuits alleging copyright infringement against which Internet MP3 sharing program? Final answer: Napster."

<hr />

HIGH NOON CAME TWO DAYS LATER, at 2 P.M. on Wednesday, July 26, 2000, in Patel's eighteenth-floor courtroom across the street from San Francisco's black-and-gold-domed City Hall. Journalists and other spectators had been lining up since 10 A.M., and two hundred were there before the hearing began. Napster's top leaders didn't seem too worried about losing, especially right away. Fanning sent an e-mail saying that even if Patel ruled against the company eventually, the order would be stayed during an appeal. He estimated there was only a 10 percent chance the higher court would also rule against Napster. Barry sent a cheery all-hands message the day before that began with the word "Greetings!" and reminded the staff to avoid speaking to the press. "We are having the hearing tomorrow. Shawn and I will be attending for the company, and we'll call you guys immediately after and let you know how it came out. There is a good possibility that nothing will happen," Barry wrote. Statistically, he was making a good guess. Preliminary injunctions, especially those likely to be appealed by one side or the other, are rarely issued in open court, before the judge has had time to digest the paperwork and craft a written ruling solid enough to withstand further challenges.

The forty-seat courtroom was so mobbed with attorneys for the various parties that many had to watch on closed-circuit television next door. Barry and Shawn, who wore a blue blazer and tie, sat behind their lawyers in the stifling room. Record-industry attorney Frackman, confident that his brief had shown his side would probably win at trial, focused his oral argument on the other half of the test for an injunction: the likelihood of irreparable harm. And now, Napster's soaring popularity was the strongest ammunition against it. "Since the court walked in several minutes ago," Frackman began, "30, 40, maybe 50,000 recordings have been downloaded using the Napster system; 14,000 recordings are downloaded a minute . . . if we take the six months that Napster has posited it will take to get to trial, there will be 3.6 billion separate recordings downloaded using the Napster system. And 90 percent of those, Your Honor, are copyrighted." By then, he said, Napster would have 75 million users, and no royalties would have gone to anyone. "The longer this goes on, Your Honor, the more impossible it will be for us, and we believe for the court, to do anything realistic." In addition to hurting CD sales, he said, the industry's efforts to get its own system of online distribution in place wouldn't stand a chance. Music publishers' attorney Carey Ramos offered a short rebuttal to Lessig's argument against stifling new technology. "All we request is that Napster be required to comply with the law, to follow the same rules of the road that other media businesses have followed for years, by obtaining permission before enabling the copying," he said. "Napster doesn't want to do that. It doesn't want to have to engage in clearances. It doesn't want to have to hire people to determine whether they need to get clearance and to seek permission. It's too much effort. It requires them to work before they become Internet billionaires."

Appearing for the first time before Patel, Boies pursued the same points laid out in his brief, starting with the language in the Supreme Court's VCR ruling that allowed technology to come to market if it could have substantial noninfringing uses. Boies handed up his charts and case citations, cleared his throat, and got out three full sentences. The last of them was: "We have at tab No. 2 of the book that the court has, a reference to a whole series of substantial noninfringing uses of which Napster is capable. And as the court is aware—" Patel cut him off. "What does that mean, 'is capable'?" she asked. "As opposed to 'is in fact' or 'has in fact been performing?'" From that moment on, Boies was crippled. Unlike in the VCR case, there was a wealth of real data about how Napster was being used right then.

It didn't get any better from there. Boies said that various courts had held service providers and others not responsible for the actions of their users. But Patel had been immersed in the early memos and e-mails from Parker and the others, and they were still staring up at her. "Isn't that the guts of what Napster was all about?" she asked, interrupting Boies for the fifth time. "'Pirating be damned,' I think, was pretty much the sense one gets in reading some of the exhibits from some of these early meetings or memos, et cetera. I mean, piracy was uppermost in their mind, right? Free music for the people, right?" Boies had little left to say, except that the facts about present-day Napster and the law were more important than the previous writings of a clever nineteen-year-old. In everything Boies brought up, from the Audio Home Recording Act to the prior year's decision allowing sales of the Rio MP3 player, Patel kept after him. The toughest jab may have come when Boies said that the VCR case permitted home copying that wasn't commercial. "They weren't sharing it with the world," Patel interjected.

Boies's sidekick from Pulgram's firm, Daniel Johnson Jr., then tried to fit Napster into the remaining DMCA exemption, the one for objective search services. To be denied that exemption, he said, you "have to have actual knowledge each time an individual consumer sends infringing material"—the unguarded remarks of a teenage cofounder notwithstanding. Again, Patel was having none of it, because all the other evidence suggested that the piracy bazaar Parker envisioned had very much come to fruition. "I don't think this system is just invested in and supported by a single nineteen-year-old," she said from the bench. In any case, "if you have in fact designed a product, a system that is in fact designed to do just what it's been doing, enabling infringing, enabling piracy, you can hardly stand back and say, 'Gee, I didn't know all that stuff on there was pirated.'" Johnson jumped to the VCR decision, which he said allowed sharing films with friends. "All 79 million of them?" Patel asked. "Seventy million or seven," Johnson ventured. "But doesn't that take it beyond personal use?" Patel asked. Johnson attempted a hop to the Rio decision in the Ninth Circuit, which had interpreted the Supreme Court's VCR ruling broadly to cover some other nonprofit copying, in that case from CDs to MP3s. Patel hadn't telegraphed her thinking, but she had already made up her mind that the Rio case dealt with certain types of hardware, not giant interactive webs of software. Sensing that the last door was closing on him, Johnson pressed so hard that instead of allowing Patel to interrupt him, he interrupted her. It was as if the internal gunfighter that lives inside each litigator had seen he was surrounded and simply decided to go out with guns blazing.

The Rio case "doesn't apply here, and I will explain why when I render my decision," Patel said.

But in that decision, Johnson persisted, "once the CD is on a hard drive, what happens to it?"

"There's no digital recording device, even by—" Patel began.

"You're not listening. Let me try one more time. Once it's on the hard drive—"

Patel interrupted him back, ending the exchange. "You're finished," she snapped. "You may have a seat." After allowing brief rebuttals, Patel called for a break that lasted half an hour.

━ ━

When she returned to the bench, Patel shocked almost everyone in the courtroom. "Plenty of time has been expended in preparing for the motion, certainly plenty of paper has been expended as well," she said. "The court is able to render a decision." Speaking off the top of her head, Patel ruled first that most Napster users were violating copyrights. "This, in fact, should come as no surprise to Napster, since that . . . was the purpose of it." Tackling next the VCR case's approval of technology capable of substantial noninfringing use, she said that even the potential for such use at Napster was minimal. "While it may be capable of some of these other things, those uses seem to pale by comparison to what Napster is actually used for, what it was promoted for, and what it continues to be used for." She conceded that the issue of acceptable personal use was a trickier one, because the technology had gotten out ahead of the law. But she said users who distributed files to large numbers of strangers "cannot be said to engage merely in the typical personal use." And she got rid of the rest of the VCR case by pointing out the huge flaw in the parallel: The VCR case involved technological devices that a manufacturer distributed to consumers and then lost control of. Napster continued to be in charge of how its service was used. Then Patel disposed of the Audio Home Recording Act in four sentences, declaring that computers were not "audio home recording devices" as defined by that law.

Satisfying herself that Napster users were breaking the law, Patel turned to what Napster knew about the behavior and if it abetted their actions, as required for a finding of vicarious or contributory infringement. Citing the internal documents about piracy and the need to remain ignorant of IP addresses for that reason, Patel ruled that the evidence "overwhelmingly establishes that the defendant had actual or, at the very least, constructive knowledge." That finding also ended Napster's attempt to get into any of the DMCA's safe harbors.

For good measure, Patel went beyond what she needed to do to shut Napster down. She said that Napster had added liability because it had "supervisory powers" over what was happening on its network, as it demonstrated by blocking hundreds of thousands of users, including those cited by Metallica and Dr. Dre. Going forward, she said, the company must find a way to make sure that none of the files available violated copyrights, even if Napster had to redesign from scratch. "I'm sure that anyone as clever as the people who wrote the software in this case are clever enough, as there are plenty of those minds in Silicon Valley, to do it, and come up with a program that will help identify infringing items," Patel said.

The ordinarily composed Boies saw everything falling apart as Patel spoke. He clutched a red pen tighter and tighter, until the ink squirted out on his hands. As Patel invited the record industry to submit proposed wording for what would become the formal injunction, Boies tried to say it would be technologically infeasible to carry out what she was ordering, and that Napster executives didn't even have a list of what songs were infringing. "That's *their* problem," Patel said. "They created the 'monster.'"

Patel asked Frackman when the industry would like the injunction to take effect. But Frackman was still recovering from his surprise at having won almost the entire case in a single day. "It was obviously a huge victory. It was one of the most public victories we had ever had. I had given one of the best arguments I had ever given, a long argument in a long day. And it had been a long eight months since we had filed the suit." Watching Frackman's next move from the audience were Hilary Rosen and other RIAA officials, plus lawyers from Universal, Sony, and Bertelsmann's BMG label. Frackman got to his feet slowly and started walking to the podium, trying to think of a way to say "immediately" without appearing ruthless. He stalled during the ten-foot walk by looking at the clock. Patel saw him do it. Frackman saw her watching and moved to take advantage. "Right now," he said, as mildly as he could. "And you're looking at the clock, not the calendar," Patel said, getting a laugh from the record-company partisans.

Frackman said that if Patel didn't act quickly, there would be "a rush to the computer and enormous amounts of downloading." Boies complained that Napster couldn't sort out legitimate use from illegitimate use quickly enough and would have to shut down. Patel's voice dripped sarcasm: "What about all those substantial noninfringing uses you were trying to convince me of?" She ruled that the injunction would take effect two days later at midnight, and she refused Boies's request for a stay of her order while Napster appealed to the Ninth Circuit. The gavel rapped, and the reporters sprinted from the court.

As Napster's lawyers huddled in the room, Shawn's eyes filled with tears. He looked down at his hands and started picking at and pinching his skin. "Oh my God," he thought. "What in the world is going on here?" The RIAA, which had been prepared for any outcome, handed out copies of a statement to reporters in the hallway. Barry scribbled out a statement on the spot, and the company's public-relations staff told journalists that he would read it to them in the lobby. Instead, the Napster crew evaded the media horde, climbed into a Lincoln Town Car, and drove off.

A dozen record-industry lawyers went to celebrate at the restaurant Jardinière. Recording Industry Association general counsel Cary Sherman found a piano and spontaneously sat down to play jazz. An associate at one of the San Francisco firms happened to sing in nightclubs, and she lent vocals to the occasion, getting extra appreciation for a Gershwin number—"They Can't Take That Away from Me." Afterward, Sherman told her that given their audience, if she couldn't get a big-label contract that night, she probably never would.

Inside Napster, Eddie Kessler sent out an unemotional e-mail relaying what Barry probably would have read to reporters: "Hi all. I just got a call from hank and milt. We are surprised and disappointed that the judge has apparently decided to issue some form of injunction, we may have to shut down all or parts of the service within 48 hours. Obviously, we will comply with the court's order and move forward. We haven't seen her order and we don't yet know what it says. You are invited to tune in to the webcast at 7 pm." Parker was in Virginia and called the office to find out what had happened, reaching Barry's assistant, Alicia Morga. "It doesn't look good, Parker," she told him, recounting the decision. "And she talked a lot about your documents."

Boies and his team threw together an emergency request for a stay from the Ninth Circuit pending a full appeal. Work at Napster pretty much ground to a halt as the forty-six employees wondered what would happen to them—if they would be laid off when the system shut down or kept around to rework it into something that complied with the injunction. The severity of the situation was glaring. In a rare e-mail from Napster recruiter Inga Kulberg to the whole staff, she urged them to hang tight: "Hi everyone. I know you have been bombarded by recruiters, and staffing managers, but don't jump ship yet! We will work it out together."

When it aired, the webcast showed a grim-faced Shawn and Barry.

"We'll keep fighting for Napster and your right to share music," Shawn said, urging viewers to e-mail the record companies. He went home and slept badly, trying to get his head around the ruling. He brainstormed about how he could change the system. Shawn had given out one of his e-mail addresses on the webcast and was rewarded with 2,626 messages in support overnight, ranging from the funereal to the defiant. "Napster was my bible for awhile, and I hold it sacred. If there's anything I can do to help, like creating some kind of a petition, please just let me know. thank you for everything you've done for us, the true fans of music," wrote New Yorker Daniel Uhl. Others suggested setting up servers in unreachable countries. Many said they had bought more CDs than ever after sampling with Napster, and more than one credited Napster's chat rooms for their romantic relationships. Within hours, there was indeed a petition: Napster staffer Nate Mordo spread the word internally about the document, in which thousands of signatories pledged not to buy CDs while Napster was down.

The day after, the Napster ruling made front pages across the country. MTV interviewed Shawn in Napster's kitchen as less-favored TV crews did stand-ups outside the building. Shawn played it populist cool for MTV, saying he was upset mostly for Napster's 20 million users. "To me, they were the ones being attacked, not necessarily me personally, or even the technology," Shawn said. He said he didn't know how Napster could comply without shutting down but didn't support a boycott. Shawn was at his best when he was both modest about Napster's innovations and mystified about the attacks on it. "It was the first application out there that demonstrated file-sharing, so I suppose I'm not surprised that it is directed toward us," he told the interviewer. "But it is surprising to me to see a technology that is based on fundamental Internet principles of exchanging information and search-engine technology and chat technology be attacked like this . . . it's just sort of a combination of technologies."

The number of Napster users soared to the highest levels yet, just as Frackman had predicted. On July 28, as the midnight cutoff neared, traffic to the website alone topped 849,000 visitors. With 22 million users and just $400,000 worth of hardware, the Napster system finally maxed out, and not everyone could connect. That week, "Napster" became the most-searched-for term on the Internet by users of one engine that tracks such figures, ending a thirty-week run by "Pokemon." In a sign that Napster's understudies were ready in the wings, "Gnutella" jumped from beneath the cutoff for Lycos's Top 50 all the way to number seven.

        ▭   ▭

FORTUNATELY FOR NAPSTER, the three-judge panel of the Ninth Circuit that was on duty to consider emergency motions included one Alex Kozinski. A Romanian immigrant who had turned fifty earlier that week, Kozinski had been appointed by President Reagan fifteen years earlier as one of the youngest appointees to the appeals court. A forceful intellect and even more forceful personality, Kozinski loved taking cutting-edge cases and was known for his aggressive interpretation of the First Amendment. He had ruled that abortion foes had the right to publicize the names of doctors who performed the operation, and he had held that a lawyer was free to criticize a judge. Kozinski was also an early fan of the Internet, having penned columns for Microsoft's online magazine *Slate* as far back as 1996. To many working at the court's offices in San Francisco when Napster's request for an emergency stay came in, the question was open-and-shut. Such emergency requests are almost always turned down with little fuss.

But Kozinski was excited about the prospect of a debate on the issues, which he argued were so important and so new that they merited a full airing. After some effort, Kozinski was able to convince one of the other two judges on duty, Barry Silverman, to vote with him to grant the stay. None of the parties in the case ever learned it, but Kozinski also tried to have the three-judge motions panel retain control of the case through the briefs and oral arguments, a step that would have kept him involved in the final ruling. The other judges didn't agree, and arguments were instead set for October, when Kozinski was unlikely to hear it.

As Napster's management spoke with Boies by conference call late on Friday afternoon about how to comply with the injunction, word came that the stay had been granted. Napster could remain online. The brief order said that the case raised "substantial questions of first impression," and noted that the appeals court would consider not just the merits but also the sweep of the injunction. In order to sway Silverman, Kozinski had resorted to arguing that even if the ruling was essentially sound, it was too harsh. Most memorably, he had cited the opinion of his son, a Napster user who had reported that forcing Napster to weed out copyrighted material "would be like trying to take the piss out of a pool."

With no idea how close they had come to failing to win the stay and no clue that their best hope on the bench would be off the case by October, the Napster crew exploded with joy. They would have months to convince the appeals judges to reverse Patel, make a deal with the labels, or develop a new system—possibly all three. Napster director John Hummer strode around the office and crowed. "This is like the playoffs," said the former NBA center. "They won the first game, and we won the second game. It's going to seven, and we're going to win it." Others in the office jumped up and down and hugged each other at the news. "It was one of the most incredible experiences of my life," Kessler said. "I was so overwhelmed afterward that I only then realized how stressed out I had been."

On Monday, Barry sent another group e-mail, thanking all for their work "under difficult and changing circumstances." He gave the schedule for paper filings and arguments before the appeals court, then dropped a bombshell: "You may well see reports in the newspapers suggesting that we are trying to get a settlement with the record companies. These reports are true. We're exploring several business models, and we'll probably be discussing them more in public as the week goes on . . . the basic options are an advertising model, a subscription model, or a hybrid of the two. Our bottom line is to keep the service convenient and easy to use for the Napster community, there is no clear response from the record companies to our overtures yet. We'll keep you informed of any developments."

━━ ━━

IN FACT, BARRY HAD BEEN TRYING to get a deal with the labels from as early as June, when his venture-firm partner and fellow Napster director Hummer called Edgar Bronfman. Bronfman was CEO of Seagram Co. Ltd., owner of the largest record firm, Universal Music. More important, Bronfman was far from being an old-school music executive, having led Seagram into the business only recently from its beverage-industry roots. Bronfman was confident that the music industry would win in court, probably even getting the preliminary injunction, but he was still predisposed to listen. "The notion was that Napster was only the first—there will be others to replace it," he said. "Here was an opportunity to maintain a large customer base, potentially, and over time migrate it into a commercially viable system."

At a California airport on July 5, 2000, Bronfman met with Barry, Hummer, and others to discuss what Napster's business model might be. The ideas came fast and furious, but there was no technology available to make Napster legitimate, and the company was reluctant to charge its users. Without charging them, Bronfman said, there didn't seem to be any way that Napster could make a profit even before it paid artists and the record companies. Yet both sides realized the prospects for a deal were best before Patel ruled one way or the other—especially if she found that Napster was breaking the law, which would give any new owners a massive liability headache. So Bronfman arranged for a summit meeting to be held with other label executives in the most conducive setting for dealmaking he could imagine—investment banker Herb Allen's upcoming annual media-moguls-only conference in Sun Valley, Idaho, birthplace of the Disney-ABC merger and countless others.

Ahead of the meeting, Hummer planned to offer the labels just 10 percent of Napster's revenue. "I urged him to be more creative and more flexible, because nobody would stand for that," Bronfman said. And Napster did up the ante dramatically, suggesting that the labels could share 60 percent of Napster's ownership. In the late afternoon on July 13, the two Napster directors met in Sun Valley with Bronfman, Bertelsmann CEO Thomas Middelhoff, Sony Corp. co-CEO Nobuyuki Idei, and Sony's U.S. chief, Howard Stringer. The meeting went well, and Idei and Middelhoff told Barry to keep dealing with Bronfman, who wanted to craft an industrywide deal. "We were very close," Bronfman said.

A week later, Hummer changed direction. "He said he had another offer for $2 billion, hinting that it was from AOL, and that unless we wanted to buy Napster for $2 billion, he would walk away," Bronfman said. Bronfman told him there was no way the record companies would pay that kind of money. He also didn't believe the AOL offer was real, that the company's directors would be willing to risk their pending acquisition of Time Warner on the Internet upstart. And that's what Bronfman told a nervous Jerry Yang, founder of Yahoo!, who also had been offered the chance to meet or beat AOL's alleged bid. After talking things over with Bronfman, Yang passed as well.

When the preliminary injunction came down and was stayed and the AOL interest evaporated, Bronfman expected Barry to return to the bargaining table and offer the labels something better. But on the Monday after the ruling, Barry e-mailed Bronfman and suggested that the record companies split 50 percent ownership of Napster, without the right to vote on the company's strategy. While more palatable than a $2 billion price tag, the offer was still less attractive than the Sun Valley summit terms, before a federal judge had concluded that Napster was probably breaking the law. It didn't make sense. "Things went backward from there," Bronfman said. Barry, who called Bronfman a visionary, said he doesn't know what went wrong that summer as he pitched variation after variation of a settlement, only to be rejected each time.

But Bronfman thinks he knows what happened between Sun Valley and the watered-down proposals after the injunction: Intel's Andy Grove. Bronfman had multiple conversations with Grove, who believed that Napster was the unstoppable way of the future. More important, Grove had multiple conversations with John Hummer.

"Andy was virulent that Napster was the next great thing, that under no circumstances would intellectual property be protected on the Internet," Bronfman said. "He was as close to God as anyone who existed in Silicon Valley, and John was going to listen to Andy harder than to me or anyone else." Bronfman is convinced that Grove persuaded Hummer not to give up control of Napster. "The two people who forfeited that opportunity were John Hummer and Andy Grove," he declared. Hummer agreed that Grove was a major booster but said it made sense not to let the record industry win the power to change Napster's direction. "They always wanted to figure out a way to tax every individual transfer, and it just wouldn't work," Hummer said. "Either you believe that Napster is super-radio, or you don't. In the end, these guys just don't believe that Napster was the best promotional tool they ever found." Hummer's own sense of high purpose couldn't have helped: His quote "I am the record industry's worst nightmare" appeared in *Fortune* around the time that the negotiations collapsed.

More than a few of Napster's employees and most of its fans would have been disappointed by any compromise with the labels. The service's popularity had always contained an element of perversity: The great attraction for many was that Napster offered an incredibly easy way to break the law. As Napster neared the end of its rope in court, that perversion intensified. The more endangered the company became, the more users flocked to the service to get what they could while they still had the chance. And that added to Napster's strategic dilemma. "Your biggest problem," Rosen told Barry, "is that instead of a business, you created a movement. And it's impossible to convert it." Every time Napster could have shifted models, Rosen said later, "they were hampered in doing so because of the perceived 'we can't do this to the community we created.'" In the end, she said, "I have never seen a brilliant idea handled so badly, bungled by such greed and so many opportunities lost."

All the traffic, combined with the Robin Hood pose, made Shawn Fanning an international celebrity. And he was beginning to enjoy the extra money he had gotten when Barry took over—eventually more than $100,000 in annual salary. He would also sell more than $100,000 in stock. He bought a BMW convertible and spent thousands of dollars constructing a makeshift recording studio to go with the gym and pool table in his plain but spacious Mountain View home. And he didn't fend off all of the women that sought him out. For much of the time after Hummer Winblad's investment, he focused on one woman who was close at hand: Alicia Morga, the beautiful young lawyer who followed Barry from Wilson Sonsini to Hummer Winblad, and who joined Napster in turn as Barry's assistant. Few within the company and even fewer outside knew about the relationship. Shawn didn't talk about it because he wanted to keep what little privacy he had. And Morga didn't talk about it because she worried that the personal and professional overlap could hurt her reputation at Hummer Winblad.

Shawn "didn't turn into an asshole. He's still a good kid," Ritter said. "But as the press kicked in, and he was on the cover of this magazine and that magazine, he had less time to code. Then he got used to not coding." Shawn sometimes frustrated Ritter and Kessler with how long he took to make modest upgrades to the Napster client. As Shawn lost some of his drive, he devoted hours to distractions like the game Quake 3, which the

Napster crew installed on a company server. Shawn entered a contest for Quake players, using the screen name "Napster." Of the hundreds of people playing, it's unlikely anyone suspected that he really was who he said he was. Shawn played with the same focus he had brought to his file-sharing program, keeping at it until he was number one, and then he quit. Shawn also tried to spread good cheer internally, requesting a Ping-Pong table for the office and a basketball hoop for outside, just like other well-funded Valley start-ups.

Parker and Ritter were having a much harder time. Parker's e-mails turned him into a scapegoat, not an appealing mascot like Shawn, and his public appearances were curtailed. "Hank was never able to forgive me for those remarks," Parker said. "If I had a chance of finding a meaningful role inside the company before that, I didn't anymore." Shawn said that Barry just wanted Parker to find "a job where he could do something tangible." But that would have been hard for Parker even without his fall from grace. After the first months, Parker had never done much that was concrete at Napster, and the tolerance for that kind of meandering was gone. "He was young and kind of immature, I guess just inexperienced," Shawn said. "Parker's more of a strategy guy, a vision guy, and he was still learning how to influence the direction of the company with his ideas."

Parker went off for a vacation in August, trying to reassess what he could do to be most useful at Napster. When he came back, Barry made it clear that he would be most useful out of the company. Parker was followed around the office like a walking liability. Devastated that he was unwelcome at the company he had helped create, Parker saw it was obvious that he would be fired. He resigned in humiliation and tried to think of what to do next. He tried writing, then consulting, but "my whole sense of identity was wrapped up in Napster," Parker said. "I was incredibly depressed. It took a long time to stop thinking about it day in and day out."

If the spotlight had been Parker's undoing, one of Ritter's gripes was that he had never gotten a chance to be in it; Ritter got almost no public recognition. What he did have was authority inside the company. Since moving west, he had the same rank as Shawn. "He did the client, and I did the server, and we didn't ask each other's permission" to make changes, Ritter said. As the company grew, Ritter was insulated from the top by more and more layers. Napster's innovation continued to stagnate. Most incredible to him, Hummer Winblad's leadership didn't seem any better than Richardson's. Barry brought badly needed money and a misguided belief that Napster would win in court. But he had little to say to the hacker staffers and barely tried. He was stiff in company meetings, and his occasional companywide messages were often sent from the mountaintop via his favorite toy, a BlackBerry wireless pager. Barry clamped down on the company's public relations, hiring President Clinton's deputy communications director from the 1992 campaign, Washington strategist Ricki Seidman, who monitored Barry's and Shawn's media contacts from afar. Barry also warned staffers that an outside law firm would investigate press leaks. "With Eileen, at least someone was out there with an opinion," Ritter said. "It may not have sounded intelligent, but at least it was a representation of the beliefs I thought the company was founded on."

Ritter had nearly quit back in April 2000, when his first six-month contract ran out and Kessler had been less than enthusiastic about paying Ritter's bonus. That was also the time when the venture deals kept falling through. "Eileen could not get John [Fanning] out of the company," Ritter said of that era. "All these things were coming to a head. There's a cliché that engineers always think they're the center of the universe, and they never are. But I look at Napster, and it had no business model, a bad legal strategy, and no value in the management. All it had was the technology." Back then, Ritter had talked to Ali Aydar about coming with him to start another firm, figuring that the two of them together could get Shawn to follow. One day after lunch, the two walked for blocks, hashing through the problems at Napster, and Ritter tried to convince him that leaving was the only logical thing to do. Aydar seemed to agree, then wavered and did nothing. "I could never get him stable enough to go to Shawn with it," Ritter said.

So Ritter, too, had stayed. Since then, he had seen Napster get both much bigger and much closer to extinction. Near the end of the summer came another blow. John Fanning accidentally sent someone inside Napster an e-mail disclosing that Napster was in talks for an investment by Bertelsmann. The e-mailed documents included the terms under discussion and an embarrassing laundry list of disclosures Napster had to make to its potential new backer. It was alarming enough to a true believer like Ritter that Napster could become an arm of a record company. Personally, it was more insulting to learn about chief operating officer Milt Olin's perks: a $50,000 signing bonus, a $1,500 monthly car allowance, and $3,200 in monthly rent for an apartment. In addition to the raft of litigation, the unresolved issues that had to be disclosed included Tom Carmody's claim "through John Fanning" that he still had the right to sell Napster-brand clothing; Draper Atlantic's recently reiterated claim of a right to get in on any new round of funding; the company's failure through June to defend the rights to its trademark; and numerous accounting and tax headaches, including the fact that Shawn, Parker, and others had never turned in receipts for their original moving expenses.

━━ ━━

BARRY RETURNED TO PROMOTING Shawn as spokesman, albeit more carefully watched than before. Far better a likable teenager than a corporate lawyer, as far as swaying the public was concerned. That fall, in a controlled setting free from hostile questions, Shawn testified before Orrin Hatch's committee at a field hearing in the senator's home territory in Provo, Utah, laying out his intentions in creating Napster and some of how the technology worked. On September 7, 2000, Shawn appeared on the MTV Video Music Awards show, introducing Britney Spears. Shawn had been nervous about it, since he tended to clam up before crowds. He sent a message to Ian Rogers, formerly of Nullsoft, explaining that his nerves might be a problem. Rogers begged him to say something significant: It was the most prominent positive exposure for a hacker in history. "Say something; I'll even write it for you. Don't just say, 'Thanks,'" Rogers implored him.

Shawn didn't end up saying much. "I was about as nervous as I've ever been," he remembered. He even called his mother, telling her he couldn't go through with it. But he did, and he was glad. "When I was walking on stage, there were a lot of people in the crowd who were in the front area, and they were saying really nice stuff," Shawn said. "I just had to read the TelePrompTer and not freeze up." After MTV show host Carson Daly introduced Shawn to massive applause, his main message was a visual appeal for peace: He wore a Metallica T-shirt, which he told Daly had been "shared" with him, though he was thinking about buying one. The onstage banter was as brief as Britney's outfit. "The sooner I can get off stage the better," Shawn said before introducing the teen pop star.

More to Shawn's liking were the concerts he got access to through Napster, and the chance to meet idols like Billy Corgan, then with the band Smashing Pumpkins. In a backstage chat after a Pumpkins show, Shawn connected to Corgan at a level that had little to do with music and more to do with the difficulties of success. "It was before the Pumpkins broke up," Shawn said. "Billy was really unhappy. It was hard to talk to him, because he was kind of in his own world. I understand it now, because I've been there. You go through a period of burnout with something, and you know you have to make a decision. You're consumed by it. You're trying to figure out how to let something go, how to move on from something. Next time I saw him was after the band had broken up and he was working on a side project, and he was incredibly happy."

Shawn himself didn't seem very happy in interviews he gave the media around that time, and he was often unsmiling in photographs. He said that he was having at least a little fun at the company, that it was just hard to do it in front of prying eyes. "I enjoy talking about Napster but not having to do press. If anybody saw me on camera, that probably means I wasn't having fun," Shawn said. "If you're, like, a musician or a sports player, you know if you do really well, you're going to be famous or there's going to be some notoriety associated with that. But if you're a computer coder, you really don't expect that kind of stuff to happen. A lot of times, I would hear about an interview, and it would just make me nervous and affect my ability to work."

That didn't diminish the sex appeal. The September 2000 issue of *Vanity Fair* included a photo feature on "enfantrepreneurs," with Shawn looking miserable. The writer described him as "shy, street-smart beefcake." Shawn's fame peaked with his appearance on the cover of the October 2 *Time* magazine. The writer had been to the offices six weeks before, when Napster spokesman Josef Robey sent a companywide e-mail asking employees to behave and to remove any "Hilary/Lars target practice signs" and other indications of revolutionary spirit. The article painted a flattering and largely accurate portrait of Shawn, though it omitted his hacker roots and the internal chaos at Napster.

With so much glory to go around, it looked as though Ritter was going to be able to get a piece of it later that month. *Wired* magazine had conducted its annual poll of techno-enthusiasts and was giving its Rave Awards October 12 at the Regency Theater in San Francisco. As with most similar awards where the public had any say, Napster cleaned up. An e-mail sent to Napster hands the day before the ceremony told staffers that Napster had won for Best Music Site, Most Innovative Web Start-Up, and Best Guerilla Marketing. In addition, fifteen thousand *Wired* readers had voted Shawn Tech Renegade of the Year, ahead of Nullsoft founder Justin Frankel and Ian Clarke, the Irish creator of FreeNet, an even more decentralized peer-to-peer system. As was the case with many Napster administrative communications, the e-mail came from Alicia Morga.

David Spade was hosting the Rave Awards, and musician Beck would perform at the party afterward. Also attending were San Francisco mayor Willie Brown and Daisy Fuentes, the MTV personality. The morning of the event, spokesman Robey e-mailed a dozen top employees, inviting them to the VIP party beforehand. An hour later he disinvited them, saying that he had "just been informed that the space for the pre-party is tight and can't accommodate all." Ritter and product marketer Brandon Barber, who had both planned on accepting awards, couldn't believe the snub. Four awards, and only Shawn and Barry would be there to bask in it? After a flurry of discussions, Robey reinvited Ritter, Barber, and marketing VP Brooks to the VIP party. When the actual event began, he wrote, "Jordan will go up with Shawn to accept best music site. Brandon and Liz will go up to accept best guerilla marketing."

It wasn't national television, but Ritter was truly excited. Bill Joy, the principal author of a popular version of the Unix programming language and a cofounder of Sun Microsystems, was getting the Wired Visionary award on the same night. And for once, Ritter would be on stage next to Shawn. The preparty went fine, and Ritter was enjoying himself as he sat at the Napster table for the awards ceremony. Then someone approached and said that Courtney Love had requested that Shawn alone come up to accept the best-music-site award. The *Wired* editors sided with Love, who was one of the night's top draws and sported a famously indomitable will. Ritter was flabbergasted, but there was nothing he could do. When

Shawn went up solo, he told the crowd he didn't know what to do onstage. A Nullsoft employee called out, "Steal something!" which Shawn didn't think was funny. Soon it grew obvious why Love, draped in a clingy white dress, had wanted Shawn by himself. She couldn't keep her hands off him, and she introduced him to the crowd as "my future husband."

To his credit, Barry brought Ritter with him to accept the innovative start-up award and graciously pushed him alone toward the microphone, where Ritter raised his fist and saluted Napster's by-then 35 million users. Afterward, Love came to the Napster table and would not go away. She sat in Shawn's lap, flirting heavily enough to get mentioned for it in the *San Jose Mercury News*. What she didn't know was that the woman seething quietly by Shawn's side, Alicia Morga, was his girlfriend.

Physical attraction aside, Love had another reason for being drawn to Shawn: He was the enemy of her enemy. In fact, if Shawn was the record industry's biggest enemy, Love was probably the runner-up. In January 2000, after Love announced that she wouldn't deliver the records she owed Geffen Records and its parent, Universal, Geffen had sued her. She countersued, arguing that the contract was "unconscionable" and there-fore unenforceable. Love's countersuit said that it was virtually impossible for bands to turn in the seven albums required in traditional seven-year deals, since the labels also require lengthy tours and sometimes insist on gaps between releases. And the record companies kept the books, charg-ing for production, marketing, and other costs before distributing any royalties. In the case of Love's band, Hole, after seven years of work, the four band members had collected a total of $375,000, less than $14,000 per year apiece.

━━ ━━

A WEEK AFTER THE Rave Awards, an old friend heard that Jordan Ritter was at Napster and tracked him down. Ritter wrote back a long e-mail explaining how worn out he was.

"Most people want to know what happened at Napster. You know, I'm sorry, not only am I personally sick of Napster (as if that weren't bad enough), but I'm personally sick of talking about Napster. I stayed only for my fellow team members (no, not the money, they jacked all of us except Shawn), and at one point even for Shawn, but my personal growth stunted the day I landed here, and hasn't really advanced since. . . . Helping lead a revolution is hard on the body AND soul, and last I checked, the revolution leaders were always killed and beheaded, so who the fuck knows what's going to happen to us. . . . Did I mention how fucked up everyone's values are here? It's a requirement, I think, on CA rental agreements or mortgage apps—Check if you are: [ ] a heartless fuck [ ] a money-grubbing sadistic fuck [ ] a techno-geek loser fuck with no life [ ] a wannabe of any discipline listed above. If you didn't check one of the above, please go the fuck away because you will be miserable here. Somehow I missed it, but I know it had to have been there. . . . Life goes on, and we all go on with it. Problem is, I have no idea where I'm going. I just look for peace of mind—constantly."

Soon after, Ritter met with the head of a private-financing start-up in San Francisco who offered to double his salary. His resistance to leaving was gone. On October 31, 2000, Ritter wrote another letter, resigning from the company he had helped build. He sent it to all the staff.

"To those most important to me, and to the company: It has been a long road for all of us, even for the few that have only been with Napster for a short time. Revolutions take energy, commitment, and sacrifice, and are, almost always, won at great cost and expenditure of effort. Napster has never been an exception to this rule; against forces of all odds—duplicitous and self-serving uncles, angry rock bands, an entire industry up in arms—we've really struggled, together, for what we believe in, for an enlightened future, for everyone. I can't express my gratitude enough for everyone's hard work—you must never forget that the sum of the parts can't amount to much without the parts themselves. Please, don't underestimate your impact on the company and the world; Napster needs you to be whole, the Revolution needs you to carry on the torch. And so it is with a very sad and weary heart that I inform you all I will be leaving Napster. . . . my departure is not a reaction to this company or events within, but a proactive change in my career and life. I must stress this again: I am leaving only to continue my personal growth and development of my professional career. For those of you who might be interested, I will be joining Round1 Inc. as Vice President of Technology, and am extremely happy to report that Round1's primary charter is to soften and streamline the process of funding companies, to make future investment experiences like Napster easier ones. Oh yeah, and to make money. Good luck, Napster, and Godspeed."

He signed it: "Jordan Ritter, Founding Developer. Joined in June of 1999."

It was Halloween, just a year after the rave in Oakland, when Napster had about 400,000 registered users. By the time Ritter served out his final two weeks, the number would pass 40 million.

Shawn thought Ritter had done the right thing. "He was getting really down and bringing people around him down," Shawn said. "He got the opportunity to move on to something that enabled him to get more responsibility and have a little more freedom, so I think that was definitely the right move for him." But Shawn wasn't there to tell Ritter any of that. He was in New York with Barry, announcing Napster's latest would-be savior.

11

bertelsmann

A HALLOWEEN DAY 2000 PRESS CONFERENCE IN NEW YORK
revealed an astonishing alliance between Napster, on its knees in court,
and the parent of one of its five archenemies. German publishing con-
glomerate Bertelsmann AG, owner of number three record label BMG
and the world's largest book publisher, Random House, had decided it
was better to join together than to fight—or perhaps best of all, to bet
both ways. BMG had been bombing financially, and Bertelsmann
thought that a Napster-like distribution system might give it an unbeat-
able advantage. As reporters gawked at Bertelsmann CEO Thomas Middelhoff hugging Shawn Fanning, they heard even more than the usual
amount of hype. "There's no question that file-sharing will exist in the
future as part of the media and entertainment industry," Middelhoff
declared. "Now the show begins." Shawn was visibly excited as well. "If
you think Napster is great now, just wait," he promised.

Of the media barons, Middelhoff was among the most predisposed to making a break with the past. Just forty-seven, he had written his doctoral thesis on new media, and he brought an intense focus on the field to old-line Bertelsmann when he joined it in 1994 as head of corporate development and multimedia. Traditions ran deep at the company, founded in 1835 as a hymnal publisher. It was at Middelhoff's urging that the giant invested $50 million in America Online in the mid-1990s, a modest gamble that would prove to be worth more than $1 billion by itself. A classic business opportunist, Middelhoff ascended to the top office at Bertelsmann and sold the investments in AOL and other dot-coms before the market fell, raking in more than $7 billion. Then Middelhoff felt left behind when his friend AOL leader Steve Case bought Time Warner. It wasn't a coincidence that in announcing the Napster deal, Middelhoff said a new version of its service could be just as big as AOL.

The alliance had begun coming together not long after Napster was crushed by Judge Patel's proposed injunction, a move that simultaneously ended AOL's remaining interest in buying Napster. After Barry drove off Edgar Bronfman and his Universal Music, he reached out to the other labels. "Hank was really about the negotiations, really enjoyed the process of flying out to meet people and these kinds of things," Shawn said. But Barry was rebuffed almost everywhere, including at Bertelsmann's BMG. "They were never serious. First they were willing to create a subscription service but not take down the pirated service. Then they said they would do it simultaneously. But they still haven't come to terms on licensing even now, which tells you something," a BMG executive said a year and a half later. As Napster's money ran low, Barry, Hummer, and John Fanning tried to attract financing, without success. Napster wooed Microsoft, Intel, and even tiny Liquid Audio. "I just got used to being turned down," said chief financial officer Lyn Jensen.

In the meantime, Middelhoff's e-commerce chief, Andreas Schmidt, was spending more and more time in Silicon Valley, chatting up digital-music firms and talking about the potential for Bertelsmann buying them. "He looked like Daddy Warbucks, with Bertelsmann's cash coming out of his ears and his breast pocket," said Gerry Kearby, head of Liquid Audio. "They were making overtures to purchase every company in the space. They were thinking about forming a giant roll-up of companies."

As Schmidt talked to Kearby, Napster's name inevitably came up, since it was the bane of Liquid Audio's existence. Kearby had known Barry for years, from when Barry had been Liquid Audio's lawyer at Wilson Sonsini. And Hummer Winblad had funded Liquid Audio. So Kearby helpfully passed on Barry's phone number.

It was also around then that Middelhoff and Schmidt discussed the potential for a Napster settlement with a discouraged Bronfman. Middelhoff and Schmidt left the meeting thinking there was some kind of deal possible, that Bronfman just wasn't seeing it. Schmidt called Barry, leaving the music people at BMG out of the loop. The talks were on again, off again, and all over the map both figuratively and literally, taking place in New York, Miami, and San Francisco. The deal died three times. At last, a handshake deal was struck. According to the draft that John Fanning accidentally sent to Napster troops, it called for a $20 million loan, convertible into 58 percent of the company.

BMG chief operating officer Strauss Zelnick was at home sleeping off the effects of oral surgery when Schmidt called him. "We're investing in Napster," Schmidt said. "We're dropping the suit and making the announcement tomorrow." Stunned out of his stupor, Zelnick couldn't believe it. "How could the music group not know about this?" he said. Zelnick and his digital-music deputy, Kevin Conroy, went into overdrive trying to convince Schmidt and Middelhoff to hold off on the deal and rethink it. They argued that if Bertelsmann made a deal with someone violating copyright protections, the company could be putting its own vast treasure of copyrights at risk under the legal doctrine of unclean hands. And they said that if Bertelsmann was still intent on such a purchase, it should simply wait for Napster to go bankrupt, then buy the assets for pennies in court. Schmidt said that Napster wouldn't go bankrupt and might even soon file for an IPO, that its legal fortunes had turned with the help of David Boies. But he passed along Zelnick's complaints to Middelhoff. "In his view, we are supporting an illegal act," Schmidt wrote.

Middelhoff agreed to delay the announcement to hear out Zelnick, Conroy, and BMG chairman Michael Dornemann. In one follow-up conversation outside a New York conference room, Schmidt told Zelnick that he was missing the essential fact—Napster had 33 million customers who would become Bertelsmann customers. "They aren't customers," Zelnick replied. "It's free. And they have zero revenue. I don't like investing in companies with zero revenue." Schmidt: "They're going to pay." Zelnick: "For them to pay, you need all our competitors too. Thomas, give me two weeks, and I'll try to bring in two other companies. If we take all the credit for this first, you're not going to get Edgar to play or Warner to play."

Zelnick ran through the numbers with Middelhoff, arguing that converting free users to paying users was incredibly difficult. Say 20 percent of Napster's users weren't kids without credit cards and could afford the service. That's 6 million people. A good conversion rate is 2 percent, he said. "Let's call it 10 percent. That's six hundred thousand consumers paying $10 a month. That's only $72 million a year in revenue." Not very exciting, Zelnick said, certainly not worth an investment of tens of millions. But looked at another way, the bet was a modest one. Bertelsmann's loan was a small piece of its $1.6 billion in annual profit.

The talks resumed for even higher stakes. At one meeting with Middelhoff in Miami, Barry passed around a half-dozen copies of the *Time* issue with Shawn on the cover. Always conscious of his own treatment by the media, Middelhoff paid attention. Bertelsmann ultimately pledged to lend Napster $60 million at just 6.1 percent interest to develop a royalty-friendly system, with the understanding that other labels would soon join in and take some of the equity that Bertelsmann could claim if it converted its loan and took 58 percent ownership. If Bertelsmann failed to convince another big label to settle in the next two years, then the loan could convert into just 35 percent of Napster's stock.

Like Yosi Amram, Ron Conway, and Hank Barry before him, Middelhoff was seduced by Napster's technology and incredible audience. But he wasn't as blinded. Unlike Barry, he didn't believe Napster was legally defensible. "It is true that this private exchange of music via the Internet has thus far infringed upon the copyrights of artists and record companies," he wrote to colleagues. And instead of a direct stock investment like those of his Napster predecessors, he was willing only to extend the loan. The reasoning was spelled out in a September 2000 briefing for Bertelsmann executives by a consulting firm. In a slide identifying the major risks of Bertelsmann's involvement, the experts wrote: "How do we avoid liability for old and ongoing copyright infringements? [Bertelsmann] provides loan and thus does not become a shareholder."

In a worst-case scenario—Napster losing in court and getting driven into bankruptcy—they predicted that Bertelsmann would emerge with Napster's valuable technology. Because the loan would be secured by those assets, Bertelsmann "gets first priority security interest," the consultants wrote. A separate task force of Bertelsmann executives assigned to "Project Thunderball" recommended that Napster's existing system stay operational until the new, copyright-friendly version was ready, even if it took six months or more. That way, the maximum number of subscribers could be pitched to switch. "Otherwise the customer base will be disbursed [*sic*]," the task force concluded in a memo sent to Middelhoff.

At Zelnick's insistence, BMG wasn't party to the deal. It would keep its part in the lawsuit alive. And the Napster project would come under Schmidt's e-commerce domain, not Zelnick's music group.

As a last step, Middelhoff treated Shawn to dinner at Manhattan's Post House, where they had steaks and a $219 bottle of Phelps Insignia Cabernet. "I had to explain the Bertelsmann culture and the Internet, the rapidity with which everything is changing," Middelhoff said. Shawn was surprisingly hard to convince. "I had a lot of concerns about it," he said. "There was this whole notion of selling out to a label." Shawn called his mother on Cape Cod, telling her he was thinking of walking away from Napster for good. "I think I want out," he told her. Shawn's mother encouraged him to stick with what he had started. Four days before the deal was disclosed, Napster added sweeteners for Shawn. The company raised his salary to $120,000, promised a November bonus of $60,000, and vested the remaining 993,000 of his 2.7 million shares. Shawn began to focus on the bright side. "Bertelsmann understood the software. They understood why it was interesting," he said months later. And "they seemed like if they got involved with a company, they gave them a lot of freedom to let them continue to do what made them successful and offer help where it's necessary—which we needed. It was a really good relationship in terms of deals and trying to get licenses and security and stuff. Those were all new issues for me that took a while to get comfortable with. Overall, it was definitely the right choice for the company. We wouldn't be here if Bertelsmann had not decided to fund the company and supported us."

⊏⊐ ⊏⊐

BERTELSMANN ANNOUNCED ITS INVESTMENT in the ballroom of the Essex House hotel in Manhattan. The press conference was long on attendees and remarkably short on details. The company said that the Napster system would continue as it was, that BMG wouldn't drop its suit for the time being, and that a new business model hadn't been worked out. The principals seemed only to agree that the new Napster would charge for membership, and Barry mentioned $4.95 a month as a hypothetical. The executives were coached not to say that Napster was running out of money. And if they were asked whether the loan would facilitate more illegal downloading, they were told to say neither yes nor no, just to parrot a line about the loan being used to develop a legitimate system. The companies revealed none of the investment terms.

As it turned out, Middelhoff had misjudged how the rest of the industry would react. Rather than racing to sign up, competing record labels were aghast, since the deal gave Napster the financial means to keep fighting them. At Bertelsmann, Zelnick and Dornemann resigned within a week—Middelhoff later said they were fired, since BMG was doing so poorly—and Conroy left two months later for AOL.

Middelhoff and Schmidt were supposed to travel to Redwood City to meet the Napster staff after the announcement, but only Schmidt made it. Middelhoff sent an e-mail instead, which Barry told everyone to keep out of the press. "You have all done an incredible amount of work in the face of significant challenges and limited resources," Middelhoff wrote. "Shawn has done an amazing thing in inventing this technology, but I know that bringing the company this far has required the talents and dedication of all of you. . . . Shawn is right when he says, 'We will always have the user's best interest in mind.' At the end of the day, Napster does not matter without its users."

Barry and Middelhoff still believed that the labels would follow them in the deal, but they were soon disappointed. Unlike Bronfman's plan from earlier in the year, Bertelsmann didn't yet have the equity to divide up among the other companies. "They never suggested anything other than a way for them to own Napster and us to pay them. It was never Thomas doing a favor for the industry," said Bronfman, who told Middelhoff the day after the announcement that he had made a mistake. Natural competition among the record companies made what was already an unlikely resolution far less achievable, Bronfman and others said. And Bertelsmann's presence didn't make up for two huge holes in Barry's plan: the lack of a business model—still—and the lack of working technology that would guard against constant pirating. Bertelsmann's move just made it the biggest victim stuck to the Napster tar baby. Middelhoff said the failure of the rest of the companies to follow him showed their poor analysis, not his. "The rest of the industry didn't see what was going on," Middelhoff said. "They don't have an end in this legal battle, and on the other hand [Gnutella successors] Kazaa and MusicCity and all the others have tremendous growth rates, and nothing can stop them."

<hr />

UNDER THE NEW NAPSTER REGIME, Barry was still in charge. But he had a new and more powerful partial master in Bertelsmann. That was good for Napster's ability to continue as a going concern, but it further complicated Barry's renewed efforts to find his own successor as CEO, someone with more operating experience. The candidates weren't sure who was calling the shots on the Napster board. Barry interviewed several prospective CEOs himself, enlisted Hummer Winblad to help, and hired an outside executive-search firm. According to several people involved in the search, Bertelsmann's ill-defined power was only part of the problem. Barry didn't seem to be sure what sort of a CEO he wanted: an entertainment-industry veteran, a Silicon Valley technologist, or a different beast entirely. Since Barry thought that a lot of the issues, and Napster's ultimate fate, might well be decided on Capitol Hill, he even gave some thought to recruiting a lobbyist for the top job.

The candidates for permanent Napster CEO ranged from former eGroups Inc. CEO Michael Klein to Mark Curcio of the film company Artisan Entertainment and even to Julie Wainwright, the former CEO of the disastrous Pets.com and a friend of Ann Winblad. Most of the people approached about the top job at Napster were too curious to reject the idea out of hand. The biggest draw may have been the enormous public exposure that would come with the job. And if the company could re-emerge, the CEO would be a hero to music fans and businesspeople alike. But many candidates who came to Napster's new offices in Redwood City ended their trip more confused than they had been before.

The CEO job would not have been an easy sell in any case. Napster was functioning only because the preliminary injunction against it had been stayed pending an appeal, and most appeals fail. Beyond the court case, Napster was in a perpetual state of uncertainty. "Hank was busily going around trying to ink deals with other labels, and he was being fairly unsuccessful doing that. At the same time, they were trying to rewrite the system to be able to conform to a royalty structure," one serious candidate said. "The issues included how they were going to transition to a pay service, how to account for it, and how it would work from a mechanical perspective," he said. "Most importantly, in talking to Hank, it was obvious they didn't know the profile of the guy they wanted, because they didn't know what the service was going to look like. At the end of the day, since they didn't know what the strategy was, they couldn't agree on who the person was."

One explanation for the confusion was that Barry and his partners had different ideas than the rest of Napster and Bertelsmann about how to proceed. A number of candidates thought they had offers from Barry, who purported to be running the show, only to find out that he had been outvoted by the Napster board or other influencers. "There were a lot of decision makers," one person close to the process said. "You had different companies with different objectives and cultures." As the search dragged on from Barry's appointment in May 2000 until past the same month the following year, a less-charitable interpretation emerged: that Barry liked being CEO, and even though he took pains to refer to himself as "interim" chief, he would be perfectly happy to continue in the job for as long as possible.

While Eileen Richardson had pushed Shawn alone in front of the cameras, Barry was allotting himself more of the spotlight. He did more of the speaking than Shawn at joint press conferences, and he made many more trips to testify in Washington and to speak at industry conferences. Some CEO candidates concluded that Barry was running such a long, thorough search just to convince his unseen superiors that he was doing as much as he could. "He was going through the motions for his partners and the boards," one candidate said. Presenting a bewildering array of potential CEOs and potential business approaches made it more likely that the board would throw up its hands and keep letting Barry do as he saw fit. "Hank enjoyed the job. He enjoyed the profile," the recruit said.

Inside Napster, more employees were beginning to chafe at Barry's autocratic style. Barry had a serious temper, especially under pressure, and the edicts emanating from his BlackBerry rubbed the engineers the wrong way. "He was often extremely charismatic and focused," one employee said. "Other days, he would just be negative and not reasonable." Eddie Kessler, who initially enjoyed strong support from Barry, said that he was, in "some respects, a breath of fresh air." But Barry's top-down style included hiring executives without the input of the leadership team, which "was kind of unheard of in the Valley," Kessler said. Shawn said Barry turned out as advertised—a solid lawyer. "He took care of the legal stuff very well. But I think the litigation was kind of a losing battle overall. Not because ultimately it went against us but because every time we expected it to go one way, it went the other. It was a roller coaster."

For whatever reason, Barry was still interim CEO, and there was still no deal with the record labels, when the U.S. Court of Appeals for the Ninth Circuit finally ruled on Patel's preliminary injunction in February 2001.

In August 2000, Napster had filed its full appeal. It asked the three-judge panel to revisit nearly every holding by Patel, including those interpreting the VCR case, the DMCA safe harbors, and the Audio Home Recording Act. And the company argued that Patel's injunction was overly broad and too harsh, in effect a form of prior restraint that would convert the network from a peer-to-peer system to "a centralized source of authorized material." Hammering on the "substantial noninfringing use" argument from the VCR case, Boies said that seventeen thousand artists had authorized their work to be distributed, at least when it came to concert recordings—even Metallica. The major labels, meanwhile, released only twenty-six hundred albums a year. Boies said Napster would enable secured-format distribution as soon as it became available. The record industry filed its own brief in response, and amicus friend-of-the-court briefs rolled in on both sides from the ACLU, the Digital Media Association, the Motion Picture Association of America, and a troupe of eighteen copyright-law professors. Even federal officials weighed in, hurting Napster when they stated flatly that the Audio Home Recording Act, which permits private noncommercial copying, didn't apply.

The climactic oral arguments came October 2 in the appeals court's ornate hearing room in downtown San Francisco. Carter-appointed circuit judge Mary Schroeder, the most senior of the three judges, sat between the two men on the panel and said the lawyers for each party would get just twenty minutes to make what could be the defining arguments of their careers. As CNN transmitted the proceedings live, Boies approached the lectern and told the judges that the record industry was asking them to make a series of rulings unprecedented in the history of copyright law. For Napster to be found liable for contributory or vicarious infringement, he said, its users would have to be found liable for direct infringement. Yet the users were deriving no financial benefit from their actions, and Napster had no financial relationship with them.

Just minutes into Boies's presentation, the judges began firing questions. Since Napster users were sharing music with millions of anonymous strangers, "you can't characterize that as personal and private use," like that allowed under the Sony VCR decision, Schroeder said. Boies shifted to the legitimate uses of Napster, which he said could be a minority but still "significant" enough to qualify the technology for protection under Sony. That protection "is particularly important in a changing technology," Boies said, and more and more artists were permitting the use of their music on Napster. Judge Robert Beezer, a Reagan appointee, jumped into the fray with questions about how Napster worked. Napster's computers might be devices with legitimate uses, he said, but the programming that linked users together was an ongoing service. That implied it didn't qualify for protection of the sort accorded the VCR, which Beezer said was "clearly, from beginning to end, a device." Boies tried dodging again, arguing that Napster's directory should be protected as free speech. "The First Amendment has never been held to prohibit the use of a directory service," Boies said. The third and least experienced appellate judge on the panel, Clinton appointee Richard Paez, said little.

Russell Frackman had enjoyed Boies's rough treatment, though he had been through enough proceedings to know it didn't foretell victory. He was feeling more pleased as he stepped to the lectern that Judge Schroeder was in charge: He had argued the flea-market case before her and won. Frackman was glad that for the first time in his career, he had brought his children to hear him argue. But he did little more than clear his throat and begin to praise Beezer for questioning the relevance of Sony when he too was interrupted. "Are you prepared to discuss the knowledge issue?" Beezer asked, thinking of the DMCA protection for Internet service providers that are merely unknowing conduits of information. "I find that extremely troublesome. . . . If this is a service, how are they expected to have knowledge of what comes off some kid's computer in Hackensack for transfer to Guam?" Frackman was prepared. "You start out talking about what they designed their system for. They designed it for piracy," he said. One last time, he read Sean Parker's smoking-gun e-mail saying that anonymity was important since Napster users "are exchanging pirated music." And moving quickly to take advantage of Schroeder's presence, he said, "This is no different than the swap meet."

The advantage immediately proved smaller than Frackman had hoped. "This is different," Schroeder told him. The flea-market operator could wander through at any time and learn that pirated goods were being sold on its premises. "Napster doesn't have any idea at any point in time," she said. The judges kept firing questions at Frackman and Boies during their rebuttals. At the end, some observers thought the questioning was tougher on the music industry than on Boies. Perhaps the suave litigator had pulled another rabbit out of his hat.

Neither side expected to wait long for a decision. But the deliberations among the judges and their clerks wore on and on. The longer it lasted, the better Napster thought its chances were and the more nervous Frackman became. In the interim, Patel appointed a mediator to try to broker a settlement: The parties met only once, and the talks went nowhere. On February 12, 2001, four months after the oral arguments, the Ninth Circuit finally handed down its verdict. It was unanimous, with

Beezer, who had asked Schroeder for the task, writing the fifty-three-page opinion on behalf of his colleagues. The panel found that Napster's users were indeed violating music copyrights, just as Patel had ruled. The Audio Home Recording Act didn't apply. The VCR case didn't help much either, because Napster had an ongoing role in its users' behavior. And the judges agreed that Napster was likely to be found to be contributing to its users' copyright violations, since its worth would rise with the number of users it drew. "The district court did not err: Napster, by its conduct, knowingly encourages and assists the infringement of plaintiffs' copyrights," Beezer wrote. The judges accepted Patel's finding that Napster was hurting CD sales. And the panel said that Napster could police its system to locate copyright-infringing material, just as it blocked people who misused the system in other ways.

The only thing the appeals court told Patel to change was the way she crafted the injunction. Patel had wanted Napster to make sure that each file offered for transfer didn't violate a copyright. The appeals court, on the other hand, moved the burden back toward the labels. Napster would still have to police its system to the best of its ability, but the record labels would have to submit the names of files with infringing works. Possibly the result of a compromise among the judges, the court may not have realized that it was calling for a logistical nightmare. As it noted elsewhere, Napster's internal documents showed it stood to win if the labels had to report every file, because each would probably be gone by the time Napster got around to disabling it, with another user's unblocked version of the same song taking its place.

Still, it was a resounding victory for the record industry. "The court of appeals found that the injunction is not only warranted, but required," the RIAA's Hilary Rosen said. "And it ruled in our favor on every legal issue presented." The ruling also made it less likely that Napster could make a deal with labels besides Bertelsmann, Schmidt acknowledged. At a San Francisco press conference, Barry vowed to ask for a rehearing and to appeal to the Supreme Court if necessary. And he amplified his calls for pressure on Congress. "We encourage members of our community to contact their representatives to let Congress know how much Napster means to them," he said. Shawn, meanwhile, said he was working on a new version that included better song-blocking and "a lot of really pretty amazing things."

▭ ▭

THE OLD NAPSTER WAS STILL RUNNING as Patel digested the appeals court's directive to modify her injunction. But in a sign of how dire things had become, Barry decided to try to give the stalled negotiations with the labels some electric-shock treatment. He called Rosen at the RIAA. "Hank said he had talked to Thomas [Middelhoff], and they really wanted to settle this thing. They were going to go to the companies. Then I got a call from a reporter who told us Barry had scheduled a press conference the next day," Rosen said. She called Barry immediately, stunned that he would be so amateurish as to make a negotiating offer in public. "It was the only time in three years of dealing with this that I lost my temper," Rosen said. "I really thought if they played it right they could have settled it. I spent an hour on the phone screaming at him from BMG's offices in L.A. I said this was going to put them back another year. He told me I was wrong."

The next day, over Napster strategist Ricki Seidman's objections, Barry held his press conference in San Francisco, joined by Schmidt and Middelhoff. Before puzzled reporters, they announced that Napster was offering the labels $1 billion over five years, to come from subscription fees on the new service, whenever it was ready. Per label, that worked out to a very small increase in revenue—a few percentage points. Per song, it worked out to pennies. Given the history of bad blood between Barry and the labels, the offer was dead on arrival. "You claim you want to be legitimate and negotiate licenses based on real business models," Rosen said in a statement. "Act accordingly. Stop the infringements. Stop the delay tactics in court, and redouble your efforts to build a legitimate system." Richard Parsons, co–chief operating officer of AOL Time Warner, added this: "They need to shut down—then we can talk." Even Barry later admitted that the press conference was a mistake.

Patel issued her revised injunction on March 6, 2001, and Napster was forced to begin blocking file names listed by the record companies. At first, it did so by each song's name. It was an imperfect solution, and the most devoted Napster users found ways around it. One popular trick used pig Latin for the names of songs and bands. A more sophisticated tool, developed by onetime message-board moderator Wayne Chang and posted at Napsterhelp.com, used encryption to trick the Napster servers into steering users to MP3 files without ever gleaning the file names. "I just wanted to bring back what was once so great," Chang said. The record industry complained about all of the holes, and Patel declared Napster's early filtering efforts to be "disgraceful." Napster's lawyers promised the company would do better, and in April it bought a cutting-edge but still-imperfect system for identifying song files by the music they contained. Patel appointed a technical adviser to baby-sit the new effort and demanded frequent updates. The fans were miserable. On one personal website devoted to all things Napster, the host wrote: "Is anyone out there besides me wincing at what's beginning to look like the cruel and unusual death of Napster? It's getting just too painful to watch."

NAPSTER WAS FAST RUNNING OUT of alternatives. In June 2001, the company's first step in further appeals, asking the full Ninth Circuit to revisit the decision of its panel, failed to muster a single judge's vote in support. That scotched talk of a long-shot petition to the U.S. Supreme Court. Instead, Napster promised that its new subscription service would be available later that summer. Until then, it was stuck trying to make its new screening system something less than a complete disaster. Patel had given Napster until June 28 to perfect the system, and the in-house engineers clearly weren't going to make it in time. Barry hired several consultants, including early Listen.com executive Richard Carey as chief engineer, and licensed still more outside technology in a frantic bid to get the new audio-fingerprinting system up and running by the deadline.

In addition to the legal pressure and the possibly insurmountable technical issues, Napster was wracked by near terror of its own upper management and by internal divisions. Some of the best engineers, led by Ali Aydar, had gotten themselves assigned to the far-more-pleasant task of developing the next generation of Napster, instead of the more-urgent but depressing task of working on the filter. And there were still true believers—"Shawn's fans," as Carey called them—who thought the company would still win the lawsuit and that any filtering was a sellout. Shawn himself tried to keep quiet about his objections.

"There were times that the company has been forced due to litigation or other things to take paths that I didn't think were ideal, and it was tough being associated with that," Shawn said. "Especially with a lot of the publicity. Because I remember when we started filtering ineffectively, sort of overblocking, I was getting recognized a lot. Kids were coming up and saying why can't I find this or why can't I find that, and that was definitely rough, because I wasn't involved in choosing whether to filter or determining how the filtering system should work, but I definitely felt the repercussions of that."

Carey had never seen anything like the mess Napster was in. "The chaos inside the organization was just strangling," he said. "It took me a week to figure out that everyone was operating based on fear—of the lawsuit, of management, of making a mistake. It was bizarre." Kessler was in charge of the screening effort, and Barry had lost faith in his ability to pull it together. "The first thing Hank asked me to do was fire Eddie," Carey said. "I said there's no way I can ship if I fire Eddie. It's all in his head." After getting berated one time too many by Barry, Kessler quit in May. Barry realized that Carey had been right: With no Eddie, there was no chance. A three-day soap opera ensued, ending only when Barry apologized and asked Kessler to come back.

The high-speed filtering effort went down to the wire. Just before the June 28 hearing, Carey and the others had it working in the lab, with "duct tape and gum holding it together." On June 27, Napster switched to the new system. As copyright-infringement notices poured in by mail, e-mail, and fax, the new audio-based system knocked out the protected songs, and the exhausted engineers congratulated each other. "The tenor of the conversation changed, to the system having a chance. And that would be the beginning of a possible settlement," Carey said.

As the Napster crew kept checking the new system's performance, they found a tiny percentage of errors—only 1 percent or 2 percent of the banned songs were getting through, mostly because of mistakes in the infringement notices. Try as they might, the engineers could not get the error rate down to zero. And Barry and Napster's other lawyers were facing the possibility that Patel would hold them in contempt of court.

Kessler was torn but eventually sided with the lawyers. "Something was going wrong," he said. "I said we should take it down until it's resolved."

Napster took down the system voluntarily on July 1, 2001, as it kept hunting for bugs, cutting off what had grown to 2 million simultaneous users, close to AOL's figures and an incredible technical achievement for such a small number of engineers and machines. Instinctively, Aydar felt the long fight was over. "Once we shut it down, we knew it was going to be hard to get it up again," he said. "It was like trying to repair the leg of a racehorse. You just shoot it. But everyone felt like it was *Napster*, so we can't let it go."

At a crucial July 11 hearing, Napster lawyer Steve Cohen told Patel that Napster could relaunch the system and weed out 99 percent of the improper songs. But Patel was adamant. "It's not good enough until every effort has been made to, in fact, get zero tolerance," she ruled. "She was furious," Kessler said. "She said it's got to be perfect. I said I can't build a system where I can guarantee that it will be perfect." Unable to promise a faultless system, Napster stayed shut. An appeal to the Ninth Circuit arguing that Patel's zero-tolerance standard was too high was rejected. And despite assurances to fans that it would soon be back, Napster's second-generation system for authorized recordings wouldn't go live until a beta test, free of major-label content, in early 2002.

After so many false deaths, Napster was truly gone, or at least in an indefinite coma. By now, tens of millions of people had been conditioned to expect free and easily accessible music, and they were willing to hunt around for new tools to use. Napster's would-be successors, meanwhile, had had plenty of time to work out the kinks in their systems. The early versions of Gnutella had difficulty in scaling to handle massive traffic. It was also slow, and it had bugs that were difficult to overcome without some user sophistication. But millions tried anyway: The number of hits to Gnutella websites ran into the tens of millions. Litigation would also target Gnutella, but its lack of centralization made it close to impossible to shut down. As Shawn had feared, the open-source effort made steady and eventually profound improvements to Gnutella. Derivatives including Amsterdam-based Kazaa and Nashville-based MusicCity Morpheus took hold in 2001, collectively surpassing the traffic Napster had at its peak. As with Gnutella, there was no practical way to stop them. The open-source versions of Napster also came into their own with the real service down. OpenNap servers began spreading in earnest. While Morpheus, Kazaa, and the other descendants of Gnutella got far more press attention, by some measures the OpenNap version of Napster draws more music seekers, according to the RIAA's Frank Creighton.

WITH NO MORE LEGAL RECOURSE and no deal with the labels in the offing, Napster's only other way out was a Hail Mary to Washington, D.C., and Barry lobbied hard for a mandatory license to force distribution of digital music. Helpfully, the record industry's unpopularity had only grown during its fight with Napster. And a law that would save Napster by making the labels share their wares in new ways was not unprecedented. The 1992 Audio Home Recording Act was the grandest of the recent compromises, expressly allowing home copies and mandating fees from the sale of blank cassette tapes that were in turn distributed among music authors, performers, and publishers. Congress had also stepped in to allow cable companies to rebroadcast shows aired by conventional networks and to sort out the rights of jukebox operators.

Much more commonly when Congress got involved, it tended to favor copyright holders—so much so that most Americans probably believed that copyrights had always been around, had no caveats, and were permanent. In fact, for most of the world's history, musicians were free to pick whatever music they wanted, earning money only by performing. The same is true of Shakespeare and other writers, who were free to copy each other or stage someone else's plays. When copyrights did come into being, it was because technology had changed the lay of the land.

Copyrights began in 1710 in England, after technology made it feasible to copy manuscripts. Since then, there has always been a balancing act between the interests of the creators and the interests of the public. The public's side of the balance, according to some scholars, probably peaked in the United States at the Constitutional Convention of 1787. It was there, at the behest of James Madison, that the framers adopted the copyright-and-patent clause of the document, giving Congress the power "to promote the progress of science and useful arts, by securing for limited times to authors and investors the exclusive right to their respective writings and discoveries."

The importance of the phrase "limited times" was not lost on early legislators, who saw copyright as a trade-off that ensured everyone would have free use of discoveries and artistic works after an appropriate period of compensation. The first U.S. copyright law provided that the exclusive rights would expire after a term of fourteen years, renewable at the author's request for another fourteen years. As copyright holders—increasingly, large publishing companies—grew in power and made return trips to Washington, that copyright term was extended eleven times in the past forty years. More than once, it happened just as Mickey Mouse was nearing his expiration date (or emancipation date, depending on one's point of view). In 1998, the Sonny Bono Copyright Term Extension Act set a new record, extending what had grown to seventy-five years of copyright for corporate works and life-plus-fifty years for works by individuals by a further twenty years apiece. The bill was challenged in court by a team including Lawrence Lessig, who argued that Congress's constant extensions were a way of sneaking around the constitutional requirement for limited time. After Lessig's side lost in lower courts, the U.S. Supreme Court in 2002 agreed to consider the case.

So far, the courts have been almost as uniformly pro–copyright holder as Washington has been. Under the Digital Millennium Copyright Act, it's illegal to hack encryption technology that protects copyrighted material. And this has been interpreted very broadly. In one of the best-known cases, that involving the DVD encryption technology known as CSS and the override program called DeCSS, it is often missed that DeCSS did not itself facilitate copying. CSS kept DVD discs from being played on computers that didn't contain the licensed technology for de-encryption. In practice, this meant that only Windows and Apple machines could play the DVDs. DeCSS just allowed Linux users to play DVDs that were purchased legally. Any DVD could be copied, legally or otherwise, without having to de-encrypt it. Yet not only were the purveyors of DeCSS found to have violated the DMCA, but journalistic websites that linked to pages *that linked to pages* that contained the DeCSS program were barred from doing so by the courts.

Likewise, the record industry won the biggest digital lawsuit besides that against Napster on far flimsier grounds. The labels went after MP3.com in the year 2000 and won a $110 million judgment over one of the dot-com's services, which allowed legitimate compact-disc owners to listen to versions of that music from wherever they logged on. The big legal issue was a small practical one: MP3.com established a database of recorded music so that when consumers electronically registered their own CDs, the company knew what music was on it. The industry argued that the very creation of that database, while made with purchased CDs, was unauthorized copying for commercial purposes and not fair use. And it won.

Oddly enough, Napster didn't start the fight in Washington that eventually was its last hope: Orrin Hatch did. The Utah Republican chaired the powerful Senate Judiciary Committee, where he had been looking to make laws on issues less divisive than those that previously had split the panel, which included ideologues from both parties. Hatch had brought together diverging interests before, when he crafted the Digital Millennium Copyright Act, which gave at least something to all sides. He had made a bigger splash by riding the Clinton-administration Justice Department to go after Microsoft. Critics pointed out that two serious Microsoft competitors happened to be based in Utah, but Hatch's brand of conservatism did call for free markets, which he felt were being strangled by the monopoly from Redmond.

During their work on Microsoft hearings, Hatch staffers led by his chief counsel, Manus Cooney, had spent many days in Silicon Valley. Cooney began hearing complaints about the difficulty in getting music licenses from the Big Five labels, and he had long conversations with Michael Robertson of MP3.com. Early in 2000, a friend suggested that Cooney check out Napster, and he downloaded the software. Cooney began tracking the RIAA lawsuit, then in its early stages. When Hummer Winblad invested in May, the entertainment industry grew more alarmed about Napster's prospects. Cooney thought the issue was something Hatch could use to forge a compromise. So he called Hank Barry at Hummer Winblad, eventually reaching the Napster CEO on his cell phone in an airport. They talked for twenty minutes, and Cooney began laying the groundwork for hearings before the Judiciary Committee.

To those familiar with reading tea leaves inside the Beltway, the witness list for those first hearings in July 2000 was strikingly pro-Napster. There was a Sony executive, and there was Lars Ulrich of Metallica. But there were also Barry, MP3.com's Robertson, and Gene Kan of Gnutella fame, representing the future of piracy if nothing was worked out. For a number of reasons, Hatch was leaning towards Napster's side. Back then, Napster had not yet lost the pivotal argument over a preliminary injunction, and the worst of the internal documents had not been publicized. And the entertainment industry is one of the largest contributors to the Democratic Party. But the most personal motivation came from a surprising place—Hatch's own musical aspirations. Probably most of his Utah constituents were unaware of it, but Hatch fancied himself a late-blooming songwriter. From the late nineties on, Hatch had cowritten some three hundred songs and recorded several CDs, many of them religious. And his early impressions of the record industry were like those of lots of aspiring musicians—frustration that bordered on anger. "I know something about songwriting. And I know something about prejudice," Hatch said at an industry conference in early 2001. "Many of the outlets that handle inspirational music won't handle mine, because they don't think Mormons are Christians."

For Hatch, anything that got obscure gospel and other kinds of unheard music in front of more people was a good thing. And if the record industry's economics didn't favor that outcome, change could be mandated from above. "Online systems provide a cheaper and easier method of self-publishing," Hatch said, citing the case of a musician friend who couldn't make a dime until he sold eighteen thousand CDs through his record label. Even then, the friend wouldn't have the rights to his work. "It's kind of like paying off your mortgage, and the bank still owns the house," Hatch said.

In private discussions with the RIAA's Hilary Rosen before the July 2000 hearings, Hatch had raised the prospect of compulsory licenses as a threat to prod the industry toward negotiating licensing deals. Barry could have seized the moment and testified for such legislation. But before the preliminary injunction hearing, Barry still believed he would win his case in court. So he explicitly asked Congress not to change the laws. It was Ulrich, instead, who pleaded for help. "Allowing our copyright protections to deteriorate is, in my view, bad policy, both economically and artistically," Ulrich testified. "We have to find a way to welcome the technological advances and cost savings of the Internet while not destroying the artistic diversity and the international success that has made our intellectual-property industries the greatest in the world." With Barry not pushing for a new law, there was little that Hatch could do. At the end of the year, Cooney left and joined Napster as a lobbyist, recusing himself for a year from speaking with Hatch.

By the time of the next hearings, in April 2001, everything had changed. Not only Judge Patel but also the Ninth Circuit had spoken against Napster. Only now did Barry ask Congress to force digital licenses on the record industry. "The Internet needs a simple and comprehensive solution, similar to the one that allowed radio to succeed—not another decade of litigation," Barry said. But it was too late. In the intervening months, an army of entertainment-industry lobbyists had descended on Hatch. They both talked tough and played to his ego. The most impressive display of the second tactic unfolded at a Washington hotel on March 21, just weeks before the new hearings. That's when the National Academy of Recording Arts and Sciences, which presents the Grammy Awards, bestowed Hero Awards on an unlikely group, including Hatch, powerful House Democrat John Conyers, and, for credibility, hip-hop star Missy "Misdemeanor" Elliott. At the lavish awards dinner, the record industry outdid itself by drafting Nashville singer Natalie Grant to croon one of Hatch's own songs, "I Am Not Alone," to the audience. According to the academy, the crowd went wild.

The industry didn't have to stall Hatch for long. He would be out of the center chair in two months, to be succeeded by Democrat Patrick Leahy of Vermont, after Sen. Jim Jeffords bolted the Republican Party and handed Democrats a Senate majority. And Leahy had bigger priorities than following the advice of a corporate lawyer turned Silicon Valley CEO, especially one whose company had been damned by a federal appeals court as a piracy profiteer.

The last Senate hearings gave Bertelsmann little hope, and the company was growing frustrated. The initial six-month estimate for a legitimate service was ending, and the product was still at least three months away. In April, Bertelsmann's eCommerce Group met to discuss two goals: getting content from the other majors and getting management control of Napster, perhaps "by replacing HB [Hank Barry] with a Bertelsmann manager." The team wrote that it would be "legally difficult, but doable" to develop a lawful way to get rid of Barry, and the executives mused about promoting Shawn to co-CEO alongside a Bertelsmann loyalist.

Just two weeks after Patel ruled that Napster would stay dark until it could block 100 percent of the infringing material, Hank Barry finally named his replacement. He remained a Napster director and went back to Hummer Winblad full-time. Successor Konrad Hilbers was the first career businessman to take the reins at the now-desperate company. A German with a doctorate in business who had worked at a U.S. bank, Hilbers's most important qualification was a stamp of approval from Bertelsmann CEO Thomas Middelhoff—just as Bertelsmann's managers had wanted. Middelhoff had cultivated a personal relationship with Shawn, one that had a strong impact on the youth, so his endorsement meant even more. "I like Thomas a lot," Shawn said. "When things got really down, he was actually a major reason that a lot of times I chose to stick it out. He believes in us so much, and he chose to put a lot of his own personal credibility and other things behind it." Hilbers, too, seemed like "a nice guy" to Shawn—perhaps too much so. "I was wondering, wow, does he know what he's getting into here? The music industry, the circumstances, the characters involved, the amount of work . . . Konrad just came off as just a nice guy, and I was wondering if he was going to be cut out for it." But Shawn decided within a few months that Hilbers was nearly perfect. "It has been the greatest decision we have ever made. The organization needed some help. We needed to be cleaned up, we needed some help with structuring engineering."

If Napster's most logical remaining exit strategy was a takeover by Bertelsmann, it could only help Barry to have someone in the lead who was known and respected by the German company. A buttoned-down but strategic thinker, Hilbers had worked for Bertelsmann's business-development team, as chief financial officer of its publisher Bantam Doubleday Dell, and as CFO of AOL Europe. A last six-month stint as chief administrative officer at Bertelsmann's BMG music division had been less pleasant, as Hilbers clashed with the rest of the bureaucracy there. During settlement negotiations on BMG's behalf with Napster, he decided the other side was more interesting than his own. He got Middelhoff's blessing to leave and his waiver of Hilbers's old pledge not to leave Bertelsmann for a competitor.

Hilbers interviewed with Barry and John Hummer and decided the Napster job was for him. "I believe in the peer-to-peer aspect, the community aspect," Hilbers said. Like many others before him, he also saw the logic of having a system for wider introduction of music to fans formerly reached only through radio. "The Internet is providing a chance for a totally new radar screen," he said. "There's a great middle ground between Britney Spears and a San Francisco garage band." Hilbers had a few big goals. With hopes fading of a rescue in Congress, he needed to work harder on a deal with the labels. And he needed to have a system to show them that was secure and controlled digital rights—something like what Napster should have had in the first place.

Not surprisingly, both priorities turned out to be much more challenging than Hilbers had anticipated. He replaced Eddie Kessler with Shawn as Napster's chief technology officer, but a secure system took six more months. It allowed for multiple payment streams, for technology that blocked duplication, and for the "expiration" of songs. It was so complex that Shawn admitted he didn't understand all of it, even at a high level of abstraction. He stayed focused on making the projected experience for the user as much like that of the old Napster as possible.

When it came out in January 2002, Napster II worked fairly well, and Shawn was satisfied with it, though most of the content was from lesser-known bands and minor labels. And while Napster had faded from the headlines and the hearts of many, who turned to new services like Kazaa and Morpheus, BearShare and LimeWire, 3 million people applied to be Napster II beta testers. The best part was that it still felt to the user like the Napster of old. "Aside from the limited content, it is actually a very seamless implementation of a system that's a thousand times more complex then the old system," Shawn said. Reviews by the users were mixed. The technology generally worked, though the payment system wasn't operating. The look and the feel were good, but there wasn't enough music. And Napster evidently planned to charge for a limited number of downloads, the majority of which couldn't be burned onto CDs or transferred to other people electronically. Many users who shopped around found that the other services were too good to give up. Hilbers declared the beta test a success. Privately, he thought a full release needed six months and $30 million.

By now, many were arguing that all of the industry's antipiracy efforts, from the Secure Digital Music Initiative to the litigation, were essentially pointless. Even if technology to prevent copying were put in place everywhere, someone could always just play the music and record it on another device, then post it to one of the Gnutella derivatives. "Copy protection on computers has been shown again and again to fail," conceded Dan Farmer, the record-industry consultant Patel used to supervise Napster's compliance efforts. "Napster has shown two things: that people don't give a rat's ass about the quality of the sound when compared to the availability and that the avarice of consumers is not bounded by sound ethical reasoning." Other industries began worrying that they were next to be Napsterized. But many were frozen in the headlights, unable to decide between taking something like the record industry's failed hardline stance and offering something small that might keep a lid on the willingness of consumers to cheat. "We're the canaries in the coal mine," warned EMI's Jay Samit.

* * *

WITH THE OLD, UNRESTRAINED NAPSTER gone, it made sense for the labels to help a new, legitimate service arise in its place. And the tone of the negotiations with the labels improved considerably with Barry's departure as CEO. But he and Hummer still had two of the four board seats, and they weren't helping to get a deal. In September 2001, Bertelsmann eCommerce CFO Bill Sorenson wrote to his boss Andreas Schmidt, complaining that Barry and Hummer were wasting Bertelsmann AG's investment. "They have done nothing to forward the business plan. They have successfully alienated the entire recording industry . . . they have failed repeatedly to deliver the project on time," Sorensen wrote. "They have wasted millions upon millions of dollars (BAG's dollars) in pursuing a strategy of litigation, litigation, litigation." Schmidt resigned in November as his eCommerce Group was merged into the Direct Group, which includes book and record clubs and electronic retailer CDNow. The Direct Group adopted responsibility for the Napster effort.

But Hilbers made progress with two of the more peace-minded labels. "By the end of this third quarter in 2001, we had two settlement and licensing deals on the table ready to be signed by AOL and EMI," Hilbers said. The deal with AOL called for $20 million in settlement money, $5 million in an immediate advertising purchase, and $20 million in future advertising. Of course, it would take Bertelsmann's money to make it happen, and Hilbers passed up word of the pacts. "Thomas Middelhoff was in favor of the deal," Hilbers said. But "he did not convince his fellow board members to give us the money." The board wanted all of the majors at once. They said, "We are not going to invest now a substantial amount of money in Napster, exercise our warrant, and then find [our]selves in litigation with Universal, Sony, and BMG," Hilbers said.

AOL, whose quest for end-of-quarter ad revenue by any means would soon land it in trouble with regulators, took the board-level reversal especially hard. "AOL is really pissed," Hilbers wrote to Middelhoff. "They backed out of the RIAA negotiation and now we took the deal off the table." It took a call from Middelhoff to AOL executive Richard Parsons to smooth things over.

The industry rebuffed Hilbers's request for a moratorium in the legal fight, wanting to close the door by winning the case against Napster in a motion for summary judgment. Given Patel's previous rulings, it seemed like a sure thing. And it would have been, were it not for the record industry's one big mistake. In forming MusicNet and Pressplay, the labels had acted very much in concert. Napster general counsel Jonathan Schwartz, a Barry recruit and a former Justice Department official, raised the last-ditch defense that since copyright law calls for a balance between the rights holders and the public, a cartel should not be allowed to set the terms by which the public will get access—that would amount to copyright misuse and a violation of public policy. For an industry already subject to antitrust accusations, the joint ventures were less than smart, and Patel let them know it. In an October 2001 hearing on the industry's request for summary judgment, a day that could well have been Napster's end, she instead took the industry to task for the joint ventures. "I'm really curious about how the plaintiffs in this came upon the idea," Patel said. "Even if it passes antitrust tests, it still looks bad, sounds bad, and smells bad." Patel put off ruling on summary judgment to allow yet another set of Napster lawyers to seek industry documents on the joint ventures. By the time she made that decision, the Justice Department said it would investigate the industry's practices as well.

Patel's unexpected reservations about the industry's conduct gave the labels more incentive to compromise.

And Napster had one more card to play—the threat of bankruptcy, which would likely leave the record labels with nothing, while Bertelsmann stood to walk away with the technology. Renewed talks between Hilbers and the RIAA picked up steam, and a consensus emerged around Christmas. The bottom line had a large number of zeroes: Bertelsmann would pay $250 million to resolve the claims in the suit. "The numbers were high but realistic," Hilbers said. The negotiations seemed so promising that both sides asked Patel to delay proceedings in the case, and at least one record company announced to its affiliates that a deal was at hand. In January, Hilbers sent a proposal to Bertelsmann based on the proposed $250 million settlement with the major labels. Like the aborted AOL-EMI deal, the resolution would have allowed Bertelsmann to convert its warrants and take full control of Napster. Hilbers sought an additional $85 million to finance the revised Napster service. Bertelsmann's Direct Group backed the idea. But the world had changed. "The bubble had burst already, but it had gotten worse since then, with the recession and September 11," Hilbers said. "Everything contributed to people being more cautious. Napster was a very bold idea, and it took a lot of money." Middelhoff's adventure had already proved more costly and more difficult than Bertelsmann's board had anticipated. Above Hilbers's head, Bertelsmann demanded more: a guarantee of future licenses with more content. "We noticed it was only a limited catalog of seventy thousand titles, but the consumer is asking for hundreds of thousands," Middelhoff said. "And we don't want to have licenses only for personal computers— we want portability" for MP3 players like the Rio.

"Bertelsmann in the end turned my proposal down," Hilbers said. Bertelsmann told Hilbers he could keep trying for more complete licenses, but he knew it was hopeless: he would never get what they wanted. "With that, this whole strategy fell apart."

The second reversal undercut Hilbers's credibility at the bargaining table. "Clearly Konrad was not speaking with any authority, and the rules seemed to be changing," a top record-industry executive said. The talks never regained momentum, due mainly to inattention on Napster's part. "It was like someone let the air out of their balloon," another record executive said. Hilbers remained outwardly optimistic. "I put together a model of what Napster needs," Hilbers said then. "We need to convince [the labels] that MusicNet and Pressplay didn't work. I think we are close." But in March 2002, Hilbers acknowledged that Napster had at least temporarily walked away from work on a deal. He stressed then that Napster had time: Patel had recently allowed Napster nine more months to obtain documents about the labels' alleged misuse of their copyrights, putting off the possibility of summary judgment until 2003. Yet with every month that passed, the rival pirate services got bigger, while the only thing getting bigger at dormant Napster was the red ink. Soon, the labels learned why Napster had suddenly grown too preoccupied to negotiate.

12

the coup

NAPSTER CEO KONRAD HILBERS HAD ABANDONED TALKS WITH
the record labels for a good reason. In Germany, Thomas Middelhoff had
decided that the time had come for Bertelsmann to make its own move.
Desperate for cash, Napster had begun laying off staff in the spring of
2002 and returned to the publisher asking for still more money. Seeing
Napster's weak bargaining position, Middelhoff suggested that Bertelsmann simply buy the company instead. He reasoned that Bertelsmann
would have a better chance of striking a deal with the other labels than
Napster would, since Napster appeared hamstrung by the Hummer Winblad directors. Before, Bertelsmann had exercised some control through
its ties to former employee Hilbers, two previous loans totaling $85
million, and the warrants that entitled it to claim a majority stake. That
one-step remove from ownership provided an extra layer of protection in

the event that Napster lost the court case. But since Napster wasn't operational, Bertelsmann began to feel that it would have no liability even if Napster were hit with a massive judgment. For a modest amount of money, Middelhoff thought, he could buy the remainder of Napster outright, eliminating the hard-line directors and positioning Bertelsmann to get all the benefits if it could work out a deal.

Bertelsmann's board members, looking ahead to a planned Bertelsmann IPO, were nervous about the figures bandied about in the lawsuit. The most recent settlement talks had called for hundreds of millions of dollars to change hands. "Some of the board is scared by the amounts," one person in the acquisition talks said. And the directors reminded Middelhoff that he had missed earlier deadlines for the birth of a new Napster. But Middelhoff stuck to his vision. He thought that even if the profits of a legitimate Napster from music distribution were small—even if no major-label settlement were ever reached—the same secure technology could be used to circulate all the content produced by Bertelsmann, including music and magazines. "It's a perfect flag in the ground to become a major distributor of media objects," Hilbers said.

Morpheus and the other pirate services might have more users and more content, but because they were so decentralized, they couldn't easily convert to a system with central control, Hilbers argued. And without central control, they couldn't have consistent search quality and legitimate rights management. The new Napster's 2002 beta test, which used twenty thousand volunteers, showed that the system worked. Bertelsmann had the content. And it could add its record club and other features to the new Napster, including links to its CDNow retailer.

So Middelhoff told Bertelsmann U.S. executive Joel Klein, the former Justice Department trustbuster, to open serious talks with Napster over an acquisition. That naturally included the Napster board, now made up of Hilbers, Hank Barry and John Hummer of Hummer Winblad, and John Fanning. Fanning had held onto his board seat when the venture firm invested but pledged to vote his shares according to the board's wishes in the event of a decision changing control of the company. Hummer Winblad had insisted on that proxy, knowing full well that he was unpredictable. But it would soon be clear that even letting him stay on the board was a mistake. Hummer Winblad would have done better to follow the lead of other venture-capital bidders who called for Fanning's complete removal.

With Hilbers's industrywide settlement shot down, Hummer Winblad was in a mood to sell. But the figures discussed were a far cry from what the venture firm had hoped Napster would bring. Instead of hundreds of millions of dollars, Bertelsmann was offering $15 million and would forgive the amount that Napster owed Bertelsmann. That offer was probably low enough by itself to enrage Fanning, never one to underestimate Napster's worth. But that was just the start of it.

Two years before, as the negotiations for Hummer Winblad's investment in Napster had dragged on and the stock market began sinking, the terms had been revised several times. In the end, Hummer Winblad won what is known as a liquidation preference in the contract. Not uncommon in venture deals, the clause meant that when a liquidation event occurred—be it a bankruptcy, an acquisition, or something more pleasant— Hummer and the smaller investors in that last Series C round would get 84 cents of every dollar received until the total reached $17.1 million, the amount everyone had invested over Napster's life. Unless they had sold shares privately, most investors who had got in early and cheaply would at least lose the benefit of those discounts. If Bertelsmann was going to pay only $15 million, Hummer would get the lion's share, and John Fanning, Shawn Fanning, Sean Parker, and Eileen Richardson would get nothing at all for their Series A Junior and common shares.

Bertelsmann had even raised the prospect of buying just Hummer Winblad's stake, an idea that confirmed to Fanning that Barry and John Hummer were looking out for themselves at the expense of the rest of Napster's shareholders, including loyal employees. (Bertelsmann Direct Group CFO Bill Sorenson testified later that the idea originated at Hummer Winblad, but Barry and another person in the talks denied that.) That discussion eventually led to the plan to buy all of Napster, according to Sorenson and the other party. "There was a series of back and forth relative to purchasing either Hummer Winblad's equity or all of the equity of Napster," Sorenson said. The very real possibility of being left with worthless paper instead of IPO riches made Shawn, who was a significant stockholder, and many other holders working for Napster very unhappy.

No one, of course, was as angry as John Fanning. He and his lawyers pored over all of the documents. Finally, they found what Fanning considered to be a sufficient loophole. As is typical with young companies, several series of stock issued by Napster had the right to convert into common shares if a majority of that class of stock agreed. The Series A Senior documents, however, appeared to have a strange twist. They said that if that class of stock wanted, it could convert not just its own shares but *everyone's* shares into common. Napster's management dismissed the wording as a careless error. No company, an ally said, would give that kind of power to one group of investors.

But it was enough for Fanning, who planned a lightning attack just as the Napster board prepared to weigh Bertelsmann's offer. Fortunately for him, the Series A Senior shares were controlled by one man—Yosi Amram. Amram, having a lot of money at stake, agreed to invoke the conversion clause. (Later, after Hummer Winblad threatened to sue him, he repudiated the conversion, saying that Fanning had pressured him to sign it before Amram left for a vacation in Brazil.) Converting Hummer Winblad's shares to common meant that its liquidation preference would evaporate, so that everything Napster took in from a sale would be divided evenly. The second phase of Fanning's scheme was to take control of the company. If Hummer Winblad no longer had special shares entitling it to name two of the company's directors, then all the other shareholders could vote them out and try their own negotiation with Bertelsmann.

So it was that the disgraced ex-chairman decided to see if he could round up a majority of all the newly common shares and vote Barry and John Hummer off the Napster board. Fanning tracked down Bill Bales in Georgia and called Richardson and other investors who were almost as stunned to hear his voice after a two-year gap as they were to hear what he had to say. Fanning proposed that they all sign documents supporting the replacement of the two Hummer Winblad directors with Amram and Martin Kay, the CEO of Fanning's NetCapital. Richardson's heart pounded at the idea: It was like a flashback to everything she had hated about Napster. But with a half-million dollars at stake, she figured that Fanning's far-fetched plan was her best shot.

One by one, other shareholders came to the same conclusion: Fanning's greed might for once work in their interest as well. He called both his nephew and Sean Parker and got their proxies. Parker had moved, then lost his lease and was staying at Shawn's house, and the two friends hashed through the possibilities until 5 A.M. Already angry that Barry would sell them out, they were incensed by a new rumor: that a key point in the negotiations was Barry's request for a clause from Bertelsmann protecting him and John Hummer from personal liability. Barry confirmed that personal indemnification was an issue in the talks, but he said he had reason to be nervous: Hilary Rosen had hinted that Hummer Winblad or its partners would be the next to be sued. Once, Barry told others, Rosen had warned him: "We know you have a nice house on Tasso Street, and we're looking forward to having it." (Rosen denied making so personal a threat.) As they counted votes the day before the Napster board would meet to vote on Bertelsmann's offer to end Napster's independence, Fanning and his allies figured they had a good chance.

One problem was Ron Conway at Angel Investors. As the value of his portfolio plummeted, the quick-dealing Conway had done the unthinkable and sworn off investing in new companies. Instead, he told his limited partners, he would dedicate himself to salvaging what could be salvaged. The glad-hander of old had been replaced by a new Conway, one who had already forced the liquidation of one Internet incubator. "I'm a mortician," he complained to one entrepreneur. Because one of Conway's multiple investments in Napster had come alongside Hummer Winblad's, he stood to get some of his money back however the millions were divided. Anything at all would exceed his expectations: A confidential year-end rundown of Angel Investors's portfolio, given to the fund's limited partners, had marked the Napster stock down to zero. Now Conway was afraid that the last-minute shenanigans would drive Bertelsmann away, leaving him and many others who had believed in the firm with nothing. Conway didn't expect good behavior from Fanning, but he fired off an angry e-mail to Amram, the professional who was supposed to know better. "I cannot believe that you are working with John Fanning when he has not invested a dollar in Napster and in fact has already profited from selling shares when you and I invested real money in this company," Conway wrote. (To be more precise, Fanning had invested a grand total of $7,000, according to statements in court.)

"BMG is offering us a gift and pretty soon BMG will get fed up and take the gift back!! Think about it, wouldn't you do the same thing if you were in their shoes!"

Parker volunteered to try for Conway's support and drove to see him at San Francisco's Fairmont Hotel on the eve of the crucial board meeting. Caught in traffic on U.S. 101 coming north into San Francisco, Parker dialed and redialed Conway's cell phone from the car, not realizing that Conway was on the phone with Shawn. When he finally got through, Parker told Conway that he had done some rough calculating and figured that Angel Investors stood to gain or lose only about $100,000 if Fanning's ploy worked, everyone's shares turned into common, and the $15 million went to all holders equally. "The only way I come out ahead is if the coup wins," Parker implored Conway. "I don't want anything to do with a coup," Conway said.

Parker finally reached the Fairmont, on top of the city's old-money Nob Hill neighborhood, and walked inside to meet Conway in the lobby bar. Conway was dressed in his usual casual style, with a shiny green jacket over a polo shirt. As expected, he continued to argue against a ninth-inning attack on the board. But as he turned the tables and argued that Parker should cast his votes against the insurrection, an idea struck Parker. He knew the math was close. But why was Conway fighting so hard, when it was clearly in Parker's interest to back the coup? It dawned on Parker that he and another shareholder he knew, Freeloader cofounder Mark Pincus, had the swing votes, that without them the coup would fail. And, he said, "Conway convinced me that Fanning was going to screw everything up. So I thought, let's use the fact that he's going to screw it up to our advantage." Parker walked outside into the blustery afternoon air and dialed Shawn on his phone, pacing back and forth. "Hey, I figured it out!" Parker told him. "I have enough votes!"

Parker believed he and Pincus, who had taken Napster shares in a swap of investment holdings with Amram, were now the key to the deal. He decided he could use his leverage either to force the upstart directors into office or, even better, to convince Hummer Winblad to fork over more of the kitty in exchange for betraying the coup. "Hummer's being greedy. Everyone's being greedy. We're all fighting over scraps," Parker said after hanging up with Shawn. "Is the coup actually going to happen?

Probably not. It's the threat that's the point." Sure enough, Shawn passed on the word that Hummer Winblad was willing to deal. Bertelsmann's offer would be tabled for the moment, and disaster staved off.

But John Fanning decided he had all the cards he needed and that Hummer Winblad wasn't going to turn generous unless forced. On March 25, as compromise proposals floated back and forth, Fanning filed a lawsuit in Delaware's Chancery Court, which hears many corporate-securities cases. The suit claimed that all the shares had been converted, that a majority of the now-common shares had voted to oust the Hummer Winblad directors and install Amram and Kay, and that the Napster board had refused to recognize the conversion as legitimate or seat the new directors. The suit named Barry and John Hummer as defendants. The two gave no comment to the press, but they and other loyalists were incensed. The suit asked for expedited review, citing an unspecified "offer to purchase the company." The *Los Angeles Times* promptly identified the offer as coming from Bertelsmann.

The suit did not go well for Fanning, especially after Amram withdrew his support. And Fanning didn't impress the judge in the case with his unique performance in a pretrial deposition. Under questioning, Fanning said he didn't recall anything of his talks with Amram about the plan to convert the Napster shares, let alone recall beseeching him to trigger the conversion. "Did you discuss with him what the effect of his conversion of his shares would be?" an attorney for the directors asked. "I don't know," Fanning replied. "You don't remember?" "I don't have a specific recollection of a discussion that I would characterize in that way," Fanning said. "How *would* you characterize your discussions with Mr. Amram on the subject of converting his Series A preferred stock?" "I'm sorry, how would I characterize them?" Fanning asked. "Yes," the lawyer said. "I wouldn't characterize them."

The memory lapse might have strained belief by itself, but Fanning didn't help his cause when he refused to give such basic information as what he did for a living between his stint at Fidelity and the creation of Napster, or even how he was making money at the moment.

"Do you have any income?" one of the opposing lawyers asked.

"How do you define income?"

"Do you have any source of income from anything whatsoever?"

"Again, how do you define income?"

"Does anybody pay you money for anything?"

"People pay me money, yes."

"For what?"

"You'd have to be more specific."

"No. I want you to answer my question. What do people pay you money for?"

After Fanning's lawyer objected, Fanning responded: "That's too broad a question."

"How do you earn your living?"

Fanning paused. "I consider that to be overly broad. I do work as a director of Napster, I'm the largest individual shareholder, and I was the founding chairman and CEO."

Fanning said he didn't know if he was still chairman of Napster and that he couldn't say which other companies he was currently a director of without refreshing his recollection. When the Napster directors complained to the judge, William Chandler, that Fanning had wasted their time, the judge agreed. Chandler ordered Fanning to sit for another deposition, answer the questions, and pay what came to $14,503 in fees for the opposing lawyers' time.

Bertelsmann didn't want to get in the middle of the firefight, and it urged the two sides to resolve their differences. Among other things, it demanded a unanimous Napster board vote and 90 percent shareholder approval. At first, Barry refused to cut any such deal with Fanning. "We don't negotiate with terrorists," he told others at Napster. But a bargain was reached in April 2002 that would give Fanning and the other early Series A Junior holders $2.4 million, while the rest of the investors split $14.1 million. All that remained was to seal the deal with Bertelsmann.

Surprisingly, even with the total $16.5 million price established and a truce in Delaware, the talks with Bertelsmann dragged on. According to people briefed on the negotiations, the stumbling block was whether Barry and John Hummer could wheedle enough protection out of Bertelsmann in the event that the record companies sued them personally. First, Barry and Hummer asked that Bertelsmann promise that if it settled with the record labels, the settlement would include pledges that the labels wouldn't sue directors and investors or that Bertelsmann would cover the first $10 million in any damages against them. Bertelsmann agreed. Second, they asked that if Bertelsmann and the labels settled during a bankruptcy reorganization, the group would get included in any similar releases from liability. Again, Bertelsmann agreed. Finally, Barry and Hummer asked that if Napster went into bankruptcy, came out the other side, and then won music-distribution licenses from the major labels, those licenses would include the personal-liability releases. That last demand was too much for the German company, according to someone on the Napster side of the talks. "They finally said, '*Basta!* [Enough!],'" the person said. Barry recalled the breakdown differently, blaming it on Bertelsmann. But Napster executives said the more fundamental problem was that Barry had difficulty accepting that Hummer Winblad would have little remaining stake in Napster when it was all over. "Hank was upset that Bertelsmann wanted them gone," one executive said.

Soon the deadline on Bertelsmann's offer expired, and it withdrew the deal, just as Conway had feared. It was like all the other negotiating experiences that Bertelsmann and the labels had with Napster before, only worse and over less. "From the beginning, it was really tough to negotiate with the Napster team," Middelhoff said. "Sometimes they changed their minds; sometimes they had different camps on their side. They continued to believe Napster had a tremendous upside and tremendous potential market capitalization."

<hr>

AFTER THE TALKS FOR AN equity deal collapsed and Fanning's lawsuit continued, Bertelsmann made a surprise, last-ditch proposal on May 3 to at least buy Napster's assets through a planned Chapter 11 bankruptcy reorganization. The creditors would get $5 million and the shareholders would get nothing, but the technology, the brand, and the employees would stay together, and Napster could escape Chapter 7 bankruptcy liquidation. As long as talks on that plan made progress, Bertelsmann promised to put in the first new money in six months, a desperately needed $50,000 per day to meet the payroll. Barry and Hummer asked questions and expressed little enthusiasm about the asset sale: They would get nothing from the deal, and they questioned Hilbers's loyalty. But they allowed Hilbers and Napster general counsel Jonathan Schwartz to keep trying, and the pair presented a finished deal document for the board to vote up or down on Friday, May 10, with the expiration on the offer three days away. Barry and Hummer hemmed and hawed, objecting that they wanted to see how Fanning's legal case played out and that they wanted to reserve Napster's right to sue BMG, along with the other record labels, on antitrust grounds.

As it became increasingly clear that the board would not meet to vote on the offer before it expired, Schwartz wrote a long e-mail on Saturday to Barry, Hummer, and Hilbers, warning them that they were coming close to breaching their fiduciary duty to get as much as possible for Napster's creditors. "Given that the company is faced with the most severe financial constraints imaginable, I do not believe that, consistent with its fiduciary duties, the board can simply reject the asset purchase agreement—either by affirmatively deciding to reject it or by not acting on it by the Monday expiration date," Schwartz wrote. "The company is insolvent."

Barry and Hummer responded that they would stick with their plan—no action by Monday, then a meeting of shareholders and creditors to discuss it later in the week. "Let's move forward with that process as the board directed," Barry wrote. And they didn't respond to Schwartz's increasingly desperate pleas that they spell out any remaining demands for him to take to Bertelsmann. Hilbers then weighed in, backing Napster's top lawyer and threatening to resign. "This is not a game," he wrote to the Hummer Winblad directors. "I am not going to abandon this buyout deal for no obvious reason and then move forward with layoffs and a road towards Chapter 7." For good measure, Napster's outside bankruptcy lawyer, Rick Cieri, the head of that practice at big firm Jones, Day, Reavis & Pogue, e-mailed an echo of Schwartz's warning about fiduciary duty.

The escalating disillusionment with Napster's leadership, which began among millions of fans who realized the game was all about money, then spread to once-supportive musicians and even to early Napster employees, was now complete. The company couldn't even keep its own CEO and general counsel on the reservation. But Barry and Hummer stood firm. There was no board vote by Monday, and Middelhoff cut off Napster's funding that day as layoffs and bankruptcy neared.

——— ———

THE NEXT DAY, TUESDAY, May 14, 2002, everything happened at once. Fanning, Barry, and Hummer were all in Wilmington, Delaware, for an anticipated three-day trial on Fanning's lawsuit against his fellow directors. In Redwood City, Hilbers knew that layoffs were inevitable. Just past 9 A.M., he announced his resignation in an e-mail to the staff. "We have put together what I consider to be a valid and beneficial deal for Napster over the last weeks. This deal would have allowed [*sic*] to keep the company's assets, including its employees, together in the long term. Unfortunately, the board has chosen not to pursue the deal. I am not agreeing with the majority of the board," Hilbers wrote. An hour later and on the other side of the continent, the Delaware judge dismissed Fanning's suit without bothering to hear from any witnesses, ruling that the company's incorporation papers made it obvious that no one class of stock could convert everyone's shares.

Just before noon, Barry called the Napster office and was placed on a speakerphone as the staffers gathered for what they knew was coming. Barry said the company couldn't meet the payroll, and each of the seventy employees had a choice: get laid off or take a week of unpaid vacation in the hope that he could resurrect a deal. Few agreed to the vacation. As they milled around after the call ended, executive after executive resigned rather than wait for the bankruptcy liquidation that would come. "It was awful. People were glad to get out of there," one said. "Everyone thought John Fanning was a fuck and what he was doing was stupid and greedy, but in the end it was really an anti-Hank sentiment." Schwartz quit, as did Milt Olin, the top operating officer and old friend of Barry. Shawn wavered. Then he resigned, too, organizing a trip that night to a San Francisco dive bar in the Mission District to toast Hilbers's efforts.

The resignations were a last demonstration of rage at Hummer Winblad. "They lost the game of chicken," Conway said that night. "The bickering of Yosi [Amram] and John Fanning versus John Hummer and Hank Barry is what caused the shareholders not to get their money back in March. Now the continued bickering between John Hummer and

Hank Barry with Bertelsmann, in refusing to approve the purchase, is causing seventy people to lose their jobs." Shawn was disgusted, too. Not only did Barry and Hummer decide to play chicken, he complained to a friend, they decided to play chicken with a Mack truck. Parker was even more blunt: "When parasites kill their hosts, they die as well," he said.

But there was still one more emergency backup plan for the system Shawn had hatched in his dorm room. "A cat has nine lives," Hilbers had said in his farewell e-mail. The bankruptcy filing would wipe out Napster's legal liability and Hummer Winblad's control, along with its investors' equity. And then Bertelsmann, as the largest creditor, would be first in line to buy the assets. Middelhoff planned to rehire Shawn, Hilbers, and forty more.

In the harsh media glare from the resignations and investor criticism, Barry went back to the office and called Bertelsmann's Joel Klein. After getting the bid up to $8 million for Napster's creditors, he agreed to the Chapter 11 sale. There were no promises of releases from personal liability. The two companies announced the deal on Friday, May 17. "We believe in the future of peer-to-peer," Middelhoff said. "This is not the end. This is the beginning of a new Napster. If this is the only way to get it done, this is how we get it done. If it takes two or three months, so what." Middelhoff said Bertelsmann would launch "a legitimate peer-to-peer service, either with the brand and the technology of Napster or not."

Barry and Hummer resigned from the board. At Bertelsmann's direction, Napster rehired its leaders, keeping a skeleton staff of eighteen from among what had been more than one hundred employees. Hilbers rejoined as CEO and the sole director. On June 3, Napster filed for Chapter 11 bankruptcy in Delaware, reporting that as of April 30, it had $7.9 million in assets and $101 million in liabilities, not counting what it might owe the record labels. The list of creditors ran in three small-print columns for fifty-nine pages, from A-A Lock and Alarm to ZZ Top. Standing out among the technical suppliers, employees, and restaurants was David Boies's law firm, owed more than $2 million. Bertelsmann was due $91 million. Napster assumed that Bertelsmann's pledge for $8 million more, for an ostensible value of $99 million, would top any competing bids for its assets.

Other technology companies by then had released secure peer-to-peer systems similar to the envisioned new Napster, including the refurbished Scour.com, without drawing many users. (They also lacked major-label content, while the new Napster would have at least BMG.) And since pirate systems housed offshore were well ahead in popularity, some questioned whether a legitimized Napster was worth even $8 million.

"Free music created Napster," Ritter said, "and free music will kill it."

But now released from both his uncle and Hank Barry, Shawn was betting on someone he saw as a kindred spirit: Thomas Middelhoff. He would have to wait through the slow-moving bankruptcy process, but at the other side would be a boss who wasn't a walking disaster. Middelhoff did more than get the technology, as Shawn put it. He showed real courage.

And Shawn and Middelhoff had a secret plan. By then the two realized they weren't likely to get licenses from the other labels at a price that would allow them to offer Napster at a low cost to consumers. Instead, Middelhoff was planning to bet big on Napster's new technology. Even though the company had failed to meet the federal judge's deadline for a version that screened out unauthorized songs, Napster still had made dramatic progress. Over the objection of some of his advisers, Middelhoff was preparing to take a giant legal risk—that the system was so good that he could get away with letting consumers offer any songs they wanted, just like in the early days, as long as it got through a filter comparing the music to a database of copyright-protected songs.

If a record company complained that an unapproved song had gotten through, Bertelsmann's Napster would simply remove it—even though it already might have been downloaded by others. Given Napster's history in court, it was a virtual certainty that when such a song got onto the system, the copyright owner would not just ask nicely for it to be pulled. The offended party would sue the company all over again, and this time Bertelsmann's money would be at stake.

Middelhoff was convinced that the Napster acquisition would make good on his pledge to turn BMG into the top music company on the planet, and he intended to spread the technology to books and videos as well. But as the summer of 2002 rolled around, the time for such grand visions was fading. The AOL Time Warner merger had proved a disaster, and AOL shares had fallen 70 percent. First AOL chief operating officer

Gerald Levin, then co-CEO Bob Pittman, resigned. Then the board of Vivendi Universal, a French water company that had swallowed Edgar Bronfman's Universal music and movie company, grew sick of CEO Jean-Marie Messier's overreaching ambition and fired him as well. The old guards were everywhere resurgent.

At Bertelsmann, Middelhoff had been pushing a historically conservative company in more and more new directions, many of them via more than $5 billion in acquisitions. Bertelsmann, thanks to Middelhoff the world's fifth-largest media company, was used to treating its various holdings as independent firms responsible for generating profit. Middelhoff was centralizing, planning to sell off traditional holdings, and willing to make quick gambles. And now he was pressing for the controlling Mohn family to give up more of its stake than it wanted in Bertelsmann's planned initial public stock offering. The Mohn family didn't like where he was going, and Napster was one of the most obvious problems they had: They didn't see how it could make any money.

After a six-week buildup in tensions, the Bertelsmann board dismissed Middelhoff at the end of July. His replacement was fifty-nine-year-old Gunther Thielen, a twenty-year veteran from Bertelsmann's printing arm, the company's oldest. Thielen ordered a review of the company's businesses and planned to reduce Bertelsmann's debts, focus on profitability, and withdraw from some of its Internet sales efforts.

None of that sounded good for Napster, and Konrad Hilbers quickly grew nervous. With Napster champion Middelhoff gone, "that left me with Joel Klein as the most prominent and highest-ranking contact partner at Bertelsmann. Then two or three days later Joel Klein was leaving, which left me with Klaus Eierhoff, the head of the Direct Group. Then a week later, Klaus Eierhoff was leaving," Hilbers complained. As the press began predicting that Bertelsmann would no longer want anything to do with Napster, Hilbers called Eierhoff's successor and was told to wait and see.

It was still better to have a reluctant buyer than no buyer at all, which is what Hilbers and Shawn feared would be the case if the Bertelsmann deal didn't go through. Bertelsmann was contractually obligated to consummate the purchase—if what had grown to a $9 million cash outlay was approved by Delaware U.S. bankruptcy judge Peter Walsh by the

September 3 deadline. The record labels and the music publishers fought the deal and won access to Napster and Bertelsmann documents and the right to conduct depositions of Hilbers, Lyn Jensen, and Bertelsmann's Bill Sorenson.

The music companies argued that Bertelsmann hadn't acted like a regular lender when it first gave Napster money, but as a disguised equity investor. In bankruptcy law, the distinction is critical. If Bertelsmann was really a secured lender, than it could count its $85 million in loans and have a giant head start on any other bidder for Napster's remains. If it was an equity investor, then the value of its holdings would be virtually wiped out alongside those of Hummer Winblad and the Fannings, and everyone would start from the same place in the bidding.

The allegations were somewhat unusual, and Napster accused the labels of vindictively trying to destroy what was left of the crippled company. Few expected the music industry's arguments to sway the judge. But once discovery got under way, the industry's lawyers turned up a raft of evidence that Bertelsmann's relationship with Napster was far different from that of a normal creditor. To begin with, Jensen testified that she couldn't get a bank loan at any interest rate before Bertelsmann stepped in. Bertelsmann not only made a massive loan, they did it at the remarkably low rate of 6.1 percent—more than three percentage points below the prime rate. And when Napster failed to make its payment, Bertelsmann did nothing more than send a letter complaining. The evidence also showed that Bertelsmann was thinking from the beginning that a bankruptcy would turn its low-risk loan into ownership.

More seriously, there was the matter of management control. Hilbers may have acted to the outside world like an independent thinker, but his e-mail was littered with direct orders from Middelhoff, his former boss, who had given Hilbers permission to take the Napster job in the first place. Then there were the internal documents, especially the Middelhoff memo from 2000, suggesting Bertelsmann knew that Napster users were breaking the law. And despite the claims that the $60 million in initial funding was going toward the development of a legally sound system, Bertelsmann executive Bill Sorenson conceded in his deposition that much of it was used for regular operating expenses during the eight months that the old Napster was around. Not only that, but Bertelsmann executives had written that they should keep the old service open so that they had the biggest potential audience when the system converted to a legitimate structure.

"Bertelsmann knew the money was being used to continue to run the infringing service until the legal service could be developed," music publishers' lawyer Andrew Rosenberg argued at a showdown hearing that began before the Labor Day weekend and concluded on the very day of Bertelsmann's deadline. Speaking for some of the record labels, attorney David Stratton went even further: Bertelsmann had such control of Napster, he said, that the labels were considering suing Bertelsmann itself. "This is not just about the bankruptcy. Bertelsmann has some real exposure here," said a third attorney familiar with the labels' thinking. Record executives confided that they were indeed weighing a suit, and lawyers in the case said it was more likely than not. The case would be similar to the never-completed claim against Napster, that it knew about the infringement and had contributed to it. The prospect made Bertelsmann's new leadership nervous: a now-wasted $85 million was bad; a potential billion-dollar liability was a whole new ball game. The other labels' three-year quest to find someone to pay for the Napster piracy might end with one of their own kind.

Judge Walsh assumed that if he ruled against the asset sale, Napster would be liquidated, with less money going to the creditors than they would have gotten from Bertelsmann. But the facts were so egregious that he had no choice. There were a number of sufficient grounds to rule as he did, Walsh said, but he cited just one—that Napster hadn't met its burden of showing that its negotiations with Bertelsmann had been at arm's length and in good faith. "It seems abundantly clear that Mr. Hilbers had one foot in the Napster camp and one foot in the Bertelsmann camp, and was so fundamentally conflicted that I believe that the transaction was tainted," Walsh said from the bench. "His contacts with Bertelsmann, I think, are just so significant."

Hours after Walsh ruled against the Bertelsmann purchase, with no more interim financing available for the skeleton crew's salaries, Napster said it planned to liquidate. "Without the engineers who created it, Napster would have no value," Hilbers said. He fired everyone but Jensen and resigned. Shawn, Aydar, and the others cleared out their desks. "It's officially over," Aydar said. "We're picking up our last paychecks." Yet even now, the reports of Napster's demise were exaggerated. A committee of unsecured creditors, including David Boies's firm, had tried in August to drum up rival bidders against Bertelsmann. They had failed in part because of Bertelsmann's claimed $85 million head start. With that advantage gone, the creditors tried some more. This time, a dozen firms were interested. Walsh was impressed enough that he allowed Napster to avoid liquidation for four more weeks. Shawn Fanning tried to raise enough money to make his own bid, but fell short.

John Fanning told others that he had arranged for $10 million to fund another takeover effort. But rather than bid in the court-approved procedure and try to walk off with the technology and brand alone, Fanning thought he could take away something even more valuable—the right to sue other people on Napster's behalf. He gathered together his old allies from the spring coup attempt, asking the Series A and common shareholders to reelect him a director of Napster. Since no one else was still on the Napster board, he planned to ask the judge for control, cut his own deal with the creditors, and sue Bertelsmann, Hummer Winblad, or both. (The gambit was an obvious long shot, since Napster's hands weren't clean.) Over the last weekend in September, just before the bankruptcy judge was to appoint a trustee to handle a sale to the top bidder, he came within a few votes and sent an angry e-mail to those who hadn't given their consent. "Needless to say, after raising 200k in DIP [debtor-in-possession] financing, 1 million in Bridge Financing, and 10 million in permanent financing in order to turn Napster Inc. around and not getting the opportunity to do just that, I am disappointed in the failure and inability of this group of shareholders to act, in what would otherwise seem clearly to be there [sic] own best interests. John."

Judge Walsh appointed an impartial trustee to dispose of Napster's assets, and the trustee began negotiating with the top bidder for Napster's brand, technology, and website. In November 2002, that bidder was revealed as Roxio Inc., which was offering $5 million in cash, $200,000 in temporary financing, and warrants for 100,000 Roxio shares. A Silicon Valley spinoff of data storage firm Adaptec Inc., Roxio made the leading software for creating CDs from MP3s or encrypted digital music files. Roxio code shipped inside tens of millions of Microsoft-based PCs, and it came with the Pressplay online service from the major record labels. Roxio CEO Chris Gorog, a former Disney and Universal Studios executive, wasn't sure what he would do with Napster. Roxio had good relations with the record industry, but it had warned in an SEC filing that if free digital music declined under legal pressure, sales of its software could fall. The biggest factor behind Roxio's bid was the recent moves by the labels to make more content available online and allow more of it to be burned to CDs. The biggest questions were whether the second-generation Napster system could be made to distribute songs with restrictions on their use, if the labels would license content that way, and if consumers would accept whatever the resulting terms were.

But the value of the brand alone was still "absolutely monstrous" nearly eighteen months after Napster's shutdown, Gorog said. In one study by Roxio, 97 percent of those surveyed had heard of Napster, more than Yahoo or Amazon. Gorog thought he could start with a client-server Napster, reviving the site in a far smaller and more controlled way, while continuing to analyze the peer-to-peer Napster II. If everything went right, Roxio would find the middle road that had eluded everyone else, satisfying both the labels and consumers. The night before he announced Roxio's intentions, Gorog sought validation from the ultimate proxy for the public's desires, reaching Shawn Fanning on his cell phone. If a now independent Shawn still wanted "free music for the people," as Judge Patel had put it, there would be no deal with the generational icon. If Shawn's remaining vision was about the "celestial jukebox," where virtually everything was available for a modest fee, than anything was possible. "One teenager not only revolutionized the way music will be distributed, but also movies and the spoken word," Gorog said. "Whatever we do will flow from that philosophy." Both sides came away impressed by the phone call and a follow-up visit to Roxio's Santa Clara headquarters, and Shawn promised to think about helping Roxio. "I'd be very surprised if this didn't result in a very positive relationship," Gorog said. "He's a brilliant kid, obviously, but I was very impressed with his speech—he's a pretty sophisticated guy. He's learned the ways of the world much faster than he intended to."

In court, John Fanning tried to stop the sale to Roxio, and his lawyers argued in a filing that their client was the "reputed owner" of some of the assets at stake, including the unused Napster.net domain name and Napster's cat-head logo. Two days before the final hearing, Fanning filed his own, more emphatic objection, one that no lawyer signed. In it, he said that he had never transferred the ownership of Napster.net or even Napster.com to the company when he incorporated Napster Inc. in 1999 and that he "never received any consideration from Napster in return for the purported assignment of his property interests in the intellectual property." Fanning also maintained that he had never signed an asset-transfer agreement to secure Hummer Winblad's investment the following year. Instead, he asserted, an older signature page had been substituted without his approval. "Mr. Fanning remains the rightful owner of the domain names," he wrote. Since Napster's trustee couldn't prove the company owned the assets in question, Fanning argued, the court couldn't very well sell them off.

At the November 27 hearing five days after Shawn turned twenty-two, Fanning didn't appear in court to testify in support of his claims, instead sending in another new lawyer. An unimpressed Judge Walsh overruled Fanning's objection and approved the sale to Roxio. Later that afternoon, the deal closed. The Napster technology went off to an uncertain future, and Napster the company belonged to history.

Epilogue:
After the Revolution

FROM THE TIME OF THE BANKRUPTCY FILING, EVEN SHAWN
Fanning suspected that Napster could never again be what it was. Napster
had begotten Gnutella. Gnutella had begotten Kazaa, and Grokster, and
MusicCity, an interlocking network of decentralized peer-to-peer file-
sharing systems. By 2002 those services were almost as easy to use as
Napster was, had as many users as Napster did at its peak, and were far
harder to shut down, though the record and movie industries were trying
through a lawsuit in Los Angeles. Because many countries didn't recognize the concept of contributory copyright infringement, Kazaa and its
ilk looked unstoppable, even with the Napster precedent. Once tapped
into one of those systems, users could trade not only music but also
movies, pirated software, and almost anything else digital. The systems
had their drawbacks as well. Some distributed invasive pop-up ads and
viruses. And their users were not just college kids looking for music. The
website GnutellaMeter, which tracks search terms on that network in
fifty-minute intervals, reported that the top thirty terms in one sweep
included valuable software Windows XP and Office XP; new movies
Harry Potter and *American Pie 2;* and the discomfiting porn terms
"Lolita," "rape," and "preteen." There wasn't a song title or rock-group
name in the bunch. More than 1.8 billion files were being transferred
monthly on the three biggest post-Gnutella networks, and Morpheus had
been downloaded 89 million times by May 2002.

MusicNet and Pressplay, the label-sponsored online music services, launched at the end of 2001 and included so many restrictions, including prohibitions on copying all but a handful of the files onto CDs, that they were quickly seen as failures: MusicNet attracted only forty thousand subscribers in its first four months. The major question was only whether their failure was accidental or deliberate, an empty gesture to Congress and the courts meant to show that the record industry was at least trying. Little by little, the labels offered more: Universal, in the biggest move, offered one thousand older albums in the unrestricted MP3 format through its subsidiary EMusic for as little as $10 a month. It said it would release far more through Liquid Audio, one of the many struggling firms that had obeyed the law but had been spurned by the big labels when they sought licenses. Other labels offered locked versions of a few songs over the pirate services, giving consumers an easy way to pay if they wanted to go legit.

But the labels also got nastier on other fronts. They seeded the unchecked pirate networks with fake MP3s from Eminem's latest CD, hoping to frustrate surfers to the point that they would open their wallets. And they hinted for the first time that they might sue consumers who posted the largest number of unauthorized tracks.

The record industry blamed the piracy explosion for a 5 percent fall in worldwide music sales during 2001, the worst drop-off since the introduction of the CD in 1983. Sales of blank CDs topped those of recorded CDs. And it was obvious that no amount of litigation would kill the hydra. "I fear we're getting into a game of Whack-a-Mole," one label executive said. In the nationally televised 2002 Grammy Awards, National Academy of Recording Arts and Sciences president Michael Greene took time out from the congratulations and gyrations to deliver a fiery condemnation of what he called "the most insidious virus" of unauthorized downloading. Greene called for a better effort to educate music fans about how they were hurting artists and stronger "leadership from Washington."

Greene's own efforts at leadership and education, which were met with scattered hoots amid the applause, could have been improved in their timing and attention to accuracy: His speech came immediately after he had bestowed a lifetime achievement award on bribe-taking disc jockey Alan Freed. And he trotted out three young people from back-stage, saying they were students who had managed to download nearly six thousand songs in two days from "easily accessible websites." It later emerged that one of the three was a technology professional, not a student, and that most of the songs had come directly from friends via instant messages. If those songs had come from purchased CDs, they might well have been sent legally. (Greene himself was forced to resign after the academy paid a reported $650,000 to head off a former executive's threatened sex-harassment suit.)

Allied with the more powerful and increasingly nervous movie industry, the record executives returned to Congress with their own demands. Before, Napster's army of users had helped the upstart get a warm reception on Capitol Hill, where Sen. Orrin Hatch had threatened the industry with legislation if it didn't open its digital vaults. As the courts discredited Napster and Hatch lost his committee chairmanship, nothing serious passed Congress. Now the momentum was reversing in a post-Napster backlash. As the threat to all manner of intellectual property rose, the entertainment companies experimented with new encryption techniques, including some that prevented legally purchased CDs from being ripped at all—even though ripping itself had been determined to be legal. Rep. Howard Berman of Los Angeles, a Democrat, went so far as to introduce a bill to allow entertainment companies to hack into consumer PCs and delete copyright-infringing files offered on peer-to-peer networks. Even if such a bill made it out of Congress, it was hard to see the wisdom of declaring war on hackers, instead of offering more cheap content to stimulate demand.

Soon came the spectacle of two of the country's most powerful industries, entertainment and technology, colliding head-on. Disney CEO Michael Eisner testified in Congress, attacking Silicon Valley for profiting from piracy-driven demand for better and faster machines and connections. "There are people in the tech industry," Eisner charged ominously, "who believe that piracy is the killer app for their business." Intel CEO Craig Barrett returned the fire, telling legislators that such restrictions on equipment would stifle innovation and prevent legitimate activity. "Peer-to-peer technologies constitute a basic functionality of the computing environment today," Barrett and Microsoft CEO Steve

Ballmer protested in a letter to entertainment CEOs that was also signed by the CEOs of IBM and Dell Computer Corp.

Sen. Fritz Hollings, a Democrat, introduced a bill that would force government-approved anticopying mechanisms on technology companies if they couldn't work out something amicable in the following eighteen months. The initial prospects for the bill and its ilk were poor, but the climate in Washington was clearly turning less hospitable for the technologists. The feud even slowed progress toward digital-television broadcasts, since the content side feared that copying would explode as broadband connections spread.

"Hollywood and Silicon Valley, it's like Israelis and Palestinians," said Napster director John Hummer. "The two groups will never see the world the same. It's a fight between content and distribution, and in the end I think distribution always wins." Now in a defensive posture, Silicon Valley tried to rally the public with such groups as DigitalConsumer.org, founded by Joe Kraus and Graham Spencer. The group's website proposed a technology consumer's Bill of Rights, which included the rights to fair use and to make copies for personal consumption on different machines. The site described Spencer and Kraus as cofounders of the Kleiner Perkins–backed Web portal Excite Inc. It didn't mention that they had also invested a combined $200,000 in Napster.

As the political balance of power shifted, the tech community divided against itself. Some looked for ways to cut the best deal with the enemy in Hollywood. Microsoft moved to the front, announcing plans to develop a new type of operating system, dubbed Palladium, that would keep content in a sort of secure vault. Secure, that is, from the computer's owner: "trusted third parties"—a movie studio, for instance—could agree to lend a video on condition that it get free rein to snoop inside and make sure everything there was paid for. (The industry already had a bot that searched for unauthorized movies, called Ranger.) The Berman bill would give entertainment companies virtual immunity for any legitimate content they damaged along the way. As hearings on the bill began, the music industry and its allies sponsored an ad campaign in which performers from Britney Spears to Luciano Pavarotti condemned file-sharing.

Digital-rights management efforts at Microsoft and elsewhere likewise devolved into a contest to give the most control to the entertainment companies. Listen to this song once, keep it for two days, and away it goes. Traditional fair use, such as making a copy of a purchased CD, was quietly heading for an early grave. Microsoft even slipped into its Media Player licensing terms the right to disable unapproved content or rival programs, such as peer-to-peer systems, on users' computers. Microsoft's monopoly power ensured that its restrictive Media Player would be widely adopted, but just to be on the safe side, exclusive songs by Peter Gabriel and Elvis Costello in the format forced downloaders to accept the new technology. "I was looking at their new innovation, and I was very much impressed," said Jack Valenti of the Motion Picture Association, after making his first visit to Microsoft's Redmond headquarters in August 2002.

With the benefit of having watching the Napster drama unfold and powerful allies in both Washington, D.C., and Washington State, the movie companies had a much better shot than the record labels at handling the crisis correctly. But they, too, were showing early signs of blowing it. They put little digitally protected content online and dictated new usage terms that were likely to annoy their customers. (In an echo of Napster's antirust claims against MusicNet and Pressplay, authorized online movie provider Intertainer Inc. sued three big studios for conspiring to drive it out of business after they set up a rival joint venture. And just like it had with the major labels' ventures, the Justice Department opened an antitrust investigation.) The pirate services, which learned the Napster lessons better, were providing an easy way to empower customers who chose to express their dissatisfaction. Because broadband connections are spreading slowly, the entertainment giants have a few years to get their answer right. In the meantime, their foot-dragging is giving people less incentive to pay for high-speed access, according to the U.S. Department of Commerce. And the broadband delay, concluded the Brookings Institution, is in turn costing the sputtering national economy an estimated $500 billion a year in lost gross domestic product.

— —

SILICON VALLEY REMAINED FULL of believers in peer-to-peer. The Napster revolution came late in the cycle of the Internet boom and continued even after the NASDAQ began shedding points almost as rapidly as it had gained them. Some experts even believed for a time that peer-to-peer technologies would be the savior of Net companies and their investors. That proved overly optimistic. But the Valley did invest in more than one hundred peer-to-peer start-ups, and such companies as IBM, Sun Microsystems, and Intel began researching and funding new efforts. The increased public awareness of the technology also helped bring attention to preexisting systems that basked in Napster's aura. The beneficiaries included attempts at what technologists called "distributed computing," the use of many small, individual processors to accomplish collectively what even supercomputers can't. Though the process was not necessarily peer-to-peer as most defined that term, the distributed-computing campaign gained momentum from the Napster phenomenon.

Perhaps the best-known instance of a wide public contribution to distributed computing was SETI@home, an offshoot of the long-running SETI project, the search for extraterrestrial intelligence. The project analyzes incoming signals from space, looking for patterns that might indicate other life. By early 2000, more than 1.6 million people in 224 countries had downloaded the program to crunch signal data on their PCs when their computers weren't otherwise in use. Other distributed-computing efforts allowed average computer users to volunteer their machines to help in cancer research and for a range of other charitable tasks.

Another recipient of Napster-fueled attention was FreeNet, a decentralized information-sharing system first described by Irishman Ian Clarke in a thesis completed in June 1999, when fewer than a thousand people knew about Napster. Clarke's goal was to defeat censorship by protecting anonymity. Some people used FreeNet for music, but it was optimized for text. Like Gnutella, FreeNet had no central index or control: Clarke said that even if someone held a gun to his head, there was no way he could disable the system. And Clarke's system avoided Gnutella's early problem with scaling to a massive size. While Gnutella forwarded requests for data to servers at random, which then forwarded those requests until traffic snarled, FreeNet's machines made educated guesses about which computers would be most responsive. Everyone who participated in the system was guaranteed anonymity in exchange for agreeing to store on his or her own computer whatever the system put there. By

2002, more than 1 million people had downloaded the FreeNet software, including dissidents in China. Clarke moved on to found a Santa Monica firm called Uprizer Inc., which hoped to use similar architecture to save companies money. The idea was that by distributing information throughout a big company's personal computers, the firm could cut down on expensive storage and server space. Intel and others invested $4 million.

Others that saw the benefits included the U.S. Army, where the technical director of the Simulation, Training, and Instrumentation Command realized that equipping soldiers with small machines that spoke to each other removed the danger of depending on a big server that was a central point of failure. "This is serious research," said the official, Michael Macedonia. "You don't want to put all your data on one server because once you take that server out, then you've got a lot of blind people with a lot of useless electronics."

In civilian life, the giants were moving, too, albeit slowly. Intel was among the fastest, moving its internal chip-development efforts and a training system to a peer-to-peer network that took advantage of unused computer time. In two years, the moves upped the rate of Intel's computer utilization from 50 percent to 90 percent, according to Chief Technology Officer Patrick Gelsinger, and saved Intel close to $1 billion. "Napster became a lightning rod, this uniformly sensible inflection point for the industry," Gelsinger said. "Peer-to-peer is to some degree a fad that labels a bigger and longer-term trend. Peer-to-peer, grid computing, and Web services are all part of a march toward distributed computing."

By late 2002, more than half of the employees who responded to a Comdex poll said their firms either were using peer-to-peer or planned to within a year. While the VC fever for peer-to-peer companies wore off in six months, real companies are saving real money with it. Drug firm GlaxoSmithKline uses Groove Networks Inc. to help employees collaborate on online documents. Big law firm Baker & McKenzie uses NextPage Inc. to skip most centralized repositories and speed the hunt for documents. The applications will keep changing, but their general use will increase over time until it becomes standard. "Peer-to-peer is not an invention. It's more of an approach," said Uprizer's Clarke, twenty-five. All the attention and money that followed Napster into the sector "created an opportunity for people with credible ideas to explore those ideas. We'll see which of those will bear fruit."

—— ——

Most of the original revolutionaries weren't around to see what followed them.

Eileen Richardson, the first of the Napster leaders to go, was exhausted and ready to move on in mid-2000, when Hummer Winblad came in. She wasn't prepared for what came next. Three months after her departure, on the heels of the preliminary injunction and its temporary stay, *Business Week* ran a long cover story on Napster that can most charitably be described as revisionist history. Largely reflecting the viewpoints of John Fanning and an unnamed former executive who sounds a lot like the terminated Bill Bales, the article made numerous errors. It said Sean Parker had "helped write" the beta version of Napster. It said that John Fanning had called Wilson Sonsini's Andrew Bridges about copyright law early on and that "those conversations" had given Fanning confidence in Napster's chances in court. In fact, Bridges had declined to represent Napster: He had only explained his arguments in the record-industry suit over the Rio portable MP3 player. For advice on Napster, Bridges had referred Fanning to another lawyer, who had referred Fanning to Seth Greenstein, of a lesser-known firm in Washington. *BusinessWeek* cited unnamed sources who reported that Richardson had been heard "screaming into the phone" at record-company executives, when in fact her only phone conversations had been with litigious RIAA officials.

Most devastating to Richardson's reputation was what passed in the article for expert opinion on what had gone wrong. It said she was "combative, inexperienced, and unable to develop a business model palatable to the record industry." It said Richardson had rejected venture-capital offers in 1999 and was able to secure funding only in May 2000, by implication because of Richardson's unexplained failure to articulate a business model. In fact, any plans about how to profit would have been pounced on by record-industry lawyers as proof of Napster's gain from illegal activity. John Fanning, on the other hand, was depicted as Napster's dedicated "chief business strategist," one whose only obvious error, besides relying on overoptimistic legal counsel, was picking the wrong person as CEO. The article failed to mention that Fanning had vetoed earlier potential CEOs alarmed at the size of his stake, driven away more substantive and larger venture offers, overruled many of Richardson's softer approaches to the industry, including the New Artist Program and the Gigabeat alliance, and generally been the one piloting Napster and his nephew into increasingly certain oblivion.

Worst of all was one simple, and false, declarative sentence: "Richardson declined to comment." She had never been reached to defend herself. The lead writer on the story had sent e-mail to her old company address, Eileen@napster.com, an inquiry that Richardson didn't receive. No reporter had bothered calling directory assistance for her home number in Palo Alto. To have her reputation savaged when she never had full control of the company was nearly more than Richardson could take. "To see the dream of these kids be undone by one greedy bastard, then have her reputation dragged through the mud, it was an unbelievable thing to have to go through," said Xtime's former CEO and current chairman, John Lee, who is still close to his former girlfriend. "If she could have given everything to the company and made no money, but had the kids be made whole, she would have done it in a heartbeat."

Richardson wrote an anguished e-mail to Amram that she never sent. "As much as I suspected one day I would be pegged as the scapegoat for Napster," she wrote, "I wasn't able to quit when I learned of all the problems at the company. I had said I'd get a job done, and by God I was going to do it. Also, there was no one to turn the company over to. Shawn, John Fanning, Bill Bales? After all the very reason I was CEO was because no one would back anyone else. . . . I know none of you have control over John Fanning and Bill Bales, so there is no blame to anyone at Napster at all. It is a situation I got myself in and there are consequences that I also now have to live with. My career may have ended this past weekend. . . . In my heart and soul I know I gave everything I had to help two bright-eyed, inexperienced teenagers get closer to their dream. And at the end of the day, this is all that matters really, to me anyway. I always said running Napster with all its press and lawsuits was dwarfed by the challenge of working with John Fanning."

Richardson took several months off to recuperate from Napster and the media attack. In late 2001, she reemerged with a Web-services start-up called Infravio Inc. Xtime was one of its first customers.

While still personally wealthy, the third original Napster director's business had taken a turn for the worse as well. Yosi Amram's ValiCert, which went public in July 2000 in a $40 million IPO, had seen its stock fall from more than $27 to less than 50 cents in the Internet downdraft. In 2001, ValiCert lost more than $28 million. It had enough current assets to last one more year; as 2002 drew to a close, Amram resigned.

Bill Bales's Flycode vanished altogether, and so did he. He and his girlfriend, Holly Shin, who had followed Bales from Napster to Flycode, were evicted from their San Mateo apartment in December 2001 for failing to pay their $2,000 monthly rent. Bales moved back to his home state of Georgia.

Jordan Ritter's first stop after Napster, private-financing system Round1, began to sputter, too. He left and founded a spam-filtering start-up called Cloudmark Inc., serving as its first CEO and successfully raising early funding. The firm's SpamNet peer-to-peer system relied on users to flag annoying e-mail as spam: If enough others voted the same way, the e-mail was blocked from reaching more subscribers. Still in beta, it had 173,000 participants by November 2002. Ritter and Jessie Garrehy planned to be married in February 2003.

Sean Parker may have been the hardest hit of all those who left. For six months, he remained obsessed with Napster, reliving the experience by writing a book proposal. Failing to sell the book, Parker consulted at Sun Microsystems and other companies, looking for a way to redeem himself. In 2001, he founded a company called Plaxo Inc. The next year, Plaxo released software that allows users to distribute contact information for themselves, building a mass network. Like Ritter, Parker worked on the project in a brutal financing environment. "Everything I did early on, I wouldn't have known to do were it not for the terrible things at Napster. You have to scrutinize every single hire. You have to have the right balance of power between the company and its investors," Parker said. "They say you learn the most from your mistakes, and Napster made every mistake in the book." He eventually won funding from Sequoia Capital Partners, a top Silicon Valley venture firm.

Better Sequoia Capital than Hummer Winblad: That firm was doing terribly, even by the washout standards of post-bust Sand Hill Road. Of the $318 million raised by Hummer for its fourth fund in 1999, $297 million had been invested by the end of 2001. The fund had realized only $5 million in gains and had $58 million left in residual value by then, according to InsiderVC.com publisher Steve Lisson. That jaw-dropping −80 percent return compared with +20 percent for a Sequoia fund, −20 percent for an Accel Partners fund, and −30 percent for a Foundation Capital fund all raised the same year. "Hummer IV is pure toxic waste," Lisson said.

━━ ━━

JOHN FANNING, ON THE OTHER HAND, accomplished a lot of what he had set out to do.

In the fall of 2000, he pitched investors in a bid to raise $50 million for new companies through his incubator, NetCapital, which was supporting the old online games firm and NetMovies, the video start-up. A draft of Fanning's presentation said that NetCapital was looking for peer-to-peer companies with viral marketing and that Napster showed NetCapital's "fundamentally value-driven approach." Napster did so well, the document crowed, because of how Shawn had been cynically marketed by the real powers at the company. "Creating a media-friendly 'Cinderella' story around a 19-year-old programmer and propagating a viral marketing strategy targeting early adopters allowed the business to grow very quickly with limited investment," it said. The presentation said that NetCapital's team, including founder and chairman John Fanning, CEO Martin Kay, and marketing chief Tom Carmody, were contributing their holdings to the portfolio. Among those holdings were $5.4 million worth of Napster stock, $300,000 worth of stock in AppleSoup (by then named Flycode), and $700,000 worth of stock in ON24.

By early 2001, NetCapital apparently had succeeded in raising $2 million, according to entertainment lawyer Howard Altholtz, who served briefly as a company vice president. Fanning's old habits still created problems, as Altholtz's experience showed. Fanning met Altholtz in mid-2000 and offered him a job as vice president for business and legal affairs. When Altholtz mentioned competing offers, he said, Fanning asked him,

"What will it take to get you to join NetCapital—does $250,000 sound right?" Altholtz negotiated a term sheet with Fanning and CEO Kay, and all three men signed it. In addition to the salary, the deal called for a $15,000 signing bonus and six months' severance pay if Altholtz were fired without cause, according to a copy of the term sheet.

The August day after Altholtz started work, Fanning met him on Nantasket Beach and handed him the $15,000—a check signed by Fanning's wife and drawn from a personal account. According to a breach-of-contract lawsuit Altholtz filed in January 2001, Fanning told him "that he had a lot of personal legal problems and that he wanted [Altholtz] to handle his personal legal matters." Fanning had reaped hundreds of thousands of dollars selling Napster shares. But in the collection cases that had gone to judgment, he owed at least $17,529 for credit-card lending by First USA Bank and $26,759 to Creditrust (though those creditors would have to refile the cases after Fanning objected that he had never been properly served).

Altholtz refused on the grounds that he had been hired to work as a business executive. He continued to work at NetCapital but never received any salary: According to the suit, Kay told Altholtz that he would be paid as soon as NetCapital won funding. After a month with no paycheck, Altholtz stopped work, demanded his six months' severance, and eventually filed suit. NetCapital claimed it had never made Altholtz a formal offer, and the case was settled for an undisclosed sum in 2002.

NetCapital and NetMovies are housed together behind grimy glass on an oceanfront street in Hull, sharing a block with restaurants that are closed except for weekends, closed except for summers, or just plain closed. Sitting nearby are an old carousel and an arcade from Hull's better days. NetCapital's front door stays locked during business hours, and employees there had ushered away people bearing legal papers. When I knocked in the spring of 2002 and introduced myself to Fanning, he shook his head, gave a half-smile, and shut the door without a word. A few days later, his public-relations woman called me. "He doesn't need a publicist," she said. "He needs a shrink."

If her opinion was based on Fanning's reluctance to follow social norms, she had more information than most of the public. The media had been timid, and Shawn had yet to fault his uncle for anything publicly.

Richardson also stayed quiet. The only negative press Fanning received by early 2003 were articles in the now-defunct *Industry Standard,* which Fanning threatened to sue for libel, and the *Los Angeles Times.* In August 2002, John Fanning fulfilled another long-held dream, to grace the cover of a business magazine. *Red Herring* trumpeted NetMovies' plan, by then one of many by technology firms, to distribute film content online—if it could get licenses from movie studios. The magazine bore the cover line "The Next Movie Mogul?" and said that Blockbuster Inc. had led a $4.8 million investment round in NetMovies, though the video-rental giant wouldn't divulge how much it had put in. The article said Fanning had "created" and "masterminded" Napster and was trying to shepherd a political solution to the music-licensing problem in his spare time. "This political activity could well be his greatest legacy," the story intoned.

The 1999-style hype notwithstanding, Fanning's firm needed more money than it had. Much of Fanning's Napster windfall had gone to pay lawyers, and NetCapital grew late in paying some bills, a creditor said. At least in part, Fanning blamed, of all people, Thomas Middelhoff, who Fanning believed would help NetMovies. "In July of 2001 we met to discuss partnering with us in the online movie deal with Blockbuster," Fanning reminded Middelhoff in an e-mail complaining that the then–CEO wasn't returning Fanning's calls. "[Eight] months later we are still having discussions and my relationship with Blockbuster has suffered because of it."

<hr>

SHAWN WAS LIVID WHEN THE *Red Herring* story came out. But even then, and even soon after, as Napster was at last melting down around him, he tried to tune out the drama. It was the one habit that most frustrated his longtime friends Parker and Ritter, all the way back to Shawn's acceptance of the 70/30 split. "John Fanning believes in the ascendancy of will," Parker said. "Shawn is the polar opposite. He thinks there's an angel on his shoulder, that everything will work out for the best. And this belief in the predestination of what was happening engendered passivity that paralyzed Napster."

But Shawn had changed in many ways, becoming more jaded about the business world and the motives and methods of the people running it. A healthy effect of that process was that he paid more attention to the rest of his life. He dated more. He actually took vacations. He looked after his teenage half brother, Raymond Verrier Jr., who had problems back on Cape Cod. Shawn had matured so much that his mother signed custody of the youngster over to him. And as another part of his new attention to loved ones, Shawn kept up the four-year-old relationship he had developed with his biological father, Joe Rando. Rando was amazed that the fame hadn't affected his son, other than to make him more polished. "I'm completely impressed with Shawn, but not because of the public reasons—because of the person he is," Rando said. "It didn't go to his head, which is pretty amazing."

Late in 2001, Shawn returned to playing with computer-security issues, the things that had interested him as a young hacker. He discovered a probable vulnerability in AOL Instant Messenger, the most popular instant-messaging system in the world. Believing the discovery might bring the wrong sort of attention to Napster, Shawn quietly passed the tip along to Matt Conover, the founder of Shawn's old hacking group, w00w00. "I don't mind the fact that I can't talk about it on a wide scale," Shawn said. "I just really do enjoy the process of securing things and finding security problems." Conover analyzed the AOL hole and made national news by writing and releasing the code to exploit it, parlaying the find into a security job in Silicon Valley.

Well before the end of Napster, Shawn was thinking about what might come next, about finding something that would keep him from being remembered as a one-hit wonder. "Technically, I understand Windows programming, and I learned a lot about architectures. And I'm not bored with computers, but in terms of some of the basic computing concepts and networking and some of those things, I feel like I'm at the point where if I want to build something, I know I can build it or find the right people to build it. I've been able to meet so many talented engineers that technology-wise, I'm really comfortable and actually looking forward to new projects in the future," he said. But none of that was the most important part of his growth. "The stuff I've learned the most about is definitely related to interacting with people," he said. "I had a chance to see some of the world, to interact with people on many different levels, and I'm a lot less intimidated by that stuff than before, when I was scared to death."

Shawn said he had no regrets about any of the choices he made. For someone who hadn't even planned on forming a company four years before, Shawn could by now take pride in the fact that he had done more to encourage young people to learn about technology than any number of presidential initiatives. "Before Napster, there was no such thing as a cool geek," said Gnutella developer Gene Kan. "Not Bill Gates, not Kevin Mitnick, not Steve Jobs. People got interested."

After the bankruptcy judge blocked the Bertelsmann sale in September 2002 and before Shawn's talks with Roxio Inc. two months later, he worked on a different idea. Shawn sought funding for what he described as a new peer-to-peer system for traffic on the Internet, one that would respect copyrights. One of his first recruits was Napster engineer Jordy Mendelson, who went scouting for San Mateo real estate. Shawn told Ritter that the system would be an open database, one that would help distribute what artists or others wanted to be sent into the world. Shawn also got some value from his former adventure, making a deal with a producer and selling the rights to his life story to MTV. The first project struck Ritter as problematic. But he told Shawn: "If anyone can do it, you can."

"Once Shawn's set his mind on something," Ritter said, "no one can talk him out of it."

Notes

▼

All oral quotes are from author interviews with the speaker unless otherwise noted. All e-mails, internal documents, and court papers referenced in the text are have been seen by the author unless otherwise noted. If any of the Web pages cited below no longer have the content listed, try http://web.archive.org, which is attempting to preserve as many old websites as possible. John Fanning declined to be interviewed; when his intermediaries spoke on his behalf, it is noted in the text.

vii **Observe my uncle** The entire text of William Shakespeare's *Hamlet* is available online and is not protected by copyright. (Neither are many old books, nor songs from the forties and before.) Hamlet's uncle killed Hamlet's father. It takes some time for the indecisive Hamlet to figure that out.

Prologue: A Party out of Control

5 **a pleasant cocoon** The account of the rave was drawn from interviews with Jordan Ritter, Sean Parker, Eileen Richardson, and Shawn Fanning.

6 **It had been a blur to Shawn** Sources included Shawn, Richard Besciak, and fellow high school students.

6 **Sponsoring it** Parker's background was drawn from interviews with Parker and others.

7 **The third member** Ritter's background was drawn from interviews with Ritter and others.

8 **Richardson was thirty-eight** Richardson's background was drawn from interviews with Richardson and others.

9 As the good feeling Sources on Fanning's history and his relationship with Shawn are given in subsequent chapters.

10 Since Amram had been burned Interviews with Amram, Richardson, and others.

1: the rebels

13 It was in a ramshackle old house The chief source for the account of the party was Coleen Verrier. Joe Rando provided details on the band.

14 "Money was always a pretty big issue" Shawn quoted in "Napster's Shawn Fanning: The Teen Who Woke Up Web Music," by Spencer Ante, available at http://www.businessweek.com:/ebiz/0004/em0412.htm. The account of the rest of Shawn's childhood was drawn from interviews with Verrier, Shawn, and other sources indicated in the text.

16 John Fanning lived an hour away Sources included several former Chess.net employees.

16 His uncle wanted to keep playing StarCraft Sources included Parker, Ritter, and a former Chess.net employee.

18 Shok's work is available See, for example, http://www.hackersclub.com/km/files/unix/.

19 "I don't see what's so bad about writing viral code" This and other w00w00 exchanges archived at http://www.w00w00.org/files/misc/w00fun/w00quotes.

20 Shawn was an aspiring hacker who was at best a gray hat These programs were available at http://www.younghackers.freeservers.com/files2.htm.

21 He badly wanted to go to Carnegie Mellon Coleen Verrier.

21 Ritter was born Ritter's background was drawn from interviews with Ritter and others.

23 BindView was publicly credited for the find by CERT See http://www.infosec.com/internet/99/internet__021399c__j.shtml and http://www.packetsormsecurity.com/9902-exploits/ftpd.txt.

23 Sean Parker's was a paragon of normality Parker's background was drawn from interviews with Parker and others.

2: a big idea

29 It was hardly worth the effort to try The description of the inspiration for Napster came from Shawn's nonpublic deposition in *A&M Records et al. v. Napster Inc.*, U.S. District Court for the Northern District of California, case number C 99-5183 MHP.

29 "The index would become out of date" These two quotes are from Shawn's declaration, available in the A&M Records public court file.

29–30 The entire point of the World Wide Web Berners-Lee's thinking and comments are from *Weaving the Web*, by Tim Berners-Lee with Mark Fischetti, Harper SanFrancisco, 1999.

30 Rob Lord and Jeff Patterson, two computer- and information-science majors The account of the Internet Underground Music Archive and Nullsoft was drawn largely from author interviews with Rob Lord. Ian Rogers of Nullsoft was also interviewed.

32 David Weekly, a Stanford University student, did just that Weekly's experiment is told in *Sonic Boom*, by John Alderman, Perseus Publishing, 2001.

33 as Michael Robertson found after he opened the website MP3.com Sources for the history of MP3.com included *Beyond the Charts*, by Bruce Haring, OTC Press, 2000.

33 Petty manager Tony Dimitriades The Tom Petty story is from Haring's *Beyond the Charts*.

34 "They won't cede control" Robertson's quote is also from *Beyond the Charts*.

35 "I wanted to make this software work" Shawn's quote is from the declaration in *A&M Records*.

36 the word "w00w00" was one of the top twenty most-searched-for terms Conover said he was told this by a friend who worked at Google.

36 "What are you going to do with it?" This was from Ritter's recollection.

36 napster is a darks1de See http://www.00w00.org/files/misc/w00fun/w00quotes.

37 "Do you realize that this is going to change everything?" This was from McGann's recollection.

37 some obvious bugs, which Ritter fixed The description of Ritter's early role was largely from his recollection.

39 Shawn came by Ritter's apartment The first business discussions between Shawn and Ritter were according to Ritter's recollection.

3: birth of a business

41 took courses at Boston College According to the college registrar.

42 Fanning bought Ed Walter's Cambridge Automation on credit Fanning lawyer Amy Hogue said the understanding was that Walter would be paid only if the business succeeded; Walter disputed that.

42 Fanning spent much of his time there Interviews with former Cambridge Automation employees, including Jack Martin and Duncan Audette.

42 Nevil had been fired The story of Aunyx Corp. was contained in *Nevil v. Aunyx*, Plymouth County Superior Court, case number CA85-21517. Attempts to locate Nevil for an interview by searching databases, visiting old addresses, and passing messages through relatives were unsuccessful.

42–43 Rockland won a judgment of more than $7 million *Rockland Trust Co. v. Jack Nevil et al.*, Plymouth County Superior Court, case numbers CA89-1228-A and CA90-1055B.

43 Key supplier Unisys ultimately sued *Unisys Corp. v. Cambridge Automation Corp.*, Suffolk County Superior Court, case number CA94-1211.

43 One regular player was a CMU computer-science professor named Danny Sleator The history of the Carnegie Mellon chess servers came from contemporaneous e-mails, interviews with Sleator and others, and the court file in

Multimedia Engineering Corp. v. Sleator Games Inc., Suffolk Superior Court, case number CV1996-03430.

44 Fanning asked how he could advertise Dzindzichashvili's tapes This was recounted in Sleator's answer to the lawsuit.

45 They told the judge Affidavit of Anthony Martin in *Multimedia Engineering v. Sleator Games.*

45 For Chess.net, Fanning used a core of Carnegie Mellon students The history of Chess.net was drawn from former employees, including McBarron, Ramme, and Dakhnovsky.

46 But Fanning also stopped making payments The story of the BMW was based on the car-financing documents, Dakhnovsky's credit report, other paperwork from the time, and interviews with Dakhnovsky and another Chess.net employee privy to the dispute.

46 a lumber-supply company won a $1,934 default judgment *Forester Moulding & Lumber v. John Fanning,* Leominster District Court, case number 0061SC0457.

46 And billing records from 1997 show thousands of dollars The records were included in the case file for *Household Bank of Nevada v. Coreen Kraysler,* Hingham District Court, case number 9858CV0623.

47 The Hull condominium where they lived and the house he was rebuilding at 2 Summit Avenue were both in Kraysler's name Hull assessor's office records.

47 The mansion overlooking the Atlantic was condemned when Kraysler bought it for $450,000 Hull assessor's office records.

47 The last straw at Chess.net came when Aydar demanded Interviews with former Chess.net employees.

47 a court entered a default judgment against him over a $17,529 bank debt. Later that year, he lost another judgment for $26,759 owed to collection agency Creditrust *CAL-SPV1/Assignee of First USA Bank v. John Fanning,* Hingham District Court, case number 9958CV0272, and *Creditrust v. John Fanning,* Hingham District Court, case number 9958CV0742.

47 The first debt would prove enough to deter Interviews with Jason Grosfeld, Ben Lilienthal, Sean Parker, and Yosi Amram.

47 Her condominium complex sued her in April 1999 for unpaid fees *Trustees of Nantascot Place Condominium Trust v. Coreen Kraysler,* Hingham District Court, case number 9958CV0292.

47 More serious was the 1998 collection case *Household Bank of Nevada v. Coreen Kraysler,* Hingham District Court, case number 9858CV0623.

49 "I'm a fighter" The quote is from "Fanning, the Elder," by Justin Hibbard, in the August 2002 issue of *Red Herring.*

49 Fanning was charged with assault and battery *Commonwealth v. Fanning,* Hingham District Court, case numbers 9958CR0016–0017.

49 He needed stitches in two places Court tape of proceedings on February 7, 2002, in *Commonwealth v. Fanning,* above.

49 Lynch was charged with malicious destruction of property *Commonwealth v. Lynch,* Hingham District Court, case number 9958CR0018.

50 **Lynch was pursuing a suit** *Robert Lynch v. Coreen Kraysler, John Fanning et al.,* Plymouth Superior Court (Plymouth), case number PLCV2001-01481.

50 **the condo complex workers' compensation insurer** *Sentry Insurance v. David Fanning and John Fanning,* Plymouth Superior Court (Brockton), case number CA01-1551.

51 **Lawrence Lessig and others have argued convincingly** In, among other places, *Code and Other Laws of Cyberspace,* Basic Books, 1999, and *The Future of Ideas,* Random House, 2001.

51 **"Through 1996, most of what happened to the Web was driven by pure excitement"** Berners-Lee, *Weaving the Web.*

53 **"He felt strongly he had something to do in the world"** Rasala's comment is from "Hi, I'm Napster," by Linda Gorov, available at http://www.boston.com/dailyglobe2/163/nation/__Hi__I__m__Napster__+.shtml.

55 **When Shawn told Sean Parker about it, Parker couldn't believe it** Interviews with Parker.

4 : getting money

57 **John Fanning may have sewn up 70 percent** John Fanning took 7 million shares and Shawn 3 million. Most internal documents said that 1 million additional shares were reserved for future employee options; at least one document says 2 million shares were reserved.

60 **Sam Hanks, twenty-seven, met Parker, Shawn, and Fanning** The story of the logo was from Hanks and Parker.

60 **Grosfeld and Lilienthal worked well as a team** The account of the pair's involvement with and study of Napster was mainly from interviews with the two men and with Parker.

62 **It called for Draper to put in $500,000** According to Grosfeld and Parker. Draper's later e-mails to Amram cited the same figure.

67 **John Fanning, also well aware of the legal hurdles, was doing his own research** Interviews with Andrew Bridges, Seth Greenstein, and Parker.

71 **Draper agreed to give Napster only a $50,000 loan** The loan was described in interviews with Amram, Parker, and Richardson, among others. The exact terms have long been disputed, but the basics of it included here were drawn from internal Napster e-mails.

77 **Andy Evans, on the other hand, was something completely different** Sources for Evans's history included "Andrew Evans Blows His Second Chance," available at http://www.redherring.com/index.asp?layout=story&channel=20000002&doc__id=110019811 and "Gates' Old Pal Evans Target of Biz2Net's Wild Fraud Lawsuit," available at http://www.observer.com/pages/story.asp?ID=2832.

79 **Fanning had met Amram years earlier** The history of Amram's relationship with Fanning was largely from interviews with Amram.

80 **Individual was based** Sources for the history of Individual included interviews with Amram and others at the company and the prospectus for the sale of its

stock by shareholders dated September 5, 1996, available from the SEC or via the EDGAR online document service.

80 **One of those companies was Freeloader** The Freeloader story was drawn from interviews with Jamie Hamilton, Mark Pincus, Amram, other Individual Inc. officers, and articles including "Start Up. Cash Out. Repeat," in the May 15, 1998 *Inc.* magazine, available at http://www2.inc.com/search/1128-print.html, and "Freeloader's Free Fall," available at http://washtech.com/washtechway/1__1/ techcap/193-1.html.

81 *Suck* **called it "era-definingly irresponsible"** Available at http://www.suck.com/ daily/96/08/01/daily.html.

82 **"Yosi pursued a wide array of investments"** Glabe was quoted by CNet, available at http://news.com/2100-1001-220513.html.

82 **Amram issued a highly unusual statement** Cited in *Steven Cooperman and Scott Sklar v. Individual Inc., et al.,* U.S. District Court in Massachusetts, case number CA96-12272 DPW. Available at http://securities.stanford.edu/ complaints/individual/96cv12272/001.html.

82 **according to the police report** Burlington Police Department case number 96-08786.

83 **"I'm not going to invest if you're the CEO"** This was from Amram's recollection.

84 **He agreed to put money in on three conditions** Also from Amram's recollection.

5: going west

85 **he misplaced his driver's license and couldn't make the flight** Shawn misplaced his license fairly frequently. But it wasn't always as much of a problem: According to Parker, Shawn once was allowed to board a flight to Los Angeles after he produced a copy of *Time* magazine with him on the cover as photo identification.

85 **When Parker arrived** This account of the stay in Sausalito was mostly based on interviews with Parker.

87 **Amram told his network** The story of Amram's hiring of Bales and Richardson was based on interviews with all three.

89 **Richardson had a personal reason** The story of Richardson and Lee was told by both. Richardson's career history was largely from her, corroborated by Atlas, JK&B, and Interwoven executives.

91 **JK&B Capital was flush with money** This was from a JK&B partner, the firm's website, and Richardson.

94 **"I've always wanted to do something big"** Bales's comments and the account of his youth are from an interview with the *Augusta Chronicle,* available at http://www.augustachronicle.com/stories/071800/bus__129-6438.000.shtml.

94 **would identify himself as a cofounder of Quote.com** See, for example, "Napster Investors Try New Venture" in the July 17, 2000, edition of *USA Today,* available at http://www.usatoday.com/life/cyber/invest/in880.htm. That article also stated that Bales "discovered Napster creator Shawn Fanning."

95 **Fikker joined them at News Direct** Sources used for the account of News Direct/ON24 included Bales, Fikker, Chen, Amram, and various news articles.

96 Bales's criminal record San Mateo Superior Court, case number SM245322A.

97 the woman's sworn statement San Mateo Superior Court, case number F-039868.

99 Soon after Shawn and Parker arrived The stories of the breakfast and rental car incident were from Parker. Parker, Shawn, and Richardson all confirmed the tale of their accidental introduction.

101 Fanning's deputy, Tom Carmody, flew out from Hull Parker's recollection.

104 Kessler and Amram had a series of meetings This was mostly from Kessler, with confirmation from Amram. Kessler was the source for his conversation with Fanning.

105 Ritter made it to the Napster offices This was primarily from Ritter, with backup from another person at the meeting.

106 Ritter returned to work out a deal with Richardson The story of the negotiation was told by both Ritter and Richardson.

107 sales by Fanning and the company According to capitalization tables from the time.

107 the Xtime employees in the adjoining cubicles thought nothing of it The story was told by Xtime's Travis Murdock. The stories from the early days in San Mateo were provided by multiple employees who corroborated each others' accounts.

108 Bales took Shawn, Parker, and Ritter to look at a house This story was told by Parker and Ritter and largely confirmed by Bales, who also provided the account of how he recruited Jensen.

108 the young men blew off steam All parts of this story were based either on one party confessing to something he did or on the accounts of two sources who were closely involved.

109 more than one romance The facts of the Richardson-Garrehy-Lee triangle were confirmed by all parties.

110 one of the very first articles Available at http://zdnet.com.com/2100-11-515433.html?legacy=zdnn.

111 it seemed remarkably easy for firms to get Conway's blessing Conway's career path is from *The Godfather of Silicon Valley*, by Gary Rivlin, AtRandom.com Books, 2001.

112 There was Pixelon For more on Pixelon, see http://www.thestandard.com/article/display/ 0,1151,16309,00.html.

113 Another Internet video firm that qualifies as a paragon of the times For more on DEN, see "How a Visionary Venture on the Web Unraveled," in the May 7, 2000, edition of the *Los Angeles Times*. A summary is available at http://pqasb. pqarchiver.com/latimes/index.html?ts=1022208002, but they want you to pay $2.50 to read the whole thing.

114 Conway would give editorial director Chris Alden This also is from Rivlin's *The Godfather of Silicon Valley*.

116 The other major financial participants According to capitalization tables.

119 **It was after another chemically enhanced rave** The anecdote was Parker's.

120 **There were other causes for celebration inside Napster's offices** Ritter, Aydar, and Garrehy were the primary sources.

122 **One of the first broader-audience publications** The story was archived at http://www.wired.com/news/technology/0,1282,32151,00.html.

124 **At the Bubble Lounge that night** This came mainly from Murdock.

124 **In mid-November, the digital music magazine** *Webnoize* **said the RIAA intended to sue . . .** *Wired* **confirmed the report** See http://www.wired.com /news/business/0,1367,32559,00.html.

124 **"We are freaking four months old"** Richardson's quote was in the story at http://www.wired.com/news/mp3/0,1285,32559,00.html.

124 **The RIAA finally filed the lawsuit** *A&M Records et al. v. Napster Inc.,* U.S. District Court for the Northern District of California (San Francisco), case number C 99-5183 MHP.

126 **Richardson clashed so badly with John Fanning** Sources included Richardson, Amram, and others present during board meetings.

129 **This three-way chat** The log was posted to the moderators' e-mail list.

132 **But Chang was ready with a quote** See CNet article from March 22, 2000, at http://news.com.com/2100-1023-238290.html?legacy=cnet.

135 **Paulson was featured in dozens of interviews** See, for example, http://www.cnn. com/virtual/editions/europe/2000/roof/change.pop/frameset.exclude.html.

136 **Chuck D of Public Enemy went further** Op-Ed available at http://www. rapstation.com/files/news/archive/print__media/april29__newyorktimes__b1__ large.gif.

136 **Napster quietly paid Chuck D** Napster disclosed the payment in the documents for Bertelsmann's loan, saying it was for "the cost of speaking engagements and support." The documents were filed as an exhibit in Napster's bankruptcy in Wilmington, Delaware. *In re Napster et al.,* case number 02-11573.

136 **Techno star Moby was also a big help** He and others quoted on http://www. napster.com/speakout/artists.html.

137 **the band wrote on its site** Still posted at http://www.offspring.com/ news/news59.html.

137 **Napster was duly mocked** On numerous websites and the front page of the *Wall Street Journal* on July 26, 2000.

140 **Napster sued Sport Service** *Napster Inc. v. Sport Service Inc.,* U.S. District Court for the Northern District of California, case number C00-04821 MMC.

140 **some, like Peter Gabriel, obliged** Posted at http://www.riaa.org/Napster__ artist__quotes.cfm.

140 **Rapper Eminem was more blunt** Also on http://www.riaa.org/Napster__ artist__quotes.cfm.

141 **Metallica filed suit against Napster** *Metallica et al. v. Napster,* U.S. District

Court for the Central District of California (Los Angeles), case number 00-03914.

141 **Richardson was quoted as saying that the band had never tried to contact Napster** Among other places, at http://www.wired.com/news/politics/0,1283,35670,00.html.

141 **Even most Metallica listeners sided with Napster** According to interviews with various fans of both Metallica and Napster, including John DiCarlo.

141 **Killmetallica.com** Other sites were listed at http://www.killmetallica.com/contents.html.

142 **Lyttle, who used the handle Pimpshiz** See "An Internet Outlaw Goes on Record" in the February 24, 2002, *San Francisco Chronicle* and at http://sfgate.com/cgi-bin/article.cgi?file=/chronicle/archive/2002/02/24/MN182931.DTL&type=printable.

142 **Lyttle reached Shawn and Ritter on IRC** According to Ritter.

142 **Parker didn't help matters** According to Paulson.

144 **"Fuck you, Lars"** This is from "The Heavenly Jukebox," by Charles Mann, in the September 2000 issue of *The Atlantic* magazine.

145 **Ulrich seemed to slump** This story came from Murdock. King said he didn't recall the words Ulrich used during the brief conversation inside Napster.

145 **After a news website linked to the comments** *ZDNet News.*

145 **A Napster fan, crying censorship, got hold of Ritter on an IRC channel and complained** Story told at http://zdnet.com.com/2100-11-520694.html?legacy=zdnn. Ritter confirmed the substance of the exchange.

7: the industry

147 **Richardson wanted to do the most** Interviews with Richardson, Parker, and other Napster executives.

149 **Morris Levy, founder of Count Basie home Roulette Records** From Fredric Dannen's *Hit Men,* Times Books, 1990.

149 **Take, for example, the matter of payola** The history of payola is best told by Dannen; for ongoing journalism on the matter, the best work is by Chuck Philips of the *Los Angeles Times.*

150 **Isgro returned to living the high life in Beverly Hills until he was sentenced** Articles on Isgro's case are available through http://www.latimes.com. The sentencing was reported on September 8, 2000.

151 **In a hypothetical example of a smash success** Contained in Moses Avalon's *Confessions of a Record Producer,* 2nd ed., Backbeat Books, 2002.

152 **The U.S. Federal Trade Commission investigated** A reasonable summary of the issues ran in the August 14, 2000, *Seattle Times.*

152 **In a 2000 settlement of the charges** FTC press release dated May 10, 2000.

155 **Glaser was brimming with confidence** A video of the speech was available over the Web at http://www.webnoize.com.

155 **But he was also a husky six-foot-three** Background from Dannen's *Hit Men*. Al
Smith declined several interview requests.

160 **Richardson gave her music-discovery pitch** Interviews with Richardson and
Cohen.

160 **Bales came down for the get-together** Interviews with Samit and Bales.

160 **Tom Gieselmann, an investor with Bertelsmann's venture-capital arm**
Interviews with Bales and Gieselmann.

164 **"Are you sure suing them is enough?"** The anecdote was told by Rosen.

167 **John Fogerty told the crowd at one benefit concert** Reported in the February
28, 2002, *Los Angeles Times.*

168 **"The record industry fiddled on the sidelines"** A copy of Henley's prepared
testimony was posted at http://www.recordingartistscoalition.com/.

8 : competition

171 **The lawyers opposed linking** According to interviews with Ritter and others.

174 **Gnutella would have had some major headaches** The story was confirmed by
McGann, Ritter, Song, and Rogers.

175 **Soon someone using Frankel's IRC handle "deadbeef"** Reported by Amy
Harmon in the March 20, 2000, *New York Times.*

176 **That worried Shawn, who wondered if AltaVista's** According to Shawn's
e-mails.

176 **Ritter went to dinner with Dodge** The story was told by Ritter.

179 **Ritter and Shawn quickly got hold of him in a private chat** According to Ritter.

184 **chairman Andy Grove, the head of the world's largest microprocessor maker**
The comment was printed by *Fortune* and other outlets and was posted on
Napster's website until Grove asked that it be removed, according to a Napster
source.

185 **Kan had applied at Napster** The story was told by Ritter and Dembo and not
disputed by Kan.

188 **soon got a call from Conway's more-organized partner** Bozeman's call was
remembered by Kan.

188 **"There was no specific business model"** Bozeman's comment is from "Can
Peer-to-Peer Grow Up?" by Justin Hibbard, in the December 4, 2000, *Red
Herring.*

189 **The moral of some of Cringely's technology stories** Robert Cringely, *Accidental
Empires,* Addison-Wesley Publishing, 1992.

189 *The Innovator's Dilemma* Clayton Christensen, Harvard Business School Press,
1997.

9 : venture games

192 **Fanning and his marketing deputy, Tom Carmody** According to Richardson
and Amram. Another executive confirmed the amount. Parker remembered
overhearing Richardson demanding of Fanning over the phone, "Why is Tom
Carmody on the payroll?"

192 **Amram's initial $250,000 investment also went to Hull** According to Richardson and Amram.

192 **Napster's junior holders included** According to capitalization tables.

193 **Fanning found an ally in Amram** According to Amram.

193 **The prospectus for the IPO** The ValiCert prospectus is available online from the SEC's EDGAR service.

194 **ValiCert angel investor and entrepreneur Gary Kremen** This much of the story told by Kremen is confirmed by Amram.

194 **Fanning and Richardson argued often** The wording of the exchanges was Richardson's recollection. Amram didn't disagree with them.

195 **he argued with Richardson and went behind her back repeatedly** Bales himself gave numerous examples.

196 **Yet Bales went ahead anyway** This was from Parker, Bales, and Richardson.

197 **Bales called New York investor Jason Grosfeld** According to Grosfeld; Richardson and Bales didn't dispute the story.

200 **he begged Richardson not to fire him** According to Richardson and other Napster staffers.

200 **Bales was spreading a rumor** Bales admitted this.

200 **The engineers told their boss, Kessler, that they would quit** According to all three.

201 **Kessler, in turn, took the threat seriously enough** This was according to Kessler. Bales said people were unduly alarmed.

203 **one director who had invested** This was according to Bales. DeVito spokesman Stan Rosenfield confirmed the initial meeting and said nothing happened afterward with his client. Avnet didn't respond to an interview request passed through his agent.

205 **Alsop wrote in *Fortune*** The November 13, 2000, issue. The column is posted at http://www.fortune.com/indext.jhtml?channel=print__article.jhtml&doc__id=00000191.

205 **The company spent $1.6 million** According to an internal income statement.

206 **Doerr gave Richardson a hug** Details of this meeting were from Richardson; Mackenzie declined to be interviewed.

207 **According to Turner's e-mails** This was what Turner said the e-mails contained after she reviewed them.

207 **Richardson returned from a meeting with Turner** This account was given by Richardson and Turner, confirmed by Amram, and supported by Richardson's e-mails and draft documents laying out the merger terms.

208 **In a tense and sometimes circular two-hour conference call** The call was described by Richardson and Amram.

211 **"If Hummer Winblad doesn't invest"** Conway and Parker told the same story.

212 **John Hummer, and another VC at the San Francisco firm drove to see Richardson** These meetings were laid out by Richardson in her deposition.

214 **The charity auction was emceed by comedian Dana Carvey** The perceptions of

Shawn and Parker were given in interviews. The surrounding events and Andreessen's quote are from a *Bloomberg News* article carried on CNet's site on May 22.

215 **Barry harbored a rebellious streak** His career was described by Barry and others in interviews.

220 **Zero Gravity, whose smaller shareholders included** The story of Zero Gravity came mainly from the 2001 lawsuit *Zero Gravity Management v. John Hummer et al.*, San Francisco Superior Court, case number 321442, with additional material from interviews and from articles in the June 22, 2001, *San Francisco Business Times* and the July 9, 2001, *BusinessWeek.* The last is available at http://www. businessweek.com/magazine/content/01__28/b3740101.htm.

220 **she said at the time** The "sticky" quote is from the March 19, 1999, *Puget Sound Business Journal.*

220 **Johnston, who had to sue for access** *Phoenix Partners IV et al. v. Rival Networks,* King County Superior Court, case number 01-2-13876-6SEA.

221 **"I am the record companies' worst nightmare"** Quoted in August 14, 2000, *Fortune* and available at http://www.fortune.com/indext.jhtml?channel= print__article.jhtml&doc__id=00000758.

10: hummer winblad

225 **Russell Frackman, the fifty-five-year-old Los Angeles attorney** Frackman, court rulings, and his firm's documents were the sources for his career.

228 **didn't stop his uncle from claiming** Napster's application for a patent on its "Real-time search engine" was filed on December 15, 1999, and granted on April 2, 2002, and given number 6,366,907. It can be found at http://patft.uspto.gov/ netacgi/nph-Parser?Sect1=PTO2&Sect2=HITOFF&u=/netahtml/search- adv.htm&r=1&p=1&f=G&l=50&d=ft00&S1=Fanning-Shawn.INZZ.&OS=IN/ Fanning-Shawn&RS=IN/Fanning-Shawn.

230 **Borkowski had been working until near midnight** This account was drawn from Borkowski, Parker, and the deposition transcript.

234 **When Napster called, Boies was out of town** The story of Boies's decision to take the case and his quotes were from the October 2000 issue of *Wired* magazine, available at http://www.wired.com/wired/archive/8.10/boies__pr.html.

241 **He estimated there was only a 10 percent chance** According to a Fanning e-mail cited in a *BusinessWeek* story of August 14, 2000, and available at http://www.businessweek.com/2000/00__33/b3694001.htm.

246 **Barry scribbled out a statement on the spot** Ibid.

246 **Parker was in Virginia and called** Parker's recollection.

247 **Shawn played it populist cool for MTV** A transcript of the MTV interview is available at http://www.mtv.com/bands/archive/n/napster00/?__requestid=260347.

247 **"Napster" became the most-searched-for term** The Lycos 50 for August 1. Available at http://50.lycos.com/080100.html.

248 **But Kozinski was excited** This account was drawn from interviews with two well-placed sources inside the appeals court.

249 **"This is like the playoffs"** Also from the August 14 *BusinessWeek* story.

250 **At a California airport on July 5** Most of the details in the account of the early talks were from an author interview with Bronfman.

251 **less attractive than the Sun Valley summit terms** This was according to Bronfman. Barry declined to address the deterioration in the talks in detail, except for saying that Bronfman stopped returning his calls. Grove declined to be interviewed.

252 **"Your biggest problem"** Rosen's recollection.

252 **more than $100,000 in stock** It was unclear how much Shawn sold overall. By around the end of 1999, he had already sold $125,000 worth, according to internal e-mails. Two of his close friends said the final figure was closer to $500,000.

255 **He sent a message to Ian Rogers** This was from Rogers.

257 **It wasn't national television** Sources for the scene at the awards included Napster employees, a Nullsoft employee, and others in attendance.

258 **She countersued** *Geffen Records et al. v. Courtney Love et al.,* Los Angeles Superior Court, case number BC 2233364, available at http://www.cappellomccann.com/courtney/courtney_cross.htm. Love settled her case on undisclosed but favorable terms in September 2002.

11: bertelsmann

261 **"There's no question that file-sharing will exist"** The quotes from the press conference were from contemporaneous news accounts.

262 **Middelhoff was among the most predisposed** For more on Middelhoff's background, see "A New Net Powerhouse?" in the November 13, 2000, *BusinessWeek,* available at http://www.businessweek.com/2000/00_46/b3707001.htm, and "Napster Meister," in the November 13, 2000, *Time* magazine, available at http://www.time.com/time/magazine/article/0,9171,1101001113-59778,00.html. Other material is from Bertelsmann's website.

262 **"I just got used to being turned down"** Jensen's deposition and Hilbers's deposition, both filed as exhibits in Napster's bankruptcy.

263 **"We're investing in Napster"** This account was based on interviews with people familiar with the conversations. For more on the internal dispute, see "Thomas Middelhoff Has a Hunch," in the June 10, 2001, *New York Times Magazine.* Middelhoff said that Zelnick and the others eventually came around and supported the Napster investment, then exaggerated their opposition after their dismissal.

263 **But he passed along** Schmidt's e-mail was filed as an exhibit in Napster's bankruptcy.

264 **"It is true that this private exchange"** Middelhoff's memo, the consultants' presentation, and the task force report were all filed as exhibits in Napster's bankruptcy.

265 **Middelhoff treated Shawn to dinner** The dinner details and Middelhoff's quote were from "Napster Meister," in *Time.*

265 **Napster added sweeteners for Shawn** The figures were disclosed in the documents for Bertelsmann's loan, filed as an exhibit in Napster's bankruptcy.

266 **The executives were coached** The coaching came in a question-and-answer preparation sheet filed as an exhibit in Napster's bankruptcy.

273 **Richard Parsons, co–chief operating officer** The comment was reported in the *New York Times* of June 10, 2001.

274 **"Is anyone out there besides me wincing"** Bo's All Things Napster, http://www.uninet.net/~blaisdel/napster.htm.

277 **when Congress got involved, it tended to favor copyright holders** Lawrence Lessig provides a good history of copyright evolution in *The Future of Ideas* and *Code and Other Laws of Cyberspace.*

278 **The bill was challenged in court** *Eldred v. Ashcroft,* U.S. Supreme Court case number 01-618. Many of the case documents are available at http://eldred.cc/.

278 **that involving the DVD encryption technology known as CSS** *Universal City Studios et al. v. Shawn Reimerdes et al.,* U.S. District Court for the Southern District of New York, case number 00-CV-277 (LAK)(RLE). Lessig's *Future of Ideas* gives a summary of the issues. Many of the case filings are available at http://www.eff.org/IP/Video/MPAA__DVD__cases/.

279 **The labels went after MP3.com** *Universal Music Group et al. v. MP3.com,* U.S. District Court for the Southern District of New York, case number 00-CV-00472. A copy of the judge's ruling is available at http://news.findlaw.com/cnn/docs/mp3/0906__mp3__unoffruling.html.

280 **"I know something about songwriting"** A Web video of Hatch's remarks was posted at http://www.webnoize.com.

280 **So he explicitly asked Congress not to change** The testimony of Barry, Ulrich, and Kan are available at http://www.senate.gov/~judiciary/search__testimony.cfm?testimony=napster.

281 **Only now did Barry ask Congress to force digital licenses on the record industry** The testimony is available at http://www.senate.gov/~judiciary/search__testimony.cfm?testimony=napster.

281 **The most impressive display of the second tactic** This was based on interviews with people who attended. The National Academy's version of events is from a press release dated April 6, 2001.

282 **perhaps by replacing HB** The eCommerce Group meeting agenda was filed as an exhibit in Napster's bankruptcy.

284 **he thought a full release needed** Hilbers's deposition, filed as an exhibit in Napster's bankruptcy.

284 **Napster has shown two things** Farmer's comment appeared in an interview available at http://www.theatlantic.com/issues/2000/09/mann-farmer.htm.

284 **Sorenson wrote to his boss** Sorenson's memo, Hilbers's description of the AOL terms, and Hilbers's e-mail to Middelhoff were filed as exhibits in Napster's bankruptcy. Other Hilbers quotes are from an author interview.

12: the coup

289 **He reasoned that Bertelsmann would have a better chance** According to interviews with Middelhoff, Hilbers, and others close to the process.

290 **Hummer Winblad had insisted on that proxy** According to interviews and an e-mail from Barry to Napster directors before the deal closed. Other big investors also had to pledge to vote their shares as the board instructed on major decisions.

291 **Hummer Winblad won what is known as a liquidation preference** The terms of the various preferences were described in interviews with Barry and other Napster investors.

291 **would get nothing at all for their Series A Junior** According to legal papers filed in *John Fanning v. John Hummer and Hank Barry,* Delaware Chancery Court for New Castle County, case number 19500 NC.

291 **Bertelsmann Direct Group CFO Bill Sorenson** The deposition was filed as an exhibit in Napster's bankruptcy.

292 **he repudiated the conversion** According to Amram's deposition in *John Fanning v. John Hummer and Hank Barry,* Delaware Chancery Court for New Castle County, case number 19500 NC.

293 **He called both his nephew** The descriptions of Fanning's calls were from the recipients.

294 **Caught in traffic on U.S. 101** Partially the author's fault; I was driving and picked a bad exit.

295 **Fanning filed a lawsuit in Delaware's Chancery Court** *John Fanning v. John Hummer and Hank Barry,* Delaware Chancery Court for New Castle County, case number 19500 NC.

295 **The *Los Angeles Times* promptly identified** On March 28, 2002. Available at http://www.latimes.com.

300 **Napster filed for Chapter 11 bankruptcy in Delaware** *In re Napster Inc., et al.,* case number 02-11573.

302 **"that left me with Joel Klein"** From Hilbers's deposition, filed as an exhibit in Napster's bankruptcy.

Epilogue: After the Revolution

310 **"I fear we're getting into a game of Whack-a-Mole"** The executive was quoted in a July 23, 2001, *Wired News* article available at http://www.wired.com/news/mp3/0,1285,45234-2,00.html.

311 **It later emerged** The *New York Times* article is available with free registration at http://www.nytimes.com/2002/03/07/arts/music/07POPL.html.

311 **Disney CEO Michael Eisner testified in Congress** Eisner's testimony was before Hollings's Senate Commerce Committee and is available at http://commerce.senate.gov/hearings/hearings0202.htm. Barrett's response came in the friendlier setting of the Judiciary Committee.

312 **they had also invested a combined $200,000 in Napster** According to capitalization tables.

313 **according to the U.S. Department of Commerce** The Commerce study and the Brookings figure were cited in "Kazaa Taunts Record Biz: Catch Us," by Brad King, in *Wired News*, September 25, 2002. Available at http://www.wired.com/news/technology/0,1282,55356,00.html.

315 **"This is serious research"** The army official was quoted in an interview by Richard Koman published on an O'Reilly & Associates website devoted to peer-to-peer efforts. The full interview is available at http://www.openp2p.com/pub/a/p2p/2001/08/28/p2pwar.html.

315 **GlaxoSmithKline uses Groove Networks** The two corporate examples are given in David Barkai's *Peer-to-Peer Computing*, Intel Press, 2001.

316 *BusinessWeek* **ran a long cover story** "Inside Napster," by Spencer Ante, in the August 14, 2000, issue. Richardson gave a detailed account of her experience with the writer after publication, including her request to him for a correction. None was ever published. In an interview by the author, Ante declined to comment. A follow-up voice-mail message was not returned.

318 **The firm's SpamNet peer-to-peer system** SpamNet was so good that in January 2003, Ritter made it back to *Wired* magazine's Rave Awards—this time in his own right, as a finalist for software designer of the year.

319 **In the fall of 2000, he pitched investors** A copy of the presentation was filed in *Altholtz v. NetCapital*, Norfolk County Superior Court, case number CA01-00169.

319 **entertainment lawyer Howard Altholtz** *Altholtz v. NetCapital*, Norfolk County Superior Court, case number CA01-00169.

321 **Fanning blamed, of all people** Fanning's e-mail was included as an exhibit in Napster's bankruptcy.

Bibliography

Alderman, John. *Sonic Boom*. Cambridge, Mass.: Perseus Publishing, 2001.

Ante, Spencer. "Inside Napster." *BusinessWeek,* August 14, 2000.

————. "Napster's Shawn Fanning: The Teen Who Woke Up Web Music." *BusinessWeek,* April 12, 2000.

Avalon, Moses. *Confessions of a Record Producer,* 2nd ed. San Francisco: Backbeat Books, 2002.

Barkai, David. *Peer-to-Peer Computing*. Hillsboro, Oreg.: Intel Press, 2001.

Berners-Lee, Tim, with Mark Fischetti. *Weaving the Web*. New York: Harper San Francisco, 1999.

Christensen, Clayton. *The Innovator's Dilemma*. Cambridge, Mass.: Harvard Business School Press, 1997.

Cringely, Robert. *Accidental Empires*. Boston: Addison-Wesley Publishing, 1992.

Dannen, Fredric. *Hit Men*. New York: Times Books, 1990.

Goodin, Dan. "Being John Fanning." *Industry Standard,* August 14, 2000.

Gorov, Lynda. "Hi, I'm Napster." *Boston Globe,* June 11, 2000.

Greenfeld, Karl Taro. "Meet the Napster." *Time,* October 2, 2000.

Haring, Bruce. *Beyond the Charts*. Los Angeles: OTC Press, 2000.

Heilemann, John. "David Boies: The Wired Interview." *Wired,* October 2000.

Hibbard, Justin. "Can Peer-to-Peer Grow Up?" *Red Herring,* December 4, 2000.

Kaplan, David A. *The Silicon Boys*. New York: William Morrow, 1999.

Kirkpatrick, David. "Thomas Middelhoff Has a Hunch." *New York Times Magazine,* June 10, 2001.

Lessig, Lawrence. *Code and Other Laws of Cyberspace*. New York: Basic Books, 1999.

————. *The Future of Ideas*. New York: Random House, 2001.

Litman, Jessica. *Digital Copyright*. Amherst, N.Y.: Prometheus Books, 2001.

Menn, Joseph. "Napster Was Gambling All the Way." *Los Angeles Times,* February 25, 2001.

Oram, Andy, ed. *Peer-to-Peer: Harnessing the Power of Disruptive Technologies.* Sebastopol, Calif.: O'Reilly & Associates, 2001.

Perkins, Anthony, and Michael Perkins. *The Internet Bubble.* New York: Harper Business, 1999.

Rivlin, Gary. *The Godfather of Silicon Valley.* New York: AtRandom.com Books, 2001.

Stross, Randall. *EBoys.* New York: Crown Business, 2000.

Tully, Shawn. "Big Man Against Big Music." *Fortune Magazine,* August 14, 2000.

Index

G

About the Author

▼

JOSEPH MENN has tracked Silicon Valley for the *Los Angeles Times* for more than four years. He is coauthor of *The People vs. Big Tobacco: How the States Took on the Cigarette Giants* (1998) and a principal editor of *The Chronology: The Documented Day-by-Day Account of the Secret Military Assistance to Iran and the Contras* (1987) and worked for *Bloomberg News* and the *Charlotte (N.C.) Observer.* He grew up in suburban Boston and was executive editor of the *Harvard Crimson* as an undergraduate. He lives in San Francisco with his wife and daughter.